The REAL King Arthur

A History Of Post-Roman Britannia
A.D. 410 - A.D. 593

Volume I

P. F. J. Turner is a Harvard-educated
scholar who has spent many years
researching post-Roman history and
the origins of Arthurian legend.  He
lives in Anchorage, Alaska, where, in
addition to pursuing his studies, he is
engaged in the practice of law.

# The REAL King Arthur

## A HISTORY OF POST-ROMAN BRITANNIA

### A.D. 410 - A.D. 593

#### Volume I

by

P. F. J. Turner

THE REAL KING ARTHUR
A HISTORY OF POST-ROMAN BRITANNIA
A.D. 410 - A.D. 593
Volume I
Copyright © P.F.J. Turner, 1993

Publisher's Cataloging in Publication
(*Prepared by Quality Books Inc.*)

Turner, Peter J.
    The real King Arthur : a history of post-Roman Britanna, A.D.
410 - A.D. 593 / by P.F.J. Turner
    2 v. cm.
    Includes bibliographical references and index.
    ISBN 0-9637434-2-2 (set)
    ISBN 0-9637434-0-6 (v. 1)
    ISBN 0-9637434-1-4 (v. 2)

    1. Arthur, King.  2. Britons--Kings and rulers--Biography.  3.
Great Britain--History--To 1066.  4. Great Britain--Antiquities,
Celtic.  I. Title.  II. Title: History of post-Roman Britannia.

DA152.5.A7T87 1993            942.01'4
                              QBI93-1013

## DEDICATION

In gratitude to
Dan Rodgers, Ron Chappel and my father,
who consented to review the early drafts of this work
and whose advise and suggestions
have proved invaluable.

BRITANNIA
in the
Time of
KING ARTHUR
*circa* A.D. 500

TABLE OF CONTENTS

VOLUME I

## VOLUME II
### LIBER QUINTUS:  The Age of Arthur
#### - The Reign of Arthur -

### LIBER SEXTUS:  The Age of Angle-Land
#### - Aftermath -

## LIST OF MAPS

"It is of this Arthur
that the Britons fondly tell so many fables,
even to the present day -
a man worthy to be celebrated not by idle fictions
but by authentic history."

William of Malmesbury
*De Gestis Regum Anglorum*
A.D. 1125

## Introduction:
## Reconstructing Post-Roman History

Yes, there really was a King Arthur.

The real King Arthur was a Briton of distinguished Roman heritage named Lucius Artorius Castus who lived in the former Roman Diocese[1] of Britannia in the late Fifth and early Sixth Centuries. At that time, most of the Roman army had been withdrawn from the Diocese, and Britannia was in serious danger of being overrun by Irish invaders from the west, Pictish invaders from the north and Anglo-Saxon invaders from the east. In about A.D. 485, Arthur rose to command of the native Romano-Briton military forces in the southern part of the Diocese, and he led them in a series of successful wars against the barbarians assailing Britannia. Several years later, Arthur became supreme ruler of most of the one-time Roman Diocese. Soon thereafter, he won his greatest victory in the Battle of Badon Hill. Arthur's victory at Badon Hill brought to Britannia a peace, at least from foreign enemies, that lasted over half a century. In order to further preserve the security of his realm, Arthur then found it necessary to campaign among the semi-barbarous Britons and the Irish colonists in the far north of Britannia beyond the Roman border. He also had to make war upon certain of his fellow Romans in the Diocese. He was successful in all these endeavors. Before his untimely death in the Battle of Camlann in about A.D. 514, Arthur had, in a very real sense, restored the Roman Empire in Britannia long after it had disappeared from the rest of western Europe.

Most people have a very different image of King Arthur. He was, they would say, a king of England in the Middle Ages. Visions of towering castles, armor-encased knights on horseback, festive tournaments, thrilling jousts and colorful fluttering banners spring instantly to mind. The popular image of King Arthur is very powerful and exciting - but almost entirely false.

The real King Arthur lived and died long before the start of the Middle Ages. He was a Briton of Roman ancestry, and he most certainly was *not* English; indeed, the Anglo-Saxons, the ancestors of the modern English, were his principal enemies. Arthur's bastions were old Roman walled towns and restored pre-Roman timber-and-earthwork forts; these structures were effective military fortifications, but they were far less imposing than the tall stone castles of medieval construction. Arthur's horsemen were fierce warriors, but they were not so elegantly bedecked nor so well equipped as medieval knights. His combats were always serious, never ceremonial, affairs. The only correct element of the popular image is that Arthur did in fact fly an impressive personal banner: a Roman windsock pennant in the shape of a dragon that writhed in the air as if alive.

We have many mistaken notions about Arthur because our knowledge of him is derived from second-hand accounts written by medieval scholars. Very few written records were kept in Britannia during the post-Roman period, and the history of that time was preserved for the most part in folk tales passed down by singers and storytellers. The scholars of the Middle Ages

---

1 The Roman Empire was divided for administrative purposes into twelve Dioceses, each of which was further divided into several provinces. Modern England and Wales are roughly comparable to the Roman Diocese of Britannia, which consisted of five provinces.

reduced some of this oral tradition to writing, but in the process they distorted the truth because they misunderstood much of what they heard. They interpreted the oral tradition in the only terms they understood, which were the terms of their own Middle Ages experience. In committing the history of post-Roman Britannia to writing, the medieval scholars produced a very confused and anachronistic description of Arthur and his times.

We should not judge the medieval scholars too harshly. They were often very conscientious in their efforts, but they were hindered by the limited historical information and narrow cultural perspective of their own times. In the political turmoil and social disruption which followed the fall of the Western Roman Empire, Classical civilization collapsed and much knowledge and learning was lost. The ensuing generations, living in the stable and slow-moving society of the Middle Ages, did not realize that earlier times were very different from their own. Lacking an appreciation of the peculiar context and situation of post-Roman Britannia, and inherently incapable of comprehending the nature of historical change, the medieval scholars misinterpreted the information available to them.

The convoluted account of post-Roman times in the medieval chronicles has caused many modern historians to dismiss the reality of Arthur altogether. Bewildered and frustrated by the Middle Ages narrative, they have in disgust consigned Arthur to the realm of myth and legend. The reaction of these historians, although understandable, really tells us more about the limits of their own historiography than it does about the trustworthiness of medieval scholarship.

We can now take a more responsible approach to the problem of post-Roman history. We possess considerable archaeological and linguistic evidence that was unavailable just a few decades ago, and we are heirs to a much more sophisticated sense of historical perspective. Consequently, we know a great deal about the times in which Arthur lived and about those in which his early chroniclers lived. Armed with a greater understanding of both the post-Roman period and the Middle Ages, we are able to take a fresh look at the medieval accounts. We can correct the errors of the medieval scholars and reconstruct the true history of the real King Arthur - the true history which the medieval scholars had before them, but have misunderstood and miscommunicated to us.

An essential part of our effort to reconstruct the true history of Arthur is to get as close as possible to the original oral tradition in which most of the genuine information about him was preserved. At the onset, we must therefore put aside some of the best-known Arthurian sagas, the Romances of the later Middle Ages.

These medieval sagas were called Romances because they were written in the then-emerging Roman-descended languages of modern Europe rather than the Latin of the Roman Empire. This choice of language is important because Latin was still the preferred language of the educated classes in the Middles Ages. The Romances were composed solely for entertainment, and they might not have been thought worthy of the language of the Caesars and of the Church. In any event, the term "Romance" soon came to encompass all non-Latin fictional writings, including those written in non-romance languages. Even sagas composed by the medieval Germans in their own language were called Romances, and to this day the German word for a novel is *Roman.* In modern English, "romance" has come to have the peculiar meaning of "love story" because of the amorous content of many of the medieval tales. We shall, however, use "Romance" in its original sense to refer to medieval vernacular fictional literature. The earliest known Romance is *Erec et Enide,* composed in French by Chretien de Troyes around 1170.

The Romances are largely responsible for keeping alive the name and memory of Arthur, but their value to us is limited. They contain far too much material borrowed from other traditions, or even created anew out of whole cloth, for us to place a great deal of credence in them as historical documents. The Romancers often sought an audience for ancient stories from pagan mythology or for contemporary tales of heroic derring-do by associating them with Arthur. They used Arthur in this fashion because Arthur was a well-known person whose name was sure to arouse the listener's attention and interest. Ironically, Arthur's very fame and reputation thus made him a magnet for the accumulation of a vast amount of extraneous and irrelevant material, which has helped obscured the truth about him. The Romances sometimes provide important clues to the oral tradition from which they sprang, so we should not ignore them altogether, but our historical inquiry must focus upon even older sources which bring us closer to the unembellished facts.

The genuine tradition of Arthur's times is most closely preserved in a relatively small number of Welsh, English and Latin sources. The most important of these sources include a series of poetic references known as the Welsh Triads, several early Welsh tales found in a collection entitled the *Mabinogion,* a Ninth Century English chronology called the Anglo-Saxon Chronicle, a handful of documents from the post-Roman period itself, and a few early medieval histories which touch upon post-Roman or early Anglo-Saxon times.

The Welsh Triads are basically lists of early Welsh tales. Each Triad consists of allusions to three, or sometimes four, different tales sharing a common theme or topic.[2] The purpose of this arrangement was mnemonic: a tale was listed in a Triad in order that it might then remind a Welsh storyteller of two or three other similar tales. The Triads were not intended to record factual data, but to aid storytellers in remembering traditional Welsh tales. Unfortunately, the tales behind the Triadic references were originally oral and very few were ever written down; the vast majority of these tales were forgotten when the Welsh oral storytelling tradition died out toward the end of the Middle Ages. Although most of the tales to which the Triads refer are now lost, we can still extract important bits of information about Arthur and his followers from the hints provided in the Triads themselves.

The *Mabinogion* is a collection of eleven early Welsh tales which did find their way into written form. Five of the tales, "Pwyll Lord of Dyfed," "Branwen Daughter of Llyr," "Manawydan Son of Llyr," "Math Son of Mathonwy" and "Lludd and Llevelys," are stories from Celtic pagan mythology. They recount the deeds of ancient gods and heroes. Another, "The Dream of Maxen," recalls the rule of Britannia in the late Fourth Century by

---

2 The Triads usually list the tales in groups of three, whence they derive their name of "Triads," but a few list a fourth tale as well, which often refers to Arthur or persons associated with him.

the Roman general Magnus Clemens Maximus. The remaining five tales, "How Culhwch Won Olwen," "The Dream of Rhonabwy," "Owein, or the Countess of the Fountain," "Peredur Son of Efrawg" and "Gereint and Enid," tell of Arthur and his warriors. The *Mabinogion* tales are valuable historical sources because they were composed and transmitted by the Welsh, who are direct descendants of the Britons of post-Roman Britannia. The composers of the *Mabinogion* tales preserved a genuine folk memory of the real Arthur.

The Anglo-Saxon Chronicle is another source based upon the folk memory of the participants in the events of Arthur's time, but in this instance the folk memory of Arthur's enemies, the Anglo-Saxons. The Anglo-Saxon Chronicle is a chronology of events in Britannia from the arrival of the Anglo-Saxons in the Fifth Century through, and in some manuscripts beyond, the Norman Conquest in the Eleventh Century. The early entries in the Chronicle, the entries for Arthur's time, were made in the Ninth Century based upon even older records. These older records were compiled by the Christian missionaries who first preached to the Anglo-Saxons of southwest Britannia around A.D. 634, just a few generations after Arthur; the missionaries obtained much of the material for their records from the heroic poems sung by their new converts in celebration of the early Anglo-Saxon leaders. Because of the antiquity of its early entries, the Anglo-Saxon Chronicle is a reliable source of information for the Fifth and Sixth Centuries in Britannia.

A very few documents survive directly from the post-Roman period. Among these documents are the laconic Latin chronicles of both Britannia and Gaul, particularly those later incorporated into the Welsh chronology called the *Annales Cambriae* (Annals of Wales). Perhaps the most important of these documents is *De Excidio Britanniae* (Concerning the Ruin of Britain), a caustic sermon written in the middle of the Sixth Century by the monk Gildas to berate several of Arthur's immediate successors for their political crimes. The information contained in these documents is very sparse, usually consisting of no more than a brief mention of then-current events, but they are invaluable guides to the interpretation of the oral tradition preserved in the other sources.

More detailed information is contained in the *Historia Brittonum* (History of the Britons), a collection of several Briton documents from the post-Roman period. These documents were assembled and translated from the Briton language into Latin by an obscure Welsh monk named Nennius in the early Ninth Century. The *Historia Brittonum* is poorly organized, being a literal hodgepodge of older material. It also suffers from the well-intentioned, but inept, efforts of later editors. As a result, its sequence of events is often difficult to follow. It also offers little that bears directly on Arthur, focusing instead on the period just before Arthur's rise to power. Despite its shortcomings, the *Historia Brittonum* is an extremely valuable source because it preserves in translated form contemporary records that would have otherwise been lost.

The *Historia Ecclesiastica Gentis Anglorum* (Ecclesiastical History of the English People) is an early Eighth Century history based upon both oral tradition and contemporary documents. The *Historia Ecclesiastica* was written by Venerable Bede, a learned and highly respected monk of the monastery of Jarrow by the River Tyne in north England.

Unfortunately, the *Historia Ecclesiastica* concentrates, as its title implies, upon religious matters in the Anglo-Saxon era which followed the post-Roman period. Its account of events before the late Sixth Century, when Saint Augustine landed in Britannia with the mission of converting the pagan Anglo-Saxons to Christianity, is therefore very brief. The *Historia Ecclesiastica* does not give an account of the life of Arthur, but it does provide meaningful insights into post-Roman and early Anglo-Saxon times.

Following in the tradition of the *Historia Ecclesiastica* is *De Gestis Regum Anglorum* (Concerning the Deeds of the Kings of the English), which was written by the monk William of Malmesbury in about 1125. William of Malmesbury, like Venerable Bede, drew upon both oral and written sources to produce a respected and scholarly history. Unfortunately, he also, like Bede, focuses upon the Anglo-Saxon era. *De Gestis Regum Anglorum* does, however, give a slightly more expansive account of the post-Roman period, and it even has a few important things to say about Arthur.

Yet another history based upon both oral tradition and contemporary documents is the *Historia Regum Britanniae* (History of the Kings of Britain), which was written in about 1136 by a Welsh scholar, Geoffrey of Monmouth. The *Historia Regum Britanniae* is, without a doubt, the single most important source of Arthurian history because it gives an extensive account of Arthur's life and times.

The *Historia Regum Britanniae* is not only the most important source of Arthurian history, it is also, sad to say, the most difficult source to use. Geoffrey of Monmouth, like Venerable Bede and William of Malmesbury, combined both oral and written sources in composing his history. The result is a clear and sensible account of post-Roman Britannia - clear and sensible, that is, to a mind shaped by the medieval experience. Being a creature of his age, and therefore lacking a full awareness of the very different circumstances in which Arthur lived, Geoffrey has misconstrued much of his material.

Despite the errors of Geoffrey's medieval misconceptions, we can find within the *Historia Regum Britanniae* a genuine history of Arthur and of post-Roman Britannia. To discover this genuine history, we must sift through the vast amount of information - and misinformation - contained in Geoffrey's *Historia Regum Britanniae* and distill from it the underlying historical reality: a formidable, but far from impossible, task.

We shall undertake precisely this task. Before we may do so, however, we must first examine the historical background against which Arthur emerged.

The history of the real King Arthur begins long before Arthur appears on the scene; it begins with the events that shaped Britannia in the late Roman period. It proceeds next through the government of Britannia by the native regimes which came to power after the departure of the Romans, first under the Briton leader known as Vortigern and then under the Roman leader named Ambrosius Aurelianus. Only at this point, when the historical context has been properly established, does it turn to Arthur himself. It finally touches upon the fate of Britannia after the death of Arthur, considering the effect of his reign upon those who came after him. The history of the real King Arthur is in essence the history of the entire post-Roman, pre-Anglo-Saxon period in Britannia.

When we have reconstructed the history of this post-Roman, pre-Anglo-Saxon period, we shall see that Arthur played a decisive role in shaping the modern nations of the British Isles. When we are done, we shall come to a full appreciation of Arthur's worthy place in authentic history.

## Population of the Late Roman Empire

| Entire Empire | |
|---|---|
| Third Century (peak) | 50,000,000 |
| Roman Europe | 25,000,000 |
| City of Rome | 1,250,000 |

| Senators | |
|---|---|
| Start of Empire (at Rome) | 600 |
| Late Empire (each half) | 2,000 |

## Size of the Late Roman Army

| Entire Army | 500,000 |
|---|---|
| Western Empire | 224,000 - 311,000 |
| In Britannia | 50,000 |
| Hadrian's Wall | 20,000 |
| Elite Mobile Troops | 94,000 - 123,800 |
| in Hispania | 10,000 |
| in Africa | 10,000 - 20,000 |
| in Gaul | 13,000 |
| in Britannia | 6,000 |

## Population of Roman Britannia

| Pre-Roman Period | 1,000,000 |
|---|---|
| Third Century (peak) | 4,000,000 |
| Fourth Century (early) | 3,000,000 |

| Fifth Century | |
|---|---|
| Romano-Britons | 2,000,000 |
| Rural | at least 1,500,000 |
| Urban | up to 200,000 |
| Industry | 50,000 |
| Villa farms | 25,000 |
| Beyond Hadrian's Wall | 500,000 |
| Anglo-Saxons | 50,000 - 100,000 |
| Britons in Armorica | 48,000 - 60,000 |

## Roman Army in Britannia

| Third Century | 63,000 |
|---|---|
| Fourth Century | 50,000 |
| Elite Mobile Troops | 6,000 |
| Hadrian's Wall Garrison | 20,000 |

# LIBER PRIMUS

# The Age of Roman Britannia

## - - Background - -

## A.D. 285 - A.D. 410

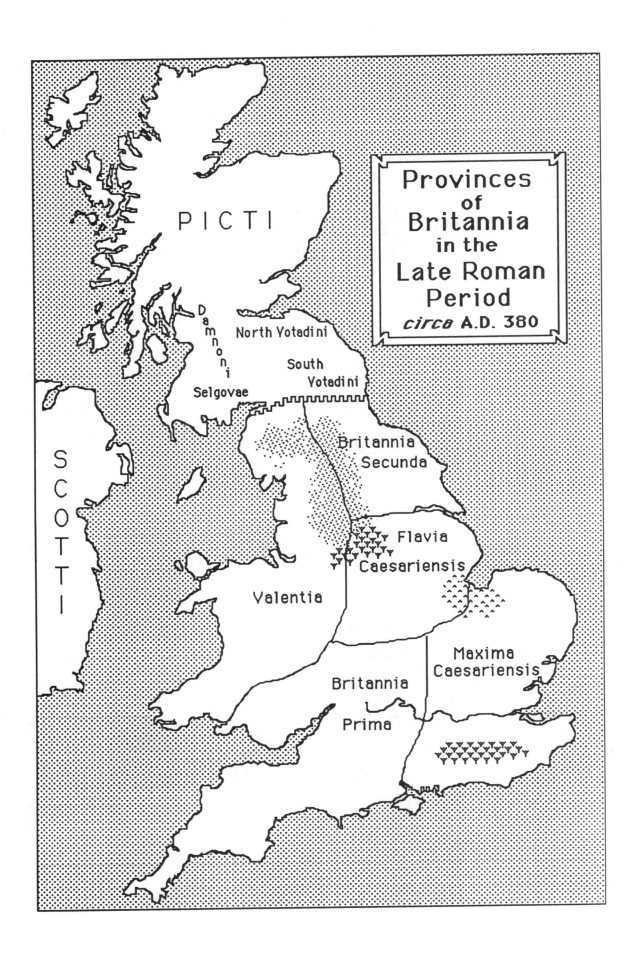

PICTI

SCOTTI

Damnoni

North Votadini

South
Votadini

Selgovae

Britannia
Secunda

Flavia
Caesariensis

Valentia

Maxima
Caesariensis

Britannia

Prima

Provinces
of
Britannia
in the
Late Roman
Period
*circa* A.D. 380

# Chapter One
## The Late Roman Period in Britannia

An account of the life of the real King Arthur must begin with a review of the last days of Roman rule in Britannia. It is against the dismal background of the decline of the Western Roman Empire that Arthur emerges and rises to power and glory. In order to understand Arthur's place in history, we shall consider the nature of Roman Imperial government and the reasons for its demise in Britannia.

Rome was not built in a day, nor did it fall in a day. Roman power did not collapse suddenly; it deteriorated gradually. Over more than two centuries, serious economic and social problems slowly and steadily sapped the vigor of the Empire. A shrinking population, the abandonment of arable land, a decline in trade, rampant inflation and disruptive class divisions all combined to undermine the commercial economy upon which the prosperity of the Empire depended.[3] Unscrupulous politicians, mentally unstable Emperors and ambitious generals aggravated the situation. Internal decay inevitably translated into military weakness. Barbarians from Germania, roughly modern Germany, Scandinavia and the low countries, took advantage of Rome's difficulties to press in upon the Empire, ultimately straining Imperial military resources to the breaking point.

When Germanic hordes began to raid and ravage the western provinces of the Empire, the Britons were still reasonably safe, and even relatively prosperous, in their island Diocese of Britannia. Roman Britannia did not altogether escape the calamities of the age, but it was touched lightly compared to most other parts of the Empire. In fact, the Emperors and generals of Rome looked to Britannia as a reliable and secure source of supplies and manpower for their campaigns in Gaul (roughly modern France) and on the German frontier.

The Britons were nevertheless alarmed by the deteriorating military situation, and they decided to fortify their towns. They erected stout stone walls about their towns; in many instances, they also installed ballista platforms.[4] By the end of the Third Century, all the large towns and many small towns in Britannia were provided with such defenses. Although the new fortifications would not have stymied a professional and well-equipped force, such as the Imperial Roman army, they were more than adequate protection against bandit gangs and barbarian warbands. Indeed,

---

3 The cause of the depopulation of the Empire is the subject of much controversy. It was probably due to the epidemic, most likely measles or smallpox, which the troops of Emperor Lucius Verus brought back with them in A.D. 166 from a campaign in the Near East. The peoples of the Mediterranean had not yet acquired any natural immunity to the new disease, and it repeatedly swept through the Empire. Some historians dispute this analysis, recognizing the decline in population, but blaming it instead upon other factors, such as moral decadence, social demoralization, soil exhaustion and even lead poisoning. The consequences of the depopulation are, however, beyond dispute. The enormous fiscal burden of defending and administering the Empire did not diminish as its population shrank, so this burden fell more heavily on fewer shoulders. A vicious cycle was thus initiated: the increased level of taxation further depressed the economy, leading to further population decline and compounding the problem for subsequent generations. The efforts of several Roman Emperors, notably Diocletian, to deal with the situation by legislating rigid price and occupational controls actually worsened matters by inhibiting the ability of the economy to adapt and grow.

4 The ballista was a stone- or javelin-throwing machine, sort of a giant crossbow.

Britannia's town walls continued to play an important military role long after the end of the Roman period and into the Middle Ages.[5] The Britons were no doubt grateful for their foresight as the Third Century progressed and a new threat to Britannia's security loomed on the southeast horizon: seaborne Anglo-Saxon raiders.

The Anglo-Saxons were barbarians from the northern part of Germania. This region is today northwest Germany, Holland, Denmark and south Sweden. The Anglo-Saxons represented several different Germanic tribes, including Angles, Saxons, Jutes, Franks, Frisians and Danes.

Some historians today do not like to use the term "Anglo-Saxon" because it implies an unjustified distinction and remoteness of these tribes from their English descendants. For our purposes, however, "Anglo-Saxon" is a perfectly valid way to refer to the various Germanic tribes which afflicted Britannia in the late Roman and post-Roman periods. Although these tribes shared a similar language and culture, and although they readily intermingled in Britannia, they did not yet truly achieve a nationhood which we would recognize as "English." We shall therefore continue to use the term "Anglo-Saxon" to refer generally to the north Germanic peoples who assailed Britannia in the declining days of the Western Roman Empire.

The Anglo-Saxons were adventurous seamen and fierce warriors. They were not unlike the better known Vikings who later came

from Scandinavia to plague the Anglo-Saxons' descendants in the Ninth Century. From the Germania coast, the Anglo-Saxons sailed across the North Sea (*Mare Germanicum* or "German Sea" in Latin) and English Channel (*Oceanus Britannicus* or "Britannic Channel" in Latin) to plunder the southern and eastern seaboard of Britannia.

Until then, the principal danger to Roman Britannia came from the uncivilized tribes living to the north of the Diocese in modern Scotland. These far northern barbarians could be, and usually were, effectively constrained by Hadrian's Wall and its associated forts. Hadrian's Wall was a massive ten foot thick, sixteen to eighteen foot high stone and brick rampart which ran seventy-two miles from the Solway Firth to the mouth of the Tyne River across the relatively narrow and defensible neck of north Britannia. This line of defense was supported by many forts constructed on, behind and even in advance of the Wall itself. Hadrian's Wall and its adjunct forts were a formidable barrier to barbarian raiding parties and even to full-scale armies of invasion. On those rare occasions when the Hadrian Wall defenses proved inadequate to contain the far northern tribes, three Imperial legions, each consisting of approximately 5,000 crack infantrymen, were stationed in Britannia in positions from which they could move up to counterattack and repel the barbarians.

The Irish, called *Scotti* (Scots) by the Romans, also sometimes attacked the Diocese, and they did so with increasing frequency and severity in the late Roman period. By the latter part of the Third Century, not even the rich farm lands of the Severn Estuary region were immune from Irish raiding parties. What started as mere plundering forays escalated into wholesale land

---

5 The repair and restoration of Roman town walls was an important part of Alfred the Great's military response to Viking invaders in the Ninth Century, and many medieval fortifications were built upon Roman foundations.

seizures during the Fourth Century. By the end of the Fourth Century, much of modern Wales, Devon and Cornwall had fallen to Gaelic invaders. Initially, however, Irish fury was hurled against the mostly rugged and economically unimportant west coast of Britannia, and a few well-placed forts on that coast were adequate to cope with the danger.

The new Germanic menace, in contrast, fell upon Britannia's open and undefended southern and eastern coasts. These coasts could not be as easily protected as the northern or western frontiers. In addition, the southern and eastern seaboard was the most heavily populated part of Britannia, where much of its agriculture and industry were concentrated. The Anglo-Saxons threatened the least defensible and most valuable part of the Diocese.

The Roman response to the Anglo-Saxon menace was to create a whole new military establishment in Britannia. This military establishment included a revamped Classis Britannica (Britannic Navy) to patrol the Diocese's coastal waters against Anglo-Saxon warships, as well as a dozen new seaside forts to house the sailors and vessels of the Classis Britannica. The Classis Britannica had been in existence since the First Century, but its size and role changed considerably in response to the Anglo-Saxon threat. Rather than consisting of a mere handful of ships to support the land armies in Gaul and Germania, the Classis was expanded to aggressively patrol the waters between Britannia and the Continent. Its new mission was to detect and intercept the marauders at sea. In order to carry out this new mission, the Classis was also provided with a number of new forts built at strategic locations in both Britannia and Gaul. The Roman response was a very practical, but a very costly, solution to the problem.

## The Revolt of Carausius

The first, or at least an early, commander of the revamped Classis Britannica was Mausaeus Carausius, a native of Roman Belgicum (modern Belgium). Carausius seems to have ably discharged his duties, but not for very long. In response to allegations of complicity with the Anglo-Saxon pirates, Carausius rebelled against the government of Rome. The allegations were probably untrue, but Carausius was unwilling to hazard his life upon the remote chance of justice at the Imperial court. He therefore declared himself Emperor, adding the Imperial names "Marcus Aurelius" to his own. After defeating the Roman Rhine fleet, which Emperor Maximian sent against him in A.D. 286, Carausius exercised independent rule over most of Britannia and north Gaul for some seven years from A.D. 287 to A.D. 293.

Carausius enjoyed considerable military support in Britannia. Legion II Augusta stationed at Isca Silurum (Caerleon) and Legion XX Valeria Victrix stationed at Castrum Deva (Chester) stood with him, as well as the important Hadrian's Wall garrisons posted near Luguvalium (Carlisle). Only Legion VI Victrix stationed at Eboracum (York), and probably the garrison troops on the eastern half of Hadrian's Wall, held aloof. In addition to two full legions and various garrison forces in Britannia, Carausius could count on the loyalty of all or part of six legions in north Gaul, including Legion XXX Ulpia Victrix in Belgicum.

Carausius did not rule his miniature Empire in peace, for the government at Rome was determined to overthrow him. The Imperial fleet sent against him in A.D. 286 was defeated, but Carausius's enemies were persistent. In A.D. 293, the Caesar, or junior Emperor,[6] Constantius Chlorus finally prevailed over Carausius in a battle fought near Bononia Morinorum (Boulogne) in north Gaul. After this setback, the admiral-turned-Emperor was murdered by Allectus, his own deputy in charge of finances. As Constantius Chlorus forcibly brought Carausius's Continental territories back within the Empire, Allectus presumed to rule what was left of Carausius's outlaw realm in Britannia.

Allectus did not enjoy the same strong military support that Carausius did. Geoffrey of Monmouth, author of the *Historia Regum Britanniae*, reports that a leader named Asclepiodotus led Briton troops against one of Allectus's officers named Livius Gallus. Geoffrey of Monmouth tells us that Asclepiodotus came from "Cornwall" and that he drew support for the opposition to Allectus from the north and west of Britannia.

What Geoffrey thought was Cornwall was actually a very different place known to the Romans as Civitas Cornoviorum (Civitas of the Cornovians).

The Civitas (plural, Civitates) was the fundamental unit of local government in the Roman Empire. "Civitas" is often translated as "Canton" and sometimes as "City-State," but a Civitas should be considered equivalent to a State within the United States. A Civitas had a great deal of autonomy in local affairs, but it was generally subordinate to the Imperial government, especially in matters of a military

nature. Most Civitates in Britannia were based upon pre-Roman Celtic tribal centers, although a few, usually bearing the more exalted title of Municipium (plural, Municipia) or Colonia (plural, Coloniae), were based upon towns founded by the Romans after Britannia's incorporation into the Empire. The political leader of a Civitas was called a Magistratus (plural, Magistrati).

Civitas Cornoviorum controlled an important and wealthy region in the west-central portion of modern England, roughly the shires of Shropshire, Stafford, Hereford and Worcester, as well adjacent parts of Powys and Clwyd in modern Wales. This region was the only "Cornwall" in Britannia in Allectus's time. Modern Cornwall was then part of Civitas Dumnoniorum (Civitas of the Dumnonians), also called Dumnonia, and it did not acquire its present name until much later, after it had been colonized by Cornovians from Civitas Cornoviorum. The chief town and capital of Civitas Cornoviorum was Viroconium (Wroxeter), not far from the headquarters of Carausius's loyal Legion XX Valeria Victrix at Castrum Deva (Chester).

Allectus's opponent Asclepiodotus was not really Magistratus of Civitas Cornoviorum, as Geoffrey implies, but a non-Briton Roman general who served under Constantius Chlorus. Geoffrey depicts the Roman Asclepiodotus as a native Briton (and the natives Allectus and Livius Gallus as foreign Romans), because he, like most medieval historians, thought Britannia had always been independent, or at least autonomous, of Rome. He therefore concluded that the victor in the conflict between Asclepiodotus and Livius Gallus must have been a Briton, and the vanquished a Roman.

---

6 Under the short-lived political reforms of Emperor Diocletian, the Empire was ruled by two senior Emperors, each called "Augustus," and by two subordinate junior Emperors, each called "Caesar."

Geoffrey's statement as to Asclepiodotus's background merely reflects a tradition that Civitas Cornoviorum and many of the soldiers and garrisons of north and west Britannia remained faithful to the slain Carausius and rallied to Constantius's general against Allectus.

Most likely, only the hitherto uncommitted Legion VI Victrix joined Allectus. Livius Gallus was probably the Legatus, or commander, of this Legion. Although Allectus also employed Anglo-Saxon mercenaries, his failure to attract wider support from the Roman army in the Diocese left him perilously short of troops. Allectus therefore did not stand a chance when Constantius Chlorus and Asclepiodotus followed up Constantius's victory over Carausius by invading Britannia in A.D. 296.

Constantius Chlorus and Asclepiodotus landed in different parts of south Britannia, where they separately engaged and defeated the forces of Allectus. According to Geoffrey, Livius Gallus assumed command of the rebel forces after the death of Allectus, but surrendered when the Imperial army appeared outside Londinium (London). Livius Gallus and many of his soldiers were then beheaded. The beheading of Livius Gallus and his soldiers may reflect the Roman practice of decimation, in which one man out of every ten in a disloyal legion was chosen by lot and executed as punishment for the crimes of the entire legion. The Classis Britannica, in order to prevent the rise of a new Carausius, was divided by the Imperial government into three smaller commands: Litus Saxonicum (the Saxon Shore) in southwest Britannia, Belgica Secunda (Second Belgian Province) in east Gaul and Tractus Armoricanus (Armorican Tract) in modern Brittany.

## The Family of Constantine the Great

The civil war between Constantius and Allectus caused the Romans to neglect the northern defenses of Britannia. The contestants diverted too many troops away from the frontier in order to do battle against each other in south Britannia, and the victors afterwards failed to restore the border garrisons to full strength. The far northern barbarians took advantage of the situation to loot the Diocese, and they carried destruction as far south as the undermanned legionary bases at Eboracum (York) and Castrum Deva (Chester).

The Diocesan military authorities were unable to reestablish control, and Constantius Chlorus, now a senior Emperor or Augustus, had to return to Britannia and campaign against the barbarians. The Romans called the far northern barbarians *Picti* (Picts). The name Pict comes from the Latin *pictus*, meaning "painted man," and is derived from the barbarians' practice of tattooing their bodies. The Picts seem to have called themselves Cruithni.

The Picts were a very ancient race of uncertain origin, probably pre-Celtic.[7] They lived in the northern half of modern Scotland, beyond the line of the Firth of Clyde and the Firth of Forth. The Romans had earlier built an earthen defensive wall, called the Antonine Wall, along this line in order to separate the Picts from the Britons, but they had long since

---

7 More recent immigrants came from Scandinavia to the northernmost parts of Pictish territory, where they built the stone forts known as brochs. This immigration lies behind Nennius's and Bede's mistaken belief that the Picts came to Britannia after, rather than before, the Britons. These later immigrants are probably the red-headed Caledonians described by the late First Century Roman historian Tacitus.

abandoned this wall. The largest tribal grouping of Picts was the Caledones (Caledonians), in remembrance of whom the modern Scottish Caledonian Airlines took its name. Of particular interest to us, and no doubt to Fourth Century Britons, is the fact that the Picts were skilled warriors. They might have even been responsible for the annihilation of Legion IX Hispania in about A.D. 119 or A.D. 130.[8]

The Pictish armies were formidable, but they were not equal to the challenge of Constantius Chlorus. The Roman Emperor won a great victory over the barbarians, decisively defeating them in A.D. 306. Quiet soon returned to the Diocese's northern frontier. Thanks to Constantius Chlorus, Britannia was able to recover from civil war and Pictish invasion, and the Diocese regained prosperity in the early years of the Fourth Century.

To say that Britannia prospered is not quite the same thing as saying that the Britons enjoyed a high standard of living. The heavy expense of the additional measures taken for the Diocese's security, as well as the burgeoning cost of defending the less fortunate parts of the Empire, consumed a great deal of Britannia's resources. The erection of fortifications, the establishment of three separate naval commands, the expansion of the army, and the related growth in the Imperial bureaucracy,[9]

all led to the imposition of a crushing weight of taxation upon a declining population and shrinking agricultural base.

The situation in Britannia was not nearly as bad as it was in Gaul. During the Third Century, large parts of Gaul had been overrun by barbarians from Germania, and many towns had to be retaken by the Imperial army. The severe devastation, coupled with the increased fiscal burden of defending the Empire, overwhelmed many Gallic farmers. Large numbers of rural people turned in desperation to a life of outlawry. Impoverished peasants, refugees from war-torn areas, army deserters and other displaced persons formed bandit gangs called bacaudae. The bacaudae even rose in armed rebellion against the Roman authorities in A.D. 284-285. The bloody tax revolt in Gaul was eventually put down, but the bacaudae rebel bands themselves were never completely suppressed.

Constantius Chlorus meanwhile died at Eboracum. His army immediately proclaimed his son Constantine as Emperor. Constantine's assumption of power was blatantly illegal under the rules of Imperial succession established by Emperor Diocletian, but the army was not to be denied. Significantly, a cohort (500 man battalion) of German warriors from the Alamanni tribe under their King Crocus led the acclamation for the new Emperor; it seems that whatever arrangements the Romans might make for their own governance were already subject to barbarian interference. Civil war followed Constantine's irregular assumption of power, but Constantine, thanks in large part to his barbarian mercenaries, was victorious. Constantine soon won grudging recognition of his illegally-assumed Imperial status, and he

---

8 Many historians today deny the Picts this victory, believing the Legion to have been simply transferred out of Britannia around the time of its alleged disappearance, only to be later destroyed in a war against Parthia in about A.D. 161.

9 The Imperial bureaucracy, although inefficient and wasteful, was necessary to handle the administrative requirements of the Roman military forces, including the collection of taxes and the procurement of supplies. These administrative requirements increased as the size and responsibilities of the military forces grew.

later eliminated all his Imperial colleagues in order to make himself sole Emperor by A.D. 324.

Constantine's rule was generally peaceful and prosperous, on account of which he has been accorded the title of "the Great." He also strengthened the social fabric of the Empire when he ended the persecution of the Christians; he even became a Christian himself. In seizing the Emperorship at the point of a sword, however, Constantine revived a dangerous precedent. Civil war sporadically broke out after Constantine's death, as various military commanders imitated his example and violently strove for the Imperial throne.

A leading military contender for Emperor in the Western Empire was Comes (Count)[10] Magnentius. Magnentius enjoyed the support of a large segment of the Romano-Briton aristocracy; he might have even been of Briton descent himself. He inaugurated his Imperial reign in A.D. 350 by murdering Emperor Constans, a son of Constantine the Great. He then proceeded to seize and independently govern most of the Western Empire. By A.D. 353, however, Emperor Constantius II, another son of Constantine, had prevailed over Magnentius and regained control of the break-away domain. The Britons then suffered grievously for their poor judgement in having backed an unsuccessful Imperial claimant.

After defeating Magnentius, the victorious Emperor Constantius II initiated savage reprisals against the rebel's supporters in Britannia. Constantius's agents employed torture, execution and property confiscation to punish those unfortunate enough to have supported (or merely to be accused of having supported) the would-be Briton Emperor. The spiteful inquisition claimed many important victims in Britannia, including the Vicarius (Diocesan Governor); the Vicarius, an admirable individual named Martinus, was forced to take his own life when his efforts to protect the unjustly accused were frustrated. Another important victim (although he was not in Britannia at the time) was the retired Comes Gratianus, father of the future Emperor Valentinian I. Many Briton landowners lost their lives, and many more their estates. Constantius II in his vengeance devastated the Romano-Briton ruling class and demoralized its survivors.

Geoffrey of Monmouth does not mention either Magnentius or Constantius II in his *Historia Regum Britanniae*, but he does describe a conflict in Britannia between their partisans. The central figure in this conflict was a certain Octavius, whom Geoffrey identifies as "Duke of the Gewissei."

Octavius was actually Magistratus of Civitas Silurum (Civitas of the Silures), a Civitas encompassing modern Gwent and Glamorgan. The medieval title Duke which Geoffrey awards Octavius comes from the Latin word *dux*. *Dux* was a high Roman military rank, rating just below Comes, and it gave rise to the medieval title of Duke,[11] but it was also an ordinary word meaning "leader." "Gewissei" was a Briton word meaning "men of Gwent." Gwent was (and still is) the name of the region about the Roman town of Venta Silurum, now called Caerwent. In Roman times, Venta Silurum was the chief town and capital of Civitas Silurum.

---

10 "Comes" (pronounced "co-mays") was a high military rank in the late Roman Empire, second only to the top rank of Magister Militum (Master of Soldiers). The medieval title Count was derived from "Comes."

11 In the medieval scheme, however, the priority of the titles was reversed and a Duke was considered superior to a Count.

The literal meaning of Octavius's title "Duke of the Gewissei" is thus "leader of the Gwentmen," which makes Octavius the Magistratus of Civitas Silurum in the Roman political system.

Octavius took advantage of the conflict between Magnentius and Constantius II to rise to prominence in Britannia. Octavius first burst into Diocesan politics with his revolt against "a certain Proconsul." "Proconsul" was an ancient Roman honorific that was sometimes applied to provincial governors and military commanders; in this instance, it probably refers to the governor of Maxima Caesariensis in southeast Britannia (or possibly of Valentia in west Britannia), who bore the title of Consularis. The unnamed Proconsul was killed in Octavius's revolt. Octavius then engaged in a contest of see-sawing fortunes against a rival leader called Trahern. Trahern is associated with the town of "Kaerperis," which is the Welsh name for Portus Adurni or modern Portchester, one of the Litus Saxonicum (Saxon Shore) forts. Trahern himself might have been Comes Litoris Saxonici (Count of the Saxon Shore). Trahern at one point managed to drive Octavius out of Britannia, apparently to a refuge north of Hadrian's Wall, but Octavius was later able to return in triumph after Trahern had been murdered. The murderer was "the Comes of a fortified Municipium" who was allied to Octavius. Geoffrey's account of the strife-filled career of Octavius reflects the political turmoil in Britannia that accompanied the greater struggle between Magnentius and Constantius II. Octavius was an early supporter of Constantius, or at least an opponent of Magnentius.

Geoffrey actually presents the Roman-named Octavius as leader of a native Briton faction and the Celtic-named Trahern as a foreign Roman leader. He even grants Octavius the title of "king" and places Trahern at the head of a Roman army of invasion. Geoffrey has thus turned a strictly local Briton rivalry into an international conflict. Geoffrey erred because he believed Britannia to have been an independent nation in Octavius's day. Since Octavius ultimately prevailed in the contest, Geoffrey has reasonably, but erroneously, concluded that Octavius must have been a Briton ruler and Trahern a Roman invader. In fact, Octavius and his rival were both Briton leaders, probably of mixed Celtic and Roman blood, who were active in the Diocese of Britannia.

Intense internal conflicts of this sort, especially when followed by vicious reprisals, destroyed the vitality and social cohesiveness of the Diocese. The suffering of the Britons was not yet over, however, because political repression soon led to military disaster.

## The Barbarica Conspiratio

Gaul suffered greatly during the civil war between the Emperors Magnentius and Constantius, but Britannia suffered even more in the peace which followed. When the armies of Constantius and Magnentius neglected their duties in order to fight each other, the German barbarians took the opportunity to plunder Gaul. When the civil war was over, Britannia was the victim of an even greater devastation at the hands of the victor. Until then, Britannia had always been able to rebound from adversity; the Diocese even managed, despite its own difficulties, to furnish supplies for Imperial troops on campaign in Gaul and to provide materials and artisans for the reconstruction of the Continental Diocese.[12] It would soon cease to do so. The stubborn resiliency of the Britons, which had repeatedly withstood the barbarians' savagery, was finally shattered by a Roman Emperor's brutality.

The Picts sensed the opportunity, and in A.D. 360 and again in A.D. 364, they conducted raids into Britannia. In response to the first raid, Caesar Julian, a nephew of Constantine the Great, dispatched a small army to the relief of the beleaguered Britons. The elevation of the militarily-able Julian to the status of Augustus later the same year boded well for the Empire,[13] but his premature death in A.D. 363 in battle against the Persians soon left the Empire virtually leaderless. As a result, there was probably no meaningful response to the second Pictish incursion in A.D. 364. Encouraged, the barbarians grew bolder in their ambitions. In A.D. 367, the Picts were joined by the Irish and the Anglo-Saxons in launching the most devastating attack which Britannia had to endure since it became part of the Roman Empire.

The great Pictish, Irish and Anglo-Saxon assault of A.D. 367 goes by the colorful name of Barbarica Conspiratio (the Barbarian Conspiracy). And conspiracy it certainly was - at least in the sense that the Picts, the Irish and the Anglo-Saxons deliberately colluded in making simultaneous attacks upon the hapless Diocese. With the Irish assailing Britannia from the west and the Anglo-Saxons attacking from the southeast, the military resources of Britannia were overburdened and the Picts were able to strike deep into the Diocese from the north.

The Barbarica Conspiratio caught the Roman military authorities completely by surprise. The military patrols and outpost garrisons who were supposed to keep watch on barbarian developments failed to warn of the massing of the Picts or the advance of the Irish and the Anglo-Saxons. The troops might have been bribed, or they might have simply been lax in the performance of their mission; either way, the disaster of A.D. 367 was the direct result of indifference to duty, a consequence of Emperor Constantius's demoralization of the Romano-Briton military and civil leadership.[14]

The barbarians quickly destroyed the Roman forces in Britannia. They ambushed and defeated the Dux Britanniarum (Duke of the Britains[15]), who commanded Legion VI Victrix based at Eboracum (York) and the garrisons of Hadrian's Wall in north Britannia. They also fought and killed the Comes Maritimi Tracti (Count of the Maritime Tract), who commanded the Saxon Shore fleet and forts in

---

12   Gaul was actually divided into two Dioceses: Galliae ("the Gauls"; roughly modern north France and Belgium) and Septem Provinciae ("the Seven Provinces"; roughly modern south and central France). For convenience, we shall nevertheless refer to Gaul as a single Diocese.

13   But not for the Church because this nephew of Constantine, the first Christian Emperor, was himself a pagan. Julian actively fostered a pagan revival during his reign, and as a result he was called "the Apostate." In Britannia at about this time, a large temple to the ancient Celtic god Nodens was erected at Lydney on the River Severn in Gwent - perhaps representing Octavius's attempt to curry favor with the new Emperor.

14   According to the Roman historian Ammianus Marcellinus, the current Emperor Valentinian was partly to blame because he failed to enforce discipline among the army commanders in Britannia. This neglect meant that the harm done by Emperor Constantius II was not repaired, but allowed to fester for almost fifteen years.

15   The Diocese of Britannia contained five provinces, hence there were five "Britains."

southeast Britannia.[16]  The Pictish, Irish and Anglo-Saxon warbands then scattered throughout the Diocese, plundering it at will.[17] The new western Emperor, a former army officer named Valentinian who had served under Emperor Julian in Gaul and Persia, found it necessary to dispatch his best general, Comes Theodosius, and four elite army units to Britannia.

Comes Theodosius implemented several important measures which had a lasting impact upon Britannia.  He first drove out the barbarians in a series of military campaigns in A.D. 368 and A.D. 369.  He then reorganized the Diocesan defenses by appointing a new Dux Britanniarum, abolishing the failed frontier outpost system, establishing signal stations on the modern North Yorkshire coast to give advance warning of seaborne raiders, and rebuilding damaged forts all over the island.  He also recovered a province in Britannia which had been considered irrevocably lost and which he renamed Valentia in honor of his Emperor. The exact location of this province is unknown, but it probably extended along the west coast of Britannia, running from Hadrian's Wall through modern Cumbria, Lancashire, Merseyside, Manchester and Cheshire into Wales; most likely Civitas Silurum (Gwent and Glamorgan) was the only part of modern Wales that lay outside the Province of Valentia.  The most important measure taken by Comes Theodosius,

or at least the one which had the greatest impact upon Britannia, was his appointment of the soldier Magnus Clemens Maximus to assume military command of the Diocese.

## Armies in Late Roman Empire

### Roman Armies

| | |
|---|---|
| Typical Late Roman Field Army | 15,000 |
| Comes Britanniarum Command | 6,000 |
| Caesar Julian, A.D. 357 in Gaul | 13,000-23,000 |
| Emperor Julian, A.D. 362 in Persia | 65,000 |
| Comes Theodosius, A.D. 368 arrival in Britannia | 4,000 |
| Magister Militum Stilicho, A.D. 405 in Italy | 20,000-30,000 |
| Riothamus of Armorica, A.D. 470 versus Visigoths | 12,000 |

### Barbarian Armies

| | |
|---|---|
| Germans (Alamanni), A.D. 357 versus Caesar Julian | 30,000 - 35,000 |
| Visigoths, A.D. 409-410 | 20,000 |
| plus, Runaway Slaves | 20,000 |
| Vandals, A.D. 428 | 15,000 - 25,000 |
| Huns, Horse Warriors | 15,000 |

---

16  "Comes Maritimi Tracti" is probably another form of the more famous title "Comes Litoris Saxonici" (Count of the Saxon Shore), although it could have been held by the officer of an otherwise unknown naval command along Britannia's west coast. If the former, the slain Comes was one of Trahern's successors in the post.

17  Some historians believe that the Anglo-Saxons did not actually land in Britannia, but instead attacked the north coast of Gaul in order to prevent Roman reinforcements from crossing the English Channel.

## Chapter Two
## Magnus Clemens Maximus
## and Flavius Stilicho

Magnus Clemens Maximus was an officer in the expeditionary force which Comes Theodosius led to Britannia in A.D. 368. Maximus originally came from the Diocese of Hispania (modern Spain and Portugal), where his family was presumably of noble Roman lineage. Geoffrey of Monmouth claims that Maximus, whom he calls "Maximianus," was a Roman Senator. Considering the high military status which he held under Comes Theodosius, Maximus must have indeed been a member of the aristocratic Senatorial Class.

Maximus apparently served with talent and distinction in the war against the barbarians because Comes Theodosius appointed Maximus to the post of Comes Britanniarum (Count of the Britains) before he returned to the Continent in A.D. 369. As Comes Britanniarum, Maximus commanded the elite, mobile field army stationed in the Diocese. He also out-ranked the Dux Britanniarum, who commanded the garrison soldiers of Hadrian's Wall, and the Comes Litoris Saxonici, who commanded the Saxon Shore defenses.[18] This post made Maximus one of the most important military leaders in the Empire, and the single most powerful man in Britannia. Comes Maximus commanded the army in Britannia for almost twenty years, and his influence upon the subsequent history of the Diocese - and of the Empire - was enormous.

### Magnus Clemens Maximus, Comes Britanniarum

One of the most far-reaching policies implemented by Comes Maximus was the installation of pro-Roman rulers over the semi-barbarian Briton tribes of far north Britannia. These tribes resided just outside the Roman Diocese in the region between Hadrian's Wall and the highland territory of the Picts, in what is today Northumberland and south Scotland. This region had been part of the Empire during the brief period when the Roman military border was the long abandoned Antonine Wall running from the Firth of Clyde to the Firth of Forth. Maximus intended to dominate the far northern tribes so he could use them as a buffer between his Diocese and the hostile Picts.

Maximus implemented his policy by giving each of the far northern tribes a loyal Roman army officer for a king.[19] He placed Quintilius Clemens, a Roman of Mediterranean origin, over the Damnonii of the Clyde River valley; he placed Paternus, son of Tacitus from Civitas Cantiacorum (Kent), over the south Votadini of Bernicia (Northumberland); he placed Catellus Decianus over the north Votadini of Lodonesia (Lothian); and he placed Antonius Donatus over the Selgovae in modern Dumfries and Galloway. Comes Theodosius might have actually selected these army officers to become far northern kings, but it was Maximus who

---

18 Comes Theodosius probably first created the post of Comes Britanniarum for Maximus. Some historians, however, believe that this post was not created until later, and that Maximus was actually Dux Britanniarum. In such case, Maximus would have commanded the Hadrian's Wall garrisons as well as the mobile troops in the Diocese, making him in effect both Dux and Comes. The rapidity with which Maximus later crossed the English Channel with his troops indicates that he also controlled the ships of the Comes Litoris Saxonici.

---

19 Although in official Roman records, the new kings were not accorded the title of Rex (King), but Praefectus Gentium (Tribal Prefect).

placed them on their new thrones and who made them secure on these thrones. Maximus's readiness to lead his army to the aid of the Roman-sponsored kings formed the basis of their power over their semi-barbarian subjects. The new monarchs immediately undertook to establish local power bases of their own, and they ultimately founded self-sufficient ruling dynasties in the far north. They were originally dependent upon their Roman patron, however, and they remained eternally grateful to him. Because of his critical role in establishing the new royal dynasties, Maximus has been accorded enduring fame and glory in Welsh legend and has even been given a place of honor in Briton royal genealogies.

A Roman military expedition in support of one of the new far northern kings lies behind the account which Geoffrey of Monmouth gives of a war between Maximus and an individual with the very Celtic name of Conanus Meridiadocus. According to Geoffrey, Conanus twice led an army from the far north of Britannia against Maximus, but Maximus defeated him each time.[20] After being thwarted in both his military attacks, Conanus agreed to make peace with Maximus. The Conanus Meridiadocus of the *Historia Regum Britanniae* was obviously a far northern Briton leader who initially opposed Maximus and his client kings, but who was finally forced to submit to the Comes Britanniarum.

With reliable army officers in command of the native realms on his northern frontier, Maximus was able to disband the garrisons of

---

20 Geoffrey actually credits Conanus with victory in the second encounter, but this assertion is an over-generous interpretation of the outcome since Geoffrey also admits that Conanus submitted to Maximus immediately after the fight - hardly the act of a victor.

Hadrian's Wall. In most cases, he did not relieve the garrison soldiers of all military duties, but required them to serve in their former posts on a part-time basis. The discharged troopers were settled on vacant agricultural land in the vicinity of the Wall, and they were allowed to keep this land only so long as they continued to render limited military service. Upon a soldier's death, the land automatically passed to his son if his son agreed to assume the same military obligations. Maximus in essence converted the garrisons of Hadrian's Wall into a territorial militia, whose soldiers were full-time farmers and only part-time warriors, not unlike the modern National Guard.

Maximus's reorganization of the Hadrian's Wall defenses was an astute economy move. The new militiamen to whom Maximus entrusted the defense of Britannia were a much smaller burden on the Briton economy than the professional soldiers whom they replaced. Unlike their full-time predecessors, whose upkeep was an enormous drain upon Diocesan resources, the militiamen were expected - and able - to provide for most of their own needs through their own agricultural activities. Maximus's new arrangement brought valuable agricultural land back into production and created a self-perpetuating class of self-supporting soldiers.

Militia troops of this type had only a limited military utility, however. Because they had to devote much of their time to tending their farms, the militiamen were necessarily less well trained than their regular counterparts. They were also inherently immobile, being tied to a specific parcel of land and reluctant to abandon their families there in times of trouble. They therefore could not be redeployed to other areas of special danger, nor were they available for aggressive counter-measures; considering their reduced level of training, they probably would not have been very effective if led to battle outside their Hadrian's Wall forts in any case. Part-time soldiers were nonetheless adequate to defend the Diocese's important frontier fortifications so long as they were not unduly pressed. The use of low-cost but ill-trained and immobile militia troops to garrison Hadrian's Wall was possible only because the military threat to the Wall had been reduced by Maximus's establishment of friendly regimes over the adjacent Briton tribes.

Maximus also established friendly barbarian regimes in west Britannia. Unlike his policy in the far north, where he constructed a buffer zone of client kingdoms by installing new, Roman dynasties over existing native tribes, Maximus constructed his western buffer zone by founding entirely new barbarian realms within the boundaries of the Roman Diocese. Maximus gave vast tracts of territory in modern Wales, Devon and Cornwall to barbarian warrior immigrants from Ireland.

The Welsh recall Maximus's policy in the *Mabinogion* tale "The Dream of Maxen." The Welsh report that "Maxen" (i.e., Maximus) "fortified" Segontium Deceanglorum (Caernarvon) in north Wales and Moridunum Demetarum (Carmarthen) in southwest Wales. Segontium and Moridunum were the chief towns in the areas turned over to Irish warlords, and their "fortification" refers to their receipt of a barbarian garrison. Maximus's policy is also reflected in the *Notitia Dignitatum*, an Imperial table of organization prepared toward the end of the Fourth Century (and last updated in the late A.D. 420's), which conspicuously omits any mention of the Roman army forts in modern Wales that are known to have been occupied prior to Maximus's time.

Maximus no doubt considered the loss of the western territories a small price to pay for Britannia's security. Although the Welsh, Devonian and Cornish districts given over to the Irish barbarians were officially Roman, they were not highly valued by the Empire. Except for Civitas Silurum, which was situated in southeast Wales and which Maximus retained under Roman control, Wales, Devon and Cornwall were not as thoroughly Romanized, nor as economically important, as the English lowlands. They were also subject to attack by Irish raiders and were already being infiltrated by Irish colonists, so Roman control was tenuous at best. In addition, north, central and southwest Wales were probably part of the Province of Valentia recently reconquered by Comes Theodosius, so Roman authority there was particularly weak. Maximus must have regarded the cession of Welsh, Devonian and Cornish territory to the Irish a matter of small significance.

Maximus then expanded his influence from the military to the political sphere by marrying into a prominent Briton family. Welsh tradition insists that Maximus took a Briton wife; the *Mabinogion* tale "The Dream of Maxen" calls her Helena, which was a common Roman woman's name in Maximus's day. Geoffrey of Monmouth tells us that she was the daughter and heiress of Octavius, the political leader from Civitas Silurum or Gwent. "The Dream of Maxen" also identifies Maximus's wife as the daughter of Octavius (whom it calls Eudav, the Welsh form of "Octavius"), but it places her home at Segontium rather than in Gwent - a change of locale inspired by the impressive ruins found by Welsh storytellers in the former Roman town (since destroyed for materials when the English King Edward I built his great castle of Caernarvon).[21] By this marriage, Maximus gained a considerable personal fortune and a valuable local connection. As a supporter of Emperor Constantius II, Octavius must have benefited from the Emperor's persecution of the supporters of Magnentius by amassing enormous wealth and power at the expense of his less astute (or merely less fortunate) fellow Britons. Maximus's marital association with Octavius's family allowed him to exercise a great deal of influence in Briton political affairs.

Maximus also made a significant alliance with the leaders of the important Civitas Cornoviorum. According to Geoffrey, a certain Caradocus and his son Mauricius supported Maximus against Conanus Meridiadocus. Geoffrey describes Caradocus as "Duke of Cornwall," which means he was the *dux* (leader) or Magistratus of Civitas Cornoviorum. Later, another "Duke of Cornwall" named Dionotus was entrusted with the government of the Diocese when Maximus was in Gaul; Dionotus perhaps succeeded Maximus as Comes Britanniarum. From Geoffrey's statements, we must conclude that Maximus established a solid relationship with the aristocracy of Civitas Cornoviorum.

Maximus's political affiliations not only enhanced his personal power in Britannia, they complemented his military policies in the western part of the Diocese. Civitas Silurum and Civitas Cornoviorum were strategically vital because they bordered on the new Irish kingdoms in Wales; after the establishment of barbarian realms in west Britannia, Civitas Silurum and Civitas Cornoviorum became, in effect, an internal frontier for the Diocese. The Civitates also possessed substantial military assets: Civitas Silurum was home to the soldiers of Legion II Augusta, which was based at Isca Silurum (Caerleon), and Civitas Cornoviorum was the recruiting ground for the elite Roman army unit called Cohors Cornoviorum (Battalion of the Cornovians).[22] Political authority over Civitas Silurum and Civitas Cornoviorum was crucial to Maximus because it allowed him to organize their soldierly inhabitants into a second line of defense for west Britannia.[23]

By A.D. 383, Maximus had made Britannia secure, both militarily for the Empire and politically for himself. Maximus's defensive arrangements preserved the Diocese from barbarian assault, and his personal alliances placed the Diocese solidly under his control. Britannia's safety and Maximus's power were based upon the joining of a major military command to a Gwentian-Cornovian political axis, a combination which would again prove to be a potent force in the Diocese.

---

21 "The Dream of Maxen" goes on to identify Conanus Meridiadocus as Helena's brother, whereas Geoffrey makes Conanus her cousin. Although these asserted relationships could be literary inventions based on the assumption that all powerful persons in Britannia had to be kin to one another, Geoffrey is probably correct because Octavius must have had friends or relatives in far north Britannia since he had been able to find refuge there when he fled Trahern.

22 Cohors Cornoviorum was originally stationed at the Hadrian's Wall fort of Pons Aelius (Newcastle-upon-Tyne), but its warriors no doubt returned home to Civitas Cornoviorum when Maximus disbanded the Hadrian's Wall garrisons.

23 Thus, "The Dream of Maxen" reports that Isca Silurum in Gwent was the third town "fortified" (i.e., garrisoned - in this case with Roman troops) by Maximus.

## Magnus Clemens Maximus, Imperator

Maximus was not content to rule only the Diocese of Britannia. Buoyed by a great victory over the Picts in A.D. 381 or A.D. 382,[24] which apparently vindicated his northern policy of relying upon client kings and inexpensive Hadrian's Wall militia, he decided to seek greater dominion. In A.D. 383, at the urging of his troops, Maximus declared himself Emperor.[25] He immediately crossed over to the Continent and seized control of the Dioceses of Gaul and Hispania. For the next half decade, Maximus governed his own small Empire consisting of the three western Dioceses of Britannia, Gaul and Hispania.

Maximus was assisted in his conquest of Gaul by Conanus Meridiadocus, his former enemy from far north Britannia. Roman generals often recruited defeated barbarians into their armies, and Maximus likewise thought to convert the defeated Conanus into an ally. Conanus and his followers were a menace to Maximus when they were free in far north Britannia, but they could be - and were - put to good use when turned against the Emperor's enemies on the Continent.

Conanus Meridiadocus served Maximus well in Gaul. According to Geoffrey of Monmouth, Maximus and Conanus together defeated a "Duke Himbaldus" who ruled Armorica (Brittany). Judging from his title and domain, Himbaldus was Dux Tracti Armoricani (Duke of the Armorican Tract). Judging from his name, Himbaldus was a German mercenary general in Roman service. In reward for his support, Maximus granted Conanus the rule of Armorica.

Although we have only Geoffrey's account of Conanus's early career, we do know from other sources that many veterans of Maximus's army did indeed settle in Armorica and that a "Cynan Meriadauc" was indeed a leader of the Briton community in Armorica. Briton refugees fleeing the Anglo-Saxon invasion of Britannia later joined the descendants of Maximus's soldiers in Armorica. Maximus's soldiers and the later immigrants ultimately transformed the Roman district of Armorica into "Britannia Minor" or "Brittany," which means "Lesser Britannia."[26]

Before Conanus Meridiadocus and his followers were comfortably settled in their new Armorican homes, Maximus again succumbed to the siren call of ambition. In A.D. 387, he invaded Italy. Italy was then ruled by Emperor Valentinian II, son of the same-named Emperor who had earlier ordered Maximus's former commander, Comes Theodosius, to Britannia. Valentinian II did not feel up to the challenge mounted by the successful Briton soldier-turned-Emperor, so he sought aid from his eastern colleague. Ironically, the eastern Emperor at the time was Theodosius, son of Comes Theodosius and a companion of Maximus's from their days together in Britannia in A.D. 368-369. The eastern Emperor Theodosius fought, defeated and slew his one-time comrade Maximus in the Battle of Aquileia

---

24 Maximus's opponents were probably Pictish leaders named Wanius and Melga. Geoffrey of Monmouth identifies these men as Maximus's barbarian enemies, although he makes Wanius king of the Huns and gives Melga sole rule of the Picts.

25 Geoffrey tells us this event occurred five years after Maximus's defeat of Conanus Meridiadocus, which dates the conclusion of the earlier conflict to A.D. 378.

26 Interestingly, the name "Conan" remained popular among the Bretons for many centuries, right down to William the Conqueror's time, when a Count Conan of Brittany fought against William in a campaign memorialized on the Bayeux Tapestry.

in A.D. 388.

The civil war between Maximus and Theodosius was not good for the Empire. In order to fight each other, the rival Emperors stripped the Imperial frontiers of troops, leaving the border provinces at the mercy of the Germans. The barbarians did not hesitate to exploit the opportunity. The Franks, a particularly fierce German tribe, took advantage of the Roman civil war to plunder Colonia Agrippina (Cologne) and expand their territory into the lower Rhine region.

Britannia, on the other hand, remained robust. As Comes Britanniarum and then Emperor, Maximus had governed Britannia well. Maximus's military measures kept the Diocese safe from its barbarian enemies, and the Britons were able to rebuild their economy after the devastation of the Barbarica Conspiratio. An eloquent testimonial to the wisdom of Maximus's policies in Britannia, and a partial explanation of his enduring fame in the island, is the fact that the Diocese remained stable and affluent as it entered the last decade of the Fourth Century, notwithstanding the departure and defeat of its Emperor.

Maximus's arrangements in Britannia were successful, but they were not a permanent solution to Britannia's problems. By A.D. 398, the Picts had recovered from the severe defeats inflicted upon them by Maximus, and they again attacked Britannia. Opportunistic Anglo-Saxon raiders also returned to plague the Diocese. It was probably at this time that the Yorkshire coast signal stations at Huntcliff and Goldsborough were destroyed and their garrisons slain. Emperor Honorius, son of the Emperor Theodosius who had defeated Maximus, found it necessary to dispatch the great Roman general Flavius Stilicho on a third, and final, military rescue of Britannia in A.D. 399.[27]

## Flavius Stilicho, Magister Militum

Britannia's rescuer, Flavius Stilicho, was half Vandal by birth, but wholly Roman by allegiance. He had served in a variety of military positions under Emperor Theodosius and he quickly rose to prominence in Imperial circles. He even became the tutor and guardian of Honorius, whom Theodosius had designated heir to the western Emperorship. At the time of his expedition to Britannia, Stilicho held the highest military rank of Magister Militum, but he was much more than just Honorius's chief army commander. Stilicho was the real power behind the Emperor's throne and, for all practical purposes, the true ruler of the Western Empire.

Stilicho defeated the Picts and restored peace to the Diocese by A.D. 400 - but only a short-lived peace. After freeing Britannia from its tormentors, Stilicho advised the Britons to tend to their town fortifications. The Britons would have been wise to have heeded Stilicho's counsel, because in A.D. 402 the Magister

27 The first "rescue" was sent by Caesar Julian in A.D. 360, and the second was led by Comes Theodosius in A.D. 368. Some historians refuse to count Julian's expedition on the grounds that the troops were recalled for Julian's rebellion against Emperor Constantius II before they could have accomplished very much. Because Nennius in chapter 90 of his *Historia Brittonum* refers to exactly three Roman "rescues" of Britannia, they believe the third "rescue" to have been a short campaign conducted by Constantius, another general of Emperor Honorius, sometime between A.D. 417 and A.D. 424. If Constantius did indeed conduct such a campaign, it had small lasting impact upon the Diocese.

Militum withdrew many troops from the Diocese. He even called away the soldiers of Legion XX Valeria Victrix, whose departure left their legionary base of Castrum Deva (Chester) virtually deserted. On balance, Stilicho did more harm than good to Britannia, because, despite his victory over the barbarians, he placed the Diocese in an extremely precarious military position when he reduced the size of its army.

Stilicho needed all the forces he could muster to resist the invasion of Italy by the Visigoths under their famous warrior-king Alaric. He might have also believed the two legions and other troops left in Britannia adequate to satisfy the short-term defensive requirements of the Diocese. Stilicho's defeat of the Picts had restored order on Britannia's northern frontier, and Maximus's Gaelic allies in Wales, Devon and Cornwall still protected the Diocese's western frontier. Stilicho was even able to redeploy elements of Legion II Augusta from Isca Silurum (Caerleon) in Gwent to the Saxon Shore fort of Rutupiae Portus (Richborough) in modern Kent, where they could be utilized against Anglo-Saxon pirates.[28] What Stilicho failed to consider was the likelihood that Legion XX Valeria Victrix and the other troops he withdrew from Britannia would never return to restore the Diocese to its full necessary military complement.

Stilicho also failed to consider the long-term consequences of other military actions which he took at this time.

In order to further bolster the defense of Italy, Stilicho recalled a large part of the army of the Rhine frontier. With the German border inadequately manned, the blood-thirsty Vandals, Suebi and Alans were able to force their way into Gaul. The damage which these barbarians did to the hapless Continental Diocese is inestimable. More to the point, at least as far as the Britons were concerned, the hostile German tribes were then in a position to cross the Channel and attack Britannia. The Britons soon found it incumbent upon themselves to free Gaul of the invaders in order to protect their own Diocese.

To meet the crisis, the Britons raised up their own Emperor, a soldier named Flavius Claudius Constantinus, but better known to history as Emperor Constantine III.

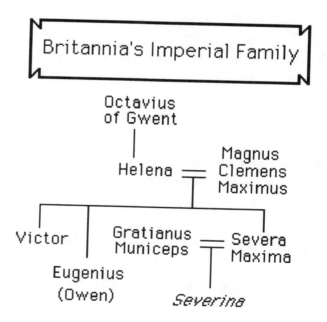

_____

28 All or part of the remainder of the Legion was then transferred to the coastal fort now known as Cardiff, which lies about fourteen miles southwest of Isca Silurum.

## Chapter Three
## Flavius Claudius Constantinus, Imperator

We can find an account of the reign of Emperor Constantine III in Geoffrey of Monmouth's *Historia Regum Britanniae*.

According to Geoffrey, Guithelinus, Archbishop of London, went to Brittany in search of a king to save the Britons from their enemies. Constantine, brother of the Breton ruler Aldroenus, answered the Archbishop's plea. Constantine arrived in Britain with 2,000 soldiers, assumed the government of the Diocese, married a local woman and had three sons: Constans, Aurelius Ambrosius and Utherpendragon.

Constantine was then treacherously slain by a Pictish assassin. Vortigern, leader of the Gewissei, contrived to have Constantine's eldest son, Constans, succeed him. Constans had earlier taken to the religious life and was living in a monastery. Vortigern persuaded Constans to leave the monastery and become king of the Britons, presumably because he thought he would be able to control the unworldly man. Later, Vortigern grew even more ambitious. He suborned the new king's Pictish bodyguards and incited them to slay their master. After the murder of Constans, Vortigern assumed the crown himself, while Aurelius and his brother wisely fled to Brittany, where they found refuge in the court of King Budicius.

Geoffrey has almost gotten the story straight.

At first blush, the tale told in the *Historia Regum Britanniae* seems irreconcilable with the known historical facts. Upon close examination, however, it becomes apparent that Geoffrey has erred in bringing together in a single tale the separate sagas of two different Romano-Briton families: the Constantini (Family of Constantine) and the Ambrosii (Family of Ambrosius).

Geoffrey's mistake was an easy one to make. There is much similarity in the backgrounds of, and the misfortunes which struck, the two families. The Constantini and the Ambrosii were probably also affiliated in some way; they were almost certainly political allies, and they might have even been related to each other. Moreover, the sources with which Geoffrey worked misled him. As a medieval scholar, Geoffrey did not appreciate the significance of Roman family names or post-Roman military titles, and he did not understand a Fifth Century shorthand reference to a distinguished family background. Geoffrey is vindicated in his account of the reign of Constantine III, not in the sense that he has been proven correct, but in the sense that his interpretation of his sources, if faulty, was at least reasonable.

Most of Geoffrey's account properly belongs to the story of the Ambrosii. We shall deal with the Ambrosii later. For now, we shall focus upon fortunes of Britannia under the Constantini.

When Constantine III came to power, Britannia was in dire straits. The Diocese had been severely weakened by Stilicho's withdrawal of many of its troops to Italy in A.D. 402. Even more devastating was Stilicho's decision to strip the Rhine frontier of defenders. Facing little opposition, the barbarous Vandals, Suebi and Alans crossed into Gaul and made ready to pounce on Britannia.

In his excessive concern for the protection of Italy, Stilicho had undermined the military strength of the Western Empire as a whole. Although Italy was the seat of the western government, it was by no means the whole, nor even any more the most important part, of the Empire. The central Diocese was certainly less vital than it had been in earlier centuries. Stilicho made a grave miscalculation, and the Western Empire was never able to control the barbarian hordes which swept over its undefended borders. In the short run, Stilicho's mistake cost the general his political influence and, in A.D. 408, his life. In the long run, Stilicho's mistake cost the Western Empire its future.

Today, nearly sixteen centuries after Stilicho's sad error in judgement, we tend to think that the doom of Roman civilization was inevitable. In fact, under wiser direction, the Western Empire might have survived - or at least struggled on a little while longer. The Eastern Empire, for instance, did manage to cope with the perils of the Fifth Century and it did not fall until 1453, almost a thousand years after the demise of the Western Empire. At any rate, the Roman citizens of the time, especially those in Britannia, were not yet ready to meekly submit to fate.

In early A.D. 406, the Roman soldiers in Britannia, realizing that the Imperial authorities in Italy had lost interest in the safety of their Diocese, decided to form their own government. They elevated a fellow soldier named Marcus to the Emperorship of Britannia. Later the same year, after the barbarians had overwhelmed the weakened Rhine defenses and entered Gaul, the army's new Emperor was found unequal to the crisis, so the soldiers sought a replacement. In A.D. 407, Marcus the soldier was ousted from power and a town official named Gratian was raised in his stead.

Gratian appears in the *Historia Regum Britanniae* as "Gracianus Municeps" who, Geoffrey tells us, was sent to Britannia by Emperor Maximus in command of two legions. He also appears in Venerable Bede's *Historia Ecclesiastica* as "Gratianus Municeps." Geoffrey is wrong, of course, in that Gratian did not immediately succeed Maximus in the rule of Britannia; he did so only after an interval of almost two decades. Geoffrey is also wrong in that Gratian did not actually bring two legions *into* Britannia; he simply took command of the two legions already *in* Britannia. Geoffrey's statement does indicate, however, that Gratian had some intimate connection to Maximus, being a protege or perhaps even a son-in-law of the former Emperor. The personal connection between Gratian and Maximus explains how Gratian, a civilian politician, was able to gain enough influence over the two legions in Britannia that they would consent to raise him to the Emperorship.

The honorific Municeps attached to Gratian's name suggests that he was the leader of a Roman town with the high status of Municipium. The Latin word *municeps* referred to the inhabitant of a Municipium, a Roman town enjoying greater prestige than an ordinary Civitas capital.[29] The only known Municipia in Britannia were Ratae Coritanorum (Leicester) and Verulamium (St. Albans), but this honorable status had certainly been conferred upon other Briton towns as well. Maximus, in fact, probably rewarded his political supporters in Civitas Silurum and Civitas Cornoviorum by bestowing the title of

---

29 Lewis Thorpe, Geoffrey of Monmouth's modern editor, mistranslates *municeps* as "freedman." Sebastian Evans had earlier and more accurately translated it as "burgess."

Municipium upon their chief towns. Gratian thus might have come from Venta Silurum (Caerwent) in Gwent or Viroconium Cornoviorum (Wroxeter). Venta Silurum is an especially strong candidate for Gratian's hometown because it is associated with both Maximus, whose father-in-law Octavius came from Gwent, and Legion II Augusta, one of the two legions still in Britannia.

The emergency facing Britannia was, however, a military crisis. This was no time for a civilian leader, no matter how well-connected his family or how prestigious his hometown. The situation demanded an experienced and capable soldier. According to Geoffrey, Gratian/Gracianus "began to exercise such tyranny over the people that the plebs [commoners] banded together to attack him and eventually assassinated him." Geoffrey may have exaggerated the circumstances, but the Britons did indeed grow disenchanted with their new Emperor. After only four months in office, the civilian Gratian was replaced by another soldier named Flavius Claudius Constantinus.

Venerable Bede describes Constantinus, or Constantine, as "a common trooper of no merit," who was selected for the Imperial honor only because of his "auspicious name." In fact, the army in Britannia would not have consented to follow any leader in that time of trouble, no matter how auspicious his name, unless they also had the utmost confidence in his ability. The Welsh, moreover, remember Constantine more fondly as "Bendigeit Custenhin" (Blessed Constantine). Constantine's subsequent actions, more than anything else, amply demonstrate that, whatever his faults, the Britons' new Emperor was at least competent in military matters.

The soldier Constantine, as Emperor Constantine III, took vigorous and effective measures against the barbarians threatening Britannia. He mobilized many of the troops still in the Diocese and crossed over to Gaul, where he intercepted the Germanic tribes as they marched toward the English Channel. Constantine and his Briton army inflicted a decisive defeat upon the savage warriors. Unfortunately for the Empire, the vanquished invaders did not retreat back to Germania. They escaped instead into the Diocese of Hispania (Spain and Portugal). Rome forever lost Hispania to these barbarians and to those who followed in their wake, but at least Britannia had been saved. But for the bold actions of Constantine III, Britannia would have certainly been invaded and destroyed.

If Constantine had been satisfied with this accomplishment, and if he had been content to govern an Empire roughly the size of that once ruled by Carausius, the history of Britannia might have taken a very different turn. If Constantine had immediately returned to Britannia, there might have never been an Anglo-Saxon England. Constantine choose instead to pursue the barbarians across Gaul and into Hispania, leaving Britannia virtually defenseless. The Picts, the Irish and the Anglo-Saxons did not fail to take advantage of the opportunity for easy plunder. While Constantine wasted his efforts in fruitless Continental campaigns, the barbarians returned in fury to devastate Britannia.

Constantine has been severely criticized by many historians for expanding the scope of his campaign beyond the simple protection of his Diocese. In defense of the Briton Emperor, we should note that Constantine did make a significant contribution to Britannia's safety when he turned back the barbarian horde in Gaul. We should also realize that a leading Roman in the early Fifth Century did not regard himself simply as a Briton (or Gaul or Italian, etc.), but as a citizen of the Empire. The error of Constantine, quite in contrast to that of Stilicho, was to consider the military welfare of the entire Western Empire and not just one part of it. Constantine's actions reflect a sincere dedication to Roman civilization rather than mere personal ambition.

At first, all seemed to go well for the new Emperor. He met early success in both his military endeavors and his efforts to rebuild Gaul. Only later did his program go awry.

Constantine remained in Gaul in A.D. 407 and A.D. 408 restoring and repairing the Rhine defenses. If Gaul was not again to become a springboard for a barbarian invasion of Britannia, such work was necessary and as much in the interest of Britannia as of the Continental Diocese. Constantine was assisted in his labors by his son Constans, who had indeed been recalled from a monastery soon after Constantine assumed the Emperorship.

The Briton Emperor made his fatal mistake in A.D. 408, when he dispatched the Briton general Gerontius to Hispania with most of his army. Constantine intended to pursue and destroy the defeated barbarians who had fled there. The Hispania campaign was initially successful, and Constantine's forces established control over most of the Diocese before the end of the year. Because of this success, Emperor Honorius begrudgingly recognized Constantine as Augustus, or equal co-Emperor, in A.D. 409. Constantine did not long enjoy his new-won status. From the height of power and glory, Constantine quickly fell into the most desperate

of circumstances. Within a few short years, Constantine lost both his Empire and his life.

While Constantine was in Gaul obtaining official recognition of his Imperial status, his fellow Briton Gerontius was in Hispania plotting against him. In A.D. 409, the very same year that Constantine received the title of Augustus, Gerontius raised up a certain Maximus as his own puppet Emperor and allied himself with the barbarians at large in Spain. He also incited the barbarians still in Gaul to attack Constantine. When Constantine was beset by Gerontius's barbarian allies, the traitor himself invaded Gaul and killed Constantine's son Constans.[30]

The Britons back home also betrayed their savior in A.D. 409. Distressed by new incursions of the barbarous Picts, Irish and Anglo-Saxons, disenchanted with their absentee Emperor and unimpressed by official recognition of his Imperial status, the ungrateful Britons repudiated Constantine's rule and evicted his administrators from the island. Nennius reports in the *Historia Brittonum* that the Britons massacred Constantine's officials and refused to pay tribute to Rome.[31]

Retaining control of only a part of Gaul and commanding only a few troops, the Briton Emperor was doomed. Constantine was finally captured and executed at Arelate Salluviorum (Arles) in south Gaul by the forces of Emperor Honorius in A.D. 411.

As Constantine was just beginning to suffer

---

30 Gerontius could have conceivably employed Pictish mercenaries to slay Constans, consistent with Geoffrey of Monmouth's report of the murder of Constans.

31 From such statements, medieval historians mistakenly concluded that the Britons had expelled a foreign army of occupation. They did not realize that the Britons had actually rebelled against and overthrown their own government.

the dire consequences of his error in judgement, Italy was already suffering the most traumatic consequence of Stilicho's error in judgement. In A.D. 410, the barbarian King Alaric and his Visigoths captured and sacked the City of Rome. For the first time in eight centuries, the birthplace of the Roman Empire suffered indignity at the hands of barbarians. Although Honorius and his court were safely ensconced in the city of Ravenna in north Italy, the disaster which befell the symbolic heart of the Empire demoralized the Emperor and Roman citizens everywhere. Stilicho's poor military decision had not only cost the Empire its western Dioceses of Britannia, Gaul and Hispania, it did not even adequately protect Italy.

The Britons must have been horrified at the fate of the Eternal City, but they were probably more concerned with their own efforts to establish a new, non-Imperial government for their Diocese. Although we do not know all the details of the Briton revolt, the overthrow of Constantine's administration was clearly not a bacaudae-type rebellion. It was an upper class *coup d'etat*. The native Romano-Briton aristocracy rejected Constantine's continued rule of their Diocese and they proceeded to independently govern their own Civitates.

A similar rebellion is described in a Rescript (Legal Decree) of Emperor Theodosius II. In A.D. 444, Valerianus, a Curialis (Assemblyman) of the town of Emesa, hired a company of barbarian soldiers, which he used to seize control of the Province of Syria. He invaded the offices of the Imperial bureaucracy, expelled the Emperor's officials and assumed for himself the role and insignia of the provincial governor. Joined by other Curiales, he then actively, and for a time successfully, prevented the collection of Imperial taxes in Syria. The rebellion of

Valerianus in Emesa ultimately failed, but that of the Britons succeeded and the Briton Curiales were able to create a new political order in their Diocese.

The viability of this new political order depended upon the ability of the Briton Civitates to defend themselves against the barbarians. Each Civitas now had to raise and support its own small army. The Civitates were able to draw upon the remaining Imperial army units in the Diocese for a ready source of trained soldiers, but the maintenance of these soldiers was a new and significant fiscal burden on the Civitates. At the same time, however, the Civitates no longer paid taxes to the Imperial government. Freedom from Imperial taxation more than offset the burden of the new military expenditures. The Briton Civitates no longer had to subsidize the Imperial bureaucracy in addition to maintaining their own local governmental apparatus, and they no longer had to underwrite remote military ventures in addition to supporting the large Roman army in Britannia. They could also seize and devote to their own purposes the extensive Imperial estates in Britannia.[32] Relieved of their obligations to the Imperial government, the Briton Civitates could well afford to provide for their own defense.

Despite the fiscal advantages of independence, not all Britons were enthusiastic about the new political arrangements in the Diocese. Important segments of Romano-Briton society gained little from the change in government except a loss of status and prestige. The Britons who did not benefit from Diocesan

---

32 The Emperor owned so much land in Britannia that he had to appoint a special official, the Rationalis Rei Privatae per Britannias, to administer it.

independence included many who were already exempt from most forms of Imperial taxation, such as former government officials, army officers, leaders of the Church and members of the Senatorial Class.[33] A large number of Britons, particularly among the educated classes, also felt a sentimental attachment to the Empire which we should not underestimate. A significant portion of the Romano-Briton leadership was definitely dissatisfied with the change in regime.

These pro-Imperial segments of the Briton population sent a delegation to Emperor Honorius in A.D. 409 or A.D. 410 requesting his military intervention in the Diocese. Historians once assumed that the delegation carried a simple plea from the Briton Civitates for assistance against renewed Pictish, Irish or Anglo-Saxon attacks, but this assumption was faulty. The contemporary eastern Roman chronicler Zosimus reports that the Britons were successful in their efforts to repulse the barbarians, so the Civitates leaders should not have been desperate enough to have so quickly repudiated their rebellion and petitioned for the re-establishment of Imperial rule. Instead, the "reactionary" elements in Briton society must have been the driving force behind the appeal to Honorius. They hoped to persuade the Emperor to send an army to restore the old order in the Diocese. They were surprised and disappointed by the Emperor's response. Rather than dispatching an expeditionary force to reclaim

the lost Diocese, Emperor Honorius in A.D. 410 wrote the Briton Civitates and told them to look out for themselves.

The legal effect of Honorius's reply, called a Rescript (*Rescriptum* in Latin), was to formally and officially grant *Imperium*, the lawful right to form a government, upon the Briton Civitates. The Emperor essentially conferred political sovereignty upon each Civitas in Britannia. Honorius also fatuously exempted the Britons from the Imperial law which permitted only members of the military to bear arms.

Another legal effect of Honorius's Rescript was to strip the two regional military commanders in Britannia, the Dux Britanniarum in the north and the Comes Litoris Saxonici in the southeast, of any valid legal authority.[34] Because they had been appointed by the usurper Constantine III, Honorius's failure to confirm them in office was probably deliberate. The Diocese's military commanders did not disband their armies and give up their power, however. They continued for many years to hold sway in their respective parts of the Diocese. The Dux Britanniarum and the Comes Litoris Saxonici no doubt sought to legitimize their continued exercise of power through the domination of the Civitates whose capitals served as their headquarters.[35]

Honorius, in issuing his Rescript, did not intend to permanently abandon Britannia. The

---

33 Roman Senators did have to pay land and other taxes directly to the Imperial government, but they were exempt from all Civitas taxes, both those required to finance local government and those required to be turned over to the Imperial government. The total fiscal burden on Senators was considerably less than that borne by their non-Senatorial neighbors, who were being crushed by the weight of governmental impositions.

34 The third major military command in Britannia, that of the Comes Britanniarum, no longer existed. The Comes Britanniarum was in charge of most of the Diocese's elite mobile forces, which had gone to Gaul with Emperor Constantine III. The traitorous Gerontius was probably the last person to hold the office of Comes Britanniarum.

35 Eboracum Colonia (York) in the case of the Dux Britanniarum, and Durovernum Cantiacorum (Canterbury) in the case of the Comes Litoris Saxonici.

Emperor made similar grants of Imperium to beleaguered Civitates in other parts of the Empire at about this same time, and those Civitates were later reincorporated into the Empire when Imperial troops were able to return after A.D. 410. The Britons' independence was still legally revocable at any time by the Emperor or his deputies.

Even so, the Imperial party in Britannia must have been disappointed by their Emperor's apparent indifference to their cause. Honorius did, of course, have other, more immediate concerns on his mind. Not least of Honorius's concerns was Alaric and his ravaging Visigoths, who sacked Rome soon after the Rescript was issued. The Briton Imperialists nevertheless did not yet surrender all hope for the re-establishment of Imperial government, and they continued for many years to work for the return of their Diocese to the Empire.

The other Romano-Briton family with whom Geoffrey confused the Constantini, the Ambrosii, were the foremost leaders of the pro-Imperial faction in post-Roman Britannia. The Ambrosii played a major role in the political affairs of the independent Diocese. Their story will, however, have to wait a little while longer. Before the Ambrosii were able to revive the fortunes of the Imperial party, Vortigern, a leader of the independence faction, came to power in Britannia.

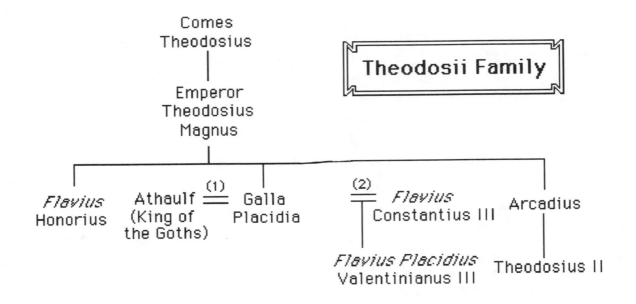

# LIBER SECUNDUS

# The Age of Vortigern

**- - The Early Post-Roman Period - -**

**A.D. 410 - A.D. 462**

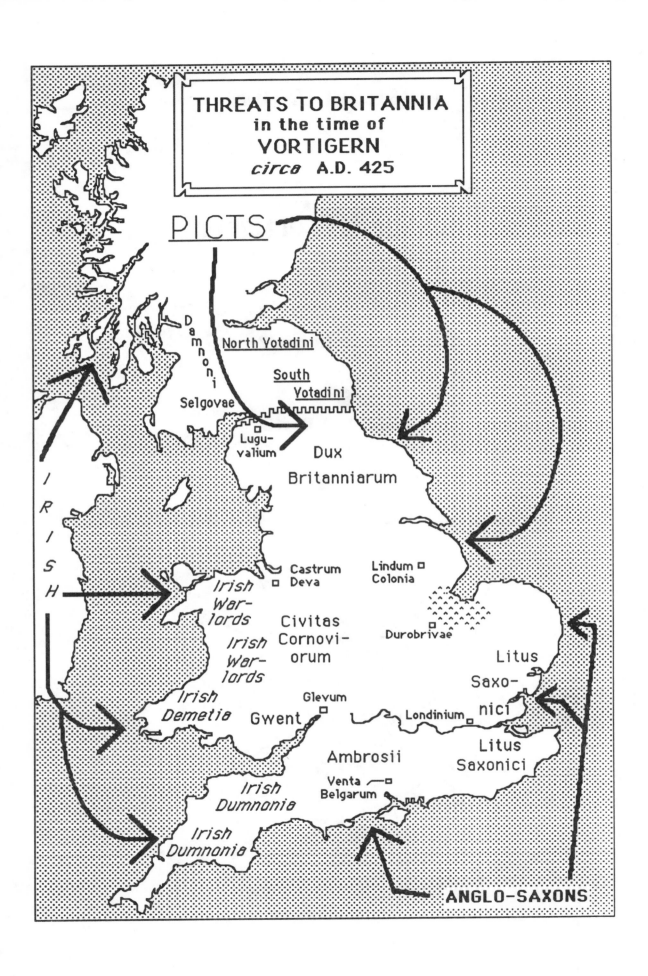

## Chapter Four
## The Rise of Vortigern

The Briton Civitates succeeded in bringing peace and prosperity to Britannia after their overthrow of Emperor Constantine III's government. They kept the Diocese's enemies at bay, and, unburdened by Imperial taxation, they even achieved a moderate level of affluence. The Britons realized, however, that their long-term security could not be ensured if they continued to rely only upon the uncoordinated efforts of the individual Civitates. The military success of the Civitates was due in large part to Magister Militum Stilicho's earlier defeat of the Picts and Emperor Constantine III's earlier defeat of the Germans in Gaul. The Britons knew that both the northern and eastern barbarians would sooner or later recover from these defeats, and that another massive assault upon the former Roman Diocese was inevitable. Many Britons began to see the need to improvise some sort of cooperative military arrangement in order to provide for the long-term security of independent Britannia.

In response to this need, a leader emerged in the A.D. 420's who was able to exercise some degree of authority throughout most of Britannia. Nennius tells us in the *Historia Brittonum* that the "reign" of this leader began in the same year in which Valentinian III became Emperor, which places his rise to Diocese-wide prominence in A.D. 425. This leader is known to us as Vortigern.

### Gerontius Catellus Durnolucius, Superbus Tyrannus

"Vortigern" is not a name; it is a title. It is derived from the Celtic words *vor*, meaning "over," and *gern*, meaning "chieftain" or "lord."[36] "Vortigern" should thus be translated as "Overlord." The Latin equivalent of the Celtic title is Superbus Tyrannus, which is how Gildas describes the Briton leader in *De Excidio Britanniae*.[37]

Vortigern's Latin title of Superbus Tyrannus could itself be translated as "Overbearing Tyrant," but this translation would be misleading to the modern reader.

Vortigern was by no means supreme in his rule of Britannia. He exercised considerable authority within the Diocese, but this authority was based entirely upon his ability to persuade or intimidate local Civitas leaders. Vortigern did not have a Diocesan administrative organization to carry out his instructions or a Diocesan police apparatus to enforce his will. Moreover, a number of powerful Britons, including the Ambrosii, emphatically rejected and strenuously resisted Vortigern's authority. Vortigern was only *primus inter pares* (first among equals), not supreme ruler, so far as the Briton Civitas leaders were concerned.

Vortigern was also not a tyrant in the modern sense of the word. The Latin word *tyrannus* did not carry all the negative connotations that our word "tyrant" does today. To the Romans, a *tyrannus* was simply a leader who acquired power outside the regular, established channels of government. Vortigern was a *tyrannus* because he exercised his authority outside the Civitas political structure upon which Imperium had been officially

---

36 Similar to the Irish *Mor Tigearna*, "Great Lord."

37 Venerable Bede, in the *Historia Ecclesiastica*, was the first historian to make the explicit connection between the "Superbus Tyrannus" of Gildas and the "Vortigern" of Nennius and the early chronicles.

conferred by Emperor Honorius. Moreover, Vortigern, as leader of the anti-Imperial independence faction in Britannia, could not even maintain the pretense of legality by using a proper Roman title. Because of our own devotion to democratic principles, we cannot abide the thought of extra-constitutional government and we really do not have a modern word equivalent to the Roman *tyrannus*, although "usurper" probably comes closest.

The most accurate translation of Vortigern's Latin title Superbus Tyrannus would be "foremost self-appointed leader" or, consistent with his Celtic title, "Overlord."

Vortigern's personal name does not appear in any surviving record of post-Roman times, but we can deduce what it was. Geoffrey of Monmouth first mistakenly introduces Vortigern in the *Historia Regum Britanniae* as the betrayer of Constans, the son of Emperor Constantine III. Constans's betrayer bore the then fairly common Briton name of Gerontius ("Geraint" or "Gereint" in Welsh). The Superbus Tyrannus must have also been called Gerontius, on the basis of which Geoffrey confused him with the same-named betrayer of Constans. In addition, the surviving fragment of a lost Welsh poem alludes to Saint Germanus receiving command of a Briton army from a ruler called Geraint. This incident occurred when Vortigern governed in Britannia, so the Geraint from whom Saint Germanus received command must have been Vortigern. Finally, a hillfort on Deeside by Llangollen in Clwyd (northeast Wales), which was recaptured by the Britons from the Irish during Vortigern's lifetime, is called Moel-y-Geraint, meaning "Fort of Geraint." This fort was probably reconquered by, and renamed for, Vortigern. The evidence thus indicates that Vortigern's

personal name was Gerontius.

"Gerontius" is, however, an individual name, not a family name. Aristocratic Romans, including wealthy Romanized Britons, usually had three names: a *praenomen*, or individual name; a *nomen*, originally designating a *gens*, or clan, but essentially a family name; and a *cognomen*, the name designating a branch of a *gens* or family. For example, the full name of Rome's first Emperor, Gaius Julius Caesar, means the individual "Gaius" of the "Caesar" branch of the "Julius" *gens*; another branch of the same *gens* produced Roman Britannia's most famous governor: Gnaeus Julius Agricola. "Gerontius" thus could not have been Vortigern's full name; he must have had one or more additional family names as well.

We shall later see that a son of Vortigern bore the impressive name of Brutus Catellus Durnolucius. "Brutus," like "Gerontius," was a Roman *praenomen*, but "Catellus" and "Durnolucius" appear to be *nomen* and *cognomen*. "Catellus" is derived from the Latin meaning "little dog," whereas "Durnolucius" could mean something like "stronghold of light." "Catellus" was a fairly common Roman family name in Britannia. Another Catellus, Catellus Decianus,[38] was, for instance, made king of the north Votadini of Lodonesia (Lothian) by Emperor Maximus in A.D. 369; Brutus could have belonged to another branch of the same family. "Durnolucius" would have been a suitable *cognomen* for a Briton whose ancestors once worshipped Lugh or Lludd, the Celtic god of light. Vortigern, of course, had the same *nomen* and *cognomen* as his son. "Catellus" was thus Vortigern's *nomen*, and

---

38 The *cognomen* "Decianus" means "pertaining to a tenth or a tithe."

"Durnolucius" his *cognomen*. The leader of post-Roman Britannia whom we know as Vortigern was Gerontius Catellus Durnolucius to his contemporaries.

Geoffrey of Monmouth tells us little about the background of Gerontius Catellus Durnolucius/Vortigern, except to say that he was "leader of the Gewissei."[39] We have seen that this description refers to the leadership of the people of Gwent. Vortigern must have ruled the Roman town of Venta Silurum (Caerwent) and its adjacent territory.

Archaeology, however, places Vortigern further north in Viroconium (Wroxeter), which was the chief town of Civitas Cornoviorum. Excavation reveals that a massive and elaborate rebuilding program was carried out in Viroconium in the early Fifth Century. The center of the town was levelled and new timber buildings, some of them quite large, were erected in Classical style over the carefully laid rubble. The nature and the extent of the reconstruction demonstrates that Viroconium was the headquarters of an important ruler, one who had access to resources beyond those of just the town and its surrounding Civitas territory. The major construction projects undertaken in Viroconium in the early Fifth Century distinguishes the town as the seat of a Diocesan-wide ruler, which means Viroconium, not Venta Silurum, was Vortigern's capital.

Archaeology, fortunately, reconciles its own evidence for Vortigern's capital being at Viroconium with Geoffrey's placing him in Gwent. Vortigern did in fact come from

Viroconium, but he also owned estates and wielded political power in Gwent.

The explanation for Vortigern's association with both Viroconium and Gwent is found in an early Ninth Century monument called the Pillar of Eliseg. The Pillar of Eliseg was discovered near Llangollen in Clwyd, north Wales. It is named for Eliseg, who was king of Powys in east Wales in the early Seventh Century. The Pillar was erected in Eliseg's honor by his grandson, King Cyngen, to commemorate Eliseg's leading the men of Powys to victory over the Anglo-Saxons in A.D. 603. The inscription on the Pillar traces Eliseg's ancestry to a certain Brittu, who was the first king of Powys. Brittu's parents are said to have been Vortigern and Severa, and Severa is said to have been a daughter of Emperor Maximus. Emperor Maximus had, of course, married the heiress of Octavius, the wealthy politician who governed Venta Silurum and Gwent. Severa must have been Octavius's granddaughter. The Pillar of Eliseg tells us that Vortigern was not a native of Gwent, but that he acquired the leadership of the Gewissei by marrying into the family of the Roman Emperor Maximus and the Briton politician Octavius.

Emperor Maximus was slain in battle in A.D. 388, so his daughter Severa had to have been in her mid-thirties in the early A.D. 420's. This age would make Severa perhaps ten or more years Vortigern's senior. Severa had also been married before her engagement to Vortigern; she even had a daughter from this prior marriage. Severa's first husband was probably Gratianus Municeps, who is associated with Maximus and who was briefly Emperor in Britannia in A.D. 407, when Severa was in her early twenties.

---

39 Geoffrey actually refers to Vortigern as the *Consul* of the Gewissei. It is impossible to know what Geoffrey thought the Roman title of Consul meant, although he obviously understood it to signify high political office. In Vortigern's case, it probably represents the office of Magistratus of Civitas Silurum.

Despite the difference in age and Severa's prior marriage, the wedding of Vortigern to Emperor Maximus's daughter was a practical way to seal an alliance between the leader of the powerful Civitas Cornoviorum and the former Imperial family living in Gwent. Neither a large age gap nor a prior marriage would have impeded a politically advantageous betrothal in ancient or medieval times. Similar circumstances and a like age gap did not, for example, prevent the marriage of the thirty year old Eleanor de Aquitaine, former wife of the king of France, to the nineteen year old Henry Plantagenet, later king of England, in 1154. Whatever Vortigern's and Severa's personal feelings about their wedding, they dutifully consummated their pragmatic marital alliance in the early A.D. 420's.

Vortigern reaped many important advantages from his affiliation with the family of Maximus. He added Octavius's estates in Gwent to the considerable property which his own family no doubt already held in Civitas Cornoviorum. He also obtained political control of the economically important area about Gwent, and gained access to the army recruiting grounds near Isca Silurum (Caerleon), former headquarters of Legion II Augusta.[40] The wealth and military manpower of Gwent, combined with the wealth and military manpower of Civitas Cornoviorum (home of Cohors Cornoviorum), made Vortigern extremely powerful. Most important of all, Vortigern received an intangible political benefit

---

40 Elements of Legion II Augusta had been transferred by Magister Militum Stilicho to Rutupiae Portus (Richborough), but the legionaries still made their home in Civitas Silurum since they would not have taken their families with them to a temporary assignment at the opposite end of Britannia. They no doubt returned home when Imperial rule collapsed in the Diocese.

in the prestige that went with a connection to the former Imperial family. This prestige neutralized at least some of the opposition which Vortigern could have anticipated from the Imperial faction in the Diocese. Vortigern in essence recreated the Cornovian-Gewissei axis which had formed the basis of Emperor Maximus's political power in Britannia, as well as taking onto himself some reflected glory from the popular Briton Emperor.

Vortigern established even wider political connections by cementing a firm alliance with the wealthy town of Glevum Colonia (Gloucester). Vortigern's alliance with Glevum was based upon distant ties of kinship. In the *Historia Brittonum*, Nennius tells us that a leader named Vitalinus fought against Vortigern's enemies in A.D. 437. "Vitalinus" is a Roman *nomen* or *cognomen* derived from the Latin *vitalis*, meaning "long-lived." Another Vitalinus appears as an ancestor in the genealogy which Nennius provides for Vortigern. This other Vitalinus is identified as a "founder" (i.e., benefactor) of the town of Glevum. Vitalinus was thus the name of a politically prominent family in Glevum which was affiliated both by blood and in arms to Vortigern. The alliance with Glevum nicely complemented Vortigern's Cornovian-Gwent political axis by securing him near-complete control over the west-central portion of Britannia.

No record of Vortigern's early career survives, but, based upon what we have been able to determine about his background, we can deduce its broad outlines.

Vortigern, or Gerontius as he was then known, first achieved prominence in local politics. He was a member of the aristocratic

The REAL King Arthur

Catellus Durnolucius family of Civitas Cornoviorum, and, as such, he began his political career in the Curia, or governing body, of the Civitas. He soon rose to leadership of the Civitas. Vortigern's rise in local politics occurred before his achievement of Diocesan-wide prominence in A.D. 425, so Vortigern must have become Magistratus of Civitas Cornoviorum around A.D. 420.

Sometime just before or just after his elevation to the position of Magistratus Cornoviorum (Magistrate of the Cornovians), Vortigern increased his personal wealth and expanded his political influence by marrying the daughter of Emperor Maximus. This marriage gave Vortigern control of Maximus's family estates in Gwent and of the economic and military resources of Civitas Silurum. It also gave him a Diocese-wide prestige through an association with the one-time Briton Emperor. Assuming that Vortigern was at least thirty when he became a major political figure in A.D. 425, he was in his mid-twenties when he wed.

An influential family background, considerable personal wealth, a distinguished political career, command of important military assets and a prestigious marriage were the assets which Vortigern exploited to make himself Superbus Tyrannus, or foremost leader, in the former Roman Diocese. Geoffrey of Monmouth begins the story of Vortigern proper, as opposed to the tale of Gerontius the betrayer of Constans, with the words:

> As soon as Vortigern realized that there was now no one at all in the realm who was his equal, he set the kingly crown upon his own head and assumed precedence over his fellow princes.

This statement is a succinct and accurate description of Vortigern's achievement of paramountcy in Britannia. Geoffrey might have even taken his summary description of Vortigern's rise to power directly from one of his ancient sources.

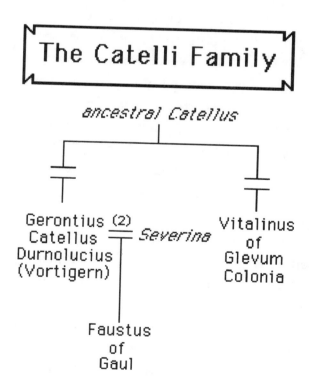

## Chapter Five
## Vortigern's Wars

Once he gripped the reigns of power in Britannia, Vortigern inaugurated a definite program for solving the Diocese's military problems. An important part of Vortigern's program was the recruitment of Anglo-Saxon warriors.

### The Adventus Saxonum

Many Anglo-Saxon warriors settled in Britannia during the Fifth Century. The date when the first Anglo-Saxons came to Britannia, the date which medieval chroniclers called the "Adventus Saxonum," is, however, something of a mystery. In the *Historia Brittonum*, Nennius tells us that the Anglo-Saxons came to Britannia in the fourth year of Vortigern's "reign," which would be A.D. 428. Nennius actually seems unsure of the correct date because he states elsewhere in the *Historia Brittonum* that Vortigern "received" the Anglo-Saxons in A.D. 447. Venerable Bede appears to endorse the later date by placing the Adventus Saxonum in A.D. 449. The Anglo-Saxon Chronicle follows Bede, but the contemporary *Chronica Gallia* (Chronicle of Gaul) contradicts both Bede and Nennius by stating that Britannia fell to the Anglo-Saxons in A.D. 441. The written sources thus confusingly date the arrival of the first Anglo-Saxons in Britannia to either A.D. 428, A.D. 441, or A.D. 447-449.

Archaeology asserts that all three dates are wrong. The evidence of excavation shows that Anglo-Saxon soldiers had been serving and settling in Britannia since the early Fifth Century. The Anglo-Saxons began to arrive in Britannia even before the Diocese gained independence in A.D. 410, which is well before the earliest date found in the written sources. We must therefore add A.D. 400 to our list of possible dates for the Adventus Saxonum.[41]

In fact, *all* the indicated dates are correct. The concept of an Adventus Saxonum had slightly different meanings to the various early chroniclers and to archaeologists, and each date marks a different phase in the long, continuing process by which the Anglo-Saxons gradually established and increased their military presence in Britannia. Despite the apparent contradiction in dates, the sources are actually consistent with each other.

Archaeology gives us the date when Anglo-Saxon artifacts first appear in Britannia. Archaeology tells us that the Briton authorities began to hire Anglo-Saxon mercenary soldiers to supplement the Diocesan forces when many of Britannia's Roman troops were serving on the Continent under Magister Militum Stilicho or Emperor Constantine III. The early chroniclers did not regard this event as particularly noteworthy because the employment of barbarian warriors, albeit not yet of Anglo-Saxons to any great extent, was a long established Roman practice. The chroniclers were much more interested in commemorating the events which marked the changing status of the Anglo-Saxons as they progressed from a small number of mere hirelings (about A.D. 400) to a large and important element in Vortigern's army (about A.D. 428), to

---

41 Archaeologists once believed that the Anglo-Saxons first came to Britannia around A.D. 360, but current re-dating of Anglo-Saxon cemeteries now places their arrival almost a half century later. In addition, belt buckles and other trappings originally thought to be Germanic military articles are now recognized as Roman civilian items.

autonomous territorial rulers in Britannia (A.D. 441), and finally to independent and hostile masters of a large part of the Diocese (A.D. 447-449).

At this point in our history of post-Roman Britannia, the relevant date is A.D. 428. In A.D. 428, a band of Anglo-Saxon warriors landed in Britannia. These barbarians were not the first Anglo-Saxons to come to the Diocese, but they were the first Anglo-Saxons to deserve special mention. The Anglo-Saxons who arrived in A.D. 428 were especially noteworthy because they joined Vortigern's army and went on to play an important role in the military affairs of the Diocese.

Nennius tells us that when Vortigern rose to the rule of Britannia, immediate threats to the Diocese were posed by the Picts and the Irish (whom he calls "Scots"). Gildas claims that the Picts intended to conquer all of Britannia. The king of the Picts at this time was Drust macErp, who reigned from A.D. 414 to A.D. 458 and who is said to have fought a hundred battles. At least some of Drust's battles were fought against the Britons. Drust could not have realistically hoped to subjugate the whole of the former Roman Diocese, but he certainly intended to ravage and loot as much of it as possible. The Irish in west Britannia took advantage of the turmoil caused by the Pictish invasions to conduct their own plundering expeditions against the hapless Britons. Vortigern thus engaged a company of Anglo-Saxon warriors in about A.D. 428 for the specific purpose of defeating a large army of Pictish invaders and putting an end to the onslaught of Irish raiders.

The Tyrannus choose to tackle the Picts first.

## Vortigern's Pictish War

All the early sources agree that Vortigern initially employed only three shiploads of Anglo-Saxons. Three Anglo-Saxon warships of this period would have carried only about 100, and certainly no more than 200, warriors. A force of this size was much more impressive in Vortigern's time than it would be today. The population of Fifth Century Britannia was much smaller than it is now, being only about 2,000,000 persons inside the Roman Diocese with perhaps another 500,000 persons beyond Hadrian's Wall, and Fifth Century armies were correspondingly smaller. Even so, a hundred or so warriors, no matter how fierce, could not have defeated the Picts all by themselves. Vortigern therefore led a large contingent of native Briton soldiers, as well as his warband of Anglo-Saxon mercenaries, when he made war on the Picts.

Vortigern raised his native troops from the substantial military populations which he governed in Civitas Cornoviorum and Gwent. The soldiers of Cohors Cornoviorum were foremost among Vortigern's followers. After being released from duty on Hadrian's Wall by Emperor Maximus, the Cornovian warriors no doubt returned home, where they served in the Pagus, or rural western district, of Civitas Cornoviorum. This area is now the shires of Powys and Clwyd in east Wales. Cohors Cornoviorum kept in good fighting trim because the Pagus was then Britannia's frontier with the Irish kingdoms in Wales, and the Cornovian soldiers saw much fighting against Irish marauders. Soldiers descended from the legionaries of Legion II Augusta, which had been based at Isca Silurum (Caerleon) in Gwent, also marched with the Tyrannus. The legionary offspring were welcome additions to Vortigern's army because they maintained at least some of the military traditions of their forebears. With access to the veterans of Cohors Cornoviorum in the Pagus and to the heirs of Legion II Augusta in Gwent, Vortigern was able to raise a considerable force of trained Romano-Briton infantry.

Vortigern also recruited soldiers from the military inhabitants of the Civitas based upon Castrum Deva (Chester). Castrum Deva was once headquarters of Legion XX Valeria Victrix, but it declined precipitously after Magister Militum Stilicho withdrew the Legion from Britannia in A.D. 402. The Civitas based upon the town ( probably called Civitas Devana) then fell under Cornovian domination. Viroconium (Wroxeter), capital of Civitas Cornoviorum, was the major town closest to Civitas Devana, and thus the nearest source of civilized government for the Civitas's Romanized residents. Moreover, the territory of Civitas Devana had originally belonged to the Cornovii tribe in pre-Roman and early Roman times. Some legionary families likely remained in the Castrum Deva area from whom Vortigern could have raised a small number of foot soldiers, but the cavalrymen stationed to the north at Bremetennacum (Ribchester) were an even more valuable military resource.

The cavalrymen at Bremetennacum were descended from a band of 5,500 Sarmatian warriors whom Emperor Marcus Aurelius had settled in Britannia in A.D. 180. The Emperor acquired this band of warriors when he defeated the Sarmatians by the banks of the River Danube ("Flumen Danubius" to the Romans) in A.D. 175. The Sarmatians were unique for their time in that they fought as heavy shock cavalry.

In combat, they relied upon the dreadful impact of the cavalry charge to sweep their enemies before them, rather than the steady advance of sword-bearing infantrymen or the harassing, hand-thrown missile fire of light, mobile horsemen. The Romans were always eager to acquire new military capabilities, and the unusual fighting style of the Sarmatian cavalry was a special curiosity to them. Indeed, the bulk of the Imperial army in the east ultimately became Sarmatian-style cavalry, an adaptation which enabled the Eastern Empire to overcome the military challenges of the Fifth Century and survive the fall of the Western Empire by almost 1,000 years. Meanwhile, the descendants of the Sarmatian warriors in Britannia adopted Roman ways and assimilated into the Romano-Briton population.[42] They maintained their native military traditions, however, and they continued to serve the Empire - and Britannia - as cavalrymen. Against the footslogging barbarian enemies of Britannia, the Sarmatian horse soldiers were an extremely potent military force.

We know from archaeology that Vortigern at one time also recruited Irish mercenary troops, and he might have already begun to do so before his Pictish war. Monuments found in Viroconium indicate that Irish chieftains were living in or near the town by the middle of the Fifth Century. The inscriptions on the monuments name in particular the Irishmen Cunorix and Ceawlin, who must have been commanders of the Tyrannus's Irish warriors. Most of these Irish troops were probably recruited in nearby Wales, but some could have

---

42 Many of the original Sarmatians were probably withdrawn from Britannia around A.D. 196 to support the usurper Emperor Clodius Albinus against Emperor Septimius Severus, but at least one *numerus*, a unit of about 300 to 500 warriors, remained behind at Bremetennacum.

come all the way from Ireland.[43]

Vortigern led his Anglo-Saxon and Briton (and possibly Irish) troops north, where he joined forces with the Dux Britanniarum. The militia garrisons of Hadrian's Wall had survived the collapse of Imperial government in Britannia, and their leader no doubt continued to employ the prestigious Roman title of Dux Britanniarum. The Dux also commanded warriors descended from the soldiers of Legion VI Victrix stationed at Eboracum (York) and from the troopers of three Imperial cavalry units deployed in northeast Britannia (Equites Dalmatae, Equites Catafractarii and Equites Crispiani). Drust macErp and his Picts were formidable opponents, but the Anglo-Saxons, Cornovians, Gwentmen, Sarmatians and Irishmen of the Superbus Tyrannus, in combination with the militiamen, former legionaries and horse soldiers of the Dux Britanniarum, could have taken on the barbarian invaders with an excellent chance of victory.

The allied Britons met and fought the Picts somewhere in the vicinity of Hadrian's Wall in about A.D. 431. We know nothing about the course of the fighting, but the Superbus Tyrannus and Dux Britanniarum won at least enough of a victory to turn back the invaders. After Vortigern's northern expedition, the Picts do not seem to have seriously troubled Britannia

any further.

Vortigern's Anglo-Saxon mercenaries were an important factor in the Britons' success. Born and raised in a warrior culture, the Germanic soldiers were tough fighters and highly effective in combat against the Picts. Even the Celtic nationalist Geoffrey of Monmouth admits that the barbarian hirelings were crucial to Vortigern's victory over the Picts.

Vortigern was now free to deal with the Irish who were assailing the Diocese from the west. He had dealt with the Pictish menace in a direct and straightforward military manner, the sort of approach in which his Anglo-Saxon mercenaries could be best employed. The Irish problem required a more subtle and long-term solution.

Vortigern was up to the challenge. He took advantage of his presence in far north Britannia to recruit the semi-barbarous people of the region for use against the aggressive Irish warlords in Wales.

## Vortigern's Irish Wars

The Roman dynasties installed by Emperor Maximus over the semi-barbarian tribes on Britannia's northern frontier still held power in Vortigern's day, but they obviously failed in their duty to shield the Diocese from the rapacious Picts of the highlands. The Votadini of Lodonesia (Lothian) and Bernicia (Northumberland) even took advantage of the Pictish invasion to engage in opportunistic raiding of their own. A hoard of broken and damaged silver objects found at Traprain Law, near modern Edinburgh, indicates that the north Votadini lifted booty or extorted protection money from their Briton neighbors. According to early Welsh poetry, the south Votadini were

---

43 Vortigern could have obtained his overseas Irish mercenaries in connection with a treaty sealed by the marriage of his daughter to a son of the Irish High King Loegaire. (Loegaire was a son of the infamous High King Niall of the Nine Hostages, who savagely raided Britannia in the early Fifth Century and who probably carried the future Saint Patrick away to Irish captivity.) A certain Foirtchern, whose name is an Irish form of "Vortigern," appears in Irish genealogies as the son of Loegaire's son Fedlimid and an unnamed Briton king's daughter. Foirtchern was born around A.D. 440.

no less piratical. When Drust macErp led his Picts against the Diocese, many Votadini marched with him.

The Irish warlords settled by Emperor Maximus in west Britannia also betrayed the Diocese by conducting raids onto Briton territory.

The full magnitude of the Irish impact upon post-Roman Britannia is seldom appreciated today. Great numbers of Irish warriors had settled in west Britannia in the Fourth Century. By the start of the Fifth Century, they easily outnumbered the Anglo-Saxons then in the Diocese. Many of the Irish warriors originally came to Britannia at the behest, or at least with the acquiescence, of Emperor Maximus, but many more came later with only their own swords for authorization. In Vortigern's day, none of the Irish in Britannia seem to have felt any allegiance to the Britons, and they steadily encroached upon Briton territory. West Britannia almost became another "Scot (i.e., Irish) -land." When Vortigern assumed power in Britannia, the Irish clearly posed the most serious long-term military threat to the independent Diocese.

The principal Irish kingdom in Britannia was Demetia in southwest Wales. Demetia was formerly the Roman Civitas Demetarum, which was based on the town of Moridunum Demetarum (Carmarthen). It was more recently known as Pembrokeshire and Carmarthenshire, and is essentially the southern part of the modern shire of Dyfed. The Irish settlement in Demetia was extensive, representing a major tribal relocation and not merely the imposition of a small warrior aristocracy upon the native population.

The Irish also colonized north and central Wales, Devon and Cornwall in southwest England, Galloway and Argyll in west Scotland, and the Isle of Man. The name of the Lleyn peninsula in modern Gwynedd bears witness to the origin of many of these colonists from the Kingdom of Leinster in east Ireland.[44] Vortigern's main concern was the Irish warlords established in north Wales because they pressed close upon the western rural district, or Pagus, of his own Civitas Cornoviorum.

Vortigern's solution to the Irish problem was very simple in concept, although no doubt complex in execution. The Tyrannus decided to set one barbarian against another, and to this end he relocated many of the unreliable Votadini from far north Britannia to north Wales.

## Cunedda of the Votadini

The leader of the migratory Votadini was named Cunedda or Cunedag, which is an early form of "Kenneth." Before relocating to Wales, Cunedda ruled the south Votadini of Bernicia, which is on the east coast of Britannia just north of Hadrian's Wall.

Welsh tradition tells us that Cunedda led many south Votadini in an extraordinary march across the breadth of Britannia in order to found a new kingdom in the territory to the west of Civitas Cornoviorum. Cunedda appears in Welsh genealogies as the grandson of the 'Paternus son of Tacitus,' whom Emperor Maximus made ruler of the south Votadini in about A.D. 370, and as the great-grandfather of the Welsh King Maelgwn, who died in A.D. 547. Cunedda's early military career and migration should therefore be placed about half a century after Emperor Maximus and about a century before King Maelgwn. This reckoning

---

44 "Lleyn" is derived from *Laigin*, "Leinstermen."

dates Cunedda's migration to the early A.D. 430's, which is around the time of Vortigern's Pictish campaign. Welsh tradition does not tell us why Cunedda and his followers chose to abandon their homeland, but the only plausible explanation is that they were compelled to do so by Vortigern. Vortigern expelled Cunedda's Votadini from Bernicia and resettled them in north Wales so they would fight his Irish enemies there.

Cunedda was one of the Votadini leaders who had repudiated the dynastic obligation to protect the Roman Diocese in order to turn bandit. Early Welsh poetry refers to Cunedda raiding towns on the Roman side of Hadrian's Wall, which means he fought against his grandfather's patrons. He most likely did so in alliance with Drust macErp. After Vortigern and the Dux Britanniarum defeated the Picts, Cunedda could have expected to pay dearly for his crimes at the hands of the victorious Briton leaders.

Fortunately for the vanquished chieftain, Vortigern planned to use the Votadini in the liberation of Wales. Vortigern offered Cunedda an opportunity to save his skin and make a new start for himself if he consented to relinquish his kingdom, move to another part of Britannia and wage war upon the Tyrannus's Irish enemies. Victorious Roman generals often extended offers of this type to defeated barbarian tribes. In just such a manner did Emperor Marcus Aurelius acquire the Sarmatians of Bremetennacum, who originally fought against him but whose Romanized descendants now served in Vortigern's army. Likewise, Emperor Maximus similarly acquired the warriors of Conanus Meridiadocus, who originally opposed the installation of Cunedda's grandfather but

who later helped Maximus conquer Gaul. Vortigern thus followed well-established Roman precedent in attempting to turn Votadini aggressiveness to his own advantage. The Tyrannus hoped to convert a northern nuisance into a western asset by unleashing Cunedda's Votadini against the Irish in Wales.

The war initiated by Cunedda at Vortigern's behest ultimately resulted in all of north Wales passing out of Irish control. Cunedda and his sons carved out a new kingdom for themselves, which they called Gwynedd (Latinized as "Venedotia"), meaning "desirable land." Cunedda's grandsons completed the formation of Gwynedd when Catwallaun seized the Isle of Mona (now called Anglesey) and Marianus captured, and gave his name to, Merioneth. The reconquest of north Wales thus took three full generations. While the long and bitter war between the far north Briton immigrants and their Irish opponents raged, neither the transplanted Votadini nor the Gaelic barbarians were in any position to threaten Cornovian or Romano-Briton interests.

As the Irish of north Wales reeled under the blows of Cunedda and his followers, Vortigern's Cornovians did not sit idly by. Cornovian soldiers had been fighting the Irish in the Pagus since the days of Emperor Maximus, and they continued to press the war. In the end, they were successful. The genealogies and place names associated with east Wales show that the region changed hands from Irish-named to Roman- and Briton-named warriors in the early Fifth Century. The restored Cornovian regime in the Pagus set down strong roots; it even managed to preserve its independence after the principal Civitas territory in the vicinity of Viroconium fell to the Anglo-Saxons in the middle of the Seventh Century. The Pagus

Cornoviorum reconquered by Vortigern's native Cornovian troops became the medieval kingdom, today the shire, of Powys.

## The Liberation of Dumnonia

With the Irish in Wales locked in combat against Cunedda's Votadini and with the Cornovians on the advance in the Pagus, the military pressure on Civitas Cornoviorum was markedly reduced. Vortigern could now devote some of his martial resources to more remote military ventures. The Tyrannus wished to keep his Anglo-Saxon hirelings under his direct personal command, but he had plenty of native warriors to spare. Vortigern felt confident enough about the situation to dispatch a large Cornovian force to free Dumnonia in southwest Britannia from Irish control.

Dumnonia, the territory of the Roman Civitas Dumnoniorum (roughly modern Cornwall, Devon and west Somerset), had also fallen to Irish warlords in the late Fourth Century. In the first half of the Fifth Century, however, new, Cornovian rulers appear in their stead. In fact, the modern place names Devon and Cornwall later came into use during the Anglo-Saxon period to distinguish the part of Dumnonia which the Anglo-Saxons had conquered from the part which the Cornovians kept independent. "Devon" is an Anglo-Saxon corruption of "Dumnonia," whereas "Cornwall" means "*Corn*ovian *Wal*es." The emergence of Cornovian rulers in territory formerly dominated by Irish warlords can only mean that Vortigern sent soldiers from Civitas Cornoviorum on a mission to liberate Dumnonia.

The Cornovian liberation of Dumnonia must have begun around A.D. 435, soon after

Cunedda's Votadini established themselves in north Wales.

About this same time, Congar Docco, a Cornovian churchman, became active in Dumnonia. Congar came from a distinguished family background. Local legend claims that he was the son of the Emperor of "Byzantium" (i.e., Constantinople, capital of the Eastern Roman Empire), which is an obvious effort to give the Saint an Imperial pedigree. In truth, he might have been a grandson of Emperor Constantine III, probably through a daughter of the Briton Emperor. Over the course of the next four decades, until A.D. 473, Congar founded several monasteries and schools in Dumnonia and elsewhere in southwest Britannia. One of his monasteries in modern Somerset was named Congresbury after him. Congar eventually became Bishop of Isca Dumnoniorum (Exeter), former capital of Civitas Dumnoniorum and chief town of liberated Cornovian Dumnonia. Congar Docco presumably moved south and became Bishop of Isca Dumnoniorum so he could minister to the religious needs of his fellow emigrant Cornovians.

Vortigern's personal prestige was greatly enhanced by the Dumnonian campaign. The expulsion of the Irish from Dumnonia eliminated a general threat to the security of southwest Britannia, which must have gained the Tyrannus grateful allies in that part of the Diocese. The Civitates based upon Corinium Dobunnorum (Cirencester), Durnovaria Durotrigum (Dorchester) and Aquae Sulis (Bath) should have been especially appreciative. The expulsion of the Irish was also another major accomplishment to chalk up to Vortigern's credit, which no doubt bolstered his reputation and stature throughout the entire

Diocese.  Civitas rulers all over Britannia must have been enormously impressed with Vortigern's talent for success.

And so should we.

Vortigern was an exceptionally perceptive and capable leader.  He had the vision to see how the limited resources at his disposal could be used to eliminate the military threats to north and west Britannia, and he had the skill to efficiently implement his vision.  He was both insightful and competent - a rare combination.  Vortigern was a formidable protagonist, and his rise to paramountcy in Britannia was no accident.

## Chapter Six
## Coelestius Senex, Dux Britanniarum

One of Vortigern's grateful allies, perhaps his most important grateful ally, was the Dux Britanniarum who governed north Britannia.

When Emperor Constantine III left Britannia in A.D. 407, military command over Hadrian's Wall and the region just south of the Wall was held by the Dux Britanniarum.  Political authority over this territory was conferred by the Rescript of Emperor Honorius in A.D. 410 upon the five Civitates within Dux's sphere of influence,[45] but the Rescript was not given much effect there.  The northern part of the Diocese had always been essentially a military district dominated by the Dux Britanniarum and other Imperial army officers, and the practical authority of the local civil authorities was correspondingly diminished.  Even the agricultural economies of the northern Civitates fell under military domination because they were devoted to supplying the needs of the Dux's soldiers.  In the circumstances, the military leaders of the region, which is to say the Dux Britanniarum and his lieutenants, naturally assumed political control after Constantine III's Imperial government was overthrown in A.D. 409.

The Dux Britanniarum himself appears as a great king in the oral history of north Britannia.  According to north Briton tradition, the region garrisoned in Roman times by the troops of the Dux Britanniarum was governed in the early Fifth Century by a semi-legendary ruler named

---

45 The Civitates based on Luguvalium Carvetiorum (Carlisle), Vercovicium Textoverdorum (Housesteads), Corstopitum Corielopocarum (Corbridge), Isurium Brigantum (Aldborough) and Eboracum Colonia (York).

Coel Hen. Coel Hen was so well regarded by the people of the region that he was claimed as founding father by several native Briton dynasties which emerged in the Hadrian's Wall and the Pennine Mountain areas in the middle of the Sixth Century. Although Coel Hen was remembered by later generations as a northern king, he no doubt governed his domain with the respected Roman title of Dux Britanniarum.

"Coel Hen" means "Cole the Old," or, more popularly, "Old King Cole." Coel is a Roman family name. It could be "Coelius" in Latin,[46] but is more likely a shortened form of "Coelestius." To his contemporaries, Coel Hen was known as Coelestius Senex.

"Coelestius" was also the name of a Briton theologian who flourished in the early Fifth Century. Coelestius the theologian was an educated Briton who went to Rome soon after A.D. 400 with the intention of practicing law. He took up theology instead, and he became a leading advocate of the religious doctrine later called the Pelagian heresy. The illustrious (or infamous) career of this Coelestius suggests that he came from an important Roman family in Britannia. Another member of the same family, perhaps the theologian's brother, could have risen to military command of north at the same time.[47]

Coelestius Senex was, without a doubt, the last officially-nominated Dux Britanniarum. The territory with which he is associated, the time period assigned to his reign, his Latin name and his probable connection to a prominent Briton theologian make it virtually certain that he used the Roman title to justify his exercise of power. His importance to later genealogists implies that his government enjoyed an aura of legitimacy which could have only been conferred by a recognized Roman authority. Coelestius Senex must have been appointed to the post of Dux Britanniarum by the Briton Emperor Constantine III before the Britons' repudiation of Constantine's government in A.D. 409.

Coelestius appears in the *Historia Regum Britanniae* as "Coillus," a leader of pre-Roman Britannia who is said to have been educated in Rome, where he learned Roman ways and developed a great admiration for the Romans. He also appears in the *Historia* a second time as "Coel" or "Cohel," a Dux of Camulodunum (Colchester) who is credited with the deeds (but not the sad fate) of Mausaeus Carausius - possibly on account of some unknown association of Carausius with Camulodunum ("Kaercolim," or "City of Coel," in Welsh).

Coelestius would have been in his late thirties or early forties when he was raised to the important military command of north Britannia. This age would put him only in his sixties when Vortigern marched north to do battle with Drust macErp and the Picts. If Dux Coelestius truly earned his nickname of "the Old," then he was still very much alive and active in Vortigern's day and he surely joined with the Superbus Tyrannus to fight the Picts.[48]

---

46 A certain Roscius Coelius once served as Legatus (commander) of Legion XX Valeria Victrix in Britannia. This Coelius made himself infamous by usurping the government of Britannia in A.D. 69-70, when the Empire was paralyzed by the chaos which followed the death of Emperor Nero.

47 Based upon statements made by his religious opponents, historians once thought that Coelestius the theologian was Irish. This theory is now rejected. Romans in other parts of the Empire often ascribed "Scottish" (i.e., Irish) traits to Britons as an insult implying that they were not proper Roman citizens.

48 Indeed, the Twelfth Century *Vita Merlini* (Life of Merlin) refers to the "Gewissi" (i.e., Vortigern's Gwentmen) coming together with the Deirans (i.e.,

As Dux Britanniarum, Coelestius commanded what was by far the largest - but also the most limited - military force in the Diocese. The vast majority of the Dux's troops were Hadrian's Wall militiamen, who were only part-time soldiers. They were poorly trained and essentially immobile. Even if Coelestius could convince his militiamen to embark on a distant military campaign, the Roman logistics organization had long ago been allowed to erode, and Coelestius would have been hard-pressed to feed and maintain his troops while they were away from home - especially since his troops were also his principal agricultural producers. Meanwhile, the far northern barbarians (including the Votadini and other former Roman allies) would have taken advantage of the situation to cross Hadrian's Wall and ravage the Ducal domain. The Dux Britanniarum was a formidable military power in Britannia, but he simply did not have sufficient military resources of the type necessary to project his influence very far outside his own northern domain.

Coelestius was hardly powerless to exert martial pressure upon his neighbors, because he did command regular army units in addition to the Hadrian's Wall militia. These regular army units included Legion VI Victrix, which was based at the Dux's headquarters town of Eboracum (York), several Imperial infantry units, which were deployed in various parts of north Britannia, and three crack cavalry units, which were stationed in the north as a strategic reserve and counter-attack force. Coelestius no doubt drew upon the training and expertise of the veteran Roman soldiers in these units to

form elite mobile warbands. The Dux's elite forces were not very numerous, however, and they were fully occupied with the effort to control Pictish invaders, Votadini traitors, Irish raiders and native bandits.

Coelestius therefore found it necessary to increase the size of his army by recruiting Anglo-Saxon warriors. He settled these Anglo-Saxon warriors on vacant lands under his control.

**The Anglo-Saxons of Deira**

Coelestius's principal Anglo-Saxon settlement ground was the territory just to the east of his headquarters at Eboracum (York). This area was then called Deira and was later called the East Riding of York, but is now known as north Humberside. Deira was an agriculturally rich land; in former days, it had been a major source of supplies for the Roman troops stationed in the north. The Deiran coastline was also vulnerable to seaborne Pictish raiding parties, however, and its population had seriously declined in the waning days of the Empire. Deira was thus a logical place to install barbarian colonists, who could bring neglected land back into production and then defend it. For over a century and a half, the Anglo-Saxons of Deira farmed and fought for the Dux Britanniarum and his successors.

Relations between the Anglo-Saxons of Deira and the Romano-Britons of Eboracum were not always harmonious. Archeology has uncovered evidence of some unrest in Deira in the middle of the Fifth Century. This unrest occurred at about the time that Coelestius, who then must have been in his seventies, is likely to have passed away. Nennius also reports that the Deiran leader Soemil "first separated" Deira

---

soldiers from modern Humberside) during the reign of "the great Cohelo" (i.e., Coelestius).

from "Bernicia," meaning from the rest of northeast Britannia.[49] Based upon Soemil's place in the Deiran genealogy, this event occurred in the middle of the Fifth Century, consistent with the archaeological evidence. Towards the middle of the Fifth Century, the Anglo-Saxons of Deira apparently demanded a change in their legal status, seeking to form their own independent government.

Dux Coelestius would have initially allowed the Anglo-Saxons to settle in Deira as laeti, warrior colonists with limited rights under Roman law. Laeti were granted land in exchange for their military services, but they were also subject to Roman legal authority and obligated to pay rent or taxes (the distinction being strictly academic at the time) to their Roman masters. The Deiran Anglo-Saxons must have demanded elevation to foederati status. Foederati enjoyed political autonomy, including the selection of their own leaders, and did not have to make tax or rent payments to the Roman authorities. The death of Coelestius was an ideal opportunity for the Deiran Anglo-Saxons to insist upon foederati rights, giving them greater control over their own affairs and relief from taxes, as a condition of supporting the Dux's successor.

Other than this one, brief period of turmoil, the Deiran barbarians remained steadfast allies of the Dux Britanniarum. As laeti and then as foederati, the Deiran Anglo-Saxons constituted an important part of the Dux's army. They were, in fact, a major pillar of support for the

49 In the Seventh Century, the Anglo-Saxon Kingdom of Bernicia (Northumberland) absorbed Deira to form the great northern Kingdom of Northumbria. The document translated by Nennius was thus speaking anachronistically of a time when Deira first established itself as an independent entity.

Ducal regime in Eboracum.

## The Anglo-Saxons of Bernicia

Anglo-Saxons were also introduced into south Votadini territory, or Bernicia (Northumberland), in Coelestius's time. The Anglo-Saxons arrived in Bernicia soon after Cunedda and his followers departed for north Wales. They made their base at Bamburgh, called Din Guayrdi by the Britons (its Latin name is unknown), on the east coast of Britannia about fifteen miles south of the River Tweed. Although not as numerous as their fellow barbarians in Deira, the Bernician Anglo-Saxons were fierce and aggressive fighters. They soon became a major factor in the history of far north Britannia. Dux Coelestius must have settled the Anglo-Saxons in Bernicia with the expectation that they would prove more reliable allies than the expelled south Votadini.

At least some of the Anglo-Saxons installed in Bernicia were recruited and sent north by Vortigern. Both Nennius and Geoffrey of Monmouth describe this event. They tell us that the Anglo-Saxon leader Hengist suggested to Vortigern that Vortigern send Hengist's "sons" Octa and Ebissa (or Ebusa) north with an Anglo-Saxon fleet to fight the Picts and Scots. Vortigern adopted the barbarian's suggestion, and the expedition was duly dispatched. Nennius and Geoffrey do not tell us why Vortigern thought it necessary to send Anglo-Saxon troops north, but we can deduce the reason for ourselves. Since the Pictish invasion of Drust MacErp had already been turned back, the barbarians must have been sent north to replace the disloyal south Votadini in Bernicia.

The medieval historians do not agree on the size of the Anglo-Saxon armada which sailed to

Bernicia. Nennius says it consisted of forty ships. Anglo-Saxon warships of this period, depending upon their size, could carry as many as seventy warriors, although a typical crew consisted of only thirty to forty warriors; the Anglo-Saxon era ship found at Sutton Hoo, which was built in the early Seventh Century, carried forty crewmen, including thirty-eight oarsmen. Forty ships would have thus carried between 1,200 and 1,600 warriors - a formidable force for those days. Geoffrey insists that the armada was even larger; he gives the number of ships as three hundred, which would have carried a highly improbable 9,000 to 12,000 warriors. The confusion stems from the fact that not all of the north-bound sailors were Anglo-Saxons; many were actually Britons.

We know that Octa and Ebissa led a joint Anglo-Briton force from the very evidence of their names. Octa could have truly been Hengist's son, because "Octa" is a Germanic name. Octa's co-commander, however, must have been a Romano-Briton leader, because "Ebissa" (or "Ebusa") seems a Celtic name. In addition, Geoffrey informs us that the expedition was accompanied by another Celtic-named individual, a certain Cherdic (or Ceretic), whom Nennius says acted as Vortigern's interpreter in meetings with the barbarians. Cherdic's presence indicates that Octa and Ebissa led a composite force, because a monolingual expeditionary force would not have placed such importance upon the services of an interpreter. Geoffrey's belief that three hundred ships sailed north was thus based upon his misreading a source which referred to Vortigern's sending 300 ship-borne barbarians to join a joint Anglo-Briton force of forty ships, or 1,200-1,600 warriors in all.

The Briton troops who sailed north under the Celtic-named Ebissa and Cherdic had the special mission of installing a new king over the south Votadini who did not go to Wales with Cunedda. A certain Germanianus appears as the first king after "Coel Hen" in the genealogy of a royal dynasty whose rule of Celtic Bernicia seems to have begun in the late A.D. 430's or early A.D. 440's. Germanianus was no doubt a Romano-Briton army officer detached from Coelestius's command and given authority over the area formerly governed by Cunedda. Dux Coelestius installed Germanianus as head of a new royal dynasty in Bernicia, much as Emperor Maximus had earlier installed Cunedda's grandfather.

Germanianus could have even been the same person as Ebissa. "Germanianus" could have been a new *cognomen* or a nickname derived from Ebissa's association with Anglo-Saxon troops. In that case, Ebissa's full Latin name was Ebissa Germanianus.

Germanianus made his capital at the fort of Yeavering Bell by Wooler, then called Gefrin. Gefrin lies about thirteen miles inland from the base of Germanianus's Anglo-Saxon allies at Bamburgh.

The Anglo-Saxons of the far north soon increased their numbers well above their original 300 warriors by attracting new immigrants from Germania. These immigrants spread throughout most of the territory just north of Hadrian's Wall. They left behind several Anglo-Saxon place names as evidence of their presence, including "Dumfries," which means "Fort of the Frisians." The Firth of Forth was even for a time called "Mare Fresicum" ("Frisian Sea"). The Frisians were Germanic barbarians from the region which is now the seacoast of Holland. The Bernician Anglo-

Saxons and their Frisian and other German colleagues quickly became the dominant military force in the far north, more important even than the soldiers of Ebissa Germanianus.

## Luguvalium Carvetiorum

Coelestius, through his sponsorship of Ebissa Germanianus and Octa, extended his influence beyond Hadrian's Wall, where his immediate predecessors as Dux Britanniarum had exercised little or no authority. At the same time, however, he lost influence over a portion of the domain originally entrusted to him by Emperor Constantine III.

After Emperor Honorius issued his Rescript in A.D. 410, the Dux Britanniarum was able to assert dominion over only the eastern and central portions of Hadrian's Wall and the territory east of the Pennine Mountains. The western portion of Hadrian's Wall and the area west of the Pennines fell away from the Dux's influence and came under the domination of the town of Luguvalium (Carlisle).

Luguvalium was the chief town of Civitas Carvetiorum, which consisted more or less of modern Cumbria. Luguvalium was also the former capital of the Roman Province of Valentia, which Comes Theodosius had earlier won back for the Empire. Although Luguvalium lost its provincial capital status when Emperor Constantine III's government collapsed in A.D. 409, it was still a town of major importance in Coelestius's day.

Luguvalium was wealthy and well-governed in Roman times, and it remained wealthy and well-governed throughout the post-Roman period. Like Vortigern's capital of Viroconium Cornoviorum (Wroxeter), Luguvalium was able to renovate many of its public buildings in the post-Roman period by reconstructing them in Classical style out of timber. It was also able to maintain its roads and aqueduct in functional condition. A prosperous Romano-Briton community thrived in Luguvalium amid Roman-style surroundings, including well-kept buildings, strong walls and operating fountains, as late as A.D. 685, when the town finally fell to the amazed Anglo-Saxons. Luguvalium sustained itself in civilized affluence for almost three centuries after the collapse of Roman rule in Britannia

Luguvalium could resist the authority of the Dux Britanniarum, maintain its political independence and preserve its prosperity because it had substantial military and economic resources of its own. It recruited trained soldiers from the many important Roman army units stationed in the vicinity of the town, including the militia garrisons of the western portion of Hadrian's Wall and the forts along the Cumbrian coast, four regular infantry units and two elite cavalry units.[50] Luguvalium supported these warriors (and its public works projects) with the bounty of the strong agricultural economy of the Cumbrian plain. The Cumbrian agricultural economy was originally developed by the Imperial government to feed the Roman soldiers who protected northwest Britannia, and it was now used by Luguvalium to feed the descendants of these soldiers who upheld the town's

---

50 The regular infantry units were Numerus Defensorum at Bravoniacum (Kirby Thore), Numerus Directorum at Verterae (Brough), Numerus Maurorum Aurelianorum at Aballava (Burgh-by-Sands) and Cohors Morinorum at Glannaventa (Ravenglass). The cavalry units were Ala Petriana Milliaria at Petriana (Stanwix) adjacent to Luguvalium and Ala Herculea at nearby Olenacum (Old Carlisle).

independence.  Luguvalium thus had ample resources with which to defend itself against both the barbarians and the Dux Britanniarum, and it made itself a major military power in north Britannia.

### The "Sons" of Coelestius

Luguvalium fell away from Ducal control during Coelestius's lifetime (or very soon thereafter), but the remainder of his realm held together for a long time after his death. Coelestius's domain did not break apart until the early Sixth Century, when it, as well as much territory just beyond Hadrian's Wall, was divided among a number of individuals identified in north Briton tradition as the "sons" of "Coel Hen."

Coelestius, despite his appellation of "the Old," had, of course, died long before his "sons" inherited his lands. Coelestius might have been long-lived, but he could not have possibly reigned in north Britannia for an entire century. His successors were therefore not literally his sons. They might not have even been his more remote descendants. The designation of "Coel Hen" as founding father in a royal genealogy was not necessarily a declaration of true blood lineage; it was usually a blatant attempt by a local ruling dynasty to trace its authority to a Roman official of unquestioned legitimacy. Because Coelestius owed his Ducal appointment to Constantine III, the last Roman Emperor to rule in Britannia, north Briton monarchs later wishing to assert the lawfulness of their rule claimed Coelestius as an ancestor.

Coelestius Senex was probably succeeded as Dux Britanniarum by his real son and then by his grandson, both of whom bore the family name Coelestius. A ruler named Coelestius thus did truly reign as Dux Britanniarum throughout the Fifth Century. His government then collapsed and strangers (i.e., his "sons") came to power in various parts of his former domain.

The exact process by which the dynasty of Coelestius was superseded in northeast Britannia is not clear. With the aid of Geoffrey of Monmouth, we shall later determine what finally became of the realm of the Dux Britanniarum.

## Chapter Seven
## Ambrosius Aurelianus the Elder

Dux Coelestius enjoyed good relations with Vortigern, but not everyone in Britannia was pleased with the government of the Superbus Tyrannus. Vortigern faced formidable opposition to his rule not only from the Pictish and Irish enemies of the Diocese, but also from certain of his fellow Britons.

It was inevitable that Vortigern's leadership of an independent Britannia would make him many enemies among his own Romanized countrymen. The Imperial faction in particular was distressed by Vortigern's efforts to maintain Britannia's freedom. The leader of the Imperial faction, and of the domestic opposition to Vortigern, was Ambrosius Aurelianus, head of the Ambrosii family.

### The Ambrosii of Britannia

The earliest surviving references to the Ambrosii are found in Gildas's *De Excidio Britanniae* and Nennius's *Historia Brittonum*. Gildas tells us that a certain Ambrosius Aurelianus led a militarily resurgent Britannia against the Anglo-Saxons in what must have been the A.D. 460's. He describes this Ambrosius as the last Roman survivor in Britannia, a man whose parents had "worn the purple" but were slain in the turmoil of the early Fifth Century. Nennius adds the surprising detail that Vortigern not only feared the Picts and Scots, but that he also dreaded "the Romans" and "Ambrosius." He further states that Ambrosius fought against a certain Vitalinus (rendered "Guitolinus" in Nennius's text) in the Battle of Wallop in A.D. 437. The

name Vitalinus was, we have seen, associated with both Vortigern and the town of Glevum Colonia (Gloucester). The strange bits of information given us by Gildas and Nennius may seem confusing at first, but they make a great deal of sense if we consider them in the context of post-Roman Britannia.

For a start, the Ambrosii clearly produced two military leaders of post-Roman Britannia. It is not physically impossible, but extremely unlikely, that the Ambrosius who caused Vortigern dread and who fought Vitalinus in the A.D. 430's was the same Ambrosius who battled the Anglo-Saxons in the A.D. 460's. Two Ambrosii were thus active in post-Roman Britannia: the elder in the A.D. 430's, and the younger, probably his son, in the A.D. 460's.

We should also take the description of Ambrosius as "the last Roman" as a statement of political affiliation, not of ethnic or cultural heritage. All Britons of this time, regardless of the relative mix of Celtic and Latin blood in their veins, considered themselves Roman citizens. They would, in fact, continue to do so for many years; indeed, the very Welsh word *Cymry*, meaning "Welsh," is derived from the Latin word *civis*, meaning "citizen." Post-Roman Briton society simply did not suffer from an ethnic or cultural division between Roman and Celtic factions. Moreover, the equally Roman name of Ambrosius's opponent at the Battle of Wallop, "Vitalinus," makes it clear that Imperial allegiance, not ancestral heritage, was at issue. The truth is that the Ambrosii were leaders of the Imperial, or "Roman," faction in Britannia.

Gildas's reference to the younger Ambrosius's parents having "worn the purple" indicates that the Ambrosii were of aristocratic background. It was also an important cause of Geoffrey of Monmouth's muddled account of early post-Roman history. In the Middle Ages, the phrase "to wear the purple" was an expression signifying royal pedigree; thus, Venerable Bede, interpreting Gildas, tells us that the parents of Ambrosius Aurelianus "were of royal birth and title." Geoffrey concluded that the royal, "purple-wearing" father of Ambrosius must have been Emperor Constantine III. Geoffrey did not know that, in the Roman Empire, Senators also "wore the purple." In the Senators' case, the "purple" consisted only of a stripe on their tunics and togas, rather than the more lavish and color-splashed garments favored by medieval kings and Roman Emperors. Senators nonetheless did "wear the purple." The "purple wearing" parents of the younger Ambrosius were not kinsmen of the Imperial Constantini family, as Geoffrey thought, but members of the powerful and wealthy Roman Senatorial class.

Besides the reference to "wearing the purple," the very name of Ambrosius Aurelianus supports the inference that the Ambrosii were Roman aristocrats of Senatorial status. Aristocratic Romans, we have noted, usually had three names: a *praenomen*, or individual name; a *nomen*, or family name; and a *cognomen*, indicating a branch of a family. In the case of the Ambrosii, "Ambrosius" was the *nomen* and "Aurelianus" the *cognomen*. We shall later see that "Aurelius" was a favorite Ambrosii *praenomen*. Such an obviously Roman name, plus the fact that it must have been used prominently in order to have survived in its Latin (rather than a debased or Celticized) form, bespeaks a very noble, a very important and a very Senatorial family.

As Roman Senators, the Ambrosii would have been predisposed to support the Imperial party in post-Roman Britannia. They would have also been affiliated with the family of Emperor Constantine III - at least as political allies, but possibly by marriage or distant blood ties as well. The Ambrosii certainly supported Constantine III in his seizure of power in Britannia,[51] and they probably stood by him even after his invasion of Gaul and loss of popularity. When Constantine III's government was overthrown in Britannia, the Ambrosii were among the voices clamoring for an Imperial restoration. They were no doubt among the Briton leaders who petitioned Emperor Honorius in A.D. 409 or A.D. 410 to send an army into the Diocese.

The statements contained in the early sources, which so confused medieval historians, thus become clear when re-examined in their proper context. There were two Ambrosii of note in post-Roman Britannia, representing successive generations of the same family. They were supporters of the Briton Emperor Constantine III, but not, as Geoffrey believed, members of his family. Instead, they were members of another noble family, a family which was important in its own right. The Ambrosii were members of the Roman Senatorial Class, advocates of the reincorporation of Britannia into the Roman Empire, and political and military opponents of Vortigern, ruler of an independent Britannia.

We can also determine that Ambrosii wealth and power were concentrated in south-central Britannia. Several sites in this part of the

---

51 Which might explain why Severa Maxima choose to align herself with the anti-Imperial Vortigern rather than the Ambrosii, since it was Constantine III who had overthrown and killed her first husband, Gratianus Municeps.

Diocese contain the place name element "Ambros," "Amber" or "Ambres," all derived from the family name of "Ambrosius." These place names memorialize the ownership by the Ambrosii of estates in the area. The principal Ambrosii estates were in the general region about modern Hampshire and Wiltshire. Key examples are Ambrosden in Oxfordshire, whose name means "Ambrosius's Hill," Amberley in West Sussex, whose name means "Ambrosius's Clearing," and Amesbury (formerly Ambresbyrig) on the Salisbury Plain, whose name means "Ambrosius's fort."[52] The Ambrosii must have dominated the several Civitates in this part of Britannia, being the Civitates based upon Venta Belgarum (Winchester), Calleva Atrebatum (Silchester), Sorviodunum (Salisbury), Dorciconium (Dorchester-on-Thames) and Noviomagus Regnensium (Chichester). The Ambrosii heartland thus lay just to the southeast of Vortigern's ally, Vitalinus, in Glevum Colonia (Gloucester), and to the east of Vortigern's Cornovian army in Dumnonia.

The Ambrosii also owned property in Roman Gaul. Two places in modern Brittany are called Macoer Aurilian, meaning "Aurelian's Wall," which suggests that the Ambrosii owned estates in the part of Gaul then called Armorica. The existence of such estates accords with Geoffrey's belief that Ambrosius's family had a Breton connection. In addition, several persons named Ambrosius appear among the leadership of Gaul in the Fifth and Sixth Centuries. Gaius Sollius Apollinaris

Sidonius, Bishop of Arverna (Clermont-Ferrand) in central Gaul, wrote a letter in the A.D. 470's to an otherwise unknown Gallic Bishop named Ambrosius, and Georgius Florentius (better known as Gregory of Tours), Bishop of Turona (Tours) in northwest Gaul, in his *Historiae Francorum* (Histories of the Franks), tells of an Ambrosius who was a leading citizen of Turona in the late Sixth Century. The Gallic Ambrosii were probably cousins of the Briton family. Based upon place name evidence, Geoffrey's account of Ambrosius's Breton background and the appearance of the name Ambrosius among the Roman aristocracy of Gaul, we may conclude that, in addition to their extensive estates in Britannia, the Ambrosii also owed property in Armorica and elsewhere in Gaul.

The Ambrosii probably at one time possessed additional acreage in other parts of the Empire. Members of the Senatorial Class, thanks to their tax exemption and political clout, were able to amass enormous wealth during the declining days of the Empire. One Senatorial family, the Valerii, is known to have owned vast estates in Italy, Sicily, north Africa and Spain, as well as Britannia, in the early Fifth Century. Even if the Ambrosii could not match the fabulous wealth of the Valerii, they were unlikely to have been strictly a Briton or Gallic family. The Ambrosii of Britannia might therefore be related to another famous Ambrosius, Saint Ambrosius (or, modernized, Ambrose), Bishop of Mediolanum (Milan) and a contemporary of the Briton Emperor Maximus.

Saint Ambrosius, like the Briton Ambrosii, enjoyed a distinguished family background. The Saint's father had held the office of Praefectus Praetorio per Gallias (Praetorian

---

52  Other Ambrosius place names are located in modern Essex and Kent, but, given their proximity to the major Anglo-Saxon population centers in Britannia, these sites were probably not agricultural estates, but military forts established by the younger Ambrosius in the late Fifth Century.

Prefect for the Gauls[53]). "Praefectus Praetorio" was the title of the Emperor's most senior civil official in a region; in status, a Praefectus Praetorio fell just below a Caesar, or junior Emperor. The title was the civilian equivalent of Magister Militum, the highest military rank. Saint Ambrosius himself served as Consularis (Imperial governor) of Liguria and Aemilia in northwest Italy before taking up religious duties. Saint Ambrosius was thus a man accustomed by both upbringing and experience to the confident exercise of power.

In A.D. 374, Saint Ambrosius was elected by popular acclaim to the position of Bishop of Mediolanum. He held this position until his death in A.D. 397. Saint Ambrosius continued to play a prominent role in secular affairs even after he became Bishop of Mediolanum. In fact, his ecclesiastical office allowed Ambrosius to thrust himself into the forefront of Imperial politics because Mediolanum was then the residence of the western Emperor and the administrative capital of the Western Empire. As Bishop of Mediolanum, Saint Ambrosius had a pulpit from which he could regularly address the leading members of the Imperial court, including the Emperor himself.

Saint Ambrosius took full advantage of his position to exhort the several Emperors of his time to maintain the peace and provide good government for their subjects. He was also instrumental in arranging a truce between the Briton Emperor Maximus and Maximus's Italian rival, Emperor Valentinian II, in A.D. 383. This truce held until Maximus invaded

---

53 Gaul, like Britannia, contained several provinces, hence there were several "Gauls." Moreover, the Praefectus Praetorio per Gallias originally had authority over the Celtic Dioceses of Hispania and Britannia as well as Gaul.

Italy in A.D. 387. In A.D. 390, the Saint even compelled the mighty eastern Emperor Theodosius to do public penance in atonement for a massacre carried out by his troops in Thessalonica in Greece. He was later instrumental in arranging Theodosius's succession to the rule of the Western Empire after the death of Emperor Valentinian II. Ambrosius then supported Magister Militum Stilicho, and he presided at the marriage of Stilicho's daughter to Emperor Honorius. Only members of the Imperial Senatorial Class, born and bred to power, could have wielded the political influence that Saint Ambrosius - or the Briton Ambrosii - did.

Saint Ambrosius was probably the great-uncle of the Ambrosius who fought Vitalinus in A.D. 437. In addition to the Saint's sharing the Briton leader's *nomen* of Ambrosius, the Saint's father bore the *praenomen* of Aurelius, a name which Geoffrey associates with the Ambrosii of Britannia. Roman families often repeated the same individual name in each generation, so the similarity in both individual name (Aurelius) and family name (Ambrosius) used by the Italian and the Briton families must be more than mere coincidence. The Italian Ambrosii and the Briton Ambrosii were almost certainly related.

The probable family relationship between the Italian Saint and the Briton military leaders suggests there was a religious, as well as a political, dimension to the conflict between Vortigern and the Ambrosii. As we shall see, strong evidence points to Vortigern being a follower of the Pelagian heresy. If the Ambrosii were devotees of the Empire's official religion, as implied by their connection to the sainted Bishop of Mediolanum, then Vortigern's Pelagian leanings made the Superbus Tyrannus doubly abhorrent to the Ambrosii and their adherents.

## The Military Forces of the Ambrosii

The animosity between the Ambrosii and the Superbus Tyrannus was political and religious in nature, but it was military in expression. The ultimate expression of this animosity was the Battle of Wallop in A.D. 437, when Vortigern's ally Vitalinus led the troops of Glevum against the elder Ambrosius.

We have already seen that Vortigern's military might was based upon native Briton soldiers seasoned in warfare against Irish warriors in the Pagus (Powys and Clwyd) and upon barbarian mercenary troops. In order to determine the nature of the military forces commanded by Vitalinus and Ambrosius in the Battle of Wallop, we must look to Gaul and its record of a remarkable Roman aristocrat active there about this time.

Ecdicius, a wealthy Romano-Gallic landowner,[54] is known to have raised a small force of highly mobile and determinedly aggressive horse warriors around A.D. 471. He recruited his troopers from the well-to-do (and therefore horse-owning and horse-riding) Romanized rural nobility. He supplied and paid these troopers out of the income from his own estates, without the benefit of any assistance from the Gallic Civitates or Imperial authorities. Ecdicius used his mounted warband very effectively to ambush the Visigoth raiding parties then afflicting south and central Gaul. He even relieved the town of Arverna

---

54 Ecdicius was the son of the short-reigned Emperor Avitus (A.D. 455 to A.D. 457), who had himself served in Gaul under the famous Roman general Flavius Aetius.

(Clermont-Ferrand) from a Visigoth siege, to the great rejoicing of the townspeople. Vitalinus and Ambrosius must have commanded similar forces: small, mobile cavalry units consisting of soldiers levied from the Romano-Briton country gentry and supported by the revenues of their own estates - although, unlike Ecdicius, they no doubt also drew upon the tax revenues of the Civitates which they dominated.

The first cavalry force to be raised in this manner was probably a Vexillatio Equitum of about 300-500 troopers which the father of the elder Ambrosius supplied to Emperor Constantine III. The *Notitia Dignitatum* identifies a unit called Equites Scutarii Aureliaci (Horsemen of Aurelius's Shieldmaker) in the command of the Comes Britanniarum. The Equites Scutarii Aureliaci does not appear before the Fifth Century and its unique name suggests that it was raised by the prominent Romano-Briton family for Constantine III's expedition to Gaul.

The Romano-Briton cavalrymen were drawn from the prosperous agricultural areas of southwest Britannia. Vitalinus's horse soldiers came from the affluent region about the lower Severn River, and Ambrosius's from the equally affluent region about modern Hampshire. Vitalinus no doubt drew upon the tax revenues of Glevum Colonia (Gloucester), Corinium Dobunnorum (Cirencester) and Aquae Sulis (Bath), while Ambrosius drew upon those of Venta Belgarum (Winchester), Calleva Atrebatum (Silchester), Sorviodunum (Salisbury), Dorciconium (Dorchester-on-Thames) and Noviomagus Regnensium (Chichester).

The Romano-Briton mounted armies were very small, a few hundred troopers at most. The

cost of maintaining larger numbers of cavalry soldiers, with their horses, gear, grooms, blacksmiths and other servants, was prohibitive. Moreover, only a tiny percentage of the Roman population, the landed upper class, had the necessary equestrian background to make good cavalrymen; in the days before the invention of the horsecollar, horses were not workbeasts, but luxury animals suitable only for riding. The Romano-Briton warriors compensated for their small numbers with tactical mobility, consummate skill (initially in horsemanship, but very soon in mounted warfare as well) and superior discipline. The aristocratic soldiers were also highly motivated and supremely confident. Against the infantry armies of their Anglo-Saxon and Irish enemies, even small numbers of Romano-Briton horsemen could be a potent and effective military force when well-led by a competent and aggressive commander.

Against fellow Roman aristocrats, the Romano-Briton horsemen enjoyed no particular advantage. Even so, when they came into conflict, as in the Battle of Wallop, their pride would not allow them to shirk the challenge. The Battle of Wallop must have been very small in scale, but very fierce in intensity.

Most of what we know about the Battle of Wallop is deduced from a brief entry in the chronology at the end of the *Historia Brittonum*, which states:

> From the beginning of the reign of Vortigern up to the dissension of Vitalinus and Ambrosius are twelve years which is Wollop that is Catguoloph, Battle of Wallop.

From this bare mention, plus the fact that Vortigern's reign began in A.D. 425, we know that the Battle of Wallop took place in A.D. 437. We also know that Wallop is a small town still bearing the same name in modern Hampshire, which was part of the region dominated by the Ambrosii. From this geographic circumstance, we may infer that Vitalinus was the aggressor and Ambrosius the defender. The sparse allusion to the Battle of Wallop does not indicate who won the Battle, although from subsequent events it is obvious that Vitalinus defeated Ambrosius.

To continue with the story of the Ambrosii, we must review what Geoffrey of Monmouth has to say about the legendary enchanter Merlin.

## Merlin and Embresguletic

Geoffrey tells us that Vortigern at one time had trouble erecting a tower in the Snowdon region of north Wales. Vortigern's "magicians" advised him that a human sacrifice, specifically of a child without a father, would somehow resolve the difficulties. This advice was a riddle, for how could there be such a thing as a child without a father? Vortigern's agents nevertheless discovered a child to fit the bill: Merlin. Merlin confounded the Tyrannus's magicians, however, by disclosing that beneath the tower site was a subterranean pool containing two dragons. The dragons were excavated, and they fought each other. Merlin then burst into a fit of prophecy, making a series of predictions which culminated in his forecasting that Vortigern would come to an ignoble end at the hands of the "sons of Constantine."

Nennius tells pretty much the same tale, although without the complete set of prophecies. Nennius limits the youth to the single prediction of a Briton victory over the Anglo-Saxons. More importantly, Nennius does not identify the prophetic youth as Merlin, but as Ambrosius, the son of "a Roman Consul."

Nennius's surprise revelation of the youth's heritage conflicts with his earlier assertion that the youth was fatherless. The original account must have merely indicated that the youth's father had died by the time of the confrontation, not that the youth never had a father. Nennius's revelation will also allow us to reconstruct the full story of the confrontation between Vortigern and the mysterious youth.

In both versions of the tale, Vortigern was impressed with the performance of the youth and decided to spare his life. Merlin is temporarily forgotten by Geoffrey in his account of the warfare which followed the incident, but Nennius tells us that Vortigern "assigned" the young Ambrosius "all the western provinces of Britain."

Geoffrey was apparently aware of the alternative version of the Merlin tale as given by Nennius, for he does remark that Merlin "was also called Ambrosius." Geoffrey does not connect the prophetic youth called Ambrosius with the great Roman-Briton military family of this name, but he should have. In the character of Merlin, Geoffrey confuses an individual of the Ambrosii family with an entirely unrelated poet named Myrddin who lived in the far north of Britannia at a much later date.

We shall deal with Myrddin, the genuine person whom we know as Merlin, later. For now, we need only focus on the Ambrosius with whom this Myrddin became confused.

We know that the youthful "Merlin" who confronted Vortigern was really a member of the Ambrosii family because the precise name given him by Nennius is "Embresguletic." "Embres" is a variation of "Emrys," a Welsh personal name derived from "Ambrosius."

"Guletic" is an early version of the Welsh *wledig*, meaning "prince" but originally carrying the connotation of "landowner." Embresguletic, or Ambrosius the Landowner, could hardly be anyone else but a scion of the Romano-Briton Senatorial Ambrosii family.

This last piece of the puzzle allows us to reconstruct the story of the Briton Ambrosii in the early Fifth Century.

The Ambrosii were supporters of the fallen Emperor Constantine III and advocates of Britannia's reincorporation into the Empire. The Imperial leanings of the Ambrosii brought them into conflict with Vortigern, leader of the independent Diocese. This conflict led to armed combat in the Battle of Wallop in A.D. 437, when Vortigern's ally Vitalinus attacked and defeated the elder Ambrosius.

From Gildas's reference to the slaying of the younger Ambrosius's parents, we know that the Ambrosii patriarch and his wife were killed in the Battle of Wallop. The elder Ambrosius might have perished in combat, but his wife was certainly murdered in the excitement which followed the victory. Vortigern's advisors urged him to kill the young son of the family as well, but the youth displayed such fine courage before his parents' conquerors that Vortigern thought it unwise or ignoble to slay him. The younger Ambrosius was then imprisoned in "the western provinces" of Britannia, meaning modern Wales.

The younger Ambrosius later escaped his prison and restored his family's prominence in the Diocese. The re-emergence of the Ambrosii in Britannia did not take place, however, for almost a quarter of a century. In the meantime, the Briton Imperial faction was crushed and Vortigern was master of Britannia.

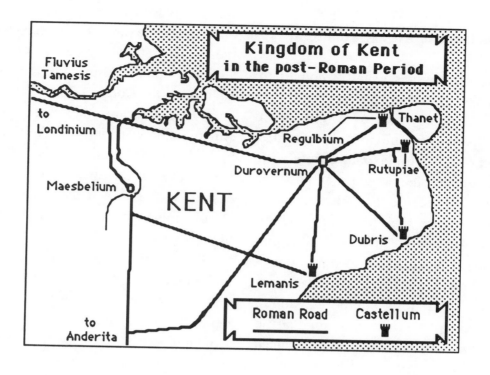

**Kingdom of Kent**
**in the post-Roman Period**

Fluvius Tamesis

to Londinium

Thanet

Regulbium

Maesbelium

Durovernum

Rutupiae

KENT

Dubris

Lemanis

Roman Road    Castellum

to Anderita

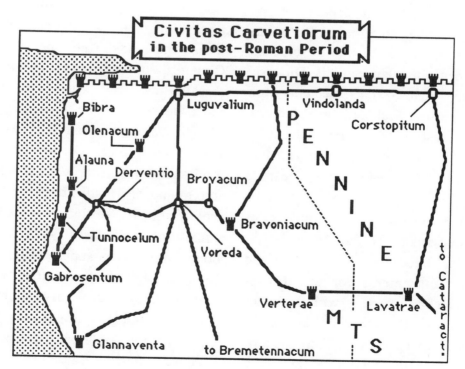

**Civitas Carvetiorum**
**in the post-Roman Period**

Bibra

Luguvalium

Vindolanda

P
E
N
N
I
N
E

Corstopitum

Olenacum

Alauna

Derventio

Brovacum

Tunnocelum

Bravoniacum

Voreda

Gabrosentum

Verterae

Lavatrae

M
T    S

to Cataract.

Glannaventa

to Bremetennacum

## Chapter Eight
## The Foundation of Anglo-Saxon Kent

One of the key issues usually thought to have divided Vortigern and the elder Ambrosius was Vortigern's employment of Anglo-Saxon mercenaries. Ambrosius might have regarded the recruitment of Anglo-Saxon warriors with suspicion, not because he thought it an unsound policy in itself, but because the barbarians were loyal only to Vortigern, their paymaster and the enemy of the Ambrosii. In fact, Ambrosius himself probably fielded Anglo-Saxon troops in the Battle of Wallop, for the hiring of barbarian mercenaries was a long-standing Roman practice. Vortigern's crime was not that he hired Anglo-Saxon warriors, but that he planned to, and did, use them against his fellow Britons.

Anglo-Saxons first came to Britannia at the start of the Fifth Century to serve the Britons as soldiers. They were soon allowed to settle on abandoned or neglected land in the Diocese. Most of the early Anglo-Saxon settlements were located on the eastern seaboard of Britannia, specifically the coastline from modern Kent up through Deira, or beside the River Thames, specifically at the River's mouth and near its upper reaches.

The regional military commanders in Britannia invited many of the Anglo-Saxon settlers into the Diocese. They hired the barbarians as replacements for the Roman troops who had gone overseas with Magister Militum Stilicho and Emperor Constantine III. The barbarians of Kent served the Comes Litoris Saxonici (Count of the Saxon Shore), who expected them to protect the Diocese's southeast coast from the unwanted attentions of their fellow-countrymen. Those of Deira worked, as we have seen, for the Dux Britanniarum. The other Anglo-Saxon settlers were employed by the Curiae (town councils) of the various Civitates upon whose lands they settled. In addition to the Comes Litoris Saxonici and the Dux Britanniarum, the chief employers of Anglo-Saxon warriors were the Civitates based upon Lindum Colonia (Lincoln) and Venta Icenorum (Caistor-by-Norwich) on Britannia's eastern seaboard, and the Civitas based upon Dorciconium (Dorchester-on-Thames) in the upper Thames region.

The Civitates based upon Lindum Colonia and Venta Icenorum established Anglo-Saxon colonies along their eastern seacoasts as a defense against piracy. The coastlines of these Civitates were exposed to seaborne raiding parties from the colonists' own homeland in Germania, and probably from Drust MacErp's Pictish kingdom as well. The establishment of these Anglo-Saxon colonies was part of the Civitates' successful response to the military threats they faced when they declared their independence from the Imperial government.

The Dorciconium Civitas was dominated by the Ambrosii in the post-Roman period, but the Ambrosii did not introduce the Anglo-Saxons into the upper Thames region. The barbarians were originally settled there by the Roman authorities in the last days of Imperial rule to protect the military supply base at Dorciconium. By A.D. 437, however, the upper Thames Anglo-Saxons probably worked for the Ambrosii, and they might have even supplied troops for the Ambrosii army in the Battle of Wallop. After the Battle of Wallop, the upper Thames barbarians seem to have shifted their loyalty to Vitalinus and his town of Glevum Colonia (Gloucester).

The distribution of Anglo-Saxon settlements did not change very much as the Fifth Century progressed, although the original settlement areas became more densely populated and expanded slightly into the interior of the Diocese. The principal expansion moved up the rivers draining into the Wash and down the ancient trail now called the Icknield Way. (The Icknield Way runs from modern Norfolk to the upper Thames region.) Anglo-Saxon colonies did, however, appear for the first time in modern Sussex and in the vicinity of Venta Belgarum (Winchester).

The Anglo-Saxons of Sussex, unlike their compatriots living elsewhere in Britannia, came to the Diocese as hostile invaders from the start, and they carved small independent domains for themselves along the Sussex coast. We shall examine the Anglo-Saxon conquest of Sussex in greater detail later. For now, we need only note that the influence of the Sussex barbarians on the rest of Britannia was slight because they could seldom make their power felt beyond the great Sussex forest called the Weald. The late-arriving Anglo-Saxons of the Venta Belgarum area were probably Ambrosius's mercenaries, although some of them might have been settled in the area by Vortigern after Ambrosius's defeat.

It was perhaps inevitable that the growing Anglo-Saxon population in Britannia would sooner or later challenge the political dominance of the Britons. As it happened, it was the Anglo-Saxons' special connection to the Superbus Tyrannus that raised them to power in Britannia.

## Hengist, son of Wihtgils

The first Anglo-Saxons employed by Vortigern were the crews of three warships which landed in Civitas Cantiacorum (modern Kent) early in the Tyrannus's reign. Geoffrey of Monmouth tells us that Vortigern just happened to be in "Durobernia, which is now called Canterbury," at the time "for it was his custom to visit that city very frequently." Actually, Geoffrey is wrong; the Roman name for Canterbury was not Durobernia, but Durovernum. Geoffrey, Nennius and Anglo-Saxon tradition are nevertheless clear that Vortigern and the barbarians first met in modern Kent. Vortigern was no doubt in Civitas Cantiacorum seeking the political support of the Comes Litoris Saxonici at his headquarters in Durovernum, and while in the vicinity he contacted the Anglo-Saxon warriors.

The Anglo-Saxons were led by a chieftain named Hengist, son of Wihtgils, and by his brother Horsa. "Hengist" and "Horsa" were not the barbarians' real names. "Hengist" is a corruption of the Anglo-Saxon word *hengest*, meaning "stallion," and "Horsa" is derived from the Anglo-Saxon word *hors*, meaning "horse." "Hengist" and "Horsa" were thus not genuine personal names, but *noms de guerre*, or warrior nicknames. Equine symbols, such as the Anglo-Saxons are known to have used in later times, probably appeared on the warlords' battle ensigns. Some scholars believe that the real name of "Hengist the Stallion" might have been Aethelbert.

Hengist explained to Vortigern that he and his companions came to Britannia in search of employment because they had been banished from their homeland on account of overpopulation. Hengist was indeed banished from his homeland, although overpopulation was merely the excuse he gave to a prospective employer. Nennius comes closer to the truth when he tells us simply that the newcomers were "exiled from Germania."

We know the truth of the matter because, even before he came to Britannia, Hengist was a legend among his own people and the subject of an heroic poem. Unfortunately, most of this poem is now lost. Fragments of the saga, called *Finnesburh* or *The Fight at Finn's Burg*, do survive in one manuscript, and additional details are preserved in summary form in the great Anglo-Saxon epic *Beowulf.*

According to the early Anglo-Saxon poets, Hengist began his military career as a young captain in the retinue of the Danish King Hnaef. King Hnaef and his troops (including Hengist) paid a visit to the king's brother-in-law and subordinate ruler, Finn Focwalding, king of the Frisians. Finn betrayed his overlord and attacked his guests. King Hnaef himself fell in the ensuing combat. Hengist then assumed command of the surviving Danes, who had barricaded themselves in the Frisian king's hall. Finn offered to spare the lives of the beleaguered Danes if they would now pledge loyalty to him. The Danes agreed. Some time (apparently several months) later, when Danish reinforcements arrived, Hengist led the defeated Danes in revolt against their new employer, slaying Finn. The incident described in *Finnesburh* shows Hengist to have been a determined warrior and a natural leader.

It also shows Hengist to have been a ruthless fighter and shameless opportunist. Under the Germanic warrior code, Hengist should not have disgraced King Hnaef's memory by surrendering to the enemy; he should have died fighting to avenge his slain master. Hengist did indeed later obtain revenge for Hnaef by killing Finn, but only after breaking his new oath to the Frisian king. Although the taking of life in revenge for a fallen leader was regarded by the Anglo-Saxons as honorable, the breaking of an oath most certainly was not. The victim of Hengist's duplicity, Finn, had also broken a vow of fealty to Hnaef, but this circumstance did not entirely excuse Hengist. Strict and absolute adherence to a pledge was a very important element in a barbarian warrior's good reputation. Hengist's standing among his countrymen was seriously undermined as a result of his overly pragmatic approach to the obligations of honor.

The ambiguous reputation of Hengist following the incidents described in *Finnesburh* explains why Hengist found it prudent to leave his homeland and seek a brighter future across the sea in Britannia. Royal employers in Scandinavia refused to engage the services of a man who, whatever his justification, had broken a sworn oath of allegiance to another king.

Hengist fought King Finn at Finn's Burg around the same time that Vortigern emerged as a Diocese-wide leader in Britannia. Nennius dates Hengist's arrival in Britannia to the fourth year of Vortigern's reign, or A.D. 428, which puts Hengist's misadventures at Finn's Burg in A.D. 426 and A.D. 427.

Nennius, translating from a contemporary account of Hengist's career, reports that Hengist and his followers resided for a time on the Isle of Thanet after they came to Britannia. Geoffrey of Monmouth supports Nennius when he tells us that Hengist's fort in Britannia was called Thanceastre; "Thanceastre" means "Thanet-fort," from Tanatus Insula, the Roman name for the island, and *ceastre* or *chester*, the Anglo-Saxon word for a walled town or fort. The Isle of Thanet lies off the east coast of Kent near the mouth of the River Thames, and the barbarians were obviously settled there by the Comes Litoris Saxonici to guard the entrance of the River Thames against their Continental kinsmen.

After Hengist and his followers had resided for a time on Thanet, Vortigern approached them. He offered to provide them with food and clothing if they agreed to fight Britannia's enemies. Vortigern's offer reflects the Roman practice of paying soldiers in goods, called *annona*. This practice arose in the late Roman period, when hard currency was scarce. Vortigern probably made his proposal after the barbarians had already lived a year or so on Thanet. Vortigern thus hired Hengist and his warband away from the Comes Litoris Saxonici, their original Briton employer, around A.D. 430.

Geoffrey tells us that the first task undertaken by Hengist and his followers at Vortigern's behest was participation in a joint Anglo-Briton expedition against the Picts. This expedition was, of course, the one which Vortigern led against the Pictish warrior-king Drust MacErp. The Anglo-Saxons in Vortigern's service were not very numerous, being only some 100 to 150 fighters, but they were very effective. Although Geoffrey indicates that Briton troops also served in the Pictish campaign, he insists that the Anglo-Saxons played the principal role in the fighting and that they were crucial to the Britons' victory.

In reward for these services against the Picts, Vortigern supposedly gave Hengist land in Lindsey, which is the area to the north and east of Lindum Colonia (Lincoln), for the support of his followers. In fact, we have no evidence to connect Hengist with the barbarian settlements then in Lindsey. The Anglo-Saxons of the region were certainly recruited and employed, not by Vortigern, but by the Magistratus and Curia (town council) of Lindum Colonia. They were hired to shield the town and its surrounding district from seaborne raiders, both Pictish and Anglo-Saxon. Hengist, as the chief barbarian in the service of the Superbus Tyrannus, no doubt enjoyed some influence with the Anglo-Saxons of Lindsey, but he was not their landlord or ruler.

Hengist was, in fact, probably known to the Anglo-Saxons of Lindsey not as an ally, but as an enemy. The "Durobernia" frequently visited by Vortigern was not Durovernum Cantiacorum (Canterbury), as Geoffrey thought, but Durobrivae (Water Newton, near Peterborough), the largest town and probable capital of Civitas Corielsoliliorum. Civitas Corielsoliliorum was a late Roman Civitas which encompassed roughly the area between Tripontium (Cave's Inn, near Rugby) and Durolipons (Cambridge); it had been carved out of the northern territory of Civitas Catuvellaunorum, which was based upon Verulamium (St. Albans). The area governed by Civitas Corielsoliliorum was principally industrial, being a major center of pottery manufacture and of iron, salt and building stone production in Roman times. The Civitas declined precipitously with the collapse of commerce in the late Roman period as its industries lost contact with their markets. It also suffered a loss of much of its farmland due to an intrusion of the sea upon the fenlands adjacent to the Wash. As a consequence, ambitious Anglo-Saxons encroaching upon its territory from nearby Lindsey would have encountered little local resistance. Vortigern must have found it necessary to frequently "visit" Durobrivae and deploy his Anglo-Saxon mercenaries against their countrymen from Lindsey in order to protect Civitas Corielsoliliorum from barbarian infiltration. Hengist's warring upon the Anglo-Saxons of Lindsey at Vortigern's behest, and his taking spoils from them, certainly underlies Geoffrey's association of Hengist with the region.

Hengist soon became associated with another part of Britannia, where Vortigern truly did give him land.

Sometime after the Pictish campaign, Hengist sent for reinforcements from Germania. These reinforcements arrived in a formidable flotilla of eighteen ships.[55] Anglo-Saxon warships of this period typically carried thirty to forty crewmen, which would put the number of Hengist's reinforcements at some 540 to 720 warriors. These numbers are certainly too high in this instance, however, because not all the barbarian newcomers were warriors. Hengist's reinforcements included at least some noncombatants, foremost of whom was Hengist's own daughter Renwein ("Hrothwina" in her own language).

Geoffrey and Nennius both claim that Vortigern fell in love with Renwein, and that he gave Hengist the "province of Kent" in exchange for Renwein's hand. In fact, the chroniclers have gotten the story backwards. Vortigern's marriage to Renwein was not an *affaire de coeur*; it was a political measure designed to ensure the continued loyalty of Hengist after the Tyrannus had already agreed to give Hengist his own foederati territory in southeast Britannia.

A capable politician like Vortigern was hardly likely to trade away a part of his realm just to acquire a wife, but he did have a number of sound military reasons for installing Hengist in Kent. Nennius reports that Vortigern was unable to deliver the promised supplies to Hengist's growing number of followers, so the Superbus Tyrannus might have intended to pay them off in real estate. He could have also used the promise of land to induce his barbarian soldiers to more vigorous efforts. More importantly, as we shall see, Vortigern had enemies in Gaul whom he hoped to counter by establishing the Anglo-Saxons in Kent. At the same time, the cementing of a political alliance with a marital union was a common and important Anglo-Saxon custom; in the Anglo-Saxon epic poem *Beowulf*, the wife of a king was even referred to as "she who was meant to establish peace." Vortigern married Renwein in order to strengthen his alliance with Hengist before he installed Hengist as ruler of his own Anglo-Saxon realm in Kent.

The wedding to Renwein was nevertheless conducted without the benefit of clergy or Roman legal sanction. Vortigern's first wife, Severa Maxima, had certainly died by this time, but, as we shall see, Vortigern had already remarried another woman in a proper Roman ceremony. Moreover, most Britons considered a familial connection to the Superbus Tyrannus an excessive honor to confer upon a mere barbarian warlord. They also feared giving a half-barbarian son of Vortigern's a legitimate claim to political power in Britannia. The wedding was therefore celebrated only according to Anglo-Saxon custom, which was not recognized under Roman law.[56] From a

---

55 Geoffrey gives the number of ships as eighteen, Nennius as sixteen or nineteen in different manuscripts. A Latin eighteen (XVIII) could have been easily converted into a sixteen (XVI) or a nineteen (XVIIII) through a slipshod error by a weary clerk.

56 When Emperor Gallienus (reigned A.D. 253 to A.D. 268) similarly married a Germanic Marcomanni

strictly legal point of view, Renwein was no more than Vortigern's mistress, but Hengist was apparently satisfied with this lesser status.[57]

Vortigern's marriage to Renwein, and Hengist's receipt of Kent, must have occurred in A.D. 441, which is when the *Chronica Gallia* (Chronicle of Gaul) reports the fall of Britannia to the Anglo-Saxons. The establishment of an Anglo-Saxon realm on Britannia's southeast coast effectively cut Britannia off from the rest of the Roman Empire, which was the appropriate event, from a Continental point of view, to mark the loss of the island Diocese.

Vortigern's grant of Kent to Hengist represented a very new and different arrangement between the Britons and their Anglo-Saxon warriors. Whereas the first Anglo-Saxon settlers came to Britannia as taxpaying laeti to serve under the command and direction of their employers, Hengist and his followers were granted foederati status in Kent. They were not incorporated into the Romano-Briton army or subordinated to the Romano-Briton government; instead, they followed their own leaders, paid no tribute to the Britons and governed their own autonomous realm. The grant of foederati status to Hengist's followers in Kent might have even inspired the Deiran Anglo-Saxons just a few years later to make a similar demand of their own employer, the Dux Britanniarum in Eboracum (York).

The transfer of "the province of Kent" to Hengist did not occur without a certain amount of difficulty. Geoffrey tells us that the grant was made without the knowledge or approval of an "Earl Gorangonus" who ruled there.

### Vorangonus, Comes Litoris Saxonici

The reference to the hapless "Earl Gorangonus" is an important clue as to what actually occurred when Vortigern transferred the "province of Kent" to his barbarian ally. "Gorangonus" is a medieval version of an older name; Nennius gives this name as "Guoyrancgonus" and William of Malmesbury as "Gorongi." The original Latin would have been more like "Vorangonus." The English title "earl" corresponds to the Continental title "count," which was derived from the Roman military rank of Comes.[58] The displaced ruler was thus a Roman called Vorangonus who held the military rank of Comes. By "province of Kent," clearly Civitas Cantiacorum, from which modern Kent takes its name, is meant. Civitas Cantiacorum was in southeast Britannia, which had been under the military jurisdiction of the Comes Litoris Saxonici (Count of the Saxon Shore) in Roman times. Taking all these facts together, it is obvious that Comes Vorangonus was the last Comes Litoris Saxonici. Vortigern

---

princess for reasons of policy, the bride was only accorded concubine status by the Romans.

57 Informal relationships seem to have been common among the Anglo-Saxons. Harold Godwinson, the last Anglo-Saxon king of England, enjoyed such a relationship with the beautiful Edith Swanneck, who bore him three sons before he took an official wife, the daughter of a former political rival. Even William the Conqueror did not consider Harold's arrangement with Edith to preclude an offer of martial alliance between Harold and his own family.

58 The English title "Earl" was taken from the Scandinavian "Jarl" in later Anglo-Saxon times. The title was retained as the English equivalent of the Continental "Count" after the Norman Conquest, when feudalism was introduced into England. Medieval chroniclers then used "Comes" as the Latin word to describe an English Earl. Geoffrey of Monmouth himself uses "Comes" to refer to "Gorangonus," although elsewhere in the *Historia Regum Britanniae* he uses the Roman civilian title of "Consul" when he seems to mean "Earl."

sent his barbarian ally Hengist to supplant Comes Vorangonus, the Roman military commander of Britannia's southeastern defenses.

From the folk traditions and genealogical records of north Britannia, we have been able to determine what became of the office of Dux Britanniarum after the end of Imperial government in Britannia: the position was held by Coelestius and then by Coelestius's successors until the Ducal domain was divided among Coelestius's self-proclaimed "sons" in the early Sixth Century. When the Britons ousted the administrators of Emperor Constantine III, the other regional military commander in Britannia, the Comes Litoris Saxonici, commanded several forts and numerous troops in southeast Britannia. The Comes, his forts and his troops did not simply vanish with the collapse of Constantine III's regime. From the accounts of Geoffrey and Nennius, we can deduce that the office of Comes Litoris Saxonici was held by Vorangonus until Vorangonus was overthrown and his commission terminated by Vortigern's barbarian foederati in A.D. 441.

Comes Vorangonus was probably a political adversary of Vortigern, most likely a partisan of the Briton Imperial faction. At the very least, the independence faction must have considered him an unreliable ally. Vortigern therefore dispatched Hengist to Kent to depose a potential opponent whom the Superbus Tyrannus, in his "frequent visits" to Civitas Cantiacorum, was unable to persuade to his side.

We can find no indication that Vorangonus contested the loss of his command. William of Malmesbury suggests, as we shall see, that at least one of the Comes's garrisons resisted barbarian take-over, but this resistance was limited and unavailing. Vorangonus probably did not have the means to offer effective opposition to Hengist.

Although the Comes Litoris Saxonici controlled extensive forces, only a small portion of them could be considered reliable in Vorangonus's time. The very nature of the Comes's command, being a coastal defense, called for the deployment of marine forces, but we have no evidence that significant numbers of Roman warships continued to ply Britannia's waters in the Fifth Century. The fleet at the Comes's disposal therefore consisted principally of barbarian galleys, such as the three ships originally stationed on Thanet under Hengist. Most, perhaps all, of the Comes's sailors and many of his soldiers must have been Anglo-Saxon mercenaries. Germanic warriors usually honored their contracts of employment with the Romans, but in this case they could not be trusted to uphold their legal commander. Vorangonus's influence over his barbarian soldiers was undermined because his opponent, Hengist, was supported by an even higher authority, the Superbus Tyrannus. The Anglo-Saxons saw Vortigern as the king of Britannia, and they no doubt considered Vorangonus a disloyal vassal who was not worthy of their support. The Comes's barbarian troops probably deserted en masse to join the new foederati leader, and Vorangonus's native soldiers were vastly outnumbered by the Anglo-Saxon warriors of the aggressive Hengist.

Vorangonus might have lost control over many of his soldiers even before his unfortunate encounter with Hengist. Lacking a dependable fleet, the Comes would have found it difficult to maintain a tight rein on the officers in charge of his more distant Saxon Shore forts. The

Comes's control over the two Saxon Shore forts in modern Norfolk,[59] where large numbers of Anglo-Saxons had settled, must have been especially tenuous. His other faraway bastions near Southampton Water[60] and in Sussex[61] probably also slipped away from him, although archaeology affirms that these forts continued to be inhabited by native Briton soldiers for many years after Vorangonus was deposed. For all practical purposes, the Comes's domain had probably shrunk to the territory in and near Civitas Cantiacorum, where most of his forts[62] and the majority of his troops were concentrated.

Comes Vorangonus nevertheless posed a serious danger to Vortigern's continued rule of Britannia. Nennius tells us that Vortigern lived in dread of, among other persons, "the Romans." The Roman leader Ambrosius had been eliminated in the Battle of Wallop, but the possibility of an invasion by the Imperial authorities in Gaul could not be ruled out. The Saxon Shore command, even in its diminished state, controlled the part of Britannia closest to Gaul, where any Imperial invasion force was certain to land. Indeed, Julius Caesar, Emperor Claudius, Constantius Chlorus and Comes Theodosius had each landed in this part of Britannia in their respective invasions of the Diocese.[63] If Comes Vorangonus, like the defeated Ambrosius, was an adherent of the Imperial faction in Britannia, or even if his loyalty to Vortigern's cause was merely suspect, then Vortigern would have feared his aiding a Roman army of reconquest to land in the Diocese. Vorangonus's continued possession of the key territory of Kent represented a military risk that Vortigern was unwilling to run. Vortigern could not allow a political enemy or an untrustworthy ally to control the strategically important southeast part of Britannia.

Vortigern could, however, depend upon his barbarian foederati to resist any Roman army which might attempt to bring the wayward Diocese back into the Empire. Vortigern's establishment of Hengist's foederati regime in Kent, besides rewarding a loyal ally, was part of the Tyrannus's program for the preservation of Britannia's independence.

Vortigern's elimination of a domestic rival and his creation of a buffer state against possible Roman re-invasion were important accomplishments, but the Tyrannus paid an enormous price for these accomplishments in the long run. If Vortigern could oust a native ruler in favor of a barbarian ally, then no Romano-Briton leader could consider himself safe. The overthrow of Comes Vorangonus in order to accommodate an Anglo-Saxon warlord did not set well with any Briton, regardless of political affiliation.

Compounding the anxiety of the Britons was

---

59 Branodunum (Brancaster) and Gariannonum (Burgh Castle), which housed the Comes's only cavalry units.

60 On Vectis Insula (Isle of Wight), a fort of unknown Roman name now called Carisbrooke (Carisium?), which was probably a militia station. Portus Adurni (Portchester) had once been a Litus Saxonici fort, but it was released from military service and raised to Civitas status in the late Fourth Century.

61 Anderita (Pevensey), base of elite Numerus Abulci.

62 Lemanis (Lympne), Dubris (Dover), Rutupiae Portus (Richborough) and Regulbium (Reculver) in modern Kent; Othona (Bradwell) in modern Essex; and a fort of unknown Roman name, now called Walton Castle (Valvaeta?), in south Suffolk. Each of these forts sheltered approximately 500 Romano-Briton soldiers.

---

63 The other major landing place in Britannia was Southampton Water, where Asclepiodotus had landed. The Southampton Water area had already fallen under Vortigern's control with Vitalinus's defeat of the Ambrosii in the Battle of Wallop.

the fact that the Anglo-Saxon warriors were no longer vital to the defense of their Diocese. The Picts were quiet, the Irish in Wales and Cornwall were on the defensive, and the Ambrosii were crushed. The Britons did not require any further services of Hengist and his followers. Meanwhile, the Anglo-Saxons, left to their own devices and in possession of their own territory, began to attract new colonists from their Continental homeland. They also expanded their land holdings in the Diocese by moving northward out of Kent along the coast to seize the Saxon Shore forts of Othona (Bradwell) and Castellum Valvaeta (Walton Castle) in modern Essex and south Suffolk - an overly ambitious interpretation of the boundaries of the realm which Vortigern had given them. Vortigern certainly intended that Comes Vorangonus be allowed to retain these two forts, which were too far north to be of much use to Roman invaders, but Hengist apparently decided that he had the right to the possession of any part of former Comital domain which struck his fancy. At the very time that their usefulness to the Britons had ended, the barbarians in Britannia were steadily increasing in numbers, in strength and in arrogance.

Vortigern had laid the foundation for a major disaster.

## Chapter Nine
## Challenges to Vortigern's Rule

Vortigern, through his establishment of Hengist's foederati realm in Kent, might have kept the Roman army out of his Diocese, but there was nothing he could do to keep out the Roman Church.

### Saint Germanus of Autessiodurum

Saint Germanus, the Bishop of Autessiodurum (Auxerre) in Gaul, visited Britannia twice during Vortigern's reign. He came first in A.D. 429 and then again in A.D. 446. The sainted Bishop's mission was to combat heresy in the Diocese.

The heresy opposed by Germanus was the product of a Briton-born theologian of the late Fourth Century named Pelagius. This heresy was called "Pelagianism" after its founder. The essence of Pelagian doctrine is the belief that a person could, through the unaided exercise of free will, choose to live a sinless life. Pelagius denied original sin and affirmed self-determination, personal freedom and individual moral responsibility. The orthodox view, espoused by Saint Augustine (a convert and student of Saint Ambrosius), is that people are by nature sinful and therefore dependent upon God's grace to achieve salvation. Pelagius also believed that the Church should consist of only a small band of dedicated do-gooders, as opposed to the catholic (i.e., universal) Church envisioned by Saint Augustine. From A.D. 394 to A.D. 410, Pelagius preached in Rome and engaged in theological debate with Saint Augustine. In A.D. 418, Pelagius's views were declared heretical.

Pelagianism was introduced into Britannia by the Briton Bishop Fastidius in the fateful year A.D. 410 through his book, *De Vita Christiana* (Concerning the Christian Life). The notion that man's fate lay within his own hands no doubt appealed to the Britons, who had just seized control of their political destiny by overthrowing Emperor Constantine III's regime and establishing their own government in its place. Bishop Fastidius even exults in the violent downfall of the Imperial administration and the rise of the new political order in Britannia.

Pelagianism quickly died out in most parts of the Empire, but it flourished in independent Britannia. The fact that the former Diocese waxed prosperous during this time, while the rest of the Western Empire continued to suffer barbarian depredations, must have seemed to the Britons a vindication of their heretical creed. Having overcome the difficulties of A.D. 410, coped with barbarian assaults and experienced a general recovery of their fortunes, the Britons had apparently demonstrated that they could indeed control their own destiny.

The Pelagian heresy was particularly popular among the Romano-Briton upper classes. At a great religious conference held at Verulamium (St. Albans), Saint Germanus argued and debated at great length against the Pelagian doctrine. His audience and opponents appear to have been wealthy and powerful: Venerable Bede and the scribe Constantius, Germanus's contemporary biographer, tell us that Germanus's listeners were well-dressed and attended by many servants and followers. In addition, as we have seen, the reigning Dux Britanniarum was probably related to the Pelagian theologian named Coelestius; in all likelihood, the great northern leader was also a devotee of the heresy. Pelagianism had an even more distinguished adherent in the Diocese. Judging by Britannia's success and prosperity under Vortigern, the apparent wealth of the Pelagian partisans and especially the poor relationship between Saint Germanus and Vortigern, the Superbus Tyrannus himself was a Pelagian.

Many Britons nevertheless remained loyal to the orthodox creed, and they must have complained about the situation to the Church officials on the Continent. In A.D. 428, the Briton Bishop Agricola was accused of "reviving" the Pelagian heresy in Britannia. In fact, Pelagianism was probably not so much "revived" as it just happened to again come to the notice of the Church hierarchy. In any event, the preaching of Bishop Agricola prompted Saint Germanus's first visit to the benighted island in A.D. 429.

The man chosen to lead the Britons back into theological orthodoxy was well-suited to the task. He was an extremely capable individual, in both religious and secular matters. Like Saint Ambrosius, Saint Germanus had embarked upon a successful political career before taking up ecclesiastical office. Saint Germanus was a civil official and military commander in Gaul, probably at one time holding the office of Dux Tracti Armoricani (Duke of the Armorican Tract), prior to his elevation to the position of Bishop of Autessiodurum.

Saint Germanus's civil and military background is important. Although he might have had the better theological position, as Saint Augustine had already demonstrated, he would not have succeeded in his religious mission had he confined himself strictly to reasoned discussion and debate. Suppression of the Pelagian heresy was as much a political as a religious matter. In order to bring Britannia back into the fold of the Church, Saint Germanus would have to demonstrate effective secular leadership, preferably at the expense of Vortigern, in order to refute the extremely persuasive argument implicit in the practical successes of the heretical ruling class of Britannia.

Germanus's first secular deed in the Diocese was, according to Nennius, the overthrow of a "tyrant" named Benlli who ruled in the Pagus, or rural district, of Civitas Cornoviorum. Saint Germanus, in response to the tyrant's impiety, called down from heaven a great fire, which consumed Benlli and his followers in their citadel. The fire was, of course, really set by soldiers under Germanus's command. The name of the roasted tyrant is preserved in "Moel Fenli," the name of a fort near Ruthin in modern Clwyd where a Roman coin horde from the late Fourth or early Fifth Century was found. Moel Fenli lies about twenty miles north of the fort of Moel-y-Geraint, which was probably reconquered and renamed by Vortigern (whose individual name in Welsh was Geraint). "Benlli" or "Fenli" is itself an Irish name, most likely a corruption of Fionnghalaigh, now Fennelly or Finnelly, which means "fair valor." The "tyrant" overthrown by Saint Germanus was thus an Irish warlord in north Wales who had encroached upon Cornovian territory.

The beneficiary of the Saint's intervention in the military affairs of the Pagus was a certain Catel Durnluc or Cadell Deyrnllug, whom the medieval kings of Powys claimed as an ancestor and the founder of their kingdom. "Catel" or "Cadell" is a Briton form of the Roman *nomen* Catellus, and "Durnluc" or "Deyrnllug" would have been something like "Durnolucius" in Latin. Catel Durnluc/Catellus Durnolucius appears in Nennius's and Geoffrey's lists of Vortigern's sons as Catigern or Katigern, which is a combination of the Roman name Catellus with the Celtic suffix *gern*, meaning "chieftain" or "lord."

The Pillar of Eliseg, the Ninth Century monument in north Wales which refers to Vortigern's marriage to Severa, does not trace the Powys dynasty back to any Catellus or Cadell or Catigern, but to a certain Brittu. "Brittu" is a Briton form of the common Roman *praenomen* Brutus. Brittu is identified on the Pillar of Eliseg as a son of Vortigern and is said to have been blessed by Saint Germanus. Brittu is without a doubt the same person as Catel Durnluc or Catigern. The full Roman name of Vortigern's son was therefore Brutus Catellus Durnolucius.[64]

Saint Germanus was thus instrumental in installing Vortigern's son Brutus Catellus as ruler of the realm which later became the Kingdom of Powys. Based upon the dates we have established for Vortigern's rise to power and for his marriage to Severa Maxima, Brutus Catellus must have been a mere child when Saint Germanus defeated the tyrant in the Pagus. The designation of Vortigern's son as ruler of the north Pagus was mostly just symbolic of the Saint's power to confer the reconquered territory however he wished. Although Brutus Catellus did receive a claim to the region which he would later make good, Saint Germanus's purpose in raising the youth to rule of the Pagus was to demonstrate superior leadership and thereby undermine Vortigern's authority.

---

64 Which, of course, makes Vortigern's full name Gerontius Catellus Durnolucius.

Saint Germanus's secular accomplishments in Britannia did not end with his defeat of Benlli in the north Pagus. The Saint went on to win his famous "Alleluia Battle" against the barbarians. Before returning to Gaul in A.D. 430, Germanus led a contingent of "newly-baptized" (i.e., newly won back to the Church) Britons against marauding barbarians. Venerable Bede and the scribe Constantius describe the enemy as Picts and Saxons. Emboldened by the Saint's battle cry of "Alleluia," the Britons charged the barbarian invaders from ambush, defeating them and winning a great victory.

The Alleluia Battle was most likely fought in the Vale of Llangollen in modern south Clwyd. Neither Venerable Bede nor Constantius name the site of Saint Germanus's victory, but the mountainous terrain described in their accounts points to Wales, and early tradition in the Llangollen area claims it as the battleground and holds Saint Germanus in special honor. Given the location of the Alleluia Battle, the barbarians must have been Irish, not Pictish or Anglo-Saxon, warriors. Constantius, who wrote the first account of the Battle around A.D. 480, probably made an incorrect assumption as to the identity of Germanus's opponents. When Constantius wrote the Saint's biography, called the *Vita Germani* (Life of Germanus), the Irish were relatively quiet while the Picts were still remembered as Britannia's traditional enemy and the Anglo-Saxons were known as Britannia's new principal enemy. In any event, the Alleluia Battle was certainly fought to clear barbarian raiding parties out of the Pagus and to enhance the security of Saint Germanus's protege in his new domain.

Saint Germanus's military successes helped preserve the Briton (or Welsh) character of west Britannia, but they also advanced the cause of religious orthodoxy. As a result of Germanus's efforts, Brutus Catellus would later become the Saint's grateful supporter, willing to provide political backing for his theological program. More importantly, Germanus's victories were seen by the Britons as a demonstration of God's favor, proving that worldly success was not peculiar to the Pelagians. Saint Germanus's secular achievements, aside from their obvious military consequences, gained enormous prestige for his religious cause.

Germanus's mission to Britannia in A.D. 429-430 was generally regarded as a triumph, but it was not a complete success. In A.D. 446, Saint Germanus felt it necessary to again visit the Diocese.

## Saint Germanus's Second Visit

Britannia presented a very different picture to Saint Germanus when he returned some sixteen years after his first mission to the island. In many ways, the changes in Britannia had been for the better, at least from Vortigern's point of view. By A.D. 446, the Superbus Tyrannus had successfully dealt with the Irish problem in Wales, initiated the liberation of Dumnonia and eliminated Ambrosius and Vorangonus, his leading political opponents. He also held a large and (so far) loyal army of Anglo-Saxon warriors under his personal command. Vortigern and the Pelagian independence party had been uniformly successful in all their policies, and they were securely in control of the Diocese.

The perceptive Saint Germanus realized, however, that all was not well beneath the surface: the Anglo-Saxons were growing increasingly powerful and arrogant, and pro-

Imperial sentiment in Britannia was only subdued, not eliminated. Vortigern had also made a number of serious misjudgements which left him vulnerable to the political wiles of the Saint.

Germanus still had the primary mission of combating heresy, and in these efforts he was assisted by the secular authorities in the person of one Elafius. Elafius is described in the *Vita Germani* as "regionis illius primus" (first man of that region). He also appears in the *Historia Ecclesiastica* as "a local chieftain named Elaphius" who hurried to greet Germanus when the Saint landed in Britannia. (The Saint then cured Elafius's crippled son.) "Elafius" or "Elaphius" is more properly "Aelafius," a Roman personal name. The name was still used by Roman aristocrats in Saint Germanus's day because Gaius Sollius Apollinaris Sidonius, Bishop of Arverna (Clermont-Ferrand), wrote a letter in the A.D. 470's to an "Elaphius" who was a leader of the town of Rutena (Rodez), and the *Historiae Francorum* (Histories of the Franks) of Gregory of Tours identifies an "Elafius" as the sainted Bishop of Durocatalaunum (Chalons-sur-Marne) in the late Sixth Century. Saint Germanus's ally was obviously a Romano-Briton ruler in south Britannia.

Judging from his willingness to assist Saint Germanus, Elafius was also an orthodox Christian and a member of the Briton Imperial faction. The Saint therefore had local support from Elafius and others in Britannia for his political program in A.D. 446, which was to make an extremely dangerous direct attack upon the personal prestige and authority of Vortigern.

On the occasion of his second visit to Britannia, Saint Germanus confronted and condemned Vortigern for the sin of incest in marrying his own daughter and having a son by her.

Vortigern certainly married only his *step*daughter, Severa's daughter by her previous marriage, and not his own flesh and blood.[65] Such a marriage would have been financially expedient because it would have allowed Vortigern to retain legal control over his deceased wife's estates in Gwent. In post-Roman Britannia and early medieval Wales, several other instances are known of rulers marrying their former spouse's relatives, and they did so invariably for reasons of wealth and property. Vortigern no doubt married his stepdaughter (Severina?) as soon as possible after Severa's death in order to ensure his continued control over her property, which is why he was later unable to sanctify his marriage to the Anglo-Saxon Renwein under Roman law. Although Vortigern's new bride was not his blood relative, the marriage was still technically incestuous and was still contrary to the laws of the Church.

Saint Germanus eventually took Vortigern's incestuously born son away with him to Gaul. The boy's name was Faustus, and he was educated by the Saint into the religious life. He later became a leader of the Church in Gaul. Vortigern's illicit offspring is probably the Faustus who was abbot of the monastery on the island of Lirinus (Lerin) off the Mediterranean coast of Gaul and who, in the early A.D. 460's, became Bishop of Reii (Reiz) in south Gaul.

In both his economically-motivated marriage to his stepdaughter and his politically-inspired marriage to Renwein, Vortigern had

---

65  If Severa's daughter was born in A.D. 407, when Gratianus Municeps died, she would have been thirty-nine when Germanus visited Britannia for the second time.

seriously miscalculated. The Superbus Tyrannus sought to preserve his wealth and power through convenient weddings rather than through continued diplomatic and military achievements. His scheming was short-sighted, gaining him immediate benefits but at great cost in the long-run. His marital affiliation to his stepdaughter, even if financially advantageous, offended the Church and its members, and his informal liaison with an Anglo-Saxon princess, even if diplomatically expedient, alienated many of his political supporters.

The displeasure of the Britons with the household arrangements of their ruler gave Germanus the tool he needed to bring down Vortigern and destroy the political strength of the Pelagian heresy in Britannia. Sensing the weakness of the Tyrannus, Germanus repeatedly raised the issue of Vortigern's improper weddings and tirelessly berated him for his marital sins. He no doubt also harped upon the undeserved fate of the hapless Comes Vorangonus. Nennius tells us that Germanus urged Vortigern "to turn to the true God," by which the Saint meant renouncing the Pelagian heresy as well as abandoning his extra-marital relationship with Renwein and his improper marriage to his stepdaughter.[66]

To escape his tormentor, Vortigern left Britannia proper and retired to the southern part of the Pagus, then called Builth. More recently, this area was known as Radnorshire and north Breconshire. Today, it is the central part of the shire of Powys. While Vortigern's son Brutus Catellus (or Catigern) recovered the northern part of the Pagus from the Irish with the aid of Saint Germanus, Vortigern himself liberated the

Builth area. Builth's post-Roman designation is preserved in the name of the modern town of Builth Wells.

Vortigern must have held extensive estates in Builth, for Nennius tells us that Builth, or at least its western part, was also called Guorthegirnaim (i.e., "Vortigernia") after the Tyrannus. Builth probably acquired this additional name, and Vortigern his estates, when the area was retaken by troops loyal to the Tyrannus. Later, one of Vortigern's sons, Pascent, became king of Builth.

## Flavius Aetius, Magister Militum per Gallias

While Germanus harassed Vortigern and drove him into hiding, other Britons, presumably including Germanus's ally Elafius, sought assistance from the Imperial government in Gaul.

Gildas has preserved for us some of the words of the plea which these Britons addressed to the Roman official then governing Gaul:

> To Aetius, now Consul for the third time: the groans of the Britons. . . . The barbarians drive us to the sea; the sea throws us back on the barbarians: thus two modes of death await us, we are either slain or drowned.

The reference to the third consulship of Aetius enables us to date the "Groans of the Britons" to A.D. 446, the same year that Saint Germanus made his second trip to Britannia, for it was in this year that the Roman leader Flavius Aetius became Consul for the third time.[67]

---

66 We may safely assume that Saint Germanus did not recommend the legitimization of Vortigern's marriage to the Anglo-Saxon princess.

67 In the Roman Republic, the two annually-elected Consuls were the chief executive officers of the Roman state. In the Empire, however, the consulship was an empty, but still eagerly sought, honor bestowed each year by the Emperor.

Geoffrey of Monmouth places the petition to Aetius out of its proper historical context in the *Historia Regum Britanniae*. Instead of placing the appeal in the middle of Vortigern's reign, Geoffrey places it before the rise to power of Emperor Constantine III, Vortigern's immediate predecessor as Geoffrey reckoned things. Geoffrey was misled by Gildas's similar ordering of events in *De Excidio Britanniae*. Gildas did not, however, write a chronicle, but a sermon, and the proper development of his theme of Britannia's woe required that the "Groans of the Britons" come early in the sermon; Gildas wished to illustrate the general nature of problem faced by the Britons before he turned to his specific attack upon the errors of Vortigern. Geoffrey's misinterpretation of his sources caused him to misconstrue the sequence of events in Britannia.

Geoffrey's mistake was reasonable considering the limited information at his disposal. He did not, and really could not be expected to, understand the ambiguous nature of the political relationship between Britannia and Rome during Vortigern's reign. Geoffrey naturally assumed that the letter to Aetius marked the earlier and (only in retrospect) final break between the Empire and its former Diocese. Geoffrey did not realize that the sundering of Britannia from the Empire was reversible, nor did he realize that many people, both in the Diocese and on the Continent, still desired and worked for the restoration of Britannia to the Empire. Geoffrey could not comprehend the plea to Aetius as having occurred when it did, so he places it much too early in the *Historia Regum Britanniae*.

Historians now recognize Geoffrey's error and they put the "Groans of the Britons" in its correct time frame, but they continue to be misled by the dire tone of the appeal. The apocalyptic image of post-Roman Britannia in the Aetius petition is exaggerated. The plight of the Britons as described in the petition is graphic, but it is also poetic; it eloquently depicts a helpless population trapped on an island with a savage warrior race, but it does not present, nor was it intended to present, an accurate and impartial account of conditions in Britannia. The purpose of the letter was to persuade the Roman Consul Aetius to send an army to Britannia in order to reestablish Imperial government, not to give a precise status report of the real situation in the Diocese. The violent and bloody uprising of the Anglo-Saxons had not yet even occurred; Gildas, for example, mentions only Picts and Scots (i.e., Irish), not Anglo-Saxons, among Britannia's enemies at this time. Saint Germanus also does not seem to have been inconvenienced in his mission or travels in the Diocese. At most, the Anglo-Saxon foederati, preoccupied with settling into their own territory in Kent, might have failed to come to the aid of the Britons against small bands of Pictish or Irish raiders - a failure which could also underlie the Britons' growing disenchantment with their barbarian hirelings. At the time of the "Groans of the Britons," Britannia might have been suffering minor barbarian attacks, but it was not in any real danger of being overrun. The complaining Britons who requested Aetius's assistance used the minor military difficulties of the moment to enhance the force of their appeal for reincorporation into the Empire.

Aetius, the recipient of the Britons' doleful letter and the person expected to bring about the restoration of the Diocese to the Empire, was a most extraordinary individual. To understand who he was and why the Britons choose to write to him, we must return briefly to the situation on the Continent.

After the death of the childless Emperor Honorius in A.D. 423, a high-ranking Imperial official (the Primicerius Notariorum, or "First Secretary of Scribes") named Johannes (John) and the Emperor's Magister Militum, Castinus, seized control of the Western Empire. Johannes assumed the title of Augustus, and Castinus rallied the Roman army in Italy behind Johannes. The eastern Emperor Theodosius II, Honorius's nephew, was displeased with the situation. In A.D. 425, Emperor Theodosius II dispatched an army to install Honorius's half-sister Galla Placidia in power as regent for her infant son, the future Emperor Valentinian III.

Galla Placidia was a fascinating character in her own right, being sister to one Roman Emperor, wife of another and mother of a third. At one time, she was even queen of the barbarous Visigoths! Galla Placidia was kidnapped during the Visigoths' sack of Rome in A.D. 410, and she made the best of the situation by marrying her abductor, Athaulf (Adolph), brother and successor to the Visigoth King Alaric. When Athaulf was assassinated by a political rival in A.D. 416, the Romans ransomed Galla Placidia so she could wed Constantius of Illyricum (roughly the former Yugoslavia). Constantius was then Honorius's Magister Militum, having replaced Stilicho in this post. It was Magister Militum Constantius who had earlier defeated and executed the Briton Emperor Constantine III in A.D. 411. As Galla Placidia's husband, Constantius briefly became co-Emperor with Honorius in A.D. 421, but he predeceased Honorius later the same year. In A.D. 425, Galla Placidia led her own

household guard and Emperor Theodosius's loaned troops against Emperor Johannes in order to seize the Western Empire in the name of her son by Constantius.

Flavius Aetius, a young Roman aristocrat, supported Emperor Johannes and Magister Militum Castinus.

Aetius had spent a part of his youth as a hostage among the dreadful Huns, then newly-arrived in Europe, and he made many friends among the barbarians. The Huns, like the Sarmatians, were deadly horse warriors, but, unlike the Sarmatians, they did not fight as heavy shock cavalry. They fought as light cavalry. The Huns did not rely upon the cavalry charge, but upon rapid maneuver and intense bowfire, to defeat their enemies. Aetius contacted his friends and raised an army of Hun horsemen in support of Emperor Johannes.

Aetius's Huns probably would have won the day for Johannes, but Aetius returned to Italy too late to affect the outcome of the contest. Galla Placidia had already defeated and captured the usurper. After the execution of Emperor Johannes, Aetius, still in command of his Hun army, made peace with Galla Placidia.

Under the terms of the peace, Aetius was appointed Comes Galliarum (Count of the Gauls). He was also supplied with a large sum of money, which he used to pay off the Huns. Aetius dismissed the barbarians, except for a small band which he retained as his personal guard when he went to Gaul. He then made himself, for all practical purposes, the independent ruler of the Diocese of Gaul. In recognition of his extraordinary power, Aetius was awarded the even more prestigious title of Magister Militum per Gallias (Master of Soldiers throughout the Gauls) just a few years later. With his control of Gaul and his command of Hun warriors, Aetius was easily the most powerful man in the Western Empire.

Aetius nevertheless had his hands full for many years just with the effort to control his own beleaguered Diocese. Aetius was principally concerned with Galla Placidia's former subjects, the Visigoths, who had settled in southwest Gaul. He also had to deal with the barbarian Burgundians and Alans who resided in his Diocese.[68] In A.D. 428 and A.D. 431, Aetius even found it necessary to campaign against the fearsome Franks, who would later conquer Gaul and rename it "France" after themselves. Not least among Aetius's worries were the native bacaudae rebels, who became active again in the mid-A.D. 430's and late A.D. 440's, and a continuing political rivalry with Galla Placidia and her supporters in Italy and north Africa. Aetius overcame all challenges. Despite his many difficulties, Aetius's shrewd mind and Hun cavalrymen made him virtually invincible.

Aetius must have nourished a secret ambition to conquer Britannia. Britannia was relatively prosperous at the time, especially in comparison to Gaul, and control of its resources would have enormously enhanced Aetius's personal power. The Magister Militum would have then been saddled with the burden of defending Britannia, but the Diocese was wealthy enough to pay for itself and still generate additional revenues for Aetius to use in Gaul. Given the right circumstances, Aetius might have spared the time, the troops and the

_____

68  Aetius inflicted an overwhelming defeat upon the Germanic Burgundians in A.D. 436, which is immortalized in the German national epic, the *Nibelungenlied*. The *Nibelungenlied*, however, misidentifies the Hun commander as Attila instead of Aetius.

energy to invade Britannia.

Concrete evidence exists to support the notion that Aetius had at least contemplated the liberation of the wayward Diocese. The *Notitia Dignitatum*, an Imperial table of organization listing all the civil and military posts in the Empire, was updated in the late A.D. 420's, about the time Aetius acquired the title of Magister Militum. Significantly, the updated *Notitia* contains provisions for the administration of Britannia, notwithstanding that Britannia had been independent of the Empire for more than a decade and a half. The Britannic chapters are not likely to have been maintained in the *Notitia* simply for academic reasons; they would, however, have been invaluable to a Roman commander planning the restoration of Imperial government in the Diocese. Aetius was the only Roman leader in a position to attempt the recovery of Britannia. The update of the *Notitia Dignitatum* chapters on Britannia suggests that Aetius hoped to someday bring the Britons back into the Empire.

When Vortigern had dread of the Romans, it must have been the specter of Aetius that haunted him most. Only the turbulent situation in Gaul and Aetius's poor relationship with Imperial Regent Galla Placidia prevented the Magister Militum from crossing the Channel and seizing Britannia. The military and political situation in Gaul began to calm in the early A.D. 440's, and Aetius could have begun to seriously plan and organize a cross-channel invasion at this time. It is no coincidence that Vortigern chose this same time to cement relations with his Anglo-Saxon allies by marrying Renwein and settling Hengist in Kent. Fear of Aetius was certainly behind Vortigern's decision to oust Comes Vorangonus from power, to install Hengist and his followers in Kent, and to turn a blind eye to the alarming increase in the number of Anglo-Saxons moving into the Diocese.

An act of God postponed the anticipated Imperial expedition. A plague swept through the Roman Empire in A.D. 443, which must have reached north Gaul in A.D. 444 (and probably Britannia in A.D. 445). The epidemic disrupted economic activity and agricultural production in Gaul, which, in turn, reduced the tax receipts available to pay and supply an army of invasion. It also made the massing of a large number of troops in a single place unwise. An outbreak of disease caused Aetius to defer any plans which he might have formulated for the reconquest of Britannia.

Meanwhile, putting it about that Britannia had passed into Anglo-Saxon control, as the *Chronica Gallia* reported in A.D. 441, helped to characterize the planned invasion as a rescue mission rather than a punitive expedition. The Imperial faction in Britannia deliberately played into this stratagem with their "Groans of the Britons" letter in A.D. 446 - although by then it was too late.

After the plague subsided, probably in A.D. 446, a brief window of opportunity opened in which Aetius might have been able to cross the Channel and invade Britannia. The window of opportunity came to a sudden and surprising close with the rise of a new menace on the Continent. This time, Aetius's own Huns, under their new and ambitious King Attila, diverted Aetius and saved Vortigern by beginning their infamous reign of terror.

Attila did not actually lead his Huns into Gaul until A.D. 451, but the barbarian king had clear designs on Aetius's domain and he encouraged the Gallic bacaudae to rebel in the late A.D. 440's in preparation for his invasion of the Diocese. While Attila ravaged the Eastern Empire and prepared to attack Aetius, the bacaudae ran amok in Gaul. The situation was so desperate that Aetius was prepared to unleash the fierce Alans (a tribe related to the Sarmatians) against the Armorican bacaudae in A.D. 448; only the personal intervention of Saint Germanus saved the Armoricans from a horrible vengeance. Aetius nevertheless managed to suppress the rebellion, and the defeated bacaudae leader Eudoxius fled to the Hun court. Aetius meanwhile had to again postpone his contemplated reconquest of Britannia. With bacaudae rebels loose in the countryside and with Hun horsemen poised to sweep into his Diocese, Aetius could ill afford to dispatch large numbers of his troops to Britannia.

Aetius ultimately inflicted a massive defeat upon the Huns in the Battle of Chalons (Chalons-sur-Marne, or Durocatalaunum in Latin) in A.D. 451. It is ironic that Aetius, who owed much of his success to his friendship with the Huns, is most famous in history for having decisively defeated these very same Huns. Attila and much of his army escaped the disaster, but the savage horde had been broken and it was never again the threat it had been. Although the Huns were able to ravage north Italy the following year, they achieved at best indifferent success in that campaign. Attila's death soon thereafter eliminated any remaining danger to Gaul. Aetius was even able to again recruit his favored Hun cavalry. With the death of Attila in late A.D. 452, the liberation of Britannia should not have been long in coming.

Fortune, however, continued to favor Vortigern. This time it was no rude barbarian, but the foolish Emperor Valentinian III, who saved the Superbus Tyrannus. The incompetent Emperor with his own hand killed the great Magister Militum in A.D. 454. Valentinian III did not long survive his victim, because the following spring one of Aetius's Hun followers avenged his master. The slaying of Valentinian III achieved justice of a sort, but it did nothing to advance the Imperial cause in Britannia. The murder of Aetius forever eliminated any chance of a Roman reconquest of Britannia.

When the prospect of a Roman expedition from the Continent evaporated in A.D. 454, Vortigern's problems were hardly over. Indeed, Vortigern was then in the midst of his greatest political crisis. The Tyrannus's short-sighted military and marital policies had finally caught up with him. A loss of faith in the Tyrannus, coupled with a rising fear and distrust of the increasingly numerous Anglo-Saxons in Britannia, led the Britons to overthrow Vortigern and raise up a new ruler.

This new ruler was Vortimer, Vortigern's own son.

## Chapter Ten
## Vortimer, Regissimus Britanniarum

One of the political accomplishments laid at the feet of Saint Germanus was his leading Vortigern's son Vortimer into rebellion against the Superbus Tyrannus. In Vortimer, Germanus found the perfect tool with which to oppose Vortigern, because, with the Saint's blessing, Vortimer did not hesitate to usurp his father's rule of Britannia.

Germanus was, of course, no stranger to the internal politics of the Tyrannus's family. He had earlier intervened in the military affairs of Civitas Cornoviorum in order to install Vortigern's son Brutus Catellus (or Catigern) as ruler of the northern Pagus (north Powys and Clwyd). He also took Vortigern's youngest son Faustus away with him into the clergy. In pursuit of his religious goals, Germanus apparently felt justified in meddling in Vortigern's personal affairs and recruiting his sons against him.[69]

According to Geoffrey of Monmouth, Vortimer required little encouragement. His father's marriage to Hengist's daughter, even if lacking legal sanction, was seen by the young man as a threat to his own political future. He worried that a half-barbarian child of the union, with Anglo-Saxon support, would eventually usurp the rule of Britannia which Vortimer saw as his own proper inheritance. Even before Saint Germanus approached him, Vortimer was seeking an excuse to seize his father's throne,

---

69 The parallels between Vortigern and King Henry II of England (who reigned after Geoffrey of Monmouth's time) are extraordinary: not only did they both marry political heiresses considerably older than themselves and come into conflict with powerful clerics, but they were both afflicted with ungrateful and rebellious sons!

spurred by the fear that he might someday find himself supplanted by an Anglo-Saxon half-brother.

Vortimer's fear was well founded. Gregory of Tours, in his *Historiae Francorum* (Histories of the Franks), reports that the illegitimate son of the late Fifth Century Frankish King Clovis was considered eligible to inherit an equal share of the Frankish Kingdom with each of his three legitimate half-brothers. The barbarians apparently did not consider illegitimacy a bar to political inheritance, so they would have not attached much significance to the fact that Vortigern's marriage to Renwein was not recognized under Roman law. A son of Renwein would have felt entitled to claim a share of Vortigern's power - and he would have had barbarian relatives to back up his claim.

The Britons were also worried about the waxing power of the Anglo-Saxons. Although we have no reason to suppose that Hengist or his followers had openly betrayed their employers as yet, the barbarians were steadily increasing in numbers and strength in Britannia. Geoffrey of Monmouth tells us that Hengist even used the promise of land in Kent to lure additional Anglo-Saxons into the Diocese. Hengist probably used the newcomers to seize the Saxon Shore forts of Othona (Bradwell) and Castellum Valvaeta (Walton Castle) in modern Essex and south Suffolk, portions of the Saxon Shore not originally contemplated as part of Hengist's foederati domain. Vortigern was unwilling or unable to restrain his barbarians or to allay the Britons' fear of them.

Geoffrey attributes Vortigern's inaction to the influence of his Anglo-Saxon wife Renwein, but the Superbus Tyrannus might have simply seen no reason to challenge the very forces which had helped establish, and which continued to uphold, his own political power. Most leading Britons were less sanguine about the situation, and they cried out for a leader to save them from the growing menace of their own barbarian soldiers. In response to Vortigern's indifference to their concerns, the Britons raised Vortimer to power.

Saint Germanus played a crucial role in Vortimer's rise to the overlordship of Britannia. He not only paved the way for Vortimer's usurpation by his persistent denunciations of Vortigern, but he specifically promoted Vortimer's succession to power. Some manuscripts of the *Historia Brittonum* report that Germanus called a synod at an unknown location identified as "Guartherniaun" (which would be "Varternia" in Latin), where he denounced and drove forth Vortigern. Vortimer then paid homage to Germanus and received the rule of Britannia. This incident may be an addition to Nennius's work inserted by a later editor, but it does accurately reflect the nature of Vortimer's political support. Saint Germanus rallied the anti-Anglo-Saxon and anti-Pelagian factions in Britannia behind Vortimer, who led them in ousting Vortigern from power.

One of the political leaders whom Saint Germanus rallied to Vortimer's cause was Vortimer's brother Brutus Catellus (or Catigern). Brutus Catellus later fought by Vortimer's side against Vortimer's enemies, which suggests that he wholeheartedly endorsed his brother's usurpation of their father's rule. Germanus had earlier made Brutus Catellus ruler of the north Pagus (north Powys and Clwyd), and the Saint no doubt urged him to show his gratitude by supporting Vortimer's assumption of power.

Saint Germanus's support of Vortimer did

not come without a price. Geoffrey reports that Vortimer, at the Saint's request, restored Christian churches in Britannia. Although Geoffrey thought his sources described the liberation of sacred buildings from pagan hands, they actually referred to Vortimer's ordering the resumption of Catholic, as opposed to Pelagian, worship in Briton churches. Vortimer obtained Germanus's backing for his seizure of power by promising to enforce religious orthodoxy in Britannia.

The Britons must have raised Vortimer to power in A.D. 447. They probably did so late in the year, just before Saint Germanus returned to Gaul. By then, the Britons would have realized that their "Groans of the Britons" plea had failed and that Aetius was not going to come to the rescue of the Diocese.

### Elafius Catellus Durnolucius, Regissimus Britanniarum

The new ruler of Britannia, like the man he displaced, is known to Geoffrey and Nennius only by his title, not by his personal name. "Vortimer" is a late variant of the ancient Briton title Vortamorix, meaning "High King." The elements of the title are *vor*, meaning "over," plus *tamo*, a superlative, and *rix*, meaning "king." The Latin equivalent of "Vortimer" is Regissimus, from *rex*, meaning "king," and the superlative suffix *-issimus*.

Vortimer probably did use the Latin title Regissimus as well as the Celtic title Vortimer. A few years later, the Roman general who governed north Gaul, Aegidius (or his son Syagrius), took for himself the title Rex Romanorum, meaning "King of the Romans" - presumably meaning "King of the Romans *in Gaul*," as distinguished from the Franks, Visigoths, Burgundians and other barbarians then in the Diocese. Vortimer, who ruled a more extensive realm and who dominated several lesser regional rulers, could with equal justification have declared himself Regissimus Romanorum (High King of the Romans), or, more likely, Regissimus Britanniarum (High King of the Britains). "Regissimus," besides being a literal Latin translation of the Briton title Vortimer, is a highly plausible designation for a post-Roman ruler of Britannia.

By consulting other sources, we can determine that Vortimer's personal name was Elafius. Vortimer was certainly the "regionis illius primus" (first man of that region) and "local chieftain" of this name who aided Saint Germanus during the Saint's second visit to Britannia. Both Elafius and Vortimer appear in the early sources as Briton rulers who championed Saint Germanus's mission, but they do not appear together in the same source. Elafius does not appear in either the *Historia Regum Britanniae* or the *Historia Brittonum*, which describe Vortimer's association with Saint Germanus, and Vortimer does not appear in either the *Vita Germani* or the *Historia Ecclesiastica*, which describe Elafius's support of Saint Germanus. Nennius and Geoffrey did not realize that the Elafius who was "regionis illius primus" and "a local chieftain" in certain sources was the same person as the Vortimer who appeared in other sources.

Vortimer would have had the same *nomen* and *cognomen* as his father and brother, so his full name was Elafius Catellus Durnolucius.

### Vortimer's War Against Kent

The principal threat to the rule of Britannia

by Elafius Catellus Durnolucius, the new Regissimus or Vortimer, was posed by the Anglo-Saxons of Kent. The tensions which had been growing for some time between the Britons and Vortigern's barbarian foederati finally came to a head, and Vortimer led the Britons to war against Kent.

Nennius and Geoffrey hold the Anglo-Saxons responsible for the rift between the barbarians and their erstwhile employers, but they are vague as to the exact circumstances that led to open conflict. Most likely, the barbarians repudiated their foederati treaty after Vortigern fell from power. The overt hostility of the new Romano-Briton regime of Vortimer probably led them to conclude that the oaths sworn by Hengist did not extend to the government which overthrew the Superbus Tyrannus. The break between the Britons and the Anglo-Saxons should therefore be dated to A.D. 447, the second date which Nennius gives for the Adventus Saxonum (Coming of the Saxons), because that is when the Britons raised Vortimer to power with the intention of curbing Hengist's power - and possibly even of cancelling his legal right to the continued possession of Kent.[70] The barbarians acknowledged the changed circumstances and officially repudiated their foederati obligations two years later. The Anglo-Saxons of Kent formally and publicly terminated their foederati treaty in A.D. 449, the date which Venerable Bede and the Anglo-Saxon Chronicle give for the Adventus Saxonum.

When Hengist and his followers terminated

_____

70 Vortigern did not *receive* the Anglo-Saxons in this year, as reported by the Anglo-Saxon Chronicle; he was probably *received by* them when he visited them in Kent in a vain effort to rally support for his continuation in power.

their foederati treaty in A.D. 449, the gradual evolution of the Anglo-Saxons from loyal employee soldiers into hostile enemy warriors was complete.

Vortimer opened the war between the Britons and their former foederati with a lightning invasion of Kent. He penetrated deep into Hengist's territory. Nennius tells us that Vortimer drove the Anglo-Saxons all the way back to the Isle of Thanet, where he three times attempted to assail the island on its western side. The Briton attacks upon the Isle of Thanet were unsuccessful, and Vortimer withdrew.

Vortimer was unsuccessful in his attacks on the Isle of Thanet because his army was composed entirely of cavalrymen. The elite Briton troops at this time fought on horseback, drawing upon the equestrian background of the Romano-Briton aristocracy and the military tradition kept alive by the descendants of the Roman cavalry soldiers stationed in Britannia. Chief among the Briton horsemen were the Romanized offspring of the Sarmatian warriors whom Emperor Marcus Aurelius had settled so long ago at Bremetennacum (Ribchester). A force of these hard-riding troopers had obviously launched a surprise invasion of Kent and advanced deep into Anglo-Saxon territory before the barbarians were able to muster their own infantry army in response. When the Anglo-Saxons finally did rally on the Isle of Thanet, the cavalrymen found the going much more difficult. A Romano-Briton cavalry army was potent in mobile warfare, but ill-suited to carry out the type of assault necessary to force a passage across the narrow straits which then separated the Isle of Thanet from the mainland.

Because Vortimer failed to conquer Hengist's stronghold on Thanet, we should classify the Regissimus's first campaign against the Anglo-Saxons as militarily inconclusive. The campaign was nevertheless a great morale victory for the Britons. It provided an enormous boost to the confidence of the Britons because the hitherto invincible Anglo-Saxons, even if not destroyed, had been humbled. Indeed, the Anglo-Saxon humiliation was so great that the Anglo-Saxon Chronicle, which steadfastly refuses to acknowledge Anglo-Saxon defeats, makes no mention of the campaign. Vortimer's campaign was not a victory in the strict military sense, but it was a triumph in the morale sense.

Hengist was not one to give up easily. Having survived Vortimer's attack, he resolutely prepared for a long war. The barbarian warlord drew upon all his resources and personal influence to raise a large army. Nennius tells us that Hengist even obtained recruits from Germania. The conflict between Vortimer's Britons and Hengist's Anglo-Saxon as a consequence lasted several years.

Nennius does not give any dates for the war between Vortimer and Hengist, but the Anglo-Saxon Chronicle does mention Hengist's fighting the Britons in A.D. 455 and again in A.D. 456 or A.D. 457. The opening campaign in Vortimer's Kentish War therefore must have taken place in the summer of A.D. 454, or perhaps a year or so earlier.

After the initial Briton strike force failed to dislodge the Anglo-Saxons from their island refuge in A.D. 454, Vortimer withdrew to gather an even larger army, no doubt including infantry as well as cavalry, to resume the struggle. By consulting both Nennius and the Anglo-Saxon Chronicle, we can deduce that Vortigern launched a full-scale invasion of Kent in A.D. 455.[71]

Nennius tells us that Vortimer's next battle took place by the River Darent or Darenth in modern west Kent. Archaeology informs us that there was as yet very little Anglo-Saxon settlement beyond the nearby Medway River, so the Battle of the River Darenth was fought as the Briton army crossed the border of the barbarian realm. The Battle of Darenth is conspicuously absent from the Anglo-Saxon Chronicle, which is mute, but eloquent, confirmation of the Briton claim of victory.

Vortimer then fought Hengist a little further to the east, which must represent a battle occurring later in the same invasion as the Briton forces followed up their victory at the River Darenth by pursuing the beaten Hengist into Kent. Nennius identifies Vortimer's next combat as the Battle of Episford, but it appears in the Anglo-Saxon Chronicle entry for the year A.D. 455 as the Battle of Aylesford.[72] Aylesford is the place where the ancient east-west track known as the Harrow Way crosses the Medway River; it is located about three miles northwest of the modern town of Maidstone, which also lay on the Harrow Way and which was occupied in Roman and post-Roman times. Aylesford was thus a logical fall-back position for Hengist to choose as his second line of defense. The sources agree that Hengist's brother Horsa was slain in the Battle, and Nennius adds that Vortimer's brother Catigern (i.e., Brutus Catellus) was also slain. Both sides claimed victory, a sure indication that the encounter was actually a bloody and inconclusive stalemate - an interpretation borne

71 Geoffrey of Monmouth also gives an account of Vortimer's war against Kent, but his account is brief

and adds nothing to what Nennius has to say.

72 The Anglo-Saxon Chronicle actually identifies Hengist's opponent as Vortigern, but this identification is obviously an error for the similar-titled, but lesser known, Vortimer.

out by the mutual loss of important commanders.

On balance, we should award battle honors for the A.D. 455 campaign to the Anglo-Saxons because the Britons again had to withdraw, allowing an independent Kent to survive a little while longer.

Hengist, at least, felt good enough about the outcome of the A.D. 455 campaign to declare himself king of Kent later the very same year. The Anglo-Saxon Chronicle reports that Hengist "received the kingdom" in A.D. 455, right after the Battle of Aylesford. "Receiving the kingdom" is the expression the Chronicle uses to mark the beginning of a king's reign. Hengist's "receiving the kingdom" of Kent in A.D. 455 could only mean that the barbarian warlord chose this year to officially proclaim himself king of Kent in his own right.

Two years later, in A.D. 457,[73] the Anglo-Saxon Chronicle reports the occurrence of the Battle of Crayford, which is not mentioned by Nennius. Crayford is located two miles from the junction of the Rivers Cray and Darenth, back again at the western border of Kent. The Anglo-Saxon Chronicle boasts that Hengist slew four thousand Britons and that the Briton survivors fled in terror to London (i.e., Londinium). Hengist no doubt only *defeated* a Briton army of the size which the Chronicle claims for the number slain. Even so, the omission of the Battle from the *Historia Brittonum* is hardly surprising because Nennius would have had small interest in preserving the

details of a major Briton defeat. Vortimer might not have been in command at the debacle, but Nennius more likely just decided to omit a setback which, in the end, did not prove to be permanent. Nennius does, moreover, admit that the war was not one-sided and that the Anglo-Saxons sometimes did take the victory. Vortimer's second full-scale invasion of Kent thus met defeat at the Kentish border and was turned back.

Despite the grave setback suffered in A.D. 547, Vortimer did win the final and decisive victory, probably in A.D. 458 or A.D. 459. Nennius reports that Vortimer defeated the Anglo-Saxons "near the stone on the shore of the Gallic Sea," which refers to the massive Roman memorial arch at the Saxon Shore fort of Rutupiae Portus (Richborough) in east Kent. This time Vortimer's victory was unequivocal, and the barbarian host was shattered.

After the Battle by the Gallic Shore, the Anglo-Saxons fled to their ships in an effort to escape across the water to their refuge on the Isle of Thanet. Geoffrey of Monmouth wrongly concludes that Hengist fled all the way back to Germania. Many of Hengist's more recently arrived recruits probably did return to their homeland, but Hengist himself remained in the Diocese. The barbarian defeat was nevertheless so severe that Hengist lost the realm which he had acquired at the expense of Comes Vorangonus and over which he had just named himself king. Hengist's domain was now reduced to the Isle of Thanet, and, after Vortimer's overwhelming victory, his grip on even this tiny island was precarious.

Hengist's position had deteriorated to such an extent that he felt compelled to sue for peace. He called upon the Briton leaders to meet him and his chieftains in a peace conference. The

---

73 Or maybe only one year later; the Anglo-Saxon Chronicle entry appears in some manuscripts under A.D. 456 and in others under A.D. 457. The later date is more likely, however, because both sides must have had heavy losses to replace after the severe fighting of A.D. 455.

Britons probably would have dismissed the barbarian's entreaties out of hand but for a small bit of good fortune which came Hengist's way: the untimely and unexpected death of Vortimer.

Vortimer must have died of a slow illness or a festering battle wound because he was able to address his supporters from his deathbed, even giving instructions for his burial. The Regissimus exhorted his soldiers to continue the fight against the barbarians, and he directed them to erect his tomb on the Kentish shore - a wish that the Briton army was ultimately unable to fulfill. Geoffrey attributes Vortimer's death to poisoning, and he blames Vortimer's Anglo-Saxon stepmother for the evil deed. We need not accept poisoning as the true cause of Vortimer's death, however, because such suspicions inevitably arose in any instance of premature death due to sickness in ancient and medieval days, when the causes and treatment of disease and infection were poorly understood. Even if the Anglo-Saxons did not poison Vortimer, as Geoffrey believes, they certainly rejoiced in his death because it brought to an end the calamitous war which Vortimer had been waging against them.

Vortimer's death must have occurred very soon after his great victory over Hengist in A.D. 458 or A.D. 459. Otherwise, Vortimer would have followed up his victory and invaded the Isle of Thanet to complete the destruction of the Anglo-Saxon Kingdom of Kent. We should therefore date the sorrowful event to A.D. 459 or A.D. 460.

Vortigern immediately stepped into the power vacuum created by the demise of his usurping son. While Vortimer prosecuted his war against Hengist, his father, the out-of-favor Superbus Tyrannus, seems to have remained in seclusion on the family estates in Builth, where he had sought refuge from the harangues of Saint Germanus. As soon as Vortimer died, Vortigern returned from Builth to resume the rule of Britannia.

Vortigern promptly agreed to the peace conference proposed by Hengist. The two leaders and their advisers were to meet at the Cloister of Ambrius, probably in A.D. 460. The Tyrannus intended to bring the war with Kent to an end, and he no doubt hoped to restore the defeated Anglo-Saxons to his service.

Hengist had other ideas.

## The Massacre at the Cloister of Ambrius

The unscrupulous Hengist instructed his men to conceal knives in their boots when they met with the Britons. Sometime during the course of the peace conference, Hengist yelled "Nimet oure saxes!" ("Grab your seaxes!"),[74] whereupon each Anglo-Saxon drew his weapon and stabbed the nearest Briton.

Nennius and William of Malmesbury report that 300 noble Britons were slain by the Anglo-Saxons, although Geoffrey gives the Briton casualties as 460. The lower number is probably correct, and Geoffrey has likely confused the year of the event with the number of murdered Britons. Either account is plausible, however. More important than the exact number slain by the Anglo-Saxons is the fact that the Briton losses were large and, being

---

74 The seax, from which the Saxons derived their tribal name, was a single-edged blade weapon, not unlike a modern machete. It was carried by all Anglo-Saxon warriors, from the most exalted nobleman to the lowliest common soldier. The seax came in several varieties, including long ones used in combat in lieu of regular swords, and short ones, such as Hengist's men must have used on this occasion.

concentrated among the native leadership, were devastating.

This exciting and dramatic tale of treachery and deceit is just the sort of story we would be inclined to skeptically dismiss as fiction, but we have a very good reason for accepting its veracity. The parallel between this incident and Hengist's experiences at Finn's Burg is uncanny, suggesting that the barbarian warlord deliberately imitated the ploy once used by his former enemy, King Finn of Frisia, against Finn's overlord and Hengist's master, King Hnaef of Denmark. This time Hengist played the role of Finn, and Vortigern that, slightly modified, of Hnaef. Hengist no doubt believed the Britons' attack upon him after his many years of good and loyal service justified his deception and the slaughter of the Romano-Briton aristocracy, just as he had earlier believed Finn's betrayal of Hnaef justified his violation of his oath to Finn.

Geoffrey informs us that the infamous act took place at the Cloister of Ambrius, near the town of Salisbury. Salisbury ("Sorviodunum" to the Romans) was the capital of a Civitas which the Ambrosii had dominated. The Cloister itself, from the very evidence of its name, was a religious establishment endowed by and named for the elder Ambrosius. It must have been located in the vicinity of the modern town of Amesbury, which was a former Ambrosii stronghold; in fact, one version of the Welsh Triads identifies "the choir of Ambrosius in Ambresbury" as one of the three "Perpetual Choirs of the Isle of Britain," where numerous monks were organized in shifts so their prayers could continue unceasingly throughout the day. Ironically, the downfall of Vortigern thus occurred on Ambrosii territory, only about ten miles west of the site of the elder Ambrosius's defeat in the Battle of Wallop.

After the Massacre, Eldadus, a monk from the Cloister of Ambrius, buried and held services for the fallen Britons.

Vortigern himself was not among the slain. The unfortunate Tyrannus was taken captive by Hengist and compelled at sword point to make territorial concessions to his former hirelings.[75] Nennius reports that Hengist received Essex, Middlesex and Sussex. In the first two instances, Nennius is referring to Hengist's acquisition of territory north of the River Thames. Hengist received legal title to the coastal territory which he had already seized between the mouth of the River and the Saxon Shore fort of Valvaeta, now called Walton Castle, (Nennius's "Essex") and to the riverside territory westward toward Londinium (Nennius's "Middlesex"). In the last instance, Nennius is referring to the contemporary arrival of new Anglo-Saxon settlers in modern East Sussex. The East Sussex barbarians were apparently allies of Hengist, whom Hengist rewarded at Vortigern's expense. In all three instances, Vortigern's "concession" was nothing more than the grant of legal sanction to land grabs which were already underway. Once their demands were satisfied, the Anglo-Saxons released the Superbus Tyrannus. When the barbarians freed him, Vortigern was a shattered and broken man.

The Anglo-Saxons of southeast Britannia then took advantage of the disarray among the

---

75 The circumstances in which the miserable Vortigern found himself were thus similar to those in which the unfortunate Aztec Emperor Montezuma would later find himself at the hands of the Spanish Conquistadors. Vortigern, like Montezuma, had no choice but to accede to the barbarians' demands, although, in doing so, he further undermined his own power and authority.

leaderless Britons to loot and plunder the Diocese. Geoffrey tells us that the countryside about York, London, Winchester and Lincoln was ravaged by marauding Anglo-Saxon warbands. These towns were still called by their Roman names of Eboracum, Londinium, Venta Belgarum and Lindum Colonia, respectively. Geoffrey's reference to "York" actually recalls the earlier successful demand of the Deira laeti for promotion to foederati status; unlike their fellow countrymen in the south, the Deirans had little cause to complain about their employer and they seem to have been content with their situation. The Londinium and Venta Belgarum areas were probably devastated by Hengist and his Kentishmen, who could have despoiled these areas as they made their way back to Kent from the Cloister of Ambrius. Lindum Colonia must have been the victim of a rebellion by its own laeti or foederati in Lindsey. Although Geoffrey says nothing about the barbarians harassing Venta Icenorum (Caistor-by-Norwich) or Camulodunum (Colchester), archaeology indicates that these towns were also attacked; Venta Icenorum, in fact, lost its freedom and was taken over by the Anglo-Saxons.[76] The whole of south Britannia was aflame.

The Briton cause was not yet without hope. One important Romano-Briton leader managed to escape the Massacre at the Cloister of Ambrius: Eldol, ruler of Glevum Colonia (Gloucester).

Geoffrey calls Eldol sometimes the "Count," and sometimes the "Duke," of "Gloucester." "Gloucester" refers to the important Roman town of Glevum Colonia, whereas the medieval titles Count and Duke are derived from the

Roman military ranks of Comes and Dux. Geoffrey's confusion as to Eldol's title could reflect his lack of familiarity with the Roman office of Magistratus, which is what the leader of a Civitas (or Colonia) was in Vortigern's day; we know that the post-Roman Britons continued to apply the label Magistratus to local rulers because the *Mabinogion* tale "Gereint and Enid" refers to a certain Gwynn Llogell, the ruler of Gower, as a "magistrate of Arthur's court," rather than a "king in attendance at Arthur's court." Mistaking "Magistratus" as a descriptive term ("magistrate") rather than the name of a public office, Geoffrey might have tried to give Eldol an appropriate medieval status. Alternatively, Eldol could have held the high rank of Dux and then the higher rank of Comes in succession. In any event, regardless of the exact title which he used, Eldol was clearly in command of the military forces of Glevum Colonia.

Eldol held the same position in Glevum which Vitalinus had once held. As we shall see, Vitalinus had resigned his political office in order to assume an important religious post. The leadership of Glevum seems to have held ecclesiastical service in high regard, because Eldol's brother, the same Eldadus who buried the victims of the Massacre at the Cloister of Ambrius, later became Bishop of Glevum.

Meanwhile, after escaping the Massacre at the Cloister of Ambrius, Eldol made his way back to Glevum. He then played an important role in structuring the post-Vortigern political order in Britannia, for he became associated with the return to Britannia of the younger Ambrosius Aurelianus.

---

76 Historians usually misdate these incidents to the late A.D. 440's, based upon their taking too literally the "Groans of the Britons" appeal to Aetius.

# LIBER TERTIUS

# The Age of Ambrosius

**- - The Middle Post-Roman Period - -**

**A.D. 462 - A.D. 490**

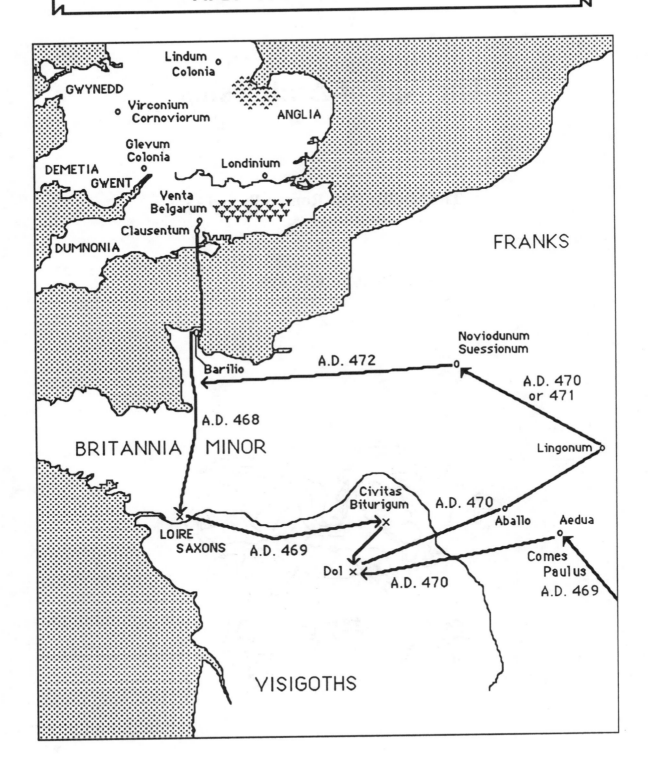

# AURELIUS'S CONTINENTAL CAMPAIGN
## A.D. 468 – A.D. 472

Lindum Colonia

GWYNEDD

Virconium Cornoviorum

ANGLIA

Glevum Colonia

DEMETIA

GWENT

Londinium

Venta Belgarum

Clausentum

DUMNONIA

FRANKS

Barilio

A.D. 472

Noviodunum Suessionum

A.D. 470 or 471

A.D. 468

Lingonum

BRITANNIA MINOR

Civitas Biturigum

A.D. 470

Aballo

Aedua

LOIRE SAXONS

A.D. 469

Dol ×

A.D. 470

Comes Paulus

A.D. 469

VISIGOTHS

## Chapter Eleven
## The Return of Ambrosius Aurelianus

Geoffrey of Monmouth tells us that after the three-times Roman Consul Aetius failed to come to the aid of the Britons, Guithelinus, Archbishop of London, went to Armorica in search of a king for Britannia. We have seen that Geoffrey places the appeal to Aetius much too early in time; Geoffrey places the appeal before the reign of Emperor Constantine III, when it really belongs in the middle of Vortigern's reign, long after Constantine's death. Likewise, Geoffrey places the Armorican journey of Archbishop Guithelinus in the wrong time period; Geoffrey places the journey immediately after the appeal to Aetius, when it really occurred some time later. The Britons would not have sent a mission to Armorica in search of a new leader in the late A.D. 440's when Vortimer was seizing control of Britannia, nor in the A.D. 450's when Vortimer was winning his victories over Hengist. They would, however, have recognized the desperate need for an experienced military commander following the terrible massacre engineered by Hengist at the Cloister of Ambrius. The Archbishop actually went abroad in search of a military savior for Britannia after the death of Vortimer and the massacre of the Romano-Briton leadership at the Cloister of Ambrius in A.D. 460.

When Archbishop Guithelinus returned to Britannia, he heralded a new era in Briton history, for the person with whom he returned was Aurelius Ambrosius Aurelianus, son of the Ambrosius Aurelianus defeated in the Battle of Wallop.

## The Mission of Archbishop Vitalinus

Geoffrey asserts that Guithelinus recruited Emperor Constantine III to be ruler of Britannia, but he has confused the story of the Constantini with that of the Ambrosii in this matter. Constantine III was already in Britannia when he began his Imperial career, so there was no need for Guithelinus or anyone else to travel abroad in search of him. The younger Ambrosius, on the other hand, fled Britannia after his father's defeat in the Battle of Wallop in A.D. 437. It was also the Ambrosii, not the Constantini, who had landholdings and relatives in Armorica and north Gaul. In addition, Gildas informs us that Ambrosius Aurelianus, not anyone named Constantine, was active in Britannia in the A.D. 460's, when Guithelinus must have returned from his search for a new ruler for Britannia. The logical object of the Archbishop's search could have only been the exiled younger Ambrosius.

The name of the man whom the Britons sent to invite the younger Ambrosius back into the Diocese sheds an interesting light on the fickleness of political fortune in post-Roman Britannia. "Guithelinus" is a Celtic version of the Latin "Vitalinus," a name we have already encountered in connection with the Battle of Wallop. Archbishop Guithelinus was, without a doubt, the very same person as the Vitalinus who fought in that Battle. If Vitalinus, the victor in the Battle of Wallop, was about forty years old when he confronted the elder Ambrosius in A.D. 437, then he would have been in his mid-sixties at the time of the mission to Armorica. At this age, an active and healthy individual could have easily made such a journey. Also, as we have seen, important secular leaders in the late Roman and post-Roman periods often took up a religious vocation later in life, as did Saint Ambrosius and Saint Germanus. The Archbishop Guithelinus who persuaded the younger Ambrosius to assume the leadership of Britannia in A.D. 460 was the former general Vitalinus who had fought and defeated the younger Ambrosius's father some two dozen years earlier.

Geoffrey calls the returnee "Aurelius Ambrosius." The individual name, or *praenomen*, of the younger Ambrosius therefore must have been Aurelius. Geoffrey most often refers to the younger Ambrosius by this *praenomen*. Geoffrey did not understand the Roman practice of using three names, and he did not realize that the first name, the individual name, of a noble Roman was the least important of the three. The Romans usually referred to a man by his *nomen* or *cognomen* (his family names), which in this case would have been "Ambrosius Aurelianus" for both the father and the son. The younger Ambrosius would have been called Aurelius only in his youth, when his father still lived and used the family names himself. We shall nevertheless follow Geoffrey's lead in this matter. To be consistent with Geoffrey, as well as to minimize confusion between the elder Ambrosius and his son, we shall refer to the younger Ambrosius by his individual name of Aurelius, notwithstanding that his contemporaries called him by his family name of Ambrosius.

When we last left Aurelius, he was in great personal danger after the death of his parents and the defeat of their cause in the Battle of Wallop.

## Aurelius's First Confrontation with Vortigern

While Vitalinus was winning the Battle of Wallop, Vortigern was, we have seen, building a fortress in the Snowdon region of north Wales. Since this region was not within Civitas Cornoviorum, but in an area recently recovered by Cunedda from Irish colonists, the Superbus Tyrannus must have been visiting the Votadini warlord. He was probably loaning the skill of his artisans and military engineers for the construction of fortifications in the reconquered territory. The Superbus Tyrannus also sent forth his agents to determine the whereabouts of the heir to the Ambrosii political fortune, and he directed that the lad should be brought before him at the new fort.

The young Ambrosius was eventually found and captured in south Wales. Nennius places the capture of "Embres" in Glevissig, now called Glamorgan, in southeast Wales. The Ambrosii probably held estates in the Glevissig area; in fact, Geoffrey tells us that Aurelius's mother was the daughter of a local "king," which implies that she was a Glevissig aristocrat. The elder Ambrosius had likely married the daughter of a wealthy Glevissig family in order to counteract Vortigern's influence in nearby Gwent. When relations between the Ambrosii and Vortigern began to deteriorate, the elder Ambrosius apparently sent his son to live with his in-laws in Glevissig, where he believed the boy would be safe.

Geoffrey actually locates Aurelius, whom he confuses with Myrddin or Merlin, a little further to the west in Carmarthen, known as Caer Myrddin to the Welsh and Moridunum to the Romans. Aurelius could not have really taken shelter in this town, however, because it is situated in Demetia, which was then in Irish hands. Geoffrey probably knew only that his "Merlin" had been captured in south Wales and he erroneously selected Carmarthen because "Carmarthen" means "town of Merlin." Geoffrey himself later places Merlin's home beside the Galabes Springs "in the territory of the Gewissei" (i.e., in Gwent) near Glevissig. We can be sure that Nennius correctly places Aurelius in Glevissig.

Despite the elder Ambrosius's precautions, Aurelius was discovered by Vortigern's henchmen. The Superbus Tyrannus's advisors then recommended slaying the youth. They no doubt feared that he might become a rallying point for the remaining adherents of the Imperial faction in Britannia. When Aurelius was brought before Vortigern, his life was considered forfeit.

Aurelius could not have been much more than twelve years old at the time and he must have realized that his life depended upon the whim of his captors. He nevertheless displayed fine courage in the grand tradition of the Roman heroes of old. Rather than cry or plead for mercy, the young Ambrosius bravely stood up to Vortigern and his court. Aurelius even went so far as to predict (or threaten) the ultimate victory of Roman soldiers over the barbarian warriors who maintained Vortigern in power.

Aurelius made his prediction in the form of a symbolic tale about a battle between two great serpents or dragons. The young Ambrosius analogized the Romans to a red dragon, a symbol taken from the serpentine windsock banner borne by Roman cavalry in the late Imperial period. The Roman red dragon emblem was adopted by the post-Roman Britons and can still be seen today emblazoned on the national flag of their Welsh descendants. Aurelius's father had likely carried such a banner in the Battle of Wallop. In the surviving form of Aurelius's tale, Vortigern and his Anglo-Saxon followers were represented by a white serpent or dragon. Considering the war names of the Anglo-Saxon leaders, "Hengist" and "Horsa" (meaning "stallion" and "horse"), the original symbol of the barbarians was probably a great white horse, an emblem which the Anglo-Saxons are known to have used in later times. The white Anglo-Saxon beast in Aurelius's tale initially dominated its opponent, but the red Roman dragon prevailed in the end.[77]

Aurelius thus prophesied ultimate victory for the pro-Roman Imperial party notwithstanding its recent defeat by Vortigern's barbarian-supported regime. This poetic way of speaking probably reflects a Celtic influence on Romano-Briton culture, or perhaps it was an imitation of Biblical parables. In any case, Aurelius's actual prediction was certainly much less wordy than the surviving accounts suggest. Aurelius's original words were no doubt a simple assertion along the lines that "the white horse may be triumphant now, but the red dragon will win the final victory."

The Superbus Tyrannus and his court were impressed with the boldness of the youth. Geoffrey tells us that "Vortigern, who was even more astonished than the others, himself spoke highly of the young man's wit and his oracular pronouncements, for that particular period in

---

77 In the *Historia Regum Britanniae*, the white Anglo-Saxon serpent actually wins the contest, but this outcome reflects Geoffrey's knowledge that Britannia was later overrun by the Anglo-Saxons; Geoffrey either misread his sources or else corrected what he thought was a clerical error in the early chronicles.

history had produced no one who was ready to speak his mind in this way in front of the king." To have murdered the helpless Aurelius after such a fearless expression of defiance would have appeared cowardly and mean. Vortigern's Anglo-Saxon troops, for whom resolute courage in the face of adversity was a cardinal virtue, would have certainly lost respect for their employer had he gone through with the planned execution. In the end, Vortigern magnanimously (or perhaps pragmatically) decided to spare the last of the Ambrosii.

Vortigern could allow Aurelius to live, but he could not allow him to go free. Loose in Britannia, the young Ambrosius would have been a focus for the Imperial sympathizers still at large in the Diocese. Vortigern therefore isolated the boy from potential supporters by shutting him up in some remote location. Nennius says that Vortigern "assigned" his recently built fort in Snowdonia to Aurelius, which suggests that Aurelius became the Superbus Tyrannus's prisoner, or "involuntary guest," in the fort.

The fort of Dinas Emrys is a very strong candidate for the prison of Aurelius. Dinas Emrys is located in the middle of the Snowdonian mountains, where both Geoffrey and Nennius believe Vortigern to have erected his fort. Archaeology confirms that Dinas Emrys was occupied by a well-to-do Romano-Briton community at this time. The fort even contains an artificial pool which could have been the site of the confrontation between Aurelius and Vortigern (i.e., the pit from which the "dragons" were excavated). The fort is also located in the middle of Cunedda's new kingdom and far from Ambrosii territory: confined there, Aurelius would have been effectively isolated from any opportunity to meddle in or affect Briton politics. The geographic position of Dinas Emrys made it a suitable place for Vortigern to have imprisoned Aurelius.

"Dinas Emrys" even means "fort of Ambrosius" in Welsh. The fort must have acquired this name from Aurelius, because he is the only Ambrosii who could have ever been at the fort. The only time Aurelius was likely to have been at Dinas Emrys was in his youth, when he was held captive by Vortigern.

The original name of Dinas Emrys was probably Dinas Brutus, meaning "fort of Brutus." "Dinas Brutus" would have been an appropriate name for a fort in an area reconquered in a joint campaign by Cunedda and Vortigern's son Brutus Catellus, ruler of the north Pagus (north Powys and Clwyd). A corruption of "Dinas Brutus," "Dinabutius," appears in the *Historia Regum Britanniae* as the name of the individual who told Vortigern's men where to find Aurelius, but Geoffrey has probably mistaken the name of Aurelius's prison for that of his betrayer.

The area about Dinas Emrys also has traditional associations, albeit indirectly, with Vortigern. The fort is located beside the Nant Gwynant valley, where local legend claims that Eugenius ("Owein" in Welsh), the son of Emperor Maximus and thus the brother-in-law of Vortigern, fought and defeated a "giant." Also nearby is Llyn Dinas, meaning "Lake Fort," where Eugenius supposedly died in combat against a "dragon." Giants and great beasts were often used in folklore to symbolize bandit chieftains and lawless warlords, descriptions which the Britons no doubt applied to the Irish warlords then ruling most of Wales. Eugenius's struggles with "a giant" and "a dragon" are thus references to battles in the long war to retake north Wales and the Pagus from the Irish. The traditional belief that Vortigern's brother-in-law engaged in military action in the vicinity of Dinas Emrys tells us that the Superbus Tyrannus had influence in this area and that he could have arranged to use the fort to hold an important prisoner.

If Aurelius had been locked up in Dinas Emrys, or any other place for that matter, then he was later paroled or somehow managed to escape, for he eventually made his way to Armorica.

Aurelius pursued a military career on the Continent. Geoffrey tells us that Aurelius was brave and hardy, and that he was formidable in personal combat. Aurelius fought well on foot, but was principally and best a horse soldier - as we would expect of an upper class Roman. Aurelius also developed considerable leadership qualities, winning the loyalty of his men by his demeanor, his generosity and his command skills. His followers were no doubt the landless younger sons of aristocratic families in Armorica, many of whom, like Aurelius, had originally come from Britannia. The turmoil in Gaul presented Aurelius with many opportunities to develop his martial talents, and he probably made himself an important factor in Armorican military affairs. Aurelius might have even served under Magister Militum Aetius, possibly as a commander of the Armorican contingent which fought with Aetius against Attila the Hun in the Battle of Chalons in A.D. 451.

Aurelius might have also engaged in other activities of a more amorous nature. In A.D. 458, a certain Ambrosius was convicted by Rogatianus, the Consularis (Governor) of Tuscia (Tuscany) in north Italy, of the crime of adultery. This Ambrosius was placed in confinement, but managed to escape. (The Ambrosii were apparently adept at prison-breaks.) Rogatianus referred the case to Emperor Majorian, who on April 17, 459 issued a Rescript (Legal Decree) confiscating all of Ambrosius's property and banishing him from the Empire on pain of death. If this Ambrosius is the same person as our Aurelius, then Aurelius's presence in Armorica could be explained as a flight from Imperial justice: at the time, Armorica was virtually autonomous of the Empire and Majorian's Rescript would not have been given effect there; the fugitive could have lived in relative safety beyond the reach of Imperial vengeance on his Armorican estates. The adulterous Ambrosius of Tuscia is not likely to be Aurelius, however, because Gildas describes Aurelius as *vir modestus*, meaning "a moderate, discreet and virtuous man." Such a man would not have been caught in an affair with another man's wife. The charge of adultery could, however, have been the cover for a political prosecution; many Romano-Gallic leaders opposed Emperor Majorian because they believed him to be implicated in the murder of his predecessor, Emperor Avitus, who was from Gaul. Aurelius could have been caught up in some political intrigue and arrested on a false charge of adultery. In that case, however, we would expect to find another reference to Aurelius's involvement in Imperial politics in some other source, but no such mention survives. In fact, the *Chronica Theodericiana*, a mid-Sixth Century history of post-Roman Italy, refers to Saint Severinus of Noricum (Austria) in about A.D. 476 obtaining from Odovacer, the barbarian king then ruling Italy, a pardon for a certain Ambrosius, who is described as "living in exile"; this Ambrosius is more likely to have been the escaped convict. Ambrosius of Tuscia is not likely to have been Aurelius, but he was almost certainly a distant relative of his Armorican namesake.

In any event, Aurelius did not, of course, remain forever in Armorica. He eventually returned to make himself master of Britannia.

## The Restoration of the Ambrosii

We should allow about a year after the Massacre at the Cloister of Ambrius for Archbishop Vitalinus to receive his commission from the Civitates of Britannia and to make the journey to Armorica, and then another year for Aurelius to gather and prepare his followers for the overseas expedition. We should therefore place Aurelius's return to Britannia in A.D. 462.

The Britannia to which Aurelius returned was in a desperate condition. The Anglo-Saxons in the southern part of the Diocese had rebelled and, joined by opportunistic adventurers from Germania, were ravaging the island from end to end. The Haestingas, a Saxon tribe, also bloodily conquered the eastern half of modern Sussex at this time. If Aurelius did not quickly restore the military situation, the Anglo-Saxons would have destroyed what was left of the economic and social structure of the Diocese, and Roman civilization would have disappeared from Britannia.

Geoffrey of Monmouth tells us that Aurelius landed at Totonesium Portus (Totnes), on the south Devon coast. Totonesium Portus then lay within Dumnonia, which had recently been reconquered by Cornovian troops from Irish warlords. Geoffrey later tells us that Gorlois, whom he describes as the "Duke of Cornwall,"

commanded a cavalry squadron in Aurelius's army. Gorlois must have been a Cornovian leader from Dumnonia and an early backer of Aurelius; he was no doubt one of the leaders who had sponsored the embassy of Archbishop Vitalinus to Armorica. Aurelius landed in Cornovian Dumnonia in order to make contact with Dux Gorlois, a powerful military ally in Britannia, before he advanced into the interior of the Diocese.

We might have expected Aurelius to land at the Roman port of Clausentum (Southampton), which was in Civitas Belgarum and close to his family's landholdings in the Venta Belgarum (Winchester) and Noviomagus Regnensium (Chichester) areas. The Ambrosii homeland had, however, been in the hands of Vortigern's supporters for over twenty years. Even if the common folk of the region still had a sentimental regard for the old manorial family, Aurelius could expect an unfriendly welcome from the new landlords whom Vortigern was sure to have installed on the Ambrosii estates. Hengist and his followers had also devastated the area about Venta Belgarum, and Anglo-Saxon raiders might have still been operating in the vicinity. Aurelius wisely landed in Cornovian Dumnonia, where he could count on a cordial reception and link up with allied forces before moving on to face his, and Britannia's, enemies.

Comes Eldol, the ruler of Glevum Colonia (Gloucester) and sole survivor of the Massacre at the Cloister of Ambrius, soon joined Aurelius's army. The town of Glevum, an important early ally of Vortigern, now threw in with the returning Ambrosius; Eldol, like Gorlois, must have been one of the leaders who had sponsored the embassy of Archbishop Vitalinus to Armorica. Aurelius probably marched his combined Armorican-Dumnonian force from Totonesium Portus to Glevum, where he linked up with Eldol and his soldiers. The advancing army also gathered to itself troops from other parts of Britannia, as adventurers and Imperial sympathizers from all over the Diocese flocked to Aurelius's banner, which was certainly a red Roman cavalry dragon.

Many of the Britons who rallied to Aurelius's banner urged that he lead them immediately against the barbarians then running amuck in the Diocese. Aurelius had another priority. The first objective of the returned Ambrosius was to eliminate Vortigern, the one man in Britannia capable of challenging his authority over the Britons.

## The Death of Vortigern

Geoffrey tells us that Aurelius was eager to avenge his father's death, so he marched north and placed Vortigern under siege in his "tower." Geoffrey mentions only Aurelius's Armoricans and Eldol's Glevum-men participating in the siege; Gorlois's Cornovians from Dumnonia probably participated as well, although it is possible that they abstained from making war directly upon their former Magistratus. At least some Cornovians of Civitas Cornoviorum did actively support Vortigern, however, and Aurelius soon realized that the siege would be long and difficult. The returned leader therefore caused Vortigern's tower to be set alight. Aurelius seized Vortigern's bastion in the confusion of the smoke and flames, only to find that the Superbus Tyrannus had perished in the fire.

The precise location of Vortigern's demise is unclear. Nennius puts the scene of

Vortigern's fiery death at the fort of Cair Guorthergirn (meaning "Vortigern's Town") by the River Towy on the Builth border with the Irish kingdom of Demetia.[78] Geoffrey places it at the fort of Genoreu or Gronwyr (now Ganarew) on Cloartius hill (now Little Doward) near the River Wye in Gwent. Archeology, on the other hand, points to Vortigern's chief town of Viroconium (Wroxeter). According to the evidence of excavation, Viroconium suffered a conflagration about this time in circumstances suggesting it was the victim of an attack: skeletons were found huddled together in the town baths, where townspeople had apparently sought refuge from attackers, only to be suffocated by fumes; one of the victims even died clutching a bag of coins, as if to protect it from looters. Only part of Viroconium was actually burnt, but many structures in the town were then deliberately disassembled and their materials removed. The only military force in Britannia which could have attacked and dismantled Viroconium is the army of Aurelius. Fortunately, Nennius provides the solution to the puzzle of the conflicting reports of Vortigern's last stand.

Nennius tells us that Vortigern, "hated by all the people of Britain" and "broken-hearted," wandered from place to place in search of refuge. The Superbus Tyrannus, knowing what he could expect at the hands of Aurelius, must have travelled across his domains in a vain attempt to rally the Builthmen, Gwentmen and Cornovians to his cause. He probably also tried to recruit Demetian Irish mercenaries against the returned Roman warrior. "Hated" and "broken-hearted" is an apt description of Vortigern's

---

78 Nennius also fails to mention Aurelius's role in the burning, simply attributing the fire to divine retribution for Vortigern's sins without giving any details.

pitiful condition as he made his way from place to place within his realm, stopping at Cair Guorthergirn, Castle Genoreu and other forts and towns in a futile effort to muster support before he withdrew to meet his fate at his capital of Viroconium.

Vortigern had ruled Britannia as Superbus Tyrannus for almost forty years, during which time he decisively shaped Briton history. Although Vortigern accomplished much that was good during his long reign, notably the defeat of the Picts, the expulsion of the Irish from north Wales and the liberation of Dumnonia, he also made several serious mistakes late in his reign which proved his undoing. He unnecessarily gave his enemies in the Church a tool to use against him when he married his own stepdaughter rather then surrender control of her mother's family estates in Gwent, and he foolishly alienated many of his Briton subjects when he took an Anglo-Saxon mistress and displaced the native Comes Vorangonus in favor of the barbarian Hengist. He then shortsightedly allowed his Anglo-Saxon mercenaries to slip from his control, further disquieting the Britons as Hengist built himself a strong base of power in southeast Britannia. Vortigern's unfortunate miscalculations caused him to forfeit his authority over the Britons and earned him a place of infamy in the annals of history.

## Vortigern's Descendants

Vortigern's family did not disappear from history after the fall of the Superbus Tyrannus. Vortigern's descendants through his son Brutus Catellus (or Catigern) still ruled the kingdom of Powys, and they would continue to do so for approximately another three hundred years; they also came to dominate the Cornovian heartland around the town of Viroconium until it fell to the Anglo-Saxons in the middle of the Seventh Century. Vortigern's son Pascent meanwhile assumed the government of Builth, which subsequently passed to Pascent's heirs. Even Vortigern's illicit son by his stepdaughter, Faustus, went on to achieve prominence in the Church in Gaul. Another extraordinary individual who might have been Vortigern's grandson through his disloyal son Vortimer later seized power in an important part of south Britannia. The several branches of Vortigern's family survived to play crucial roles in post-Roman affairs even after the disgrace and downfall of their forebear.

Nevertheless, it was Vortigern's enemy, Aurelius Ambrosius Aurelianus, who now assumed the leadership of post-Roman Britannia.

## Chapter Twelve
## Aurelius's War Against Kent

After destroying Vortigern and burning his town, Aurelius spent the next several years consolidating his power in Britannia. He repossessed his family estates in south-central Britannia and he levied Briton troops to augment the forces which he had brought with him from Armorica. He probably also led periodic military expeditions against the Anglo-Saxon raiders loose in the Diocese. Three years after he set sail from Armorica, Aurelius was secure in his control of Britannia and ready to strike at the source of the barbarian problem. In A.D. 465, Aurelius invaded Hengist's Kent.

### The Battle of Maisbeli

Hengist was ready to meet the new Romano-Briton ruler in battle. Geoffrey of Monmouth tells us that the barbarian leader had assembled a "hand-picked army" in anticipation of the conflict with Aurelius.

Geoffrey also tells us that Hengist retreated north across the Humber River to flee the advance of Aurelius's army. Such a maneuver makes absolutely no sense, however, because it would have only distanced Hengist from his strongholds and supporters in Kent. Geoffrey must have been confused by the fact that Anglo-Saxons from far north Britannia later fought for Hengist against Aurelius. Hengist did not flee north across the Humber River, but east across the Medway River, because, without a doubt, the barbarian leader made his stand in his own realm of Kent.

Aurelius and Hengist first met in combat in the Battle of Maisbeli. We do not know where Maisbeli was, but it had to have been somewhere in west Kent. A likely location is the modern town of Maidstone.

Maidstone lies in west Kent near the important ancient trail later called the Harrow Way. The Harrow Way was the principal east-west route in Britannia south of the River Thames since long before the arrival of the Romans, and it was the logical path of invasion into Kent from Dumnonia (Devon and Cornwall), Glevum Colonia (Gloucester) and Venta Belgarum (Winchester), the areas from which Aurelius drew his support. Maidstone itself was occupied in both late Roman and post-Roman times, and it lies near Aylesford, where Hengist had earlier fought Vortimer. We do not know Maidstone's Latin name, but it could have been something like "Maesbelium," which evolved into (or from) the Briton "Maisbeli." "Maesbelium" could have later become the Anglo-Saxon "Maisbel's-towne" and then "Maidstone." The Battle of Maisbeli was probably fought in a clearing near the town.

Geoffrey tells us that the invading Briton army amounted to 10,000 men, including 3,000 Armoricans, and that the defending Anglo-Saxon army mustered 200,000 men. Medieval historians were hopelessly incapable of dealing with large army sizes, but, with a little help from the Anglo-Saxon Chronicle, we can deduce the actual number of combatants from the information found in the *Historia Regum Britanniae*.

We can deduce the size of the two forces in the Battle of Maisbeli based upon the different descriptions of Vortimer's army found in two different manuscripts of the Anglo-Saxon Chronicle. The army in question is the one which Vortimer led in the Battle of Crayford in

A.D. 457. One manuscript states that Hengist "slew" (i.e., defeated) "four thousand" Britons, whereas the other manuscript claims that he "killed four companies." In the early chronicles, the word "thousand" thus seems to be synonymous with the word "company" or "military unit."

Briton infantry units of the post-Roman period did indeed have a nominal complement of 1,000 warriors, based upon the late Roman infantry unit of this size. We know that the Welsh later organized their infantry on a decimal basis, which indicates that the post-Roman Britons and their Welsh descendants continued to follow the late Imperial model of military organization. They therefore would have attempted to raise Roman-style infantry units of 1,000 men. In practice, however, their infantry units were probably closer to half their professed strength and could have seldom exceeded 800 soldiers. The decline in population and the break-down in social organization did not permit the maintenance of large army units at full strength. A reference to "ten thousand" Briton warriors thus means a force of ten military units, which would have been no more than 8,000 foot soldiers.

As for cavalry, the Welsh in slightly later times considered 300 horsemen to be the proper military escort for a king. Many references to warbands of 300 horseborne warriors appear in early Welsh sources, including the poem *Gododdin*, the biographical *Vita Cadoci* (Life of Saint Cadoc) and the *Mabinogion* tales "Owein, or the Countess of the Fountain," "The Dream of Rhonabwy" and "Peredur Son of Efrawg." Geoffrey also tells of a Briton commander of Arthur's time leading a charge of 300 cavalrymen. (The commander was Hyrelgas, nephew of Arthur's companion Bedwyr.) Especially powerful kings seem to have had mounted warbands of 900 men, apparently three units of 300 soldiers each. The early Welsh poem *Cath Palug* (Clawing Cat), for example, refers to Arthur's companion Bedwyr commanding 900 men but bringing only 600 of them into battle, as if he led two units of 300 into combat and held another unit of 300 back in reserve. Cunedda, before he emigrated to Wales, also supposedly commanded 900 horsemen. A Romano-Briton cavalry unit thus numbered about 300 horse soldiers.

Cavalry units also included a large number of grooms and other servants. The "Owein" tale, for instance, refers to Arthur at one time leading 3,000 men "not counting servants." The servants cared for the unit's horses and equipment, thereby freeing the riders to concentrate on training and on fighting. They also reinforced the elite status and morale of the aristocratic cavalrymen by relieving them of menial tasks. The cavalry servants were not frontline warriors, but neither were they strictly non-combatant. In addition to their non-military duties, the servants guarded baggage camps, escorted supply trains and generally assisted the mounted soldiers in battle. In the Middle Ages, similar functions were performed by the squires who served the horseborne knights. Allowing for these semi-combatant servants, a Briton cavalry unit was not much smaller than its infantry counterpart.

Since three Briton leaders were present at the Battle of Maisbeli (Aurelius, Eldol and Gorlois), three of Aurelius's ten units must have been cavalry units, for a total of approximately 900 horse soldiers. To these 900 horsemen, we should add perhaps an equal number of semi-combatant servants. The remaining seven units in Aurelius's army were infantry units, for a total of approximately 5,000 foot soldiers.

Geoffrey tells us that three "thousands" of Armorican warriors served in Aurelius's army, so, in addition to his personal Armorican cavalry band, Aurelius must have commanded two Armorican infantry units. The Armorican contingent in Aurelius's army thus came to about 300 cavalry and 1,400 infantry. An additional 300 servants would bring the total size of the Armorican contingent to approximately 2,000 men, which corresponds to the number of Breton soldiers which "Constantine" (whom Geoffrey confuses with Aurelius) was supposed to have brought to Britannia.

The Romano-Briton invasion force led by Aurelius thus totaled in the neighborhood of 6,500 soldiers, including about 1,400 Armorican infantry (two units), 300 Armorican cavalry (one unit), 3,500 Briton infantry (five units), 600 Briton cavalry (two units) and several hundred semi-combatant servants.

As for Hengist's barbarian army, the early chronicles most often quantify Anglo-Saxon forces in terms of the number of "keels" or "warships." The complement of Anglo-Saxon warships of the period varied considerably, ranging from as few as twenty to as many as seventy crewmen. A warship which we could consider typical held between thirty and forty warriors. We should therefore allow about thirty-five combatants for each Anglo-Saxon military unit. The Anglo-Saxon force commanded by Hengist thus consisted of 200 military units, meaning 200 ships' crews or approximately 7,000 warriors.

Hengist's army was entirely an infantry force. Wealthy Anglo-Saxons often rode to combat on horseback, but they dismounted as soon as they arrived at the battlefield. Like their more humble countrymen, Anglo-Saxon aristocrats only fought afoot with sword (or seax), shield and spear. Although Anglo-Saxon noblemen were fine horsemen, they simply lacked the training and experience, and even the proper weapons and harness, to wage war effectively as cavalrymen.

Anglo-Saxon warriors compensated for their lack of horseborne mobility by maintaining a strict martial tradition. All Anglo-Saxon males, both commoners and noblemen, were literally bred to war. Raised in a warrior culture, they were from an early age familiar with the handling of weapons, accustomed to military discipline, trained in simple close-order infantry formations, and, most important of all, psychologically prepared to endure the rigors and hardship of combat. Hengist's foot soldiers were all tough fighters.

Briton infantrymen were generally inferior to their barbarian counterparts. Roman Britannia was essentially a civilian society, and very few of its inhabitants had any meaningful army experience. Only the descendants of the Imperial soldiers formerly stationed in the Diocese had any military background, and this military background was often very limited. For the most part, the professional Roman fighting men of former days had been replaced by part-time militiamen. These militiamen had long ago abandoned the severe training regimen that once made the Imperial army invincible in the ancient world. They had also become accustomed to elite mobile units and barbarian mercenary units doing most of the hard fighting. Foot soldiers recruited from the heirs of these semi-professional Roman soldiers usually did not make very good warriors. Only Cohors Cornoviorum in the Pagus (Powys and Clwyd) and Dumnonia (Devon and Cornwall), Legion VI Victrix in Eboracum (York), Legion II Augusta in Gwent and Glevissig (southeast Wales), and possibly remnants of Legion XX Valeria Victrix in Castrum Deva (Chester) and a handful of other Roman army units scattered across north Britannia produced high quality infantrymen. The leaders of post-Roman Britannia simply did not have access to a large reservoir of well-trained or experienced infantrymen.

The Romano-Briton cavalrymen were, however, superb warriors. Aurelius's fellow aristocrats, steeped in a cavalier tradition and experienced equestrians, made excellent horse soldiers. Likewise, the descendants of the Imperial cavalry troopers stationed in Britannia seem to have preserved their ancestor's martial standards. The Romano-Briton cavalrymen were not nearly so well equipped as the heavily armed and armored knights of the Middle Ages, but their swiftness and their ability to strike unexpectedly at the flanks or rear of an enemy formation were important advantages in post-Roman warfare. These advantages more than compensated for the poor quality of the Briton foot soldier. If a Romano-Briton army was led by a competent commander, its elite cavalry component gave it a definite advantage over an equal-sized Anglo-Saxon force, despite the outstanding caliber of the Anglo-Saxon infantry.

The two armies at Maisbeli were thus well matched in effective strength. Hengist had a slight edge in total army size and in the quality of his infantry, but Aurelius's Romano-Briton cavalry gave him a tactical flexibility which could prove decisive.

Hengist, after his many years in Britannia,

knew the value of Romano-Briton cavalry, and he was determined to deny Aurelius the opportunity to deploy his horsemen. When Aurelius invaded Kent, Hengist did not assume a defensive stance; he seized the initiative. He aggressively advanced to intercept the Briton force while it moved eastward along the Harrow Way. As the Britons approached the field of Maisbeli, the Anglo-Saxons suddenly fell upon them, hoping to catch them by surprise. An unexpected assault upon an army strung out in road-marching order could be devastating if the attackers struck quickly before the enemy was able to react. Aurelius was not to be taken quite so easily.

The Roman leader must have been warned of Hengist's plan by his advance scouts, or else he was simply alert and cautious. Before the full force of the barbarian attack was delivered, Aurelius deployed Gorlois's Dumnonians[79] on the hilly ground on one flank of the army, and Eldol's Glevum-men[80] by the wooded area on the other flank. He kept his Armorican troops and the Briton infantry near him in the middle. Aurelius obviously intended to engage the Anglo-Saxons with his foot soldiers in the center of the army, while the allied Briton cavalry circled around the enemy flanks and his own Armorican cavalry stood back in reserve.

Hengist soon saw that Aurelius was ready for him. Rather than snaring his enemies in a trap, he was about to be trapped himself. After some sharp initial fighting, Hengist wisely chose to withdraw.

---

79  Being the more southerly Britons, which is no doubt what Geoffrey's source said and which he mistranslated as "Demetians," the south Welsh in his day.

80  Being the more northerly Britons, which is no doubt what Geoffrey's source said and which he mistranslated as "Venedotians," the north Welsh in his day.

Geoffrey tells us that Hengist and his army fled toward the town of "Kaerconan, which is now called Cunungeburg," by which he means Conisbrough in South Yorkshire. Because Geoffrey mistakenly believed that the Battle of Maisbeli was fought in north Britannia, he misidentifies the town toward which Hengist retreated. The full Roman name of any town in Kent would have included the Civitas designation "Cantiacorum," and this designation must have caused Geoffrey to look for a similar-seeming name in Yorkshire. He found Kaerconan/Conisbrough. Hengist actually withdrew in the direction of Maidstone, which lay near the border of Hengist's Kent and the probable battle site.

Aurelius vigorously pursued Hengist, and the barbarian was unable to make good his escape. Before Hengist could retreat behind the safety of Maidstone's walls, he was overtaken by Aurelius's horsemen. Hengist had realized that the flanking movement of Aurelius's allied cavalry was intended to surround and destroy his army, but his reaction came just a little too late. His foot soldiers were unable to outrun the Romano-Briton cavalry. Cut off from their refuge, the Anglo-Saxons turned at bay, and a new phase of the Battle commenced.

The Anglo-Saxons in this situation would have formed up in a dense infantry formation called a shieldwall. In a shieldwall, the Anglo-Saxon warriors stood literally shoulder-to-shoulder, holding their round wooden shields in front of them. The shields' edges touched and slightly overlapped, thus presenting a solid line to the enemy; it was from this solid line of shields that the formation derived its name. If any warrior in the line was killed or wounded, several ranks of additional warriors stood behind him, ready to move up and take his place. A shieldwall was an extremely strong defensive formation. It was very difficult to push aside and virtually impossible to overrun. At the Battle of Hastings approximately six hundred years later, the very same Anglo-Saxon battle formation, although eventually overcome, resisted and repulsed with heavy losses many repeated assaults by the much better equipped and more strongly armed Norman knights of William the Conqueror.

With the Anglo-Saxons on the defensive and in their traditional - and formidable - battle array, the Battle of Maisbeli was joined in earnest. Both sides fought hard, with the Anglo-Saxons maintaining their cohesion and steadily gaining the upper hand. The barbarians appeared to be on the verge of winning a great victory. Then, at precisely the right moment, Aurelius struck. When the Anglo-Saxon shieldwall was just slightly disordered as the barbarians pressed forward against the faltering Briton infantry, Aurelius ordered in the Armorican cavalry. Striking hard at the decisive instant before the Anglo-Saxons could again tighten their ranks, the Armorican charge shattered the shieldwall and scattered the barbarian warriors. Once the integrity of their close-order battle formation was lost, the individual Anglo-Saxon foot soldiers were easy prey for the hard-riding and aggressive Romano-Briton horsemen. Many Anglo-Saxon warriors were cut down by their enemies' long, slashing cavalry swords. Only a lucky few managed to elude bloody death. The timely commitment of the Armorican cavalry, a decision requiring cool, steady and experienced judgement in the heat and confusion of combat, turned the tide of battle and won the day for the Britons.

The Briton victory at Maisbeli was decisive, and the survivors of the defeated Anglo-Saxon host bolted in two different directions.

## The Battle of Wippedesfleot

We are able to draw upon the Anglo-Saxon Chronicle to learn the fate of the warband which fled under Hengist's personal command. After the Battle of Maisbeli, Hengist and some of his followers managed to elude the Romano-Briton army. They made their way due east. The Britons pursued Hengist, and the resulting combat found its way into the Anglo-Saxon Chronicle.[81]

The Anglo-Saxon Chronicle reports that Hengist fought the Britons at Wippedesfleot in A.D. 465. "Wippedesfleot" means "Estuary of Wipped." The Estuary of Wipped is the Wantsum Channel near Richborough ("Rutupiae Portus" to the Romans), which then separated the Isle of Thanet from the Kentish mainland. The Anglo-Saxons named the Channel after Wipped, a thane (nobleman) who fell in the Battle. Today, the Wantsum Channel has largely silted in, but in the Fifth Century it was still a major waterway meriting the description of "estuary"; Venerable Bede tells us that in his day the Wantsum was fordable in only two places. The second battle in Aurelius's invasion of Kent thus took place in the far eastern part of Hengist's realm. The Battle of Wippedesfleot was obviously fought as Hengist attempted to flee to Thanet, where he had twice managed to elude Vortimer's wrath.

Geoffrey associates only Eldol and Gorlois

---

[81] The Battle of Maisbeli itself does not appear in the Anglo-Saxon Chronicle, but the omission is hardly surprising because the Chronicle studiously ignores barbarian defeats.

with the pursuit of Hengist after the Battle of Maisbeli, so Aurelius must have dispatched his two allies and their personal warbands to run the Anglo-Saxon warlord to ground. The entire Briton pursuit force was therefore mounted. Hengist and his chieftains would have also been on horseback since they were in headlong flight. Anglo-Saxon noblemen were fine horsemen, but, as we have noted, they were neither trained nor equipped to fight from horseback. If the Romano-Briton cavalry force had caught up with the routed barbarians, it would have cut them to pieces. The prelude to the Battle of Wippedesfleot was a long, furious horserace.

Wipped, the Anglo-Saxon thane for whom the barbarians named the battle site, rallied some of his fellows to make a desperate stand against their pursuers. He chose to make his stand at one of the crossing points over the Wantsum to Thanet. The Anglo-Saxons would have dismounted and formed a shieldwall at the ford in order to present a strong front to the onrushing Romano-Briton horsemen. In this way, Wipped hoped to slow down the pursuit and buy time for Hengist and the rest of the warband to escape to Thanet. A similar tactical situation is described in the Anglo-Saxon poem *Exodus*. In this poem, a very Anglo-Saxon-like Moses instructed companies of picked Israelite warriors to make an identical defensive stand against Pharaoh's pursuing hordes in order that their people might safely cross the Red Sea. It was a very brave thing for Wipped to do. The Anglo-Saxon shieldwall was a formidable defensive formation, but it was also immobile. By forming a shieldwall, the Anglo-Saxon defenders could indeed slow down the Briton pursuers and buy time for their comrades to escape, but they would also give up any chance of making their own escape. Wipped's heroic effort was doomed, but it did delay the Romano-Briton horsemen long enough for Hengist and the rest of his followers to reach their island refuge.

Wipped, before he fell, slew twelve enemy "thanes" according to the Anglo-Saxon Chronicle. "Thane" was the title which the Anglo-Saxons gave their noblemen. The Briton "thanes" were obviously Romano-Briton cavalrymen. Because only wealthy Anglo-Saxon warriors could afford to own horses, the barbarians assumed the same for their enemies and counted all Romano-Briton horsemen as "thanes." They were more or less correct since post-Roman Briton horse soldiers were indeed recruited from the Romanized aristocracy. Wipped thus sold his life dearly, taking some of his enemies with him when he sacrificed himself to cover his leader's retreat.

Geoffrey nevertheless asserts that Gorlois captured Hengist after the Battle of Maisbeli. He also claims that Eldadus, the Churchman who had buried the victims of the Massacre at the Cloister of Ambrius and who was then Bishop of Glevum, urged the execution of the barbarian warlord. Eldadus's brother Eldol supposedly heeded this advice and beheaded the self-styled king of Kent. The Anglo-Saxon Chronicle, however, credits Hengist with another battle eight years later in A.D. 473. If Hengist was a young man when he came to Britannia in A.D. 428, then he would have been in his late sixties or early seventies at the time of his last fight: an advanced age for those times to be sure, but one at which he still could have been quite active. Geoffrey has mistakenly merged two different battles, almost a decade apart, into a single combat, and Hengist did not yet meet his fate in A.D. 465.

## The Siege of Durovernum

While Eldol and Gorlois chased Hengist to Wippedesfleot, Aurelius occupied Maidstone. He called a temporary halt there to give his weary soldiers a rest. At the same time, Hengist's son Octa and his "kinsmen" Eosa led the main force of Anglo-Saxon survivors to Durovernum Cantiacorum (Canterbury). Geoffrey actually tells us that the two barbarian leaders retreated into the town of "York" (i.e., Eboracum), but he clearly errs. Eboracum was much too far away from the scene of the fighting to have been Octa's and Eosa's true destination - to say nothing of the fact that the town was already occupied by the Dux Britanniarum. Geoffrey's source must have reported that the Anglo-Saxons fled into the "chief town of those parts," which would have been Eboracum if they had been in the north of Britannia as Geoffrey thought, but was actually Durovernum in Kent. After three days, Aurelius marched his army from Maidstone to Durovernum, where he proceeded to put Octa and Eosa under siege.

Octa was, of course, leader of the Anglo-Saxons of Bernicia. He had obviously come south, no doubt with as many warrior companions as he could rally, to assist his father against Aurelius. Octa now found himself in command of the defeated remnant of a once-proud Anglo-Saxon army and surrounded by enemies in a Kentish town, many of whose inhabitants, being Britons, must have also been hostile to him.

The army of Aurelius, while a far cry from the mighty Roman legions of old, should have nevertheless possessed sufficient skill in siege-craft to have eventually taken Durovernum.

Aurelius could have also appealed to the Briton inhabitants of the town to throw open the town gates. Even if Aurelius was unable to capture Durovernum outright or to persuade its citizens to deliver it up to him, he could at the very least have used his infantry to bottle Octa and his followers up in the town, slowly starving them into submission. The morale of the defeated Anglo-Saxons could not have been very high in the circumstances. Octa took the only logical course of action available to him:  he surrendered.

Aurelius accepted the barbarian's surrender. He then, according to Geoffrey, "granted" to Octa "the region near Scotland." Aurelius, in other words, allowed the defeated Anglo-Saxon to return to Bernicia. He also extracted a treaty from Octa. Aurelius's treaty no doubt contained Octa's promise to keep the peace with the Britons and to stay out of the southern part of the Diocese.

When Octa headed north, he took most of the surviving warriors of Hengist's army, including a large number of Kentishmen, with him. The defeated Anglo-Saxon warriors would have gladly accompanied Octa to Bernicia because they now had little prospect of martial gain or glory in the south. Aurelius's decisive defeat of Hengist in the Battle of Maisbeli meant that the expansion of Kent was, at least for the moment, checked. It also meant that the barbarian warriors could expect small profit if they were foolish enough to again challenge the Roman leader. Denied military success in the south, the Anglo-Saxon warriors sought new opportunities elsewhere.

Some of the vanquished Anglo-Saxons even joined Aurelius's army. The *Mabinogion* tale "How Culhwch Won Olwen" reports that a chieftain named "Osla Big Knife" later fought under Arthur's command. "Osla" is probably a Celtic version of "Eosa," which suggests that Octa's co-commander took service with his conqueror. "Osla" is certainly an Anglo-Saxon name in any case, whereas "Big Knife" is an excellent description of the Anglo-Saxon seax. Osla Big Knife, even if he was not the same person as Eosa, was clearly an Anglo-Saxon mercenary in Briton service, and he was probably a follower of Octa who entered Briton service after the Battle of Maisbeli. With Hengist defeated and Kent overrun by the Britons, the prospect of pay and booty in Aurelius's army appealed to at least some of the barbarians.

Overall, Aurelius's Kentish War was a great victory for the new ruler of Britannia. Although Hengist had once again escaped Briton vengeance and although he still ruled an independent Anglo-Saxon realm in east Kent, he had been gravely humiliated. Hengist lost most of his soldiers to death in combat, expulsion to the north or defection to Aurelius. He also forfeited the territories of "Essex" and "Middlesex" which he had recently received in exchange for Vortigern's freedom;  the Ambrosius-named forts in these areas were no doubt established there by Aurelius at this time. Besides, as Aurelius and his advisors must have known, the complete elimination of the Kentish kingdom was no longer a realistic objective. Many of the barbarians had been living in Britannia for over three decades by then, working farms, raising families and intermarrying to at least some extent with the native population; they were as firmly established in the Diocese as the Britons themselves. The breaking of Hengist, the dispersal of his army and the diminution of his realm, in combination with the submission of Octa and the recruitment of Eosa/Osla, qualifies Aurelius's A.D. 465 campaign as an enormous success.

The greatest tribute to the success of Aurelius's Kentish War is the fact that the Anglo-Saxons for some time thereafter ceased their aggression against the Britons. They continued to consolidate their position within their allotted territories, but they generally remained within the confines of their authorized settlement areas and they refrained from making war upon the Britons. Even the trailing-off of battle entries in the Anglo-Saxon Chronicle confirms the unusually pacific nature of the barbarians at this time.

Archbishop Vitalinus, Comes Eldol and Dux Gorlois could be satisfied that their decision to invite Aurelius back to Britannia had been wise.

## Chapter Thirteen
## The Early Reign of Aurelius

After his triumphant Kentish campaign, Aurelius concerned himself principally with re-establishing the Imperial party in control of Britannia. Geoffrey of Monmouth tells us that Aurelius set about "restoring to their rightful heirs the scattered possessions of long-dead folk." Geoffrey's statement could only mean that Aurelius reinstated the Imperial partisans in their ancestral property. He no doubt reinstated them in their political privileges as well. Aurelius demolished the pro-independence political establishment which had grown up during the forty years of Vortigern's reign and replaced it with a more traditionally-oriented regime. Aurelius then governed as much as he was able along conventional Roman lines, earning in the process the epithet of "the Last Roman."

Aurelius's first official peacetime act was to order the repair of the churches in Kent[82] and the general renovation of the former Diocesan capital of Londinium. The upkeep and maintenance of the Kentish churches must have been ignored by the barbarian rulers of the region, while Londinium appears to have also suffered neglect. Aurelius collected carpenters and stone-masons from every part of Britannia for the reconstruction; he might have even used some of the materials which his army had removed from Vortigern's former capital of Viroconium Cornoviorum (Wroxeter). Aurelius then retired to Londinium, where he could oversee both the restoration of the Kentish churches and the rehabilitation of the one-time

---

82 Which Geoffrey again misidentifies as the area near "York" or Eboracum.

Roman capital. While in Londinium, Aurelius formally and officially assumed the government of Britannia.

Aurelius initially governed Britannia with the title of Magister Militum per Britannias (Master of Soldiers throughout the Britains). "Magister Militum" was the top Roman army rank, suitable for the highest military authority in a Roman Diocese. Aurelius's title was equivalent to the title of Magister Militum per Gallias (Master of Soldiers throughout the Gauls) which Aetius, and then Aetius's successor Aegidius, had used to govern Gaul.[83] It also proclaimed Aurelius's devotion to the Roman Empire, in notable contrast to the independent regime which Aurelius had superseded. Aurelius preferred the title of Magister Militum because it was a prestigious Roman military rank and because it reaffirmed his loyalty to the Empire.

Geoffrey of Monmouth says that Aurelius governed Britannia from Londinium, but all Aurelius's subsequent actions, other than certain of his military campaigns, actually took place in or near Venta Belgarum (Winchester). Venta Belgarum is situated within the Ambrosii heartland, close to Aurelius's family estates and where Aurelius would have naturally preferred to locate his headquarters. Even Geoffrey admits that Aurelius took a special interest in the renovation of that town (which could have been another beneficiary of the materials taken from Viroconium). Geoffrey only assumed that the Roman warlord made his headquarters in Londinium because Londinium had been the chief town of Roman Britannia and was again the foremost urban center of Britain in Geoffrey's time. Venta Belgarum, not

_____
83 Although Aegidius (or his son Syagrius) later took the more exalted title of Rex Romanorum.

Londinium, served as Aurelius's capital.

One of the actions which Aurelius took near Venta Belgarum (specifically at the Cloister of Ambrius, which his family had endowed near Amesbury) was the appointment of new Bishops for Britannia. According to Geoffrey of Monmouth, Aurelius appointed Samson to be Archbishop of "York" and Dubricius to be Archbishop of "the City of the Legions." Geoffrey's "York" could not be Eboracum, which was then in the hands of the Dux Britanniarum who had succeeded Coelestius; it must be an error for some other town in south or central Britannia which Aurelius controlled - perhaps Venta Belgarum, Aurelius's capital, or Viroconium, Vortigern's former capital and the northernmost town dominated by Aurelius. The "City of the Legions" in this case was Isca Silurum in Gwent, which was within Aurelius's sphere of influence; the modern name of the town, "Caerleon," even means "City of the Legion" in Welsh. Aurelius obviously took an interest in the religious affairs of his realm, and his appointees were no doubt orthodox, anti-Pelagian clergymen.

Britannia, thanks to the defeat of Hengist and the surrender of Octa, was at peace for much of Aurelius's reign. The Magister Militum therefore had plenty of time to devote to the restoration of traditional Roman government and religious orthodoxy in the Diocese. He did not, however, neglect military matters. Aurelius also initiated a very important rebuilding program which enhanced the military security of his realm.

During Aurelius's time, and certainly at his direction, ancient hillforts throughout south Britannia were refurbished and reoccupied. These ancient hillforts were timber and earthen structures erected on strategically situated hills by the native Britons before the Roman conquest. The Imperial authorities had long ago ordered the abandonment of the hillforts, but many of them were refurbished and reoccupied in the second half of the Fifth Century. More than forty such sites are known to have been reoccupied in south Britannia, including over a dozen in modern Somerset alone. Some of the sites bearing Ambrosii place-names were among the restored hillforts. In particular, the Ambrosii sites in modern Essex, an area which had just been wrested from Hengist, must have been hillforts reconstructed at Aurelius's order. A number of the restored hillforts, such as the Ambrosii sites in Essex, were suitably placed to defend the interior of Britannia against the Anglo-Saxons of southeast Britannia, while others were obviously intended to guard against seaborne Irish raiding parties from the west.

Militia forces were adequate to garrison these hillforts. With a minimum of training and organization, local farmers and agricultural workers could be pressed into sentry duty on the hillfort walls, and they would be able to hold off enemy attacks for at least brief periods of time. In this regard, the refurbished hillforts resembled the *montana castella* (small hillforts) erected by Romano-Gallic aristocrats on their country estates in Gaul; the *montana castella* were built as refuges for landowners and their dependents against barbarian raiders and lawless *bacaudae*, being more practical to defend than the luxurious (and now-abandoned) villas. With local militia garrisons, the hillforts thus became ready refuges for rural civilians against hostile raiding parties. They also served as forward observation posts to keep watch on the barbarians and secure bases for operations by Aurelius's elite cavalry forces when they came

into the area. Aurelius took advantage of the ancient hillforts scattered across south Britannia in order to implement a comprehensive strategy for the protection of his frontiers.[84]

Geoffrey tells us that Aurelius also ordered the erection of a monument to the Romano-Briton leaders slain by Hengist in the Massacre at the Cloister of Ambrius. Tremorinus, the Archbishop of "the City of the Legions" (Dubricius's predecessor in this office), suggested that Merlin the magician had the skill to create a worthy memorial.

## Merlinus Ambrosius

Merlin first appears in the *Historia Regum Britanniae* in the guise of the youth who confronted Vortigern at peril of his life when the Superbus Tyrannus was attempting to construct a fortress in north Wales. We have seen that this youth was not really Merlin (or "Myrddin" in Welsh), but the young Aurelius facing Vortigern after the death of his parents and the destruction of his family fortunes in the Battle of Wallop.

Merlin appears several more times in the *Historia Regum Britanniae* to play a role in the political affairs of Britannia. He appears with greater frequency in the medieval Romances to play an even greater role in the politics of Arthur's court.

Geoffrey was the first author to associate Merlin with Arthur. In the *Historia Regum Britanniae*, however, Merlin has little direct contact with Arthur, but is mainly associated with Arthur's predecessors in the government of

---

84 A similar defensive strategy relying upon timber and earthen forts was later followed with success by the Anglo-Saxon King Alfred the Great against Viking invaders in the Ninth Century.

Britannia. Even in the *Vita Merlini* (Life of Merlin), which was written soon after the *Historia Regum Britanniae* (probably by Geoffrey, although his authorship is disputed), Merlin's connection with Arthur is slight. It is only later, in the medieval Romances, that Merlin achieves prominence as court magician to King Arthur, and only later still, in modern novels, that he becomes important as Arthur's tutor. Once Geoffrey introduced Merlin into the Arthurian saga, the wizard quickly became a major figure in literature. Merlin was, and still is, a character of special fascination to storytellers.

What, then, is the truth about the legendary sorcerer?

Merlin was, in fact, a very real - and a very important - person. Unfortunately for those of us who are enthralled by the literary reputation of the famous enchanter, Merlin actually lived and thrived long after Arthur was in his grave. The historic Merlin was a bard who lived in far north Britannia toward the end of the Sixth Century.

A bard was a Celtic songster whose vital function was to preserve and orally transmit the laws, culture and history of his society in rhyme and verse. He was, in essence, a living library and archive. In a non-literate society, such as Britannia was both before and briefly after the Roman period, bards enjoyed high social status and great influence.

Drawing upon the vast wealth of historical and psychological information contained in the lore entrusted to his memory, a bard on occasion anticipated the deeds of political leaders and projected the future consequences of current actions. Today, historians, economists and sociologists attempt to perform more or less the same function - with, we might suspect, considerably less success. Instances when a bard had successfully drawn upon his store of wisdom to make accurate predictions were exaggerated in the retelling, giving rise to legends of bardic prophetic powers.

The particular bard with whom we are concerned was called Myrddin (pronounced "mur-thin") in his own Briton tongue. Geoffrey softened the name to "Merlin" for the benefit of his French-speaking Anglo-Norman audience because, in writing, the bard's true name bore an unfortunate resemblance to the French word *merde*. Merlin/Myrddin was a member of the household of King Gwenddolau.

Gwenddolau ("Wintholey" in English) was king of a Briton realm situated just beyond Hadrian's Wall. He ruled the area about Liddel Water on the modern English-Scottish border near Luguvalium (Carlisle). Gwenddolau, like many of his contemporaries in north Britannia, claimed descent from "Coel Hen," whom we know as Coelestius Senex, the last Roman Dux Britanniarum. Gwenddolau was probably in fact a descendant of Antonius Donatus, whom Emperor Maximus had appointed to rule the semi-barbarous Selgovae of modern Dumfries and Galloway.

King Gwenddolau fought a battle in A.D. 573 or A.D. 575 against his neighbor, King Urien of Rheged. Rheged was a Briton kingdom located next to Gwenddolau's realm, but on the Roman side of Hadrian's Wall. Rheged was based upon Luguvalium and then consisted more or less of modern Cumbria. The battle was fought about eight miles north of Luguvalium at Arfderydd, now called Arthuret,[85] over possession of the nearby

---

85 No connection with Arthur; many seemingly Arthurian place names are actually derived from the

fortress of Caerlaverock, whose name means "fort of the lark." The Battle of Arfderydd is remembered in the Welsh Triads as one of the "Three Futile Battles of the Isle of Britain," so called because it was fought over "a lark's nest": a bitter joke referring to the fort's unusual name.[86] Urien defeated Gwenddolau and conquered his realm, extending Rheged's rule for the first time over territory outside the former Roman Diocese. Myrddin's patron fell in the fighting.

Myrddin was appalled at the carnage of the Battle of Arfderydd. Half-mad with grief, the bard retired into hermitage in the Forest of Celidon, also called the Caledonian Wood, about the headwaters of the Rivers Clyde and Tweed near modern Lanark and Peebles. On account of his time in the Caledonian Wood, Myrddin is sometimes called Silvester (meaning "woodsman" in Latin) or Celidonius. During his forest wanderings, Myrddin periodically encountered King Rhydderch of Strathclyde (the area about modern Glasgow) and other notables, to whom he delivered mysterious prophecies.[87]

These prophecies were the link which Geoffrey saw between the Sixth Century Celtic bard and the Fifth Century Roman aristocrat. Geoffrey has obviously mistaken the young Aurelius's prediction (or perhaps "threat" is more accurate) of the downfall of Vortigern's Anglo-Saxon-supported regime as one of the bard Myrddin's prophecies.

The misidentification of Myrddin with Aurelius was abetted by the fact that Myrddin was also called Ambrosius, as Geoffrey claims.

"Ambrosius," or "Emrys" in Welsh, was a personal name, but it was also an ordinary word meaning "immortal." Just as we may today refer to Shakespeare or Homer as "immortal," so too did Welshmen at one time refer to Myrddin. Myrddin appears with this appellation in the early Welsh poem *The Stanzas of the Graves*. Geoffrey apparently mistook a reference to "the immortal Myrddin" ("Myrddin Emrys" in Welsh or "Moridunus Ambrosius" in Roman Latin) as a rendering of the bard's full personal name, rather than his personal name plus an honorific.

"Myrddin" itself was not even the bard's true personal name; it was a formal name conferred by the Britons upon all important poets. Taliesin, another leading northern poet of a slightly later time, is, for instance, also known to have been called "Merddin." Moreover, certain early stories from the far north of Britannia describe an individual named Lailoken whose life strongly resembles that of Myrddin. Many of these stories are preserved in the *Vita Kentigerni* (Life of Kentigern), a medieval biography of the Glasgow area Saint Kentigern.[88] The Lailoken stories suggest that Myrddin and Lailoken were the same person and that "Lailoken" was the real name of the historical bard. The "immortal Merlin" was thus not a single popular poet, but a series of leading poets, the Poets Laureate of ancient and post-Roman Britannia.

The original Myrddin was probably the pagan Briton god of poetry, whose name was later bestowed upon preeminent bards. This conclusion is suggested by the early north Briton poem *Gododdin*, which opens with a reference to the "blessed inspiration of

---

Briton/Welsh word *arth*, meaning "bear."

86 In fact, Caerlaverock was strategically situated at the mouth of the River Nith.

87 King Rhydderch, as well as the Romano-Briton rulers of Eboracum (Peredur and Gurci), probably fought in alliance with Urien in the Battle of Arfderydd.

---

88 *Vita Kentigerni* is believed to have been written by Herbert, Bishop of Glasgow from 1147 to 1164.

Myrddin," much as ancient Greek poems often open with invocations to the Muses. The town of Carmarthen ("Moridunum" in Latin and "Caer Myrddin" in Welsh) seems to have been named for this god, and Stonehenge was probably a site of his worship. The connection of the god Myrddin to Carmarthen and to Stonehenge explains Geoffrey's association of these two places with his one particular bard (Lailoken) who bore the honorific "Myrddin."

Geoffrey's confusion of the bard (or bards) Myrddin with Aurelius also explains why his account of the young Ambrosius's predictions goes far beyond the version found in Nennius's *Historia Brittonum*. Geoffrey has inserted into the *Historia Regum Britanniae*, and attributed to his Merlin, a completely unrelated work that has no proper place there. Geoffrey has inserted into the *Historia Regum Britanniae* a collection of the historical Myrddin's (i.e., Lailoken's) prophecies called the *Prophetiae Merlini* (Prophecies of Merlin).

The *Prophetiae Merlini* does not properly belong in the *Historia Regum Britanniae*, but it is an authentic masterpiece of literature in its own right. It is an authentic masterpiece because it preserves traditional Celtic mystical lore and because its predictions, being well-crafted, often appear accurate in hindsight.

We may put little stock in prophecy today, but it was generally considered reliable in Geoffrey's day. The contemporary chronicler Giraldus Cambrensis (Gerald of Wales), for example, reports on the popularity of a certain soothsayer named Meilyr in Twelfth Century Wales. In fact, a belief in the gift of "second sight" persisted in Celtic countries until fairly recent times. By examining a famous prediction of a renown Scottish seer of a later period, we can learn something of the nature of Celtic prophecy.

The renown Scottish seer was Coinneach Odhar (Kenneth the Sallow), who was active in the late Seventeenth Century. Coinneach is said to have predicted the Highland Clearances of the early Nineteenth Century. The Highland Clearances was a movement by Scottish landlords to expel tenant farmers from their lands so the fields could be converted to more profitable sheep-raising. Coinneach warned, "The clans will become so effeminate as to allow themselves to be driven from their native land by an army of sheep."

The style of Coinneach's prediction is typical of traditional prophecies: vague and ambiguous, so that, through after-the-fact rationalization, it can be interpreted to conform to subsequent events. Although the prediction does seem to presage the expulsion of Scottish clansmen from their land in order to make way for flocks of sheep, it also seems to foretell other events equally well. If the Highland Clearances had never occurred, Coinneach would have no doubt been credited with predicting one of the Eighteenth Century military defeats of the individualistic Highlanders by the regimented ranks of English soldiers in their red woolen uniforms.

Merlin's prophecies fit this same pattern. For example, his prediction that "Monks in their cowls shall be forced into marriage," was considered, in hindsight, to foreshadow the dissolution of the monasteries by King Henry VIII. Likewise, his warning that "The baths shall grow cold at Bath and its health-giving waters shall breed death," was seen as foretelling the bacterial infection which has caused the baths to be closed in modern times. If, however, neither of these events had occurred, some other religious crisis and some other disturbance at Bath would have been found to satisfy the prophecies. Today, we may find relevant Merlin's promise that "The sea over which men sail to Gaul shall be contracted into a narrow channel; a man on any one side of the two shores will be audible to a man on the other, and the land-mass of the island will grow greater." This prophecy seems to anticipate the integration of Britain into the Continental economy pursuant to the European Economic Community's plans for European unity. If, however, these plans fail, then we can easily reinterpret the prophecy as a more mundane forecast of technological improvements in British transportation, communications and agriculture. The *Prophetiae Merlini* is basically a collection of riddles which the quick-witted may gleefully analogize to any of a number of actual events.[89]

After making the predictions of the *Prophetiae Merlini*, Merlin's next task in the *Historia Regum Britanniae* was to assist Aurelius in erecting a monument to the Briton leaders treacherously slain by Hengist at the Cloister of Ambrius. Merlin proposed that Aurelius send his brother Utherpendragon to arrange the relocation of Stonehenge from Ireland to Britannia.

Merlin's proposal reflects a genuine folk memory of the ancient transportation of certain of the Stonehenge stones, the so-called bluestones, from the Prescely mountains in southwest Wales (near Moridunum or Caer Myrddin) to the Amesbury area for the worship of the god Myrddin. In Aurelius's day,

southwest Wales was the Irish kingdom of Demetia; it was thus correctly described as "Ireland," or, more precisely, "land of the Irish." Geoffrey has confused the true story of Stonehenge and its patron deity Myrddin with an expedition to the Irish-ruled part of Wales by Aurelius's general, whom Geoffrey calls Utherpendragon.

Geoffrey's source must have said something to the effect that "Utherpendragon led an army into the land of the Irish, whence came Myrddin's stones at Stonehenge." Geoffrey misconstrued this statement as a reference to an invasion of Ireland and a concurrent movement of the stones by Merlin. In fact, Geoffrey's source meant that Utherpendragon led an expedition into Demetia, which was then ruled by the Irish, and that it was from Demetia that certain of the stones at Stonehenge had been taken in more ancient days.

Geoffrey exploits his character of Merlin at this point to explain how Utherpendragon was able to transport the Stonehenge monoliths from Ireland to Britannia. Geoffrey had, of course, overestimated the distance over which the stones had to travel. He also underestimated the skill and ingenuity of his ancestors. Geoffrey therefore seized upon his mistaken association of the bard Myrddin with the Magister Militum Aurelius for an answer to the mystery: Merlin's magical arts could suffice when the brute strength of Utherpendragon's soldiers would prove unavailing.

Merlin thus became a sort of *deus ex machina* ("god by machine," a reference to the theatrical device by which supernatural beings were made to appear to fly on stage), or perhaps more accurately *magus ex machina* ("magician by machine"), to account for events in history which were incomprehensible to the medieval

---

89 The prophecies contained in the *Vita Merlini* are not nearly so clever; they merely "predict" events which will occur in the future of the speakers, but which are already history to the author.

understanding. Merlin was such a convenient device for explaining enigmatic elements in Arthurian history that the Romancers readily followed Geoffrey's lead, making the poet-turned-sorcerer into a leading (some would say *the* leading) character in Arthurian literature.

## Utherpendragon

The general who allegedly oversaw the movement of the Stonehenge monoliths to Britannia is called Utherpendragon by Geoffrey. "Utherpendragon," sometimes written as the two words "Uther Pendragon," is not a name. Like "Vortigern" and "Vortimer," "Utherpendragon" is a title.

Geoffrey almost admits as much. He tells us that "Utherpendragon . . . in the British language means 'a dragon's head'." Aurelius's general supposedly acquired the name "dragon's head" from a comet seen in the heavens when he later succeeded Aurelius on the throne of Britannia.

Geoffrey is close, but not quite on the mark, in translating Utherpendragon as "dragon's head." *Pen* in this instance actually means "head" in the sense of "chief." *Dragon*, while having the same meaning it does in modern English, was also applied by the Britons to war leaders - no doubt because of the dragon banner carried by Roman and post-Roman cavalry units.[90] "Pendragon" thus means "chief war leader." *Uther*, or more properly *uthr*, means "terrible" in the sense of "awe-inspiring"; in this context, *uther* seems to be a superlative. "Utherpendragon" could be translated as "terrifying dragon head," but should be more

accurately rendered as "foremost chief warlord."

The Latin equivalent of "Utherpendragon" is "Magister Militum," the highest Roman military rank. The man called Utherpendragon in the *Historia Regum Britanniae* would have been called Magister Militum per Britannias (Master of Soldiers throughout the Britains) by his Romano-Briton contemporaries.

Who, then, was this Utherpendragon or Magister Militum per Britannias?

He was different persons at different times.

The first, and most obvious candidate, for the office of Magister Militum per Britannias is Aurelius himself. Although Geoffrey identifies Utherpendragon and Aurelius as brothers, they are never together: either Aurelius does something while Uther is nowhere to be seen, or Uther does it while Aurelius is said to be elsewhere. The "brothers" never play independent, simultaneous roles. In addition, they both share the same fate, each falling sick and then dying of illness amid suspicions of poisoning. They even share the same grave, at the Cloister of Ambrius near Amesbury. Geoffrey has obviously assembled a number of stories about Aurelius, some referring to him by name and others by title, which he then mistakenly divided into two separate biographies on the assumption that they referred to two different persons.

Aurelius no doubt took the title of Magister Militum per Britannias when he first landed in Britannia. It was, we have seen, an appropriate designation for Aurelius to use as an autonomous regional ruler of Roman heritage. His contemporaries, Aetius and Aegidius, had each governed Gaul under the equivalent title of Magister Militum per Gallias. Aurelius's adoption of a Roman military rank was also an

---

90  The warrior assigned to carry the cavalry standard was called the *draconarius* (dragon-bearer), just as the bearer of the eagle standard of the infantry Legions was called the *aquilifer* (eagle-bearer).

affirmation of loyalty to the Roman Empire. As a representative of the Imperial faction in Britannia, Aurelius initially governed under the familiar Roman title of Magister Militum, somehow imagining himself to be holding the Diocese in trust for the Empire.

Aurelius later assumed the grander title of Regissimus Britanniarum, which Vortimer had already used. After he consolidated his political power in Britannia, and when he realized that Rome no longer had any intention - or ability - to reclaim its former Diocese, Aurelius apparently saw no reason to maintain the fiction that Britannia was still part of the Empire. He therefore assumed a more exalted title which carried greater prestige. In doing so, Aurelius was still following Gallic precedent, because Aegidius (or his son Syagrius) had by then put aside his Roman army rank in order to rule north Gaul as Rex Romanorum (King of the Romans).[91] When Aurelius promoted himself to the status of Regissimus Britanniarum, he appointed another person to the position of Magister Militum per Britannias.

One person who served as Aurelius's Magister Militum was Arthur.

The evidence for Arthur's having held the position of Magister Militum under Aurelius is overwhelming. Ten years before Geoffrey wrote the *Historia Regum Britanniae*, William of Malmesbury wrote in *De Gestis Regum Anglorum* (Concerning the Deeds of the Kings of the English) that Arthur assisted Aurelius in defeating the Anglo-Saxons. William's statement indicates that Arthur was not always a "king," but had once been a high-ranking army officer under Aurelius. In addition, the title Utherpendragon, the Briton form of Magister

Militum, is traditionally associated with Arthur: Geoffrey and the medieval Romancers thought that Arthur's father was named Utherpendragon. This belief came about when an early Welsh historian, failing to recognize the post-Roman period title, mistook a reference to "Arthur *the* Utherpendragon" to mean "Arthur *son of* Uther Pendragon." Geoffrey also refers to "Utherpendragon" opposing a large-scale Irish invasion of south Wales in a campaign that was actually fought by Arthur. The "Utherpendragon" in this campaign was undoubtedly Arthur because the same campaign is described in much greater detail in the *Mabinogion* tale "How Culhwch Won Olwen," which calls the Briton war leader by the name of Arthur rather than by the title of Utherpendragon. The connection of Arthur to Aurelius, to the title Utherpendragon and to a campaign which Geoffrey ascribes to "Utherpendragon," all indicate that Arthur at one time served as Aurelius's Magister Militum.

Arthur was not Aurelius's chief general at the very beginning of Aurelius's reign as Regissimus Britanniarum, however. Based upon the dates firmly connected to Arthur, Arthur was much too young and inexperienced to have held such an important and powerful position until late in Aurelius's reign. Someone else preceded Arthur in the office of Magister Militum per Britanniarum.

We can find the identity of Aurelius's first Magister Militum in the *Vita prima Carantoci* (First Life of Carannog), a medieval biography of the Welsh Saint Carannog.

The *Vita prima Carantoci* tells us that Arthur once served as a junior officer under a military leader named Cadwy. This statement is credible because it concerns a matter that is irrelevant to the religious moral of the *Vita*

---

91 Presumably Rex Romanorum *per Gallias*, meaning "King of the Romans *throughout the Gauls*."

*prima Carantoci*; it is an incidental detail which medieval hagiographers would have had no reason to fabricate and which they could have only taken from a contemporary source. We also know that Cadwy was a real person of note because he is remembered in Welsh tradition: the Welsh Triads remark upon his courtesy, and the *Mabinogion* tale "How Culhwch Won Olwen" names his father as Gereint ("Gerontius" in Latin) and his son as Berth. In Latin, "Cadwy" was probably "Catavia," a plausible Roman family name derived from the Latin literally meaning "intelligent road," but more accurately translated as "the smart way."

The *Vita prima Carantoci* further states that Cadwy/Catavia was active in the region of modern Somerset, where the important hillfort of Cadbury Castle is located. Cadbury Castle was the largest of the hillforts reconstructed during Aurelius's reign. Its size denotes it as the base of operations for a large military force; it was clearly Aurelius's chief military base. It was just as clearly Catavia's headquarters because it was named for him: "Cadbury" is short for "Cadwy's Bury," an anglicization of the Latin "Castellum Cataviae" or the Welsh "Dinas Cadwy," both meaning "fort of Catavia." Catavia's association with the large and important hillfort of Cadbury Castle tells us that Catavia was a major military leader in southwest Britannia in Aurelius's day.

From the statements in the *Vita prima Carantoci* and the evidence of the place name Cadbury, we can deduce that Catavia was Aurelius's Magister Militum when Arthur was still a young soldier rising through the ranks.

"Utherpendragon" was thus not a single person, but three different persons at three different times: first Aurelius, then Catavia and finally Arthur. Failing to realize that Utherpendragon was not a name, but a title, Geoffrey attributes certain of the deeds of these persons to a separate, discrete - but wholly fictitious - individual whom he calls Uther Pendragon.

"Utherpendragon's" first action according to Geoffrey was an invasion of "Ireland" for the purpose of carrying off Stonehenge, which Aurelius wished to reconstruct in Britannia as a memorial to the Briton leaders slain by Hengist. We have already seen that this expedition actually went to Demetia in southwest Wales, and that the reference to Stonehenge is an anachronism. "Utherpendragon's" invasion of "Ireland" was in truth a seaborne punitive raid conducted by Catavia against the Irish of Demetia, and the real reason for the expedition was a rebellion against Aurelius's authority by the ruler of Builth, Vortigern's son Pascent.

## Pascent of Builth

Geoffrey tells us that sometime after the defeat of Hengist and Octa, Aurelius summoned the religious and secular leaders of Britannia to a great festival at Amesbury, where he "placed the crown upon his head." Aurelius apparently took the occasion to put aside his military rank of Magister Militum and assume the royal title of Regissimus Britanniarum.

Not all Britons rejoiced in Aurelius's assumption of this high office. The reigning Dux Britanniarum, heir of Coelestius Senex in Eboracum (York) and commander of the powerful army of northeast Britannia, was unlikely to have offered his congratulations; he certainly did not submit to Aurelius's rule. Likewise, Pascent, the son of Vortigern who ruled the Kingdom of Builth, did not truckle to his father's slayer. Pascent of Builth was, in fact, openly hostile to the new Regissimus.

Pascent might have been the only son of Vortigern who remained loyal to the Superbus Tyrannus. He does not seem, for instance, to have joined his brothers Vortimer and Brutus Catellus (or Catigern) in their rebellion against their father. He then succeeded to a part of Civitas Cornoviorum which must have supported Vortigern, or at least more fondly remembered him, since it bore the name Guorthegirnaim (Vortigernia) from the Tyrannus's Celtic title, as well as Builth. Geoffrey also tells us that Pascent (whom Geoffrey calls "Paschent") desired to avenge his father. In any event, Pascent did not assent to Aurelius's assumption of the overlordship of Britannia, and he proceeded to raise an army against Aurelius.

Geoffrey claims that Pascent went to Germany in order to recruit Anglo-Saxon troops. The Builth leader made no such journey. Geoffrey did not realize that large numbers of Anglo-Saxons still resided in Britannia after Aurelius's defeat of Hengist, so he assumed Pascent had to go to Germania in his quest for barbarian allies. In fact, Pascent remained in Builth and dispatched envoys to the Anglo-Saxons living along Britannia's eastern seaboard.

The east coast Anglo-Saxons were laeti who shed their allegiance to their Romano-Briton masters during the rebellion of the early A.D. 460's. They seized the town of Venta Icenorum (Caistor-by-Norwich) during the rebellion, and they established their own independent realm on territory formerly belonging to Civitas Icenorum, Civitas Trinovantum and Civitas Corielsoliliorum. Civitas Icenorum was based upon Venta Icenorum; Civitas Trinovantum was based upon Camulodunum (Colchester); and Civitas Corielsoliliorum was probably based upon Durobrivae (Water Newton, near Peterborough). Today this region comprises roughly the shires of Norfolk, Suffolk, Cambridge and north Essex; in Anglo-Saxon times, it constituted the Kingdom of East Anglia. In Pascent's day, the east coast region was probably called Anglia, after the barbarians' tribe, the Angles.

Unlike the Kentishmen, who were chastened by Aurelius's defeat of Hengist, the Angles of Anglia were still keen to assert themselves. They were logical allies for Pascent.

Between his own troops in Builth and his allies from Anglia, Pascent might have hoped to crush the new Regissimus in a vise. If so, then he poorly coordinated his plans with those of his co-conspirators because the Angles marched before the Builthmen were ready. On the other hand, the two opponents of the new regime might have acted independently of each other; Geoffrey might have inferred a formal conspiracy when Pascent and the Angles merely shared a common enemy. The Builth leader and the barbarians were nevertheless likely to have been at least casual allies. Even if Pascent did not plan a joint Anglia-Builth attack upon Aurelius, he no doubt encouraged the Angles to make war upon the Regissimus Britanniarum.

Whether on their own initiative at Pascent's urging or as part of a planned two-prong offensive, the eastern barbarians did indeed march against Aurelius. The Regissimus responded quickly and aggressively; he set forth to engage the barbarians before they could go very far or make any rendezvous with rebel Builth forces. We do not know exactly where the resulting battle took place, but it had to have been somewhere north or northeast of Londinium. It probably took place on the ancient trail known as the Icknield Way, which runs from modern Norfolk to modern Oxfordshire. In the Battle on the Icknield Way, Aurelius attacked, defeated and routed the barbarians.

Undaunted by Aurelius's trouncing of his Angle accomplices, Pascent turned to another source of barbarian troops. Geoffrey has Pascent again travelling overseas in search of allies, this time to "Ireland." The Builth ruler actually had to go no farther than his own western border if he wanted to recruit Irish warriors. The "Ireland" to which Pascent went in his quest for new allies was Demetia.

Geoffrey tells us that Pascent made contact with an Irish king named Gillomanius. "Gillomanius" is not a personal name, but a warband designation. The prefix *gill* or *gilla* means "servant" or "follower" in Irish, so Geoffrey's source referred to the warriors of an Irish chieftain with a name something like "Manius." "Manius" is the latinization of some Irish name, most likely an early form of "Mannion," which has ancient roots. Pascent thus attempted to obtain the services of the Irish leader Mannion ("Manius") and his warband ("gilla").

This prospective coalition of Pascent and the Irish of Demetia prompted the "Stonehenge Expedition" into Demetia by Catavia, Aurelius's Magister Militum or Utherpendragon. Catavia's expedition was a preemptive strike intended to dissuade the Demetian Irish from consummating their military alliance with Pascent.

Catavia's raiding force was certainly seaborne, as Geoffrey asserts, because the hostility of Builth made the overland route to Demetia much too dangerous. A land-bound expedition across the mountainous terrain of south Wales would have been vulnerable to ambush by Builth forces. It would have also moved much too slowly for Catavia to have maintained the element of surprise. Instead, Catavia launched a swift hit-and-run amphibious attack upon Demetia; he probably used some of the same ships which had earlier carried Aurelius and his Armoricans to Britannia.[92] Catavia sailed to Demetia, surprised the Irish there and wrought a great deal of destruction before escaping again by sea.

Catavia's punitive expedition dissuaded the Demetians from backing Pascent. Having felt the fury of Aurelius's army, they began to doubt the wisdom of an alliance with the Builth leader. The Demetians were subdued, and Pascent, denied support, was forced to make peace with Aurelius.

The peace between Aurelius and Pascent was based upon a mutual recognition of each other's titles. Nennius reports that Aurelius "granted" Pascent "the province of Builth." Aurelius, in other words, confirmed Pascent's right to rule the domain which he had already received from his father. This confirmation must have occurred soon after Catavia's successful "Stonehenge Expedition." Although Aurelius held the upper hand at this point, he had good reasons to avoid pressing his advantage. In coming to a negotiated settlement, Aurelius avoided a civil war which could have been as ruinous for the victor as for the vanquished. He also gained an important measure of political legitimacy for his own government because his official recognition of

---

92 Aurelius must have kept these ships with him in Britannia because the Welsh Triads refer to him as a fleet-owner.

Pascent's regime in Builth was certainly given in exchange for the son of Vortigern acknowledging Aurelius as Regissimus Britanniarum. For Pascent's part, submission to Aurelius was a small price to pay for the security of his own realm. Pascent must have known that, without Angle or Irish allies, he could not possibly withstand Aurelius's power for very long. Aurelius's confirmation of Pascent as ruler of Builth and Pascent's acknowledgement of Aurelius as Regissimus Britanniarum were the terms of a practical accommodation which ended (at least for a time) the conflict between the rival Briton leaders.

The victory in the Battle on the Icknield Way, the success of the Stonehenge Expedition into Demetia and the submission of Pascent occurred soon after the conclusion of Aurelius's War against Kent, or in about A.D. 466, A.D. 467 and A.D. 468, respectively.

With these achievements, Aurelius affirmed the peace achieved by his victory in the Battle of Maisbeli and brought political and military stability to the beleaguered Diocese of Britannia. He was now free to pursue more glorious adventures outside the Diocese. The Regissimus Britanniarum took advantage of the respite which he had won for Britannia to lead a large Briton army across the English Channel to Gaul in support of one of the last western Roman Emperors.

# Armies in Post-Roman Britannia
## I

### Romano-Briton

| | |
|---|---|
| Octa and Ebissa, A.D. 434-440 | |
| expedition to Bernicia | 1,200-1,600 |
| Romano-Britons | 900-1,300 |
| Anglo-Saxons | 300 |
| Vortimer, A.D. 457 | |
| Battle of Crayford | 2,700-4,000 |
| Aurelius Ambrosius, A.D. 460 | |
| return to Britannia. | 2,000 |
| Aurelius Ambrosius, A.D. 465 | |
| Battle of Maisbeli | 6,500 |
| Riothamus of Armorica, A.D. 470 | |
| versus Visigoths | 12,000 |
| Eldol and Gorlois, A.D. 472 | |
| against Kentish raiders | est. 600 |

### Anglo-Saxon

| | |
|---|---|
| Hengist and Horsa, A.D. 428 | |
| three ships | 100-150 |
| Hengist and Horsa, A.D. 434-440 | |
| nineteen ships | 600 |
| Hengist and Octa, A.D. 465 | |
| Battle of Maisbeli | 7,000 |
| Hengist, A.D. 472 | |
| Kentish raiding party | est. 1,000 |

### Irish/Scottish

| | |
|---|---|
| Fergus Mor, *circa* A.D. 501 | |
| arrival in Dalriada | 150 |
| Dalriada, *circa* A.D. 660 | |
| per *Senchus Fer nAlban* | 2,000 |

## Chapter Fourteen
## Riothamus of Britannia Minor

For the next major event in the life of Aurelius, we must skip ahead several chapters in the *Historia Regum Britanniae*. Geoffrey of Monmouth reports on a Briton military expedition to Gaul which he attributes to Arthur, but which was actually undertaken by Aurelius.

Geoffrey tells us that the Gallic expedition began after Arthur received an insulting letter from one Lucius Hiberius, who is described sometimes as Procurator and sometimes as Emperor of Rome. In reply, Arthur mustered all of his forces, gathered all of his allies, and embarked on a massive invasion of Gaul. Arthur fought, defeated and killed the Roman leader.

Geoffrey has in fact confused a campaign which Arthur fought against rebellious Romans in Britannia with a very different campaign which Aurelius waged in support of one of the last Roman Emperors to rule in the west. We can find no evidence to support Geoffrey's assertion that a Briton army campaigned in Gaul in Arthur's time, but the contemporary chronicles of Gaul do report that a Briton army fought in Gaul in Aurelius's time. Geoffrey obviously came across an account of this campaign, and he mistakenly attributed it to Arthur. In order to sort things out, we shall have to briefly review the events which occurred in the rest of the Western Empire while Britannia was absorbed with its own concerns.

### Afranius Syagrius Aegidius, Rex Romanorum

After the assassination of Emperor Valentinian III by a Hun follower of the murdered Aetius in A.D. 455, the Western Empire suffered through a series of short-lived and ineffectual Emperors. These hapless Emperors exercised very little real power because they were dominated by their barbarian generals. When Aurelius governed in Britannia, the *de facto* ruler of what was left of the Roman Empire in the west was the barbarian general Ricimer.

Ricimer had earlier raised a Roman named Majorian to the western Emperorship in A.D. 457. Once firmly established on the throne, however, Majorian proved too independent and vigorous to suit Ricimer. Disappointed with his puppet Emperor, Ricimer executed Majorian in A.D. 461 and raised up a more docile Libius Severus.

Majorian's single most far-reaching accomplishment during his brief reign was his appointment of the Romano-Gallic general Afranius Syagrius Aegidius to the position of Magister Militum per Gallias (Master of Soldiers throughout the Gauls). Aegidius was extremely capable in political and military matters, and he was steadfastly loyal to his Emperor. After the murder of Majorian, Ricimer attempted to depose Aegidius, but he could not suborn the Magister's troops and had to abandon the effort. Aegidius retained the title of Magister Militum despite the hostility of Ricimer, and, from his headquarters in the town of Noviodunum Suessionum (Soissons), he effectively made himself the ruler of an independent north Gaul.[93]

---

93 Another appointee of Emperor Majorian, Magister Militum Marcellinus, at the same time established an independent government in Dalmatia on the shore of the Adriatic Sea across from Italy. Marcellinus and Majorian had earlier served together in Gaul under

Aegidius had to cope with many threats to his small domain. He faced potentially hostile barbarians in south and east Gaul, as well as the ever-present danger of attack from Ricimer's portion of the diminished Empire in Italy. Aegidius nevertheless managed to establish and maintain a fair degree of security and stability for north Gaul. Aegidius, or his son Syagrius who succeeded him in A.D. 464, eventually abandoned the military rank of Magister Militum in favor of the more exalted title of Rex Romanorum (presumably short for Rex Romanorum *per Gallias*), meaning "King of the Romans (*throughout the Gauls*)."

An important element of Aegidius's strategy was the maintenance of good relations with the powerful German tribe of the Franks, who had expanded into northeast Gaul. Aegidius was so successful in this policy that, when the Frankish King Childeric was exiled to Thuringia for excessive philandering with the daughters of his subjects, the barbarians took the extraordinary step of electing Aegidius to be their king. Childeric was later restored to his kingship, but he does not seem to have borne Aegidius any ill will on account of the latter's assumption of his crown. Childeric remained a dependable Gallo-Roman ally until his death in A.D. 481. Childeric and his Franks readily accepted Aegidius's domination, and they gladly fought his enemies for him.

Aegidius died of plague in A.D. 464, soon after Aurelius's return to Britannia, but he was succeeded by his equally capable son Syagrius. Syagrius continued his father's policy of maintaining close ties with the Franks, and the Franks were still willing, at least for the time being, to submit to Gallo-Roman overlordship.

---

Magister Militum Aetius.

## Emperor Anthemius

The eastern Emperor Leo I had meanwhile become disgusted with the shameful condition of the Western Empire. Disregarding the wishes of Ricimer, Leo himself appointed a new western Emperor after Emperor Libius Severus died in A.D. 465. In A.D. 467, Emperor Leo I conferred the dubious honor of ruling the west upon a Greek nobleman from Constantinople named Anthemius.

Anthemius must have often felt that Leo had done him no favor in bestowing the Imperial dignity upon him. In addition to dealing with the dangerous Ricimer, Anthemius had to contend with the various barbarian tribes then occupying most of his nominal realm.

Anthemius's most powerful and deadly foes were the Visigoths, who had recently come under the rule of the decidedly anti-Roman Euric. The Visigoth kingdom at this time included much of Hispania (Spain and Portugal) and southwest Gaul. Euric had clear designs on the rest of Gaul. He was also a heretic, following the Arian brand of Christianity which was hostile to the Roman Church.[94] Euric vigorously persecuted the Church throughout his reign; among his many religious crimes was his later driving into exile the Churchman Faustus, the son of Vortigern who had accompanied Saint Germanus to Gaul. The resources of the depleted Western Empire were hopelessly inadequate to cope with the Visigoth menace.

Anthemius therefore sought allies. Fortunately for the Emperor, Euric posed a threat to many other people who had interests in Gaul, including Syagrius and Childeric in north Gaul and the barbarian, but pro-Roman,

---

94 Arianism deemphasized Christ's divinity, stressing instead His human nature.

Burgundians in east Gaul.[95] Anthemius took advantage of the situation to form a grand alliance of several Roman and barbarian factions against the Visigoths. One of the Roman factions which Anthemius lured into his coalition consisted of the Britons who had emigrated to Armorica in northwest Gaul.

## Britannia Minor

Armorica was then part of the Roman province of Lugdunensis III in northwest Gaul, whose capital was the town of Turona (Tours). The official name of the region was Tractus Armoricanus (the Armorican Tract). At the time of the Emperor's plea for assistance, Armorica was, under the influence of expatriate Britons, rapidly undergoing an enormous social transformation. This social transformation sundered Armorica culturally and linguistically from the rest of Gaul. Armorica became a separate and distinct realm, which was called after its Briton immigrants "Britannia Minor" or "Brittany," both meaning "Lesser Britannia."

The transformation of Armorica began, according to Welsh and Breton tradition, with the settlement there of the Romano-Briton soldiers who had survived the defeat of Emperor Maximus in A.D. 388. This tradition is reflected in Geoffrey of Monmouth's account of the deeds of Conanus Meridiadocus. The first Briton migration to Armorica was, however, relatively small and unimportant.

_____

95 The pro-Roman attitude of the Burgundians was influenced by their belief that they were descended from the garrison soldiers of the Roman general Drusus. Drusus was the stepson of Emperor Augustus, brother of Emperor Tiberius and father of Emperor Claudius; he had conquered much of west Germania up to the Rhine River. The Romans, for obvious reasons, did nothing to dissuade the Burgundians from this belief.

The Briton colonization of Armorica began in earnest in the A.D. 440's and A.D. 450's, when large numbers of immigrants came to Armorica from Britannia. Many of the immigrants came from the modern Hampshire area, which suggests that they were Ambrosii supporters fleeing persecution by Vortigern's followers; some of them no doubt rallied to Aurelius's standard when he was in Armorica and later returned with him to Britannia. The Britons in Armorica are said to have eventually numbered 12,000 fighting men; with their wives, children, old folk and servants, the total immigrant population could have numbered some 48,000 to 60,000 people. The Bretons, as we should now call the Armorican Britons, became so numerous that they were entitled to send their own bishop, Mansuetus, to a Church council held at Turona in A.D. 461.

Flavius Aetius, when he was Magister Militum per Gallias, welcomed the Britons to Armorica. The unruly Armorican bacaudae had repeatedly rebelled against the Empire during the first half of the Fifth Century, including a very serious revolt in the mid-A.D. 430's and another in the late A.D. 440's. Aetius expected the emigrant Britons to keep the peace in Armorica. He also expected them to supply him with troops from time to time, as they did when he marched against Attila the Hun in the Battle of Chalons in A.D. 451. Aetius, and then Aegidius and Syagrius, allowed the Bretons to administer their own government in Armorica on condition that they maintain order in their district and render occasional military assistance against the barbarians afflicting the other parts of Gaul.

For his part, the new western Emperor Anthemius hoped to induce the Bretons to make a further contribution to Gallic security by joining him, Syagrius's Gallo-Romans and the Burgundians in a great anti-Visigoth coalition.

## Riothamus of Armorica

The name of the Breton leader who responded to the Emperor's call appears in the contemporary chronicles of Gaul as Riothamus. "Riothamus" is a Latin corruption of the Celtic "Rigotamos."

"Rigotamos" is yet another purported name, like "Vortigern," "Vortimer" and "Utherpendragon," which turns out to be a title. "Rigotamos" is derived from the Celtic word *rix*, meaning "king," and the superlative *tamos*. "Riothamus" or "Rigotamos" thus means "High King." It is a variation on the more ancient title Vortamorix or Vortimer, and, in the form "Rigisamus," is attested on pagan inscriptions in Britannia as an epithet of some of the Celtic gods. A leader known to the Celtic Gauls as Rigotamos would have been called Regissimus by his Latin-speaking followers.

The Riothamus of the Gallic chronicles was none other than Aurelius, the Regissimus Britanniarum.

Some historians have assumed that Riothamus and all his soldiers were Bretons, but this assumption is erroneous. The contemporary Gallic accounts state that Riothamus led his troops to Gaul from across the sea, a journey which no local leader or strictly Breton force would have had to make. The Bretons were also not yet numerous enough by themselves to field a large army capable of operating for a prolonged period of time outside their own territory. Although they might have been able to muster as many as 12,000 fighting men, these

fighting men were needed to defend their own Armorican territory; if too many Bretons remained too long away from from home, Armorica would have been quickly overrun by Saxon pirates and thoroughly ravaged by bacaudae rebels. Many of Riothamus's soldiers were Bretons, but the general himself and a large part of his army were overseas travellers who could have only come to Gaul from Britannia.

The title Rigotamos/Regissimus used by the army commander also militates against his having come from Armorica. While a Breton leader might have assumed the title of Rex (King), he would not have assumed the very lofty title of Regissimus. This title would have elevated him above his more powerful neighbor and overlord, Rex Romanorum Syagrius. In fact, the genealogies of Brittany give an Armorican ruler of about this time, Johannes (John) Reith, only the diminutive title of Regulus, meaning "petty king" or "under-king"; "Reith" itself is a corruption of the Celtic *rix*, meaning "king" (not high king). One ruler of Britannia, Vortimer, had already assumed the august title of Regissimus, so the army commander who later also did so was certainly another ruler of Britannia, Aurelius Ambrosius Aurelianus.

Some historians have suggested that the genuine Briton leader behind the title Rigotamos was not Aurelius, but Arthur. This theory is not credible. Placing Arthur in Gaul at this time precludes his participation in the campaigns of the A.D. 480's and A.D. 490's, including the crucial Battle of Badon Hill, with which tradition and the early written sources so strongly associate him. Only Aurelius, ruler of Britannia and leader of the Briton Imperial faction in the A.D. 460's and A.D. 470's, could have been the Rigotamos/Regissimus whom Emperor Anthemius lured into his grand anti-Visigoth coalition.[96]

Aurelius must have received the Emperor's petition for assistance soon after Anthemius took the throne in A.D. 467. He promptly mustered a small but powerful expeditionary force in Britannia and sailed to Armorica; the Regissimus's eagerness to campaign in Gaul might have even been a factor in his decision to make peace with Pascent of Builth. Aurelius arrived in Gaul at the start of the A.D. 468 summer campaign season. Geoffrey tells us that "Arthur" (i.e., Aurelius) sailed from "Southampton" (i.e., Clausentum) to the Gallic port of "Barfleur" (i.e., Barilio) on the Manche peninsula of Normandy, which was then part of Armorica. After landing in Gaul, Aurelius marched south to rendezvous with old friends in Armorica, whom he had no doubt alerted of his coming and of his desire for reinforcements. Aurelius should have been ready to march against the enemies of the Empire with a combined Briton-Breton force sometime in the summer of A.D. 468, which is indeed when "Riothamus" first took the field.

Aurelius's first military undertaking in Gaul was a campaign against the Saxons who had settled along the lower Loire River on the southern border of Armorica. Aurelius led his Briton and Breton soldiers in an attack upon the barbarians soon after he arrived in Armorica. The Regissimus defeated the Saxons and drove them from the Loire region in A.D. 468. After defeating the Loire Saxons, Aurelius marched his army east along the River Loire into Civitas Biturigum (more recently called Berry) in

---

96 Aurelius could have also taken the opportunity to obtain an Imperial pardon for himself if he was the allegedly adulterous Ambrosius of Tuscia.

central Gaul. In A.D. 469, Aurelius expelled the Visigoths from Civitas Biturigum.

Aurelius spent the winter of A.D. 469-470 in the town of Biturigae (Bourges). Biturigae offered a strong strategic position from which Aurelius could dominate central Gaul. The town sat upon the junction of five major Roman roads which spread out in all directions across Gaul. From Biturigae, Aurelius could keep a close watch on the Visigoths in southwest Gaul. He could also establish contact with the Rex Romanorum in north Gaul and the pro-Roman Burgundians in east Gaul. In fact, Geoffrey tells us that part of "Arthur's" (i.e., Aurelius's) strategy in Gaul was to "conquer" (i.e., link up with) the Burgundians (whom Geoffrey calls "Allobroges," from the name of the original Gallic tribe of the region). In occupying Biturigae, Aurelius seized the key strategic position in Gaul.

Aurelius probably occupied Biturigae with only his own Briton followers and a small number of Breton volunteers. Most of Aurelius's Breton soldiers would have returned to Armorica once the immediate danger to their own homeland ended with the defeat of the Saxons by the River Loire and the expulsion of the Visigoths from Civitas Biturigum. Battle casualties must have further depleted the Regissimus's manpower, for even victories are costly in blood. Aurelius and his army were nevertheless the most formidable military force in Gaul. Despite the reduction in the number of his troops, Aurelius held the balance of military power in Gaul because he controlled the key strategic position in the Diocese with a small, but elite, corps of combat-hardened veteran cavalrymen.

Aurelius had, until then, been virtually

invincible on the field of battle. He was, however, about to be bested in a very different sort of contest. This contest involved underhanded political intrigue rather than an honest clash of arms. The Regissimus was about to fall victim to treachery of the lowest sort.

## The Battle of Dol

Aurelius had come to Gaul as the savior of the Western Empire at the request of Emperor Anthemius, but not all the Romans in Gaul were happy to see him active in their Diocese. Arvandus, the Praefectus Praetorio per Gallias (Praetorian Prefect for the Gauls), saw Aurelius as a threat to his own status - and a serious impediment to his ability to continue looting the public coffers. Arvandus conspired with the anti-Roman Visigoth King Euric to overthrow Aurelius.

The perfidious plot was discovered, and Arvandus was arrested, tried, fined and banished. But too late. The damage had already been done. Euric had already received one or more letters from Arvandus detailing the size, location and plans of the Briton-Breton force. Euric planned to take full advantage of Arvandus's information, even if Arvandus was no longer able to reap any profit from his treason.

In A.D. 470, Euric moved against Aurelius. At this time, as Arvandus had no doubt informed Euric, the Briton Regissimus was marching from his headquarters at Biturigae to a rendezvous with his allies prior to an invasion of Visigothic Gaul. Euric moved rapidly and fell unexpectedly upon Aurelius with an overwhelming force near the town of Dol (or, more properly, Vicus Dolensis, modern Bourg-de-Deols) on the River Indre across from modern Chateauroux.

Even the greatest generals may be overcome by treachery and sufficiently large numbers, and Aurelius was defeated. The Briton army was smashed. Euric pursued the beaten Britons, and drove them from Civitas Biturigum. Aurelius fled with the battered remnant of his once-mighty army northeast across the River Loire into the adjacent territory of the friendly Burgundians. Aurelius escaped with the Briton survivors, and "Riothamus" disappeared from Continental history.

The *Historia Regum Britanniae* gives an account of the downfall of Aurelius which supplies us with the details of the treason that led to Aurelius's defeat. Geoffrey tells us that Aurelius was brought low by a perfidious Saxon named Eopa, who was in the pay of Pascent of Builth. Eopa disguised himself as a monk in order to gain access to the Regissimus. Pretending to be skilled with medicines, the sinister pretend-monk administered a deadly poison to Aurelius. The Regissimus died from this poison. Geoffrey's story of the poisoning of Aurelius is certainly based upon the true events which led to the betrayal of the Briton army in Gaul to Euric.

The details of the treachery - a traitorous Saxon, a Romano-Celtic paymaster and a spy disguised as a Christian cleric - are elements of the elaborate plot which Arvandus hatched against Aurelius. Eopa was probably a hostage taken from the Loire Saxons. As such, he would have been eager for revenge against the conqueror of his people; he would have gladly betrayed the hospitality of Aurelius in order to provide damaging intelligence to Arvandus. Arvandus was, of course, the evil Roman paymaster.

Arvandus must have sent a spy into Aurelius's camp in the guise of a Christian clergyman. A pagan Saxon could not have deceived Christians by falsely donning clerical garb, but a Gallic spy sent by Arvandus could have easily posed as a clergyman in order to gain access to the court of Aurelius. The spy might have even been a genuine, but insidious, priest. In any event, Arvandus's secret agent made contact with the disgruntled Saxon hostage Eopa in Biturigae. Eopa revealed Aurelius's military strength and plans to the spy, who reported them to Arvandus, who in turn passed the information on to Euric.

Euric certainly knew that Aurelius would be at Dol with a small force awaiting Roman, and possibly Breton, reinforcements on that fateful day in A.D. 470. Euric was thus able to launch a surprise attack upon the Briton force, catching Aurelius unawares before his allies arrived. Because Euric knew exactly where he had to go, he was able to quick-march directly to the planned rendezvous spot, arriving before word of his unexpected invasion reached Aurelius. Surprised and outnumbered, the Briton force was decimated.

Emperor Anthemius did not long survive the defeat of his Briton champion. Ricimer deposed and murdered the Emperor in A.D. 472. Four years and four Emperors later, the Western Empire itself came to an ignominious end.[97]

---

97 Ironically, the last western Emperor, Romulus Augustulus, was deposed by a barbarian warlord named Odovacer. Odovacer had been a leader of the Loire Saxons whom Aurelius defeated in A.D. 468. The Franks absorbed most of the Loire Saxons into their own tribe after Aurelius's victory, but Odovacer and his followers refused to submit to Childeric; they wandered across western Europe, ultimately establishing themselves in Italy.

Euric was meanwhile unable to convert his victory in the Battle of Dol into the conquest of Gaul. He had hardly defeated Aurelius when a certain Comes Paulus arrived on the scene at the head of Anthemius's Imperial forces. Paulus was accompanied by Syagrius's Frankish allies and presumably by some of Syagrius's native Gallic troops. Judging from Geoffrey's account of "Arthur's" campaign, Paulus had established a base at Aedua (Autun) in late A.D. 469. He was joined there in early spring of A.D. 470 by his Frankish and Gallo-Roman allies. The Comes then advanced with this composite force from Aedua to Dol, where he expected to link up with Aurelius. He arrived at Dol too late to help Aurelius, but not too late to fight Euric. Comes Paulus engaged and defeated the Visigoths, once again expelling them from Civitas Biturigum.

Come Paulus was unable to achieve a complete victory because, instead of following up the success against Euric, the anti-Visigoth allies fell to fighting among themselves. For reasons unknown to us, the Frankish King Childeric attacked and killed Comes Paulus. Childeric's quarrel seems to have been personal and not political, however, because the Franks then rejoined the remaining Romans and Gallo-Romans to resume the war against the Visigoths. The reconciled allies finally managed to drive Euric out of central Gaul, but they left him in possession of the southwestern part of the Diocese.

The victory over Euric was incomplete, but it was enough to allow Syagrius to preserve his kingdom throughout the A.D. 470's and early A.D. 480's. Syagrius was, however, unable to make his realm permanent. In A.D. 481, Syagrius's Frankish ally Childeric died and was succeeded by his able son Clovis. Clovis was extremely aggressive and ambitious; he eventually betrayed his Roman overlord. In A.D. 486, Clovis led the Franks in revolt against Syagrius. He defeated the Gallo-Roman forces in battle, seized Noviodunum Suessionum and executed the Rex Romanorum. In A.D. 486, the independent Gallo-Roman kingdom came to an end, and all of north Gaul fell to the Franks.

Clovis steadily expanded the borders of his domain throughout his long and active reign. By A.D. 496, he had conquered the Alamanni of southwest Germania, occupied Bohemia and established himself on the River Loire in Gaul. By A.D. 507, Clovis had driven the Visigoths completely out of Gaul, confining them thereafter to Hispania. In the same year Clovis became a Catholic, the only major barbarian leader who was neither a pagan nor a follower of the anti-Catholic Arian heresy. Clovis thus became the only major barbarian leader to receive the political backing of the Church. The support of the Church was important, because it ensured Clovis the cooperation of the native Gallo-Roman populace of his new kingdom. His regime thus stood on a more secure foundation than did those of the other barbarians with whom he competed for control of Gaul. By his military conquests and choice of religion, Clovis almost single-handedly transformed Roman Gaul into medieval "Frank-land" or France.

Large numbers of Britons meanwhile continued to leave their homeland and emigrate to Armorica through the middle of the Sixth Century. Armorica, or more accurately by then Brittany, avoided Frankish conquest, but it had to accept Frankish suzerainty. After A.D. 507, the Breton rulers found it expedient to give up the title of Rex (King), taking instead the lesser title of Comes (Count). The great Frankish Emperor Charlemagne officially ended Breton independence in the late Eighth Century, but the Bretons nevertheless managed to retain a large degree of autonomy and to preserve their unique culture.

Of more immediate concern to us, Aurelius and the shattered remnant of his army made good their escape into Burgundian Gaul. Based upon what Geoffrey has to say about "Arthur's" movements in Gaul, the Britons retreated in a northeasterly direction from the battlefield of Dol to Andematunnum Lingonum (Langres). Andematunnum Lingonum, as "Leigrys," is specifically mentioned by Geoffrey in his account of "Arthur's" campaign in Gaul. En route, Aurelius might have rested in the Gallic town of Aballo (Avalon). "Aballo" was a fairly common Celtic place name, essentially meaning "Apple-town." Gallic Aballo had a counterpart in north Britannia, the Roman fort of Aballava (Burgh-by-Sands) near Luguvalium (Carlisle) on Hadrian's Wall, which enjoys Arthurian associations; in fact, it was probably Aurelius's stopping at the Gallic Aballo which misled Geoffrey into identifying "Riothamus" as Arthur. From Andematunnum Lingonum, the Britons turned north to Syagrius's capital of Noviodunum Suessionum, which Geoffrey calls "Siesia."[98]

At Noviodunum, the Britons met the regional Gallo-Roman army. The Britons did not, as Geoffrey thought, seek battle with the Gallo-Romans; they sought refuge with them.

---

[98] The town also appears as "Suesia," "Soissie," "Sessoyne" and "Assnessia" in different manuscripts of the *Historia*, which resemble its Roman name (Suessionum), its modern name (Soissons) and its modern Department (Aisne). Lewis Thorpe, Geoffrey's modern editor, mistranslates the town name as "Saussy."

From Noviodunum, Aurelius eventually led his followers back to Britannia, but not for some time. The Regissimus Britanniarum had been seriously wounded in the Battle of Dol, and he remained two or three years in convalescence as Syagrius's guest at Noviodunum.

Geoffrey describes Aurelius, both by name and by his former title of Utherpendragon, as infirm and unable to ride a horse during the latter part of his reign. A genuine folk memory of an incapacitated ruler must underlie these accounts of Aurelius's disability; Aurelius must have suffered a crippling injury after he became Regissimus Britanniarum. The most likely source of the royal injury was the Battle of Dol.

While Aurelius recovered from his wounds, his soldiers might have participated, albeit in minor supporting roles, in the several battles then being fought in Gaul. The contemporary Gallic accounts are confused, but they seem to imply that the Britons continued to fight as allies of Syagrius for at least some time after the Battle of Dol as the relationships and rivalries among the Romans, Gallo-Romans, Visigoths, Burgundians and Franks played themselves out.

With the Regissimus defeated and wounded in Gaul, rumors of his death inevitably spread to Britannia. While Aurelius recuperated in Burgundian Aballo and Gallo-Roman Noviodunum, his prolonged absence from Britannia seemed to confirm the stories of his demise. The situation in Britannia began to deteriorate. Encouraged by the defeat and presumed death of the once invincible Aurelius, the Anglo-Saxons in Britannia again went on the rampage.

## Chapter Fifteen
## Catavia and the Anglo-Saxon Uprising

While Aurelius was *hors de combat* in Gaul, the Anglo-Saxons saw their chance to prey upon his subjects in Britannia. Word of the disaster at the Battle of Dol would have reached Britannia late in A.D. 470. A few opportunistic warbands might have begun raiding Briton territory as early as the summer campaign season of A.D. 471. The prolonged absence of Aurelius from Britannia encouraged the barbarians, and they massed for a full scale attack upon the Diocese in the spring of A.D. 472.

### Catavia's Northern Campaign

The Anglo-Saxon attackers gathered in the north under the leadership of Octa of Bernicia.

Geoffrey of Monmouth tells us that Octa no longer felt bound by his treaty with Aurelius when "Utherpendragon" rose to power in the Diocese. Octa thought that Aurelius - and his treaty - had expired in Gaul. When Aurelius failed to return to Britannia, Octa assumed that he had been killed. In Octa's mind, the promises made after the Battle of Maisbeli were strictly personal to himself and Aurelius, and Aurelius's death would release him from any obligation to keep the peace with the Britons. Octa, to his way of thinking, was freed by the presumed death of Aurelius to resume his piratical ways and to again attack the Britons, who were now led by Catavia, the Magister Militum or Utherpendragon.

Octa led the Anglo-Saxons of Bernicia across Hadrian's Wall to the town of Eboracum (York), where the Dux Britanniarum had his headquarters. Octa was joined there by Angles from Anglia. Geoffrey actually tells us that Octa allied himself with "the Saxons whom Pascent had brought over." These "Saxons" were, of course, the Angles whom Aurelius had earlier defeated in the Battle on the Icknield Way; Geoffrey, like the contemporary Britons, did not properly distinguish between the Angles, the Saxons and the other Germanic tribes in the Diocese. The Dux Britanniarum made no effort to oppose the barbarian army.

The northeast of Britannia, under the rulers who had succeeded Coelestius Senex as Dux Britanniarum, remained independent and aloof of Aurelius's government in south Britannia. Spared the ravages of the Anglo-Saxon revolt of the A.D. 460's and maintained in power by their own political and military institutions, the northeastern leaders saw small reason to concern themselves with the affairs of the south. They saw absolutely no reason at all to submit to a southern ruler. The northeastern leaders were also unaffected by Vortimer's support for Saint Germanus's mission, so they no doubt continued to follow Pelagius's heretical theology.[99] Pelagianism would have united the northeastern Romano-Briton aristocrats against their orthodox southern counterparts. Political and religious differences thus separated the two parts of Britannia. The reigning Dux was definitely not going to risk the peace and security of his own realm in order to defend Aurelius's rival regime.

The Dux Britanniarum might have even instigated the Anglo-Saxon invasion of south Britannia. He could have recruited the barbarians for his own army of conquest, or he could have simply induced them to attack the southern part of the Diocese on their own. Either way, he would expect the Anglo-Saxons to destroy the remnant of Aurelius's army in the south, thereby paving the way for conquest by his own forces. Alternatively, the Dux might have granted the invaders uncontested passage through his territory only to spare his own lands from devastation, much as certain eastern Emperors are alleged to have saved their own realm by encouraging barbarians to attack the Western Empire. The Dux Britanniarum facilitated the invasion in any case by permitting the Anglo-Saxons to cross his realm unmolested, and he certainly planned to take advantage of the circumstances to enrich himself one way or another at the expense of his Romano-Briton neighbors.

Regardless of his motives, the Dux Britanniarum was not going to save Britannia from the barbarians. The only other person in the Diocese capable of dealing with the resurgent Anglo-Saxons was Catavia, Aurelius's Magister Militum.

Catavia decided to meet the barbarian challenge head-on. To this end, he led the southern army to Eboracum. Aurelius's allies, Comes Eldol of Glevum Colonia (Gloucester) and Dux Gorlois of Dumnonia (Devon and Cornwall), accompanied him. Geoffrey tells us that "Utherpendragon" (i.e., Catavia) caught the Anglo-Saxon marauders as they were attempting to besiege the Ducal capital. If the town leaders were not incompetent, and if the town garrison was loyal, the besiegers stood little chance of success. More likely, however, the barbarians were simply camped near the town. They were probably awaiting supplies from the Dux Britanniarum and the arrival of barbarian - or

---

99 Pelagianism was resilient in Britannia; according to the Twelfth Century chronicler Giraldus Cambrensis (Gerald of Wales), it was still to be found in parts of Wales even in the late Sixth Century.

even Ducal - reinforcements before they continued their march into Aurelius's territory. As soon as he neared Eboracum, Utherpendragon Catavia charged the enemy.

Catavia obviously hoped to engage the Anglo-Saxons before all their forces were mustered. His hopes were misplaced. Most of the barbarian warriors had already arrived, and they were able to repulse Catavia's repeated attacks. The Anglo-Saxons then went over to the offensive, defeating the Britons and putting them to flight. They pursued the fleeing Britons for as long as daylight permitted. The beaten southern army withdrew in good order, the sign of well-trained soldiers and competent leadership. Catavia rallied his men to make a stand on nearby Mount Damen.

The Eboracum garrison and the Deiran foederati failed to join Catavia in the Battle of Eboracum. If an Eboracum force had sallied forth from the town to aid Catavia, the Battle would have certainly gone in Catavia's favor; few armies, particularly barbarian ones, are able to cope with simultaneous attacks from different directions. Likewise, the Anglo-Saxons could not have vigorously pursued the fleeing southerners if they feared the sudden appearance of a hostile Deiran force. The lack of assistance from the Ducal army is a clear indication that the current Dux Britanniarum was at least a passive supporter of the Anglo-Saxon invasion. If Eboracum or Deiran troops did participate in the fighting, they did so as allies of Octa and enemies of Catavia.

While his soldiers were encamped for the night on Mount Damen, no doubt counting the number of campfires lit by the adjacent barbarian army, Catavia held a midnight conference with his officers. Gorlois of Dumnonia proposed an early morning attack upon the enemy camp. The Anglo-Saxons were fierce warriors, but not very well organized. A sunrise attack just might catch them before they were prepared to resume the fight. Catavia adopted Gorlois's plan. The Britons made their way in the late night darkness towards their sleeping enemies, maneuvering into position for an all-out assault at dawn.

At first light, the Britons launched their attack. It was a complete success. The barbarians were taken by surprise and were unable to offer effective resistance. The Anglo-Saxon army was destroyed, and Octa was captured.

Geoffrey, in his description of Catavia's campaign, continues to pair Eosa with Octa, but he does so simply out of habit. Having once associated the two Anglo-Saxon leaders, Geoffrey continues to do so, not realizing that Octa and Eosa had probably parted ways. Eosa, as "Osla," probably entered Briton service after the Battle of Maisbeli; he might have even served with Catavia against Octa in the Battles of Eboracum and Mount Damen. Geoffrey could not conceive of one group of Anglo-Saxons fighting under Briton command against another group of Anglo-Saxons, so he erroneously persists in lumping the two barbarian leaders together.

## Catavia's Expedition to Alclud

While Catavia was engaged in combat against Octa near Eboracum, other barbarians were assailing another part of Britannia. Geoffrey tells us that after the Battle of Mount Damen, "Utherpendragon" (i.e., Catavia) advanced all the way to the River Clyde, where he imposed order upon the "Scots" and "pacified the northern provinces." By "Scots," Geoffrey must mean the Irish warriors then colonizing modern Argyll and modern Galloway in west Scotland. They had apparently raided Briton territory and needed to be taught a lesson. Catavia no doubt also fought Octa's allies from the Anglo-Saxon settlements in the Dumfries area. Skirmishing against various barbarian warbands occupied Catavia's attention through late A.D. 472 and into A.D. 473.

Catavia's base of operations in the far north was the town of Alclud, now called Dumbarton. "Alclud" is derived from the Briton *Alt Clut*, meaning "Rock of the Clyde." The town was named for the volcanic plug in the Clyde River upon which it sits. "Dumbarton" itself comes from the Scots Gaelic meaning "Fort of the Britons." Alclud was fortified by the Britons of the Clyde Valley ("Strathclyde" in local dialect) in the late Fifth Century, and it remained virtually impregnable in their hands until it fell to the Vikings after a long and difficult siege in A.D. 870-871. In Catavia's day, and for a long time afterward, Alclud was capital of the Celtic Kingdom of Strathclyde.

In the A.D. 450's, the ruler of Strathclyde was named Coroticus. "Coroticus" is the Latin form of the Celtic name Ceretic or Ceredig, also occasionally written "Cherdic" or "Keredic." It is probably derived from the name "Corotiacus," which was borne by one of the many Celtic war gods associated with the Roman war god Mars on pagan inscriptions in Roman Britannia. "Coroticus" was a popular name among the Britons of the post-Roman period; it was, for instance, the name borne by the interpreter who had gone north with Octa and Ebissa in the late A.D. 430's. Coroticus of Strathclyde was the grandson of Quintilius Clemens, whom Emperor Maximus made king over the Damnonii of the Clyde River region in the late A.D. 360's.

Coroticus earned a dubious place in history by arousing the ire of Saint Patrick. Coroticus incurred the Saint's wrath for raids conducted against Patrick's Christian converts in Ireland. Saint Patrick sent an angry letter to Coroticus castigating him for his monstrous behavior in murdering and enslaving fellow Christians. The text of Saint Patrick's letter, called *Epistula ad Coroticum* (Letter to Coroticus), survives to this day. Although Saint Patrick's letter depicts Coroticus in an unflattering light, it also indicates that the Strathclyde leader was an aggressive and capable leader. Coroticus was powerful enough to turn the tables on the Irish barbarians who were then plaguing the rest of Britannia.

Strathclyde was governed in Catavia's time by Coroticus's son Cynnwyd (also spelt "Cinuit"). Cynnwyd was the ruler who fortified Alclud and established it as the Strathclyde capital, on account of which Briton bards later regarded him as the founder of the Kingdom of Strathclyde.

Catavia's purpose in marching to Alclud and in fighting the far northern barbarians was to establish diplomatic relations between Aurelius's Romano-Briton regime and Cynnwyd's Celtic realm. Although situated almost at opposite ends of the island from each other, south Britannia and Strathclyde had a common interest in opposing the Dux Britanniarum and his barbarian associates. The Dux's willingness to collaborate with the far northern Anglo-Saxons posed a serious threat to both governments. Catavia had just averted a ducal-supported Anglo-Saxon invasion of south Britannia, but he did so only with difficulty and only for the moment. The Magister Militum knew that the Dux and his barbarians might make another attempt in the future. The Dux's cosy relationship with the far northern Anglo-Saxons was an even greater problem for Strathclyde. Strathclyde's lands were within easy raiding distance of both the Bernician and the Dumfries Anglo-Saxons, and Ducal support would allow the barbarians to conduct ever bolder incursions onto these lands. Because the barbarians did not fear counter-attack by the Dux while they were lifting booty from the Strathclyders, they could make much deeper and more frequent forays into Strathclyde. Cynnwyd was therefore very receptive to an offer of friendship with the south Britons. Catavia was able to form a military alliance with Cynnwyd against the enemy which both he and Cynnwyd shared in the Dux Britanniarum and his Anglo-Saxon allies.

Catavia also formed a military alliance with Civitas Carvetiorum, which was based upon the town of Luguvalium (Carlisle) in northwest Britannia. Civitas Carvetiorum was the wealthy Civitas which had slipped away from the control of the Dux Britanniarum in, or very soon after, Coelestius Senex's time. Civitas Carvetiorum's defiance of the Dux Britanniarum made it very receptive to Catavia's overtures. It was eager for military allies against the possibility that the current Dux might attempt to regain control over the Civitas. Civitas Carvetiorum, like Strathclyde, shared with south Britannia a common enemy in the Dux Britanniarum.

Catavia consummated the alliance with Civitas Carvetiorum by turning his noble Anglo-Saxon prisoner Octa over to the rulers of the Civitas. Surrendering Octa to the Carvetians was a generous gesture because Octa was a valuable hostage against the good behavior of the far northern Anglo-Saxons. Catavia's gesture was generous, but it was not extravagant. The gift of the barbarian leader was a small price to pay in order to gain the friendship of the northwest Civitas.

Geoffrey actually claims that "Uther-pendragon" imprisoned Octa in "London" (i.e., Londinium), but Geoffrey is mistaken. In order to have jailed Octa in Londinium, Catavia would have had to drag the barbarian leader with him all the way from Mount Damen up to Alclud and then all the way back down again to Londinium. The transport of a dangerous enemy over such long distances through territory in which he had many followers and allies would have been extremely foolhardy. Luguvalium, by contrast, was fairly close to the site of the Battle of Mount Damen; Catavia could have easily transported and safely imprisoned Octa in this town. Geoffrey has obviously confused the former provincial capital of Luguvalium with the former Diocesan capital of Londinium, no doubt because the Welsh name for Luguvalium was "Kaer Luilid," which is similar to "Kaer Lludd," a Welsh name for Londinium. Catavia did not haul his Anglo-Saxon prisoner back and forth across the entire length of Britannia; he used him instead to gain influence in nearby Luguvalium.

Catavia went to Luguvalium and Alclud with only part of his army. He released some of the Briton cavalry to return home under Comes Eldol and Dux Gorlois. The Magister Militum probably thought it unwise to leave south Britannia too long unguarded. Besides, once the immediate threat to their own domains in the south had been averted, Eldol and Gorlois would have lost interest in any further northern adventures. Comes Eldol and Dux Gorlois led their own forces homeward soon after the Battle of Mount Damen.

A good thing, too, that the Briton cavalry returned south. While the Romano-Briton army was engaged in the north, the first Anglo-Saxon king to rule in Britannia had not been idle. Hengist was not one to pass up an opportunity for easy plunder, and he raided the undefended southern portion of the Diocese.

## Hengist's Last Battle

The Anglo-Saxon Chronicle tells us that Hengist ended eight long years of abiding quietly in Kent in order to wage war upon the Britons in A.D. 473. The Chronicle states that the Kentish king "seized countless spoils of war," although it does not say where he took these "countless spoils." The reference to "countless spoils," and the absence of a specified geographic location, indicate that Hengist did not fight a regular, set-piece battle against the Britons. Instead, he raided over a wide area of south Britannia. The Britons, unprepared for the onslaught, fled from the Anglo-Saxons, the Chronicle reports, "as one flees fire."

Hengist probably expected to encounter little resistance. After all, Aurelius and a large part of his army were either slain or stranded overseas, and most of the rest of the Romano-Briton military forces were far away in the north. Hengist thought he would have an easy time of it. Hengist was wrong; he should have stayed home.

In A.D. 473, the fatal encounter between Eldol and Hengist, which Geoffrey mistakenly places after the Battle of Maisbeli, occurred. Comes Eldol, the Glevum commander, and Dux Gorlois, the Cornovian leader from Dumnonia,

raised their small cavalry forces and set out after Hengist. The Romano-Briton cavalry leaders defeated the Anglo-Saxon warlord, and Eldol captured and executed him.

Hengist's last battle was not a major engagement involving large numbers of troops. Because most Briton soldiers were committed elsewhere, only a handful of warriors were available to Eldol and Gorlois. They probably commanded no more than their own personal warbands of about 300 horsemen each. Small troops of mobile horse soldiers were, in any case, the most effective type of force to deploy against a wide-ranging raiding party. The barbarian army likewise numbered only in the hundreds, for Kent could not have fully recovered from the severe battle losses and defections which followed Aurelius's victory in A.D. 465. Hengist probably led only his own company of household troops and a few hundred loot-hungry adventurers. In all likelihood, the two Briton leaders commanded only about 600 cavalrymen, and Hengist perhaps just under 1,000 horse-riding infantrymen.

Eldol and Gorlois seem to have led their horsemen separately against the raiders, patrolling the countryside in hopes of intercepting Hengist and his followers as they returned home laden with booty. Burdened with plunder, the barbarians were moving slowly and were most vulnerable. As Hengist made his way back to Kent with his "countless spoils," Eldol and Gorlois fell upon him.

Geoffrey informs us that Eldol and the Glevum cavalry were the first to encounter Hengist. Eldol's troopers and the Anglo-Saxon raiders then fought for some time without either side making any headway. The Briton horsemen were apparently unable to break the Anglo-Saxon shieldwall, while the barbarians could not pin down the fast-moving horse soldiers. Gorlois and his riders finally arrived on the scene and charged into the fray. The added pressure of the Cornovian reinforcements turned the tide, and the Anglo-Saxon battle formation fell apart. As the barbarians broke and fled, Eldol managed to capture Hengist.

Aurelius was clearly not present at Hengist's last battle, for he played no role in deciding the fate of the barbarian king. The important choice between executing or ransoming the ruler of Kent was one that Aurelius would not have delegated to another had he been on the scene, yet it was Bishop Eldadus, brother of Eldol of Glevum, who determined that the barbarian's life should be forfeit. Upon the Bishop's advice, Comes Eldol led Hengist away and beheaded him. Geoffrey says that Aurelius arranged Hengist's funeral, but this task is something the Regissimus could have done later. Aurelius was probably still en route to Britannia from Gaul when Hengist was captured and executed.

Aurelius's desire to pay Hengist final honors may seem surprising, but the Regissimus probably felt some obligation toward the Anglo-Saxon leader going back to the day when he was brought before Vortigern after the Battle of Wallop. The admiration of Hengist and his followers had most likely saved the life of the courageous young Aurelius when Vortigern's advisors proposed his murder. Indeed, Aurelius's regard for the Anglo-Saxon warlord might have prompted Bishop Eldadus to urge Hengist's immediate beheading before the Regissimus could intervene to spare the barbarian's life.

Hengist's death must have occurred in A.D. 473, the same year for which the Anglo-Saxon Chronicle records his last military success. It could not have occurred much later, because the Kentish king was already quite old. Hengist had been in Britannia for some forty-five years by A.D. 473. Even if he was a young man when he first landed on Thanet, he must have been well into his late sixties or early seventies when he conducted his last raid onto Briton soil. We have no reason to suppose that a man as dynamic as Hengist would not have still been active at this age, but he was nonetheless quite advanced in years according to the life expectancy of the time. Given the circumstances of Hengist's defeat and execution, we should not be surprised that the Anglo-Saxon Chronicle merely makes note of his final bold defiance of the Britons and remains silent as to his passing. The barbarian chroniclers had small interest in preserving the memory of Anglo-Saxon humiliations, so they reported Hengist's taking of spoils but deliberately neglected to mention his defeat and execution.

## The Succession to the Kingship of Kent

After Hengist's death, Kent was left essentially leaderless. Hengist's natural heir was his son Octa, then a prisoner in Luguvalium. Although Octa eventually escaped captivity, he could not have made his way to Kent until some time after his father's death. The Anglo-Saxon Chronicle does not even name any successor for Hengist until A.D. 488, when it reports that Hengist's "son" Aesc "received the kingdom."

Nennius also acknowledges Aesc, whom he calls "Ossa," as king of Kent, but he does not identify him as Hengist's son or immediate successor. Nennius identifies Aesc as Hengist's *grand*son and the third king of Kent. He also tells us that Octa was Hengist's immediate successor and the father of Aesc. The leadership situation in Kent after Hengist's death thus seems confused.

The clue to unraveling the mystery lies in the fact that in later times the Kentish dynasty identified itself as "Aescingas" (the people of Aesc), not "Hengistingas" (the people of Hengist) as we would expect. The use of the dynastic name Aescingas indicates that Aesc was not a direct descendant of Hengist and that he founded his own royal dynasty in Kent in A.D. 488. Political disturbances must have occurred in the Kentish kingdom, disturbances which resulted in Hengist's descendants being displaced by a new ruling family headed by a warrior named Aesc or Ossa.

Aesc must have been a local Kentish leader who seized the throne of the kingdom at the expense of the natural heirs of Hengist. He was most likely an ambitious nobleman of undistinguished heritage, although he could have been a grandson of Horsa; William of Malmesbury tells us that Hengist had a nephew, presumably Horsa's son, and this nephew could have been Aesc's father. In addition, a variant version of the *Historia Regum Britanniae* reports that Ossa was a cousin of Octa, the son of Hengist, which further suggests descent from Horsa. In any event, because Octa spent so much time in the north, including the early part of his reign as a prisoner in Luguvalium, Aesc had ample opportunity to make himself *de facto* ruler of Kent in the true king's absence. After Octa's death, Aesc took the royal title, as well as the royal power, onto himself.

The original keepers of Kentish history did not wish to lay out the sordid details of the treason against Hengist's family, so they simply skipped a generation in the Kentish king list. They could not ignore the semi-legendary founder of the Kentish kingdom, but they could omit any mention of his direct descendants, whom Aesc overthrew, or at least pushed aside, in establishing his own dynasty. Venerable Bede confirms that unworthy monarchs were indeed sometimes deliberately omitted from Anglo-Saxon king lists; Bede reports that two Seventh Century Northumbrian kings who had repudiated Christianity and revived pagan worship were intentionally left out of the Northumbrian king list, and that the year of their joint reign was attributed to their Christian successor. With Octa deliberately omitted from the Kentish king-list, later generations of scribes erroneously made Aesc into Hengist's son in order to explain his succession to the kingship.

The Britons were indifferent to the political sensitivities of the barbarian kingdom, so their version of the Kentish king list, which fell into Nennius's hands, continues to list Octa as a King of Kent. The early account used by Nennius must have simply reported that "Ossa" (i.e., Aesc) succeeded Octa, which statement was mistaken by Nennius to mean that Aesc/Ossa was Octa's son.

Venerable Bede gives a slightly different version of the Kentish king list, which sheds further light on the dynastic situation in Kent. Bede, like Nennius, shows Octa as a king of Kent, but he also shows an individual named Oeric or Eric as king after Hengist and before Octa. Bede claims that Eric was Kent's second king and a son of Hengist, and that Eric was also known as "Aesc."[100]

---

100 Bede then brings his king list into agreement with Nennius's by making Aesc's son Eormenric into Octa's son and continuing thence through the subsequent kings of Kent.

The appearance of Eric in the Kentish royal family tells us that Hengist had a son named Eric who was next in line after Hengist for the kingship of Kent. From the dates associated with Octa - specifically his participation in the northern expedition with Ebissa in the late A.D. 430's - Octa could not have been Hengist's grandson, but must have also been his son. Eric was thus Hengist's elder son, and Octa his younger son. This circumstance explains why Octa went to Bernicia; Octa expected Kent to pass to his older brother Eric upon his father's death, so he went north in order to carve out his own realm in the former Votadini lands beyond Hadrian's Wall. Eric, as it turned out, predeceased Hengist or died childless soon after Hengist, and Octa found himself heir to the Kingdom of Kent as well as ruler of his own domain in Bernicia.

Bede's making Aesc into an alter ego of Eric merely represents Bede's effort to find a place for the upstart Aesc in the Kentish genealogy. Bede never considered the possibility that Aethelbert, Aesc's grandson and the first Christian Anglo-Saxon king, was the scion of a usurper dynasty; to Bede's mind, a king who saw the light of Christianity could have only come from a legitimate ruling family. In order to make sense of the Kentish royal succession, Bede concluded that Aesc had to have been the same person as the otherwise unremarkable Eric.

While the leaders of Kent sorted out their dynastic problems, the Anglo-Saxon kingdom remained militarily inactive. Only many years after the death of Hengist, when Aesc was secure in his power, did Kent again assert itself and again play a major role in the history of post-Roman Britannia. Long before then, Aurelius recovered his strength, assembled his surviving soldiers and resumed his rule of Britannia.

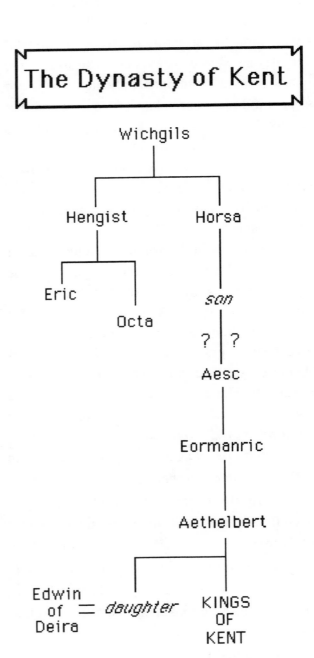

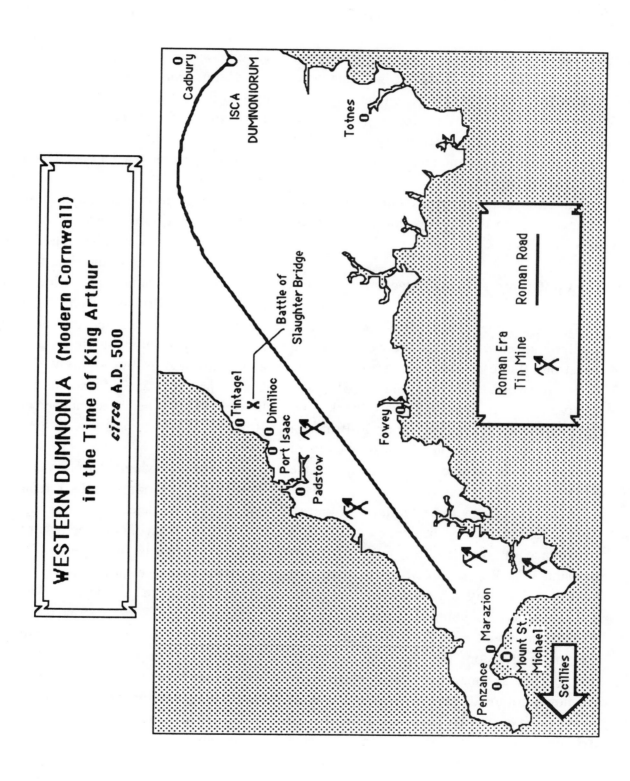

**WESTERN DUMNONIA** (Modern Cornwall)
in the Time of King Arthur
*circa* A.D. 500

Cadbury

ISCA DUMNONIORUM

Totnes

Battle of
Slaughter Bridge

Tintagel
Dimilioc
Port Isaac
Padstow

Fowey

Roman Era
Tin Mine

Roman Road

Penzance
Marazion
Mount St.
Michael

Scillies

## Chapter Sixteen
## The Rebellion of Dux Gorlois

The Magister Militum and the local rulers whom Aurelius left in charge of Britannia were able to deal with the Anglo-Saxon threats which arose in the Regissimus's absence. New, more serious barbarian dangers were soon to afflict Britannia, but for the moment the Diocese was safe from foreign enemies.

Aurelius did not return home to peace, however, but to the most pernicious form of strife: civil war.

### The Conference at Venta Belgarum

Before coming back to Britannia, Aurelius required several years to recover from the disastrous Battle of Dol. He needed time to allow his wounds to heal and to whip the survivors of his shattered army back into fighting shape. He did not return to Britannia until A.D. 473, too late to adjudicate the fate of Hengist, but just in time to order an honorable burial for his former enemy.

After tending to Hengist's funeral, Aurelius's first order of business was to call a conference of the leading men of south Britannia. The Regissimus wished to reacquaint himself with the military situation in the island and to reassert his political dominance within the Diocese. Geoffrey of Monmouth places this meeting in "London" (i.e., Londinium), but he probably just assumed that it took place there; the newly-returned Aurelius was much more likely to have met the assembled nobility of Britannia in his own stronghold of Venta Belgarum (Winchester). Regardless of where the conference of Romano-Briton leaders was

held, it became the scene of a bitter confrontation between Aurelius and Gorlois, the Cornovian Dux from Dumnonia and one of Aurelius's earliest supporters.

Gorlois must have reckoned himself too exalted to submit any longer to the authority of an overlord. As the military commander who had come up with the plan that defeated Octa and as the general who had put the dread villain Hengist in his grave, Gorlois probably overestimated his own importance. After all, he might have reasoned, it was he, together with Vitalinus and Eldol, who had raised Aurelius to the rule of Britannia in the first place, and he, together with Catavia and Eldol, who had recently saved Britannia from the barbarians. He no doubt also realized that his Cornovian troops were crucial to Aurelius's early victories and continued military might. Moreover, Gorlois probably decided that Aurelius forfeited his right to rule when he abandoned his duties in Britannia in order to pursue a personal quest for glory in Gaul. Whatever Gorlois's precise justifications, when Aurelius returned to Britannia, the Cornovian Dux repudiated his allegiance to the defeated Regissimus.

Geoffrey's account of the resulting conflict became the basis of a pivotal incident in Arthurian Romance and legend.

According to Geoffrey, Aurelius, as "Utherpendragon," met Ygerna, the wife of Dux Gorlois, at the assembly of the leaders of his kingdom. Aurelius conceived an obsessive passion for Ygerna. Gorlois was not blind to the Regissimus's amorous attentions to his wife, and he left the conference in a rage. Furious at being rebuffed by Ygerna's husband, "Utherpendragon" invaded "Cornwall."

Gorlois's hasty departure from the meeting

was not really prompted by jealousy; it was prompted by ambition. The Cornovian Dux had no doubt made known his refusal to accept Aurelius as ruler of Britannia. Geoffrey concluded that the conflict between Aurelius and Gorlois was motivated by Aurelius's lust for Ygerna because the Regissimus later married his adversary's wife. The fact that Aurelius took Ygerna to be his wife does not mean the Briton civil war was caused by sexual passion, because Aurelius's motivation in wedding Ygerna was certainly political.

Aurelius must have known that the military defeat of Gorlois was only half the job facing him; the other half was to regain the allegiance of the Cornovians of Dumnonia. The Cornovian warrior aristocracy was a valuable military asset, one which Aurelius should have been extremely loath to lose. The wedding with the wife of the defeated Dux was a gesture of goodwill and a plea for reconciliation between the Romano-Briton ruler and the Cornovian soldiers. In similar circumstances, Canute, the Danish conqueror of England in the early Eleventh Century, married the queen of the defeated Anglo-Saxon King Ethelred Unraed in order to reconcile the English to his rule. The ability of wedding bells to heal political wounds was well-known to the post-Roman Britons; in the *Mabinogion* tale "How Culhwch Won Olwen," the storyteller thought it perfectly natural for a king to marry the wife of a defeated opponent. Aurelius hoped to mend fences with the Cornovian warriors and win back their support by taking Ygerna as his wife.

Ygerna was also politically well-connected in her own right. A surviving Welsh genealogy identifies her as a granddaughter of Cunedda, the Vòtadini leader who founded the Kingdom of Gwynedd in north Wales. The parallel to Canute's situation is thus especially strong because Ethelred Unraed's widow was also a member of a powerful ruling family, in her case the dynasty then governing Normandy. After vanquishing Gorlois, Aurelius seized the opportunity of Ygerna's widowhood to cement relations with Ygerna's powerful Welsh relatives, as well as to regain the loyalty of the Cornovians of Dumnonia.

Before he could implement a policy of reconciliation with the Cornovians, Aurelius, of course, had to defeat their rebellious Dux. The Regissimus promptly set out to do just that.

## The Siege of Dimilioc

Aurelius gathered an army and marched on Dumnonia as soon as possible after Gorlois's expression of defiance. The acrimonious conference at Venta Belgarum occurred in the winter of A.D. 473-474, immediately following Aurelius's return to Britannia. We should therefore date the invasion of Cornwall to the spring of A.D. 474.

Geoffrey identifies the commander of the Dumnonian invasion force as "Utherpendragon," so Catavia, Aurelius's Magister Militum, must have led the vanguard of the invading army. The prominence of the Magister Militum in this campaign explains why Geoffrey attributed the conflict to the reign of his fictitious "Utherpendragon" rather than to the reign of Aurelius.

Aurelius does not seem to have fully recovered from the wounds he received in the Battle of Dol. Indeed, he does not seem to have ever fully recovered. Geoffrey tells us that "King Utherpendragon" fell "ill" soon after the Dumnonian campaign and that he even had to be carried in a litter when he went on campaign. "King Utherpendragon" was, of course, Aurelius. Moreover, "the king's illness" must actually relate to a time before the A.D. 474 campaign, because otherwise Aurelius, not his Utherpendragon, would have led the invasion of Dumnonia. The Regissimus probably received a debilitating leg wound at Dol, which was a fairly common injury among horsemen in combat against foot soldiers and which could have made it difficult for him to ride or fight on horseback. The returned Aurelius, like the Grail King of the Romances, was a crippled ruler, often forced to rely upon able assistants to command his armies.

Gorlois, for his part, chose not to meet Aurelius's army in battle. He decided to deploy his forces in fortified positions throughout Dumnonia, hoping that the long and difficult task of besieging the many Cornovian forts and hillforts would deplete the invasion army. Gorlois also sent to "Ireland," probably meaning Demetia, for reinforcements. The Cornovian Dux thus adopted a strategy of attrition against his enemy. Gorlois intended to conserve his strength and muster allies while Aurelius engaged in a costly effort to reduce the Cornovian strongholds one by one.

Gorlois meanwhile sent his wife to the remote citadel of Tintagel for safekeeping. Tintagel was then a small fort of little strategic importance in west Dumnonia (modern Cornwall).[101] Isolated on a rocky peninsula and accessible by a single narrow path, Tintagel could, however, be defended by just a few men. It was, for all practical purposes, impregnable.

---

101 Archaeologists originally interpreted the Fifth Century remains at Tintagel as a Celtic monastery, but recent re-examination of the evidence indicates that it was indeed a fort, as Geoffrey asserts.

Gorlois, in sending Ygerna to Tintagel, was simply taking a sensible precaution to keep his wife out of harm's way.

Gorlois himself was not far away at the fort of Dimilioc, now called Castle Dameliock, near the village of Pendoggett some five and one-half miles southwest of Tintagel. Dimilioc lies close to the port towns of Padstow and Port Isaac, either of which was a likely place for an overseas army from Demetia or Ireland to land. Gorlois abided at Dimilioc awaiting his Irish allies.

Gorlois's plan was sound and might have worked against a lesser opponent. Aurelius was not to be so easily confounded. Gorlois had gravely underestimated the caliber of his enemy. Before his plans could come to fruition, Gorlois found himself trapped and besieged in Dimilioc by the Regissimus's forces.

Aurelius's troops bypassed all the Cornovian strongholds and penetrated deep into Dumnonia in order to attack Gorlois personally. Aurelius's maneuver was bold, but risky. He had obviously sent a strike force of fast-moving cavalry under the command of Catavia directly against Gorlois at Dimilioc, while he himself followed up with his more numerous and slower-moving infantry. The horsemen, in pressing so far into hostile country, were able to catch Gorlois by surprise, but they also ran a serious risk of being cut off and destroyed by Gorlois's soldiers. The objective of Aurelius's offensive was to capture or kill the rebel Dux at the very outset of the campaign, thereby bringing a quick and easy end to a potentially ruinous civil war.

Aurelius had a reasonable chance of achieving this objective because many Cornovian warriors in Dumnonia remained loyal to the Regissimus. They even aided him against their Dux. Catavia could not have surprised Gorlois in the heart of his own domain otherwise. Without the aid of Cornovian loyalists, Catavia would not have even known where to find the rebel leader, let alone make his way there without alerting Gorlois. Indeed, the officers in command of many of the hillforts which were to bar Aurelius's advance must have immediately rallied to the Regissimus's cause. The existence of Cornovian factions loyal to Aurelius made his invasion strategy feasible.[102]

Aurelius's aggressiveness disconcerted Gorlois and upset his plans. Gorlois intended to use Dimilioc as a safe command post from which he could direct the war and gather allies, but the unexpected appearance of Aurelius's horsemen outside Dimilioc cut Gorlois off from the rest of his domain. The fort became Gorlois's prison instead of his campaign headquarters. Lest his rebellion die for lack of leadership, Gorlois had to cut his way out of the fort and join his main forces to the east. In desperation, the Cornovian Dux sallied forth with a small band of warriors to engage his besiegers in combat.

Geoffrey tells us that Gorlois's sortie was prompted by the royal army's ill-advised attempt to attack Dimilioc in the "king's" absence. Geoffrey is, of course, correct in asserting that the Regissimus was absent, but he has misunderstood his sources. Geoffrey has mistakenly concluded that his fictitious "Utherpendragon," not Aurelius, was "the king" and that "Utherpendragon" had abandoned his troops. The Utherpendragon was actually Magister Militum Catavia, and Catavia certainly

remained at his post while Aurelius was elsewhere with the main army. Geoffrey is also wrong in his evaluation of the attack upon Dimilioc. While an assault upon a fortified position is an expensive and inefficient use of cavalry, the success of Aurelius's strategy depended upon Catavia destroying Gorlois quickly. Catavia had to destroy Gorlois before Gorlois's Irish allies and Cornovian supporters could rally to his rescue. As it turned out, the royal army was fortunate and the rebel forces unlucky, for Gorlois was slain early in the fighting.

The most extraordinary incident of the Dumnonian campaign, however, concerns "Utherpendragon's" actions during the absence of "the king" from the Siege of Dimilioc. Geoffrey narrates a series of events which are flat-out unbelievable. An important truth nevertheless lies behind Geoffrey's strange account.

## The Legend of Arthur's Birth

Geoffrey tells us that Uther Pendragon's lust for Ygerna grew unbearable, so he sent to Merlin for advice. The mage had a plan, one that was much more elaborate than a cold shower. Using "drugs," the great magician put the appearance of Gorlois upon Uther, that of Gorlois's servant Britaelis upon himself, and that of Gorlois's aide Jordan upon Uther's soldier Ulfin. In these guises, Uther and his companions fooled the guards at Tintagel and were admitted into the fort. Deceived by Merlin's enchantment and believing Uther to be her husband, Ygerna's took the randy king into her bed. Arthur was conceived that very night.

If nothing else, Geoffrey has preserved for

---

102 The continued loyalty of these Cornovian warriors reinforces the conclusion that Gorlois was wrong to defy Aurelius and that illicit sexual desire was not really the cause of the rebellion.

us the names of three individuals who would have otherwise been lost to history: Ulfin, probably "Ulfinus," and Jordans, alternatively "Jordanus," who were army officers under Aurelius and Gorlois, and Britaelis, a servant of Gorlois. The rest of Geoffrey's account is, of course, quite untrue.

The appearance of Merlin tells us what Geoffrey is up to. The author of the *Historia Regum Britanniae* has employed his *magus ex machina* to reconcile conflicting information in his sources. Geoffrey for some reason felt a strong need to show how "the king" (i.e., Aurelius) came to have an heir from Dumnonia, a fact which somehow seemed difficult to explain.

The evidence is clear that Arthur was a noble Cornovian warrior from Dumnonia. All the early Welsh sources associate Arthur with this region, insisting that Arthur had his home there. The *Vita prima Carantoci* also reports that Arthur served in Dumnonia as a young army officer under "Cadwy" (i.e., Magister Militum Catavia). Geoffrey was aware of these traditions. Lacking any clear account of how Arthur the Cornovian warrior became the chosen successor of "Utherpendragon" (i.e., Aurelius) the Armorican Regissimus, Geoffrey resorted to the wizardry of Merlin.

Geoffrey was no doubt confused by the Roman practice of adult adoption. Roman aristocrats often legally adopted their designated successors, even when the intended heir was already a fully-grown adult. Many Roman Emperors, for example, adopted the men whom they wished to rule after them. Thus, Julius Caesar adopted Augustus, Augustus adopted Tiberius, and Tiberius adopted Caligula. Later, Claudius adopted Nero, Nerva adopted Trajan, Trajan adopted Hadrian, Hadrian adopted Antonius Pius, Antonius Pius adopted Marcus Aurelius, etc. In like manner, Aurelius must have adopted Arthur.

Gildas refers to the existence of living descendants of Aurelius in the mid-Sixth Century, so Aurelius obviously had a son or a son-in-law who was his natural heir. Yet Aurelius was not succeeded by any blood or marital relative, but by Arthur. Aurelius apparently designated Arthur as his choice for Regissimus Britanniarum in preference to his own descendants; he certainly did so by adopting the young adult Arthur. By legally adopting Arthur, Aurelius conferred upon Arthur a strong recognized claim to rule south Britannia and he provided for the orderly transfer of power from himself to the Cornovian warrior.

Arthur thus had two fathers: his natural father, a Cornovian soldier from Dumnonia, and his adoptive father, the Regissimus from Armorica. Geoffrey did not realize that Aurelius had adopted Arthur, so he seized upon the wizardry of Merlin and upon the ambiguous association between Arthur and the title Utherpendragon in order to explain how the Breton "king" could have had a son who was also said to have been the son of a Cornovian warrior.[103]

Aurelius meanwhile married the widow of the slain Dux Gorlois. Aurelius and Ygerna seem to have found personal happiness in the pragmatic political union, for Geoffrey tells us that "King Utherpendragon" and his new wife held "great love for each other" and "lived

---

[103] Geoffrey's solution to the mystery of Arthur's conception might have been inspired by the myth of Heracles and the legend of Alexander the Great: each hero was said to have been fathered by the god Zeus in the guise of his mother's human husband.

together as equals." Aurelius and Ygerna had a daughter whom they named Anna.

Ygerna was certainly Aurelius's second wife. If Aurelius had been about twelve years old at the time of the Battle of Wallop, then he was now close to fifty years of age. A wealthy aristocrat like Aurelius would not have remained unwed until so late in his life. Aurelius must have married earlier when he was in exile in Armorica. Aurelius's descendants to whom Gildas refers sprang from his first marriage.

Aurelius was fortunate enough to enjoy several years of peaceful rule of Britannia with his new wife.

## Chapter Seventeen
## The End of Aurelius's Reign

Once the unhappy, but mercifully short, Cornovian civil war was over, Britannia settled into what, in those troubled times, could pass for peace and security. The biographer of Saint Germanus even describes Britannia around A.D. 480 as prosperous. Britannia's good fortune did not last, however, for serious trouble loomed on the horizon.

Aurelius had broken the military might of the Anglo-Saxons in Britannia, but he did not expel them from the island. The barbarians were too long and too well established on the eastern seaboard of Britannia, and it was simply not possible to evict them from their new homeland. While the Britons prospered, the Angles and Kentishmen were therefore able to replenish their own strength. The barbarians steadily increased their numbers in Britannia, both through their own growing population and by attracting new immigrants from Germania.

The Romano-Briton military position was nevertheless very strong. The Britons held all the key strategic strong-points which blocked the potential avenues of Anglo-Saxon advance. Londinium (London) checked the expansion of Kent; Lindum Colonia (Lincoln) prevented the westward migration of its former laeti in Lindsey; and Camulodunum (Colchester), Durobrivae (Water Newton, near Peterborough), Verulamium (St. Albans) and several small towns scattered across east-central Britannia barred the progress of the Angles of Anglia. These towns were supplemented by the many small hillforts which Aurelius had ordered refurbished and reoccupied in east Britannia. Part-time citizen militia defended these frontier towns and hillforts, while the towns and hillforts themselves served as forward supply bases and campaign headquarters for Aurelius's elite mobile forces from the Romanized west and southwest of the Diocese. The barbarians were secure in their own territories, but their movement out of these territories was effectively blocked.

The Anglo-Saxons were, moreover, handicapped by a lack of unity. Despite what medieval historians thought, the Anglo-Saxons were not a single, unified nation. Although Anglo-Saxon warbands often collaborated in pursuit of mutual advantage, usually at the expense of the Britons, they did not respond to a single leader and they only poorly coordinated their actions. Each warband was independent and acted solely for its own self-interest. The chief danger to Britannia was that any Anglo-Saxon military success would inspire imitation by other barbarians, unleashing a torrent of greedy and opportunistic raiders upon the hapless Diocese. If, on the other hand, the first wave of any invasion was timely and decisively defeated, the barbarians would be discouraged and a potential explosion of trouble averted. The separate Anglo-Saxon warbands were vulnerable to destruction in detail by a well-led professional Romano-Briton army, such as Aurelius and Catavia commanded.

Some of the Anglo-Saxon inhabitants of Britannia could even be counted upon to fight for the Britons against their fellow barbarians. Adjacent to many Roman towns at this time were small Anglo-Saxon settlements. These settlements were much too small to pose a threat to the nearby town, which suggests that the barbarians were there with the permission of the townspeople. They must have been laeti or foederati in the employ of the town Curia (town council). A group of larger Anglo-Saxon settlements in the upper Thames region, near the Civitas town of Dorciconium (Dorchester-on-Thames), also sheltered loyal Briton allies. The upper Thames Anglo-Saxons fought for the Britons against their own countrymen throughout the Fifth and Sixth Centuries; they worked first for the Imperial authorities at the Dorciconium military supply depot, then for the Ambrosii, and finally for the Curia of nearby Glevum Colonia (Gloucester). Even former enemies could on occasion become Briton allies, such as the Anglo-Saxon mercenary captain Eosa/Osla.

To take full advantage of the strategic situation and to fully exploit the weakness of the barbarians, the Britons had to maintain a strong, mobile and ready army. They also had to ensure that command of this army was entrusted only to loyal, aggressive and capable leaders. Aurelius and his Magistri Militum maintained this army and provided the necessary leadership in the A.D. 460's, A.D. 470's and A.D. 480's. So long as the Britons could field a large national cavalry force under a competent commander, the prospects for the continued survival and prosperity of the former Roman Diocese were favorable.

## Loth of Lodonesia

Although Aurelius's Romano-Briton military establishment was able to protect its own territory in south Britannia, it could not control events in far north Britannia. In the late A.D. 480's, a threat to the peace of Britannia emerged in the far north in the familiar form of Octa.[104]

---

104 Geoffrey continues to pair Eosa with Octa, although

Geoffrey of Monmouth reports that the barbarian leader and his prison guards together escaped from "London" to "Germania." What Geoffrey must mean is that the prisoner somehow managed to bribe or elude his wardens at Luguvalium (Carlisle) and make his way back to his own "German" territory in Bernicia. As we have seen, Geoffrey confuses Luguvalium ("Kaer Luilid" in Welsh) with Londinium ("Kaer Lludd" in Welsh), and he obviously confuses Bernicia with Germania. Octa, once free, resumed his piratical ways and waged war upon Loth of Lodonesia.

"Lodonesia" was the name of the region now known as Lothian in southeast Scotland. Lodonesia was the realm of the north Votadini, whose ruling dynasty had been installed by Emperor Maximus more than a century earlier.

Loth would one day become ruler of Lodonesia, but he did not yet hold this position when Octa made war upon him. In the A.D. 480's, Loth governed Alclud (Dumbarton) and Strathclyde. Loth was the son of Cynnwyd and the grandson of Coroticus, and he succeeded them as King of Strathclyde. When Octa made war upon Loth in the A.D. 480's, he fought against him in Strathclyde.

Octa did not limit his war-making to a single raid against Loth in Alclud; he initiated a major conflict which ranged across all northwest Britannia and on both sides of Hadrian's Wall. Octa rallied the Frisians of Dumfries and the other Germanic barbarians of the far north, as well as his own Anglo-Saxons of Bernicia, and he led them against the Romano-Briton regime of Civitas Carvetiorum based upon Luguvalium (Carlisle), as well as against Loth's realm of Strathclyde. Octa no doubt wished to punish

by this time Eosa, as "Osla," was certainly in Briton service.

Civitas Carvetiorum in revenge for its having held him prisoner in Luguvalium, and he apparently nursed territorial ambitions which could only be satisfied at Strathclyde's expense. Civitas Carvetiorum and Strathclyde were also allies by virtue of their mutual friendship with Aurelius's regime in south Britannia, a fact reflected in some manuscripts of the *Historia Regum Britanniae* which claim that Loth was "Earl of Carlisle." In order to retaliate against his former captors and expand the boundaries of his far northern realm, Octa therefore plunged the entire northwest of Britannia into war by leading the Anglo-Saxons beyond Hadrian's Wall against the two Romano-Briton realms of Civitas Carvetiorum and Strathclyde.

The fortunes of the northern war were fickle, favoring first one side, then the other, and then back again. Geoffrey tells us that Loth was sometimes defeated and forced to retire behind his fortifications, but that on other occasions he was able to repulse the Anglo-Saxon raiders. Overall, the Strathclyde and Carvetian warriors had the worst of the fighting, for they were always on the defensive and reacting to the barbarians. Loth and his Carvetian neighbors had nothing to gain, but much to lose, each time they took the field.

The barbarians must have been supported by the Dux Britanniarum in their war against Loth and Civitas Carvetiorum, because Geoffrey tells us that the Britons, in their arrogance, refused to cooperate against the Anglo-Saxons. Geoffrey's statement could refer to the difficulty of coordinating the common defense between Alclud and Luguvalium, but it more likely refers to the outright hostility of the Ducal regime to the neighboring Romano-Briton realms. Even if the Dux did not actively assist the barbarians in the fighting, he at least aided them by refusing to attack their lands when their warriors were away ravaging Strathclyde or assailing Civitas Carvetiorum. The reigning Dux Britanniarum no doubt supported Octa in the hope that Octa would destroy his rival Romano-Briton regimes in the north.

Despite their misfortunes, Aurelius did not forsake his northern allies. Geoffrey claims that "Utherpendragon" gave Loth command of the "British army," which, stripped of hyperbole, means that Aurelius sent military assistance to the embattled Strathclyder. Aurelius even reaffirmed his alliance with Strathclyde by giving his young daughter Anna to Loth in marriage.

Anna Ambrosia was probably fourteen years old on her wedding day. Although we may think a girl of this tender age much too young to wed, political marriages were often arranged in ancient and medieval times as soon as a girl reached sexual maturity. People also seem to have reached adulthood quicker in those days; under medieval Welsh law, for example, a girl was deemed to come of age when she was only twelve years old. The marriage of Anna Ambrosia and Loth of Strathclyde should therefore be dated to about A.D. 489, or approximately fifteen years after Aurelius's Dumnonian campaign against Dux Gorlois.

Aurelius obviously saw some advantage to south Britannia in continuing his alliance with Strathclyde. This advantage was principally military. Aurelius wanted Loth to keep the far northern barbarians fully engaged so they would not be available to join the Dux Britanniarum for another attempted invasion of south Britannia. Immunity from such an invasion was especially important to Aurelius at this time, because he had serious military problems of his own in the south. Aurelius wanted Loth to occupy the energies of the far northern Anglo-Saxons so he could deal with a resurgence of military activity on the part of the Angles of Anglia on Britannia's east coast.

## The Battle of Verulamium

Geoffrey tells us that the Anglo-Saxons who had been allied to Pascent, which is to say the Angles of Anglia (modern Norfolk, Suffolk, Cambridgeshire and north Essex), sent for, and received, reinforcements after their defeat by Aurelius in the Battle on the Icknield Way. Nennius agrees, adding that the barbarians also sent for kings and army commanders. Even the *Vita Merlini* refers to the Angles arriving in Britannia when "Uther Pendragon" was king (i.e., late in Aurelius's reign). Archaeology confirms the written accounts. Excavation reveals that burials in the Angle homeland of Angeln (south Jutland in modern Denmark) virtually ceased before the end of the Fifth Century, coinciding with a sharp increase in the number of burials in Anglia in Britannia. Towards the close of the Fifth Century, all the Angles still in Germania, including commoners, nobility and king, emigrated to the former Roman Diocese. Procopius of Caesarae, a Sixth Century eastern Roman historian, claims that Angeln was depopulated by the emigration, a condition still true in the Eighth Century according to Venerable Bede.

The newcomers were called Icelingas after Icel (or Ickel or Hickel), their king. We know the name of the Angle leader because the Anglo-Saxon epic poem *Beowulf* lists the kings of Angeln down to Icel's father Eomer, but not beyond. This same king-list appears in the

Anglo-Saxon Chronicle and other sources as a genealogy of the Anglo-Saxon royalty of Britannia, but in these sources it continues from Eomer through Icel to the later kings of Anglo-Saxon England. The clear implication is that King Icel did not reign in Angeln, but that he led his people to Britannia instead. We can also find evidence of the settlement of King Icel and his followers in several "Hickel" and "Ickel" place names in east and east-central Britannia. Based upon the literary and archaeological evidence, Icel arrived in Britannia in the late A.D. 460's, and he reigned there until the early A.D. 480's.

The Icelingas migration, in addition to bolstering the Angle population of Britannia, brought the prestige and authority of an ancient and honored royal dynasty to the Diocese. King Icel's lineage was especially distinguished because Icel's ancestors included Offa, a legendary late Fourth Century conquering king of Angeln, and Offa's grandfather Wiglaet or Wihtlaeg, the dynastic founder[105] who defeated and killed the Jutish King Amlethus - more familiarly known today as Shakespeare's "Prince Hamlet." The venerable and august Icelingas dynasty provided an important morale boost to the barbarians in Britannia and served as a focal point for the unity of the Angles in the Diocese. It is no accident that the Anglo-Saxon people and their language are today known as "Anglish" or "English," rather than "Saxonish."

The resurgent Angles, now led by Icel's successors, made war upon Aurelius. They advanced from Anglia in a southwesterly direction, no doubt marching down the ancient Icknield Way into the south-central heartland of Britannia. Geoffrey, because he saw the Anglo-Saxons as a single nation, places Octa and Eosa in command of these barbarians, but this assumption is clearly erroneous. The year was A.D. 490.

Aurelius was seriously ill, but he decided to take the field himself. Geoffrey tells us that Aurelius, as "Utherpendragon," was not well enough to ride his horse, so his men had to carry him about in a litter. Aurelius did not allow his infirmity to interfere with his conduct of the war, and he directed the campaign from his carriage.[106]

The Regissimus caught up with the raiding Angles in the vicinity of Verulamium, now called St. Albans. The barbarians had somehow gained admittance into the town, but they were careless and Aurelius found the town gates open. Geoffrey suggests that the Angles were too proud to close the gates against a "half-dead" opponent (a reference to Aurelius's poor health). In fact, the barbarian's lack of military discipline probably caused them to neglect the town's security. Alternatively, a patriotic citizen within the town might have courageously thrown the gates open to the advancing Briton army. In any event, Aurelius was able to enter Verulamium without having to overcome its defenses. Aurelius's troops rushed into the town and engaged the raiders within its walls. The Angles managed to repulse the Britons, but only after much heavy fighting.

The Angles regained control of Verulamium, but they did not establish a tenable position. The barbarians could not hold out very long besieged in a hostile Briton town, and they knew it. Loyal townsmen would have

---

105 Wiglaet must have been the founder of the Angle dynasty because he is the first king listed in the Angle royal genealogy after the god Woden.

106 About half a century after Geoffrey wrote, a gravely ill King Henry II similarly insisted on going on campaign, thereby hastening his own death.

undermined the Angles' efforts to mount a defense and would have eventually betrayed the town to their Regissimus. The Angles therefore resolved to bring Aurelius to battle at the earliest opportunity. At first light the very next day, the Angles sallied forth against the Britons in a bold effort to break out into open country.

The barbarian attack did not catch the wily old campaigner Aurelius by surprise. As soon as the Angles emerged from the town, the Briton army attacked them and forced them onto the defensive. The Angle army put up a stout resistance, but was defeated.

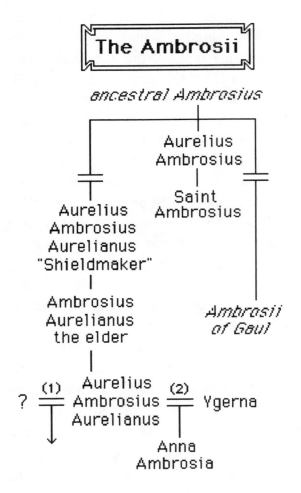

Geoffrey avers that Octa and Eosa were killed in the battle. The barbarian leaders were not even at the battle, let alone slain there. As we shall see, Eosa was indeed slain that year, but in another battle many miles away, while Octa had already died in combat some two years earlier.

After his victory over the Angles, Geoffrey tells us that "Utherpendragon" (i.e., Aurelius) resolved to march north to the relief of his son-in-law Loth. Aurelius, who was ill and who must have been in his mid-60's, was only buoyed up by the exhilaration of his triumph. He was not really capable of carrying out his intentions. Old injuries and the strain of the campaign had taken too great a toll on the Regissimus, and Aurelius died at Verulamium.

Geoffrey attributes Aurelius's death to the poisoning by Anglo-Saxon spies of the well from which he drew water. Other soldiers using the same well also died, he claims. Aurelius might have indeed taken a drink from a tainted pool, one which made other wounded Briton soldiers ill. Given the imperfect sanitary measures of the time,[107] however, we have no reason to believe that Aurelius was deliberately poisoned. An old battle wound, combined with the rigors of the campaign, should bear the greater share of responsibility for the death of Aurelius Ambrosius Aurelianus, Regissimus Britanniarum.

The government of Britannia now passed to Arthur.

---

107 Although the Romans were very sophisticated in such matters, the public facilities of Verulamium and other Briton towns had seriously deteriorated by Aurelius's day.

# LIBER QUARTUS

# The Age of Arthur

### - - The Rise of Arthur - -

**A.D. 475 - A.D. 504**

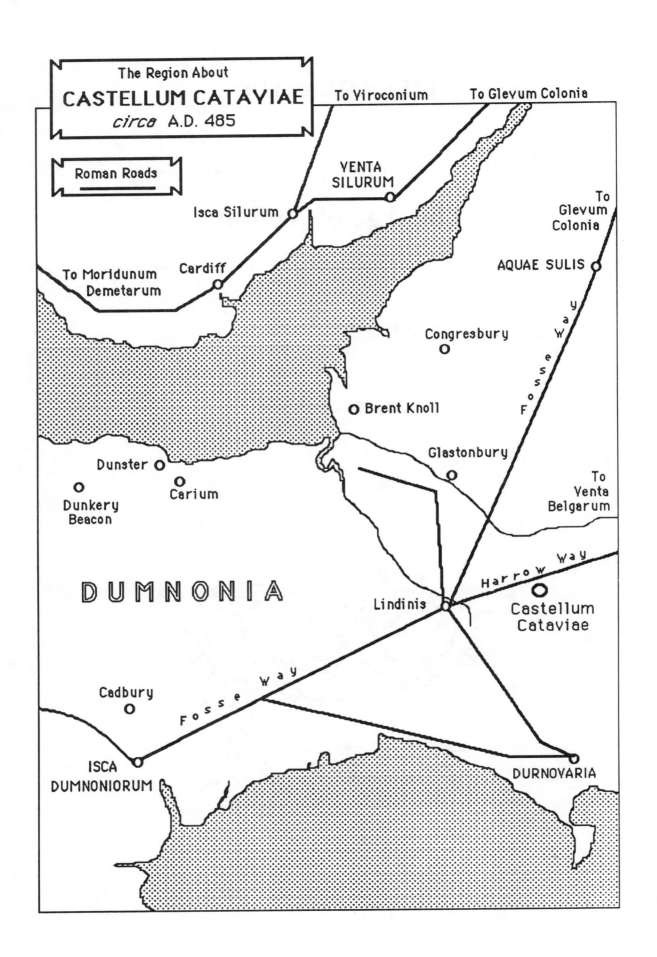

The Region About
**CASTELLUM CATAVIAE**
*circa* A.D. 485

Roman Roads

To Viroconium
To Glevum Colonia

YENTA SILURUM

Isca Silurum

To Glevum Colonia

AQUAE SULIS

Cardiff

To Moridunum Demetarum

Congresbury

Brent Knoll

Glastonbury

Fosse Way

Dunster

Carium

To Venta Belgarum

Dunkery Beacon

DUMNONIA

Harrow Way

Lindinis

Castellum Cataviae

Cadbury

Fosse Way

ISCA DUMNONIORUM

DURNOVARIA

## Chapter Eighteen
## Arthur's Background

In "Arthur," unlike "Vortigern," "Vortimer," "Rigotamos" and "Utherpendragon," we have a genuine personal name rather than merely a title. "Arthur" is a Celtic form of the Roman family name Artorius.

### Lucius Artorius Castus

The Artorii family had a long and distinguished history in Britannia. The family first appeared in the Diocese around A.D. 180, when a certain Lucius Artorius Castus served as Praefectus Castrorum (Prefect of Camps) of Legion VI Victrix, based at Eboracum (York).

The Praefectus Castrorum was a high-ranking officer in a Roman Legion. He was superior to the Centurians (who were equivalent to senior sergeants in modern armies), but junior to the Legion's overall commander, the Legatus. Artorius Castus was a member of the prestigious Equestrian Order, and, as such, he was eligible for promotion to high rank within the Imperial army. He could not, however, have realistically aspired to full command of a legion. That senior post was reserved for members of the even more prestigious Senatorial Class. The distinction between Equestrian and Senatorial status was based upon both wealth and birth. The Equestrians could be considered "upper-middle class," a high, but still limited, status. The post of Praefectus Castrorum would have normally been the highest military office to which an Equestrian's ambition could lead him. Artorius Castus had, in effect, reached the top of his profession.

Artorius Castus was one of the many dedicated servants of the Empire who labored so long and so hard over the centuries to build and preserve the glory of Rome. In almost all cases, the names of these steadfast Romans are lost and forgotten today. Artorius Castus was saved from historical obscurity only by a peculiar circumstance which allowed him to rise to the level of his ability, rather than to merely that of his birth.

In A.D. 184, Artorius Castus was ordered to lead two legions from Britannia to Armorica to suppress one of the many revolts which the unruly Armoricans were wont to initiate from time to time against Imperial authority. It was very unusual for an Equestrian to hold such an important command or to play such a prominent role in Imperial military affairs. At the time, however, Emperor Commodus was attempting to undermine the political influence of the Senate by appointing Equestrians to high administrative and military positions. Because Imperial policy then happened to favor the advancement of the Equestrian Order, Artorius's ability was given due recognition and Artorius was saved from historical oblivion.

Artorius Castus was also associated with the cavalry forces stationed in Britannia. Before being posted to Britannia, he served in Pannonia (roughly modern Hungary) under Emperor Marcus Aurelius, father of Commodus. During the course of the Pannonian campaign, Marcus Aurelius defeated the barbarian Sarmatian tribe in A.D. 175. The Sarmatians were unique for their time in that their military forces consisted of heavily armored cavalry rather than foot soldiers or light-armed horsemen. Soon after defeating the Sarmatians, Marcus Aurelius dispatched several thousand captive Sarmatian warriors to Britannia, where they were attached as auxiliaries to Legion VI Victrix. The barbarians were stationed at Bremetennacum, now Ribchester in Lancashire. Artorius Castus accompanied the Sarmatian cavalrymen to Britannia as their first Roman commander.

The Sarmatian horsemen were a significant addition to the Roman military forces. They established for the first time a heavy cavalry tradition within the Imperial army. The foot soldiers of the Legions continued to be the premier arm of combat for another two centuries, but mounted forces became increasingly important in the later days of the Empire - setting the stage for the predominance of horseborne knights in the warfare of the Middle Ages. In addition to bringing heavy cavalry into the Imperial army for the first time, the Sarmatians also introduced the Romans to many new military fashions.

The most important military fashion introduced by the Sarmatians was the use of the dragon as a martial emblem. Carried as a windsock pennant fixed atop a pole, the dragon caught the wind and wriggled in the air when the Sarmatian horsemen moved forward. When the Sarmatians charged, the writhing dragon seemed alive. It must have been a thrilling sight. The red dragon soon became the symbol of the Roman cavalry, the horse soldier's equivalent of the golden eagle borne by the infantry Legions. It remained in use in Britannia through the post-Roman period, and Geoffrey of Monmouth reports that Arthur himself bore dragon devices into battle. The Sarmatian/Roman red cavalry dragon still flies today on the Welsh national flag.

The Sarmatians also used the symbol of a sword thrust into the ground or into a wooden platform. The thrust-sword symbol was very ancient. Herodotus, the Fifth Century B.C.

Greek historian, describes its use by the Scythians of his day, who were the ancestors of the Sarmatians. This symbol represented military leadership and was originally the icon of the Sarmatian war god. Arthur was, as we shall see, a cavalry commander, and, as such, he was probably associated with the Sarmatian sword emblem. This symbol may lie behind the legend of Arthur's "Sword in the Stone."

We may think it improbable that Artorius Castus of Second Century Britannia could have any connection to his namesake Arthur some three hundred years later, but time and change moved much more slowly in the ancient past. In those days, custom dictated that a son should follow the same profession as his father, and this custom was particularly strong during the long stability of the Roman Empire. Moreover, family traditions ran very deep among the Romans, especially among the minor Equestrian aristocracy and Imperial army soldiers; as in all times, the upper middle class and the army tended to be among the more conservative elements in society. These traditions even became a matter a law by the time of Emperor Constantine the Great, when it was decreed that the sons of soldiers should enlist in the army; special emphasis was placed upon the sons of horse soldiers joining the cavalry. It is not only possible, but indeed virtually certain, that for generation after generation the Artorii remained in Britannia, serving in the army and maintaining strong ties to the Sarmatian cavalry forces stationed at Bremetennacum.

We can also find evidence in the Romances supporting Arthur's presumed connection to the Romano-Briton Artorii family. In the medieval Romances, Arthur's foster father, who raised the boy while his real father Utherpendragon ruled

Britannia, is named Ector. The original Ector was, of course, Arthur's natural father, and "Utherpendragon," or Aurelius, was merely his adoptive parent. "Ector" would be "Ectorius" in Latin, which, like "Arthur," seems a corruption of the Roman family name Artorius. Some of the early Romances even give the name of Arthur's foster father as "Antor" or "Auctor," which more closely resemble "Artorius." The Romances thus indicate that Arthur's natural father, like Arthur himself, bore the Roman personal name Artorius, which suggests the Roman custom of referring to the head of a family in each generation by his *nomen* or family name.

The *praenomen* or individual name of the Second Century Artorius, "Lucius," is also associated with Arthur in several different contexts. As we shall see, Arthur in his youth and Arthur's son were both called Lucius. Roman families tended to have favorite *praenomina*, which they repeated in each generation. The appearance of the individual name Lucius in connection with Arthur further suggests a relationship between Arthur and Artorius Castus.

Arthur of the Fifth Century was without a doubt the descendant of Lucius Artorius Castus of the Second Century, and Arthur's full Roman name was certainly also Lucius Artorius Castus.

## Artorius's Sarmatian Cavalry

When Emperor Constantine III crossed to Gaul with most of the Roman field army of Britannia in A.D. 407, the Bremetennacum cavalry remained behind. The cavalrymen had become thoroughly Roman by then, although their military unit still bore the designation of Sarmatian.[108] Declining economic conditions

made it impossible to maintain the heavy cavalry in its former style, and the horsemen served in less expensive, lighter armor made of leather rather than metal. This armor was also confined to the soldiers themselves, rather than being draped as well over their horses as in the past. Even so, the fast-moving and hard-hitting mounted warriors must have been greatly feared by the foot-slogging Anglo-Saxon and Irish marauders assailing Britannia in the Fifth Century. In mobile warfare against barbarian raiders, the Romano-Briton horse soldiers descended from Marcus Aurelius's Sarmatians were highly effective, and the Britons were no doubt glad to have them.

The Sarmatian cavalry probably came under the nominal command of the Dux Britanniarum in A.D. 407, but the Dux was unable to exercise any real authority over the horsemen. The cavalry base at Bremetennacum and the Dux's headquarters at Eboracum (York) were separated by the Pennine Mountains. The Pennine Mountains were more than just a physical barrier; they were a strategic division between north Britannia and west Britannia and their very different military situations. East of the Pennines, the Dux's forces at Eboracum and on Hadrian's Wall were principally concerned with the possibility of invasion by Pictish armies from the far north, but west of the Pennines, the Bremetennacum cavalrymen were more worried about the danger of attack by Irish raiders from the west. In fact, when Magister Militum

---

108  The theory, favored by some historians, that the Sarmatians somehow remained a separate and distinct nation within the Empire is implausible. It is also inconsistent with the experience of other barbarian units recruited by the Roman army in the early Imperial period, before large numbers of barbarian immigrants overwhelmed the Latin population.

Stilicho withdrew Legion XX Valeria Victrix from Britannia in A.D. 402, he probably also redeployed the horse soldiers to a new station to the southeast, perhaps even to the Legion's former base at Castrum Deva (Chester), where they could better fill the security vacuum created by the departure of the Legion - and where they would be further removed from Ducal influence. The Bremetennacum warriors therefore drifted away from the Dux and into the orbit of another legal authority in west Britannia which faced the same Irish threat. Just as the Dux lost control over the western garrisons of Hadrian's Wall, which fell under the domination of the wealthy former provincial capital of Luguvalium (Carlisle), so too did he lose control over the Sarmatian cavalry, which fell under the domination of Vortigern's town of Viroconium Cornoviorum (Wroxeter).

As chief town of Civitas Cornoviorum, Viroconium had a legal basis for taking command of the Sarmatian cavalry under the Rescript of Honorius. More importantly, Viroconium was wealthy enough to support the horsemen and willing enough to do so. The Curia (town council) of Viroconium certainly appreciated the tactical value of heavy cavalry against the Irish foot soldiers afflicting west Britannia, and it might have been amassing military power in anticipation of the wider political ambitions ultimately realized by Vortigern. These same legal, economic and military considerations made a Cornovian alliance attractive to the Sarmatian horse warriors. The Sarmatian cavalry unit therefore transferred its allegiance and service to the rising political star of Viroconium and Civitas Cornoviorum soon after the collapse of Imperial government in the early Fifth Century.

Castrum Deva was actually the chief town of the Civitas wherein the Sarmatian troopers resided, which gave its Curia a greater legal claim to their loyalty, but the former legionary base was in no condition to assume command of the cavalry unit. The town had severely declined after Magister Militum Stilicho withdrew Legion XX Valeria Victrix from Britannia in A.D. 402, and it was in sad shape. It could not even properly maintain its own urban amenities, let alone take responsibility for supporting a heavy cavalry force. In fact, Castrum Deva itself no doubt fell under the political domination of Viroconium and Civitas Cornoviorum.

Allied to Civitas Cornoviorum, the Sarmatian cavalry fought in the reconquest of the Pagus Cornoviorum (north Powys and Clwyd) and in Vortigern's war against the Picts. Formal command of the unit might have been officially transferred to the Superbus Tyrannus during the Pictish War under the terms of Vortigern's alliance with Dux Coelestius - if a formal grant of authority was then even thought necessary. After the Irish in north Wales were put on the defensive by the arrival of the aggressive Votadini from Bernicia, Sarmatian horsemen were among the Cornovian soldiers dispatched to liberate Dumnonia from the Irish of southwest Britannia.

If our conclusions about the family of Lucius Artorius Castus are correct, then his early Fifth Century descendant, in accordance with family tradition, should have been serving as an officer of the Sarmatian cavalry when it relocated to southwest Britannia. We could then surmise that Arthur, the late Fifth Century Artorius, was born and raised in Cornovian Dumnonia.

And so he was.

The evidence connecting Arthur to Cornovian Dumnonia is overwhelming. Geoffrey, of course, associates Arthur's origin with Dumnonia, or more specifically "Cornwall," where "King Utherpendragon" kept his illicit tryst with Ygerna, wife of the Cornovian Dux Gorlois. Various Saints' Lives also place Arthur in the region, and, in A.D. 1113, more than two decades before Geoffrey wrote the *Historia Regum Britanniae*, the medieval traveller Hermann of Tournai reports being told in Devon and Cornwall that he was in "Arthur's country." To this day, local folklore and place names in Devon and Cornwall argue strongly for an Arthurian connection.

Welsh tradition is even more insistent on Arthur's Cornish origin. The Welsh tales and Triads claim that Arthur came from the fort of Kelliwic in Cornwall. Kelliwic is a pre-Roman hillfort now called Castle Killibury; it is located east of Wadebridge near modern Padstow and about ten miles roughly southwest of Tintagel. It is a defensive position likely to have been reoccupied by the Cornovian liberators of Dumnonia. Although the Welsh would have preferred to claim Arthur as one of their own, they nevertheless admit that his home was in Cornwall, where we would expect to find a Fifth Century Artorii in service with the Sarmatian cavalry.

Arthur was thus an Artorii, a member of an old Roman military family long established in Britannia with a strong tradition of service in the cavalry. The Artorii survived the collapse of Imperial authority in the Diocese, and they maintained their family tradition. When the Sarmatian cavalry came within the orbit of the powerful Civitas Cornoviorum based upon the nearby town of Viroconium, the Artorii offered their allegiance to the Civitas and served in its military campaigns. When Vortigern dispatched Cornovian troops to Dumnonia in order to expel the Irish colonists who had settled there, the Sarmatian cavalry and the Artorii went along. Arthur was then born in the military fort of Kelliwic in west Dumnonia. In the course of time, the young Arthur, following family tradition, became a cavalry officer and began his military career in service to Britannia in Dumnonia.

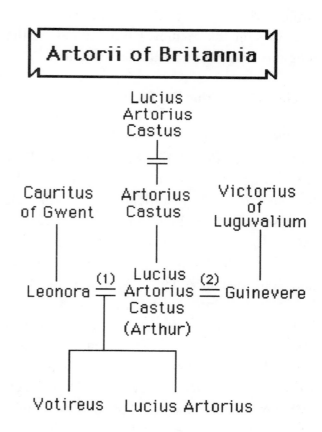

## Chapter Nineteen
## Arthur's Early Military Career

Geoffrey of Monmouth tells us that Arthur became ruler of Britannia at the youthful age of fifteen. In fact, the Britons would have never entrusted their fate to someone so young and inexperienced. Arthur might have been fifteen when he first took up his sword and joined his father's cavalry unit, but he was at least twice that age when he received the government of Britannia from Aurelius.

How, then, did Arthur occupy the early years of his military career? By what path did he rise to the highest political office in Britannia? We can find the answers to these questions in the medieval biographies of the religious leaders of post-Roman Britannia.

### Lucius, Procurator Rei Publicae

These medieval biographies are called Saints' Lives (*Vitae Sanctorum* in Latin). They were written in the Middle Ages by monks who had no interest in historical fact. Their sole purpose was to extol the sanctity of the various saints. Each century, the monks recopied earlier versions of the Saints' Lives, making changes and additions in order to reinforce the holy image of the saints. For the most part, the result is heavy-handed, slow-reading and extremely dull. Nevertheless, the medieval monks off-handedly preserved many important facts about Britannia's post-Roman period. These facts were not crucial to the moral point of the Saints' Lives, so they were repeated each time the Lives were recopied without serious thought or consideration. They are survivals from the original stories, ultimately based upon first-hand or near-contemporary knowledge. If we ignore the main theme of the Saints' Lives, and focus instead on the incidental details, we can learn a great deal about the life and times of Arthur.

The Saints' Lives, consistent with Welsh tradition, place Arthur in Cornovian Dumnonia. They locate him specifically in the Glastonbury region of modern Somerset, which was then northeast Dumnonia. More importantly, the Saints' Lives give us valuable clues to the young Arthur's activities.

In the Saints' Lives, unlike the early chronicles and the Romances, Arthur's authority is obscure and limited, and never unquestioned. The Saints' Lives usually describe Arthur as only a warband leader or a local ruler, but even when they acknowledge him as "king" of Britannia, his authority seems circumscribed or uncertain. They point to a time when Arthur had not yet achieved full dominion over Britannia. The Saints' Lives depict Arthur as a leader of some importance, but one whose power is restricted or parochial - as it would have been when Arthur was merely a cavalry officer in Aurelius's army. The Arthur in the Saint's Lives is Arthur in his early military career.

Surprisingly, Arthur does not come across very favorably in the Saints' Lives. He is presented as a greedy and grasping warlord, a vindictive tyrant who frequently attempted to ride roughshod over the devoted servants of the Church.

The Eleventh Century *Vita Cadoci* (Life of Cadoc) shows Arthur in a particularly bad light. According to the *Vita Cadoci*, Arthur disputed the right of Saint Cadoc to grant sanctuary to a fugitive in the Saint's monastery at Llancarfan in Glevissig (Glamorgan). The fugitive was a "great general" named Ligessauc Longhand, son of Eliman, who had killed three of Arthur's soldiers. Arthur demanded that Cadoc compensate him with 100 cows before he would recognize the Saint's right to grant sanctuary. To make Cadoc's task difficult, Arthur insisted that each cow be half red and half white. With divine assistance, Cadoc managed to assemble the necessary cattle. He sent the herd across the River Usk towards the waiting Arthur. God then punished Arthur and vindicated Saint Cadoc by turning the tribute cows into bundles of fern as soon as they crossed the river. Arthur is thus portrayed as malicious, arrogant and greedy.

Saint Cadoc, from what we know of him from other sources, could not have been the abbot of a monastery before the middle of the Sixth Century, which is after Arthur's time. Elsewhere in the *Vita Cadoci*, Arthur is said to have encountered Cadoc's parents before Cadoc's birth - an encounter which did in fact occur. When Cadoc reached adulthood, however, Arthur was already dead. The selection of Arthur as the villain of the *Vita Cadoci* was thus a later invention inspired by Arthur's association with Cadoc's parents. The hagiographer wished to show that God favored His saint over grasping secular leaders, and, interestingly, Arthur was regarded as the archetype of a spiteful and avaricious despot.

Arthur comes off just as badly in the *Vita prima Carantoci*, a Twelfth Century biography of Saint Carannog. According to the *Vita prima Carantoci*, Saint Carannog one day decided to let God choose the next place where he should preach. To this end, he cast a portable altar into the Severn River. The altar floated across the Bristol Channel ("Sabrina Aestuarium" to the Romans) and washed up near Dindraethou, now Dunster, on the north coast of modern Somerset. At the time, Arthur governed in the region as the subordinate of Cadwy, whom we have identified as Catavia, Aurelius's Magister Militum. Arthur found Saint Carannog's altar while unsuccessfully hunting a giant snake which was harassing the people of nearby Carrum (Carhampton). Arthur seized the altar, intending to use it as a dinner table. Only after Saint Carannog banished the great serpent that Arthur was unable to defeat, did Arthur reluctantly return the altar to its owner.

Arthur might have actually encountered Saint Carannog. Saint Carannog was a grandson of Cunedda, the Votadini leader who relocated to north Wales in the early Fifth Century. Carannog therefore thrived in the latter part of the Century, which corresponds to Arthur's early military career. Local traditions also reinforce the belief that Arthur was active in the north Somerset area; he is particularly associated with Brent Knoll, which lies just up the coast from Dunster and Carrum. The location of Arthur in the Dunster region, the identification of Arthur as the subaltern of Cadwy, and even Arthur's rapacious nature, are no doubt genuine elements preserved from the original biography of Saint Carannog.[109]

Another tale of Arthur's greed is preserved in the Twelfth Century *Vita Paterni* (Life of Padern). Arthur is described as "a certain tyrant" from "foreign parts" who came to Saint Padern's monastery near Aberystwyth on the west coast of Wales in Ceredigion. Ceredigion

---

[109] Arthur did not, of course, really hunt a giant snake. Fantastic beasts were often used in medieval stories to symbolize bandits and pirates, so Arthur must have been in pursuit of Irish raiders operating in the Bristol Channel.

was later known as Cardiganshire and is now the northern part of Dyfed. Arthur burst into the Saint's cell and demanded that Padern turn over a fine tunic given him by the Patriarch of Jerusalem.[110] At Padern's command, the earth swallowed Arthur up to his neck, releasing him only when he apologized and begged the holy man's forgiveness. Once again, Arthur's avarice was frustrated by God's intervention on behalf of one of His saints.

The only saint who seems kindly disposed towards Arthur is Saint Illtud. The *Vita Iltuti* (Life of Illtud) identifies Illtud as a cousin of Arthur who came to Britannia from Armorica. According to the *Vita Iltuti*, Illtud was attracted to Britannia by the "magnificence" of Arthur, and he joined Arthur's army. Illtud served Arthur as a soldier for several years before he turned to the religious life.

The overall picture of Arthur preserved in the Saints' Lives is thus quite different from that of the highly respected and capable ruler we find in the early chronicles and the Romances. Yet the Saints' Lives, no less than these other sources, are ultimately based upon a living memory of the real Arthur. We must somehow reconcile these conflicting appraisals of Arthur's character.

The answer to the contradiction in the sources lies in the fact that the original monkish scribes encountered Arthur at an early stage in his military career. Arthur's purported avarice in the Saints' Lives reflects a genuine, but biased, account of clashes which the religious establishments and monasteries of post-Roman Britannia had with Arthur when Arthur was a junior military officer assigned to requisition materials and supplies for Aurelius's army.

As a young cavalry officer from a distinguished and noble family, Arthur was the perfect subaltern to whom Aurelius and Catavia could entrust the important, but distasteful, job of obtaining provisions. Arthur was certainly capable of performing this vital mission, as his later career amply demonstrates; his military superiors would have perceived this fact early on. Arthur was also junior enough in rank at the time that he did not have other duties to occupy his attention - or the authority to delegate the disagreeable task to another.

In the performance of his duties, Arthur must have devoted a great deal of time and effort to the collection of tribute from the primitive monasteries then established in various parts of Britannia. These monasteries were not the rigidly organized institutions which we usually associate with the Middle Ages; those institutions were established later under the Rule of Saint Benedict, who was born about the same time that Arthur was requisitioning supplies for Aurelius.[111] The early Briton monasteries were simple communities of devout men and women governed by loose, and sometimes eccentric, rules. Like their medieval counterparts, however, they were characterized by hard work, sexual abstinence and a repudiation of luxury. The simple lifestyle of

---

110  Venerable Bede, in his *Historia Abbatum* (History of the Abbots), reports that silk cloaks from Mediterranean lands were so valuable in his day that Abbot Benedict Biscop was able to trade two of them for three hides of land. Three hides was enough land to feed and support three families. Padern's imported tunic was thus a prized and expensive item.

111  Saint Benedict was a Roman nobleman who withdrew from secular life shortly after A.D. 500, when he was about twenty years old. Around A.D. 530, Saint Benedict founded the important monastery at Monte Cassino, which became the model for the monasteries of the Middle Ages. Monasteries electing to follow the rules established by Saint Benedict at Monte Cassino constituted the Benedictine Order.

the monasteries made them a special target of post-Roman tax assessors, including the young Arthur. A community of unmarried, celibate and able-bodied men and women was capable of producing an abundance of food and goods in excess of its own needs, and the post-Roman civil authorities sought to use this excess to sustain the army in its struggle against the barbarians.

The monks, on the other hand, considered their excess production to be dedicated to God's work - and, indeed, in most cases it was. The monks used their surplus to support many uneconomic activities, such as the copying and preservation of ancient books, the conduct of agricultural and animal breeding experiments and the performance of a multitude of charitable activities. In this way, the monasteries made very substantial contributions to the advancement of knowledge and the improvement of the human condition; they kept well their commitment to serve God. The civil authorities nevertheless saw the maintenance of the army in troubled times as a more immediate and critical need to which the monastic surplus should be devoted. Conflict between monastic and secular officials was inevitable.

Since Emperor Constantine the Great's day, the Church had been exempt from taxation in the Roman Empire, so the monks considered any suggestion that they "render unto Caesar" to be unprecedented as well as sacrilegious. They were, however, powerless to resist the demands of the military establishment. The monks' anger and frustration therefore found expression in unflattering portrayals of secular tax officials in the Saints' Lives. Arthur was not spared this indignity. Having ably discharged the unpleasant task of obtaining provisions for Aurelius's military forces, and consequently having endured many bitter confrontations with abbots who resisted the payment of monastic dues, Arthur paid for his devotion to duty with all the infamy which monkish pens could heap upon his name.

The reputation of the great Frankish general Charles Martel similarly suffered in the monastic writings. In A.D. 732, Charles Martel led the Christian armies of early medieval France to victory over Moslem invaders from Spain. The Moslems were only narrowly prevented by Charles's victory from overrunning all of western Europe. The monks were nevertheless scandalized that the Frankish leader dared to requisition Church property to finance his war. They were mollified not in the least by the holy purpose to which he put their contributions. The parallel treatment of Charles Martel and Arthur in monastic tradition confirms that the mere act of tax-collection, and not necessarily any genuine character flaw, was enough to arouse monkish ire and lead to accusations of arrogance and greed.

In some fairness to the hagiographers, we should note that the monks were not the only ones to depict Arthur as overly acquisitive. The Welsh Triads refer to Arthur and three comrades (Bedwyr, Cai and Marchell) trying (albeit unsuccessfully) to make off with a herd of pigs belonging to someone else. The story of Arthur's attempted porcine theft is fictitious, but it does reflect a genuine period in Arthur's early career when he sometimes undertook expedient measures in order to bring home the army's bacon.

Arthur's early tax collection activities also found their way into the *Historia Regum Britanniae*.

Geoffrey of Monmouth at one point in his

narrative refers to a Roman opponent of Arthur as "Lucius, Procurator Rei Publicae." The title used by this Lucius is significant. "Procurator" was the title of a Roman civil official responsible for financial matters, principally tax collection. It comes from the Latin verb *procurare*, meaning "to take care of, to attend to," from which we derive our verb "procure." The title Procurator remained in use at least through the Seventh Century; it appears on an inscription dated to about A.D. 508 and found in modern Morocco, which had been part of the Roman Diocese of Africa, and it appears in an early Seventh Century Welsh charter as the title of an official who levied dues and services from an estate. The Latin term *Res Publica* (*Rei Publicae* being the genitive form) is the direct ancestor of our modern word "republic," but it had a very different meaning to the Romans. *Res Publica* in the original Latin simply referred to public institutions in general and did not imply any particular form of government; the Empire could, and often did, refer to itself as *Res Publica*. A more accurate translation of *Res Publica* would be "Commonwealth." The Lucius who appears in the *Historia Regum Britanniae* thus held the peculiar office of "Tax Collector for the Commonwealth."

"Procurator Rei Publicae" was an appropriate title for a post-Roman Briton tax official. In post-Roman Britannia, taxes still had to be collected in order to feed and support Aurelius's cavalry forces. These taxes were collected in goods and produce rather than in coin, but they were taxes nonetheless. The official who collected these taxes performed the function of a Procurator. "Res Publica" was meanwhile a suitably vague description of Aurelius's government, which was neither in the Empire nor rejecting it. A military officer assigned to requisition supplies for Aurelius's Romano-Briton army could have been correctly called Procurator Rei Publicae.

Geoffrey's Procurator Rei Publicae was certainly Arthur. We have seen that the young Arthur was Aurelius's supply requisition officer, which made him, in Roman terms, Aurelius's Procurator. We have also seen that Arthur's full Roman name was probably Lucius Artorius Castus. Arthur would have been called Lucius in his youth, while his father still lived; he would not have been called by his family name of Artorius until later in his career, after he became the senior surviving male, and thus the head, of the Artorii family. Arthur, as a young military supply officer with the individual name of Lucius, was referred to as "Lucius, Tax Collector for the Commonwealth," or, in Latin, "Lucius, Procurator Rei Publicae."

Geoffrey was unfamiliar with the Roman custom whereby Arthur would have originally been known to his contemporaries as Lucius, and only later as Artorius or Arthur. Geoffrey also did not appreciate the significance of the title Procurator, nor did he understand that Arthur could have held a Roman title like Procurator before he became "king" of Britannia. When Geoffrey came across a reference in his sources to a "Lucius, Procurator Rei Publicae," he therefore never considered the possibility that this "Lucius" and his hero Arthur were the same person; he concluded that the "Lucius" with the strange Latin title must have been a rival Roman leader. Geoffrey did not realize that the person appearing in his sources as "Lucius, Procurator Rei Publicae" was Arthur himself, identified by his youthful name and early military title.

Arthur's holding the position of Procurator Rei Publicae, or supply requisition officer for Aurelius's army, marked him as an exceptional officer with a promising future. The post of Procurator Rei Publicae carried important responsibilities which would have been entrusted to only a very capable individual. It also provided excellent "hands-on" training in the political and economic realities of post-Roman Britannia - invaluable experience for any military leader who hoped to someday wield greater civil authority. Certain of Arthur's monkish taxpayers bore a deep resentment toward him because of his impositions upon their religious establishments, but their pique represents anger only at the very notion of the Church having to support the Romano-Briton army and reflects unfairly upon Arthur's character. Arthur's appointment to the position of Procurator resulted in abuse being heaped upon his name by disgruntled taxpayers, but it also made him an up-and-coming leader of Britannia in the eyes of his contemporaries.

Before we can proceed any further in our examination of Arthur's early military career, we must review the military arrangements which Aurelius made for the defense of southwest Britannia. To determine what these military arrangements were, and to understand their importance, we must turn to archaeology.

## Castellum Cataviae, the Hillfort of Cadbury Castle

In the southern part of modern Somerset, near the Dorset border, is a pre-Roman hillfort known as Cadbury Castle. Cadbury Castle lies adjacent to the ancient east-west track later called the Harrow Way, and close to the north-south Roman road now called the Fosse Way.

The hillfort was thus well sited to give ready access to the entire southwest region of Britannia. This region was an economically important part of the Diocese in the post-Roman period; it was also where Aurelius recruited many of his soldiers and warhorses. In the circumstances, we should not be surprised to find that Cadbury Castle was one of the hillforts refurbished in Aurelius's day. Archaeology tells us that Cadbury Castle was reconstructed and reoccupied around A.D. 470 and that it remained in use until about A.D. 550.

Although the hillfort is today called Cadbury *Castle*, it was not the sort of castle which we normally associate with "King Arthur" or the Middle Ages. It was an impressive defensive structure nonetheless. The hillfort consisted of an eighteen acre hilltop plateau surrounded by a sixteen foot thick earthen wall. The earthen wall ran nearly three-quarters of a mile around the 250 foot high summit of the hill. The wall incorporated dressed-stone and unmortared masonry within a wooden beam framework, and was surmounted by wooden breastworks and platforms - and probably by watchtowers as well. Three lines of trenches were dug into the sides of the hill, increasing the natural defensive strength of the hillfort's slope. A sophisticated Roman-style military gatehouse was constructed on the southwest side of the hill to guard the main entrance to the fort. The refurbished hillfort represented a massive commitment of labor and resources, and it was an important military base.

Many other hillforts were rebuilt and reoccupied during the Fifth Century, but very few were reconstructed using the same advanced stone-and-timber method employed at Cadbury Castle. Alclud (Dumbarton), capital of

Strathclyde, and a handful of much smaller sites in modern Scotland utilized similar building methods, but none of these other hillforts were as large or elaborate as Cadbury Castle. Moreover, only Cadbury Castle had a Roman-style gate-house. Cadbury Castle was unique for its period in its sophistication, size and structure.

Cadbury Castle seems to have been designed to shelter about 1,000 soldiers, plus their families and servants. The hillfort's residents would have been mostly cavalrymen and their dependents, but would have also included a considerable number of blacksmiths and other craftsmen, as well as a small company of foot soldiers to serve as lookouts and sentries. If we assume two men to defend every three yards of wall, then the lookouts and sentries at Cadbury Castle numbered about three hundred guardsmen. Three hundred guardsmen would leave room for about six to nine hundred cavalrymen, that being the approximate complement of two or three Romano-Briton cavalry units. If six to nine hundred mounted warriors were normally stationed at Cadbury Castle, plus a permanent detachment of several hundred guards and support personnel, then we have accounted for the apparent size of the Cadbury Castle garrison.

Cadbury Castle was an important army post, but it fulfilled more than just a military purpose. Within the hillfort enclosure was a major building used for civil functions.

The non-military building at Cadbury Castle was a large timber hall now referred to as "Arthur's Palace." The "Palace" measured 63 feet long by 34 feet wide. It was divided by a screen about a third of its length from the east end, which marked off a spacious private chamber for the personal use of the hillfort's commander. The main portion of the "Palace" was obviously intended for meetings and celebrations involving large numbers of people, which are activities not normally conducted in a purely military facility. The existence of a large residence and meeting hall at Cadbury Castle indicates that the refurbished hillfort was an important political, as well as military, headquarters.

Cadbury Castle was even intended at one time to be a leading religious center of Britannia. A trench was dug within the hillfort enclosure for the foundation of a cruciform church of Fifth/Sixth Century design. Some archaeologists have speculated that the planned church might belong to the Tenth Century, when the Anglo-Saxon King Ethelred Unraed made temporary use of the site for a coin mint, but the style of the church is anachronistic for the Tenth Century. The planned church clearly belongs to Arthur's time. It would have been a major shrine in the Diocese, but, mysteriously, it was never completed. The sudden abandonment of the church-building project suggests that the commander of the hillfort lost interest in his headquarters, as if distracted or lured away by other concerns - a possibility which we shall examine later.

For the moment, we need only note that Arthur spent a great deal of his early military career at the Cadbury Castle hillfort. He was initially a soldier in its garrison, but he later became its commander.

We know that Arthur operated out of Cadbury Castle because the hillfort has for many centuries been identified in local folklore as Arthur's headquarters. John Leland, a renowned antiquarian,[112] visited Cadbury Castle

---

112 An antiquarian was a scholar who studied the past by examining ancient sites and artifacts; antiquarianism

in 1532 and discovered that the people of the area associated the hillfort with Arthur. Leland reports that the site was called "Camallate" as well as "Cadbyri," and that the locals insisted "Arthur much resorted to Camallate."

By Leland's time, "Camelot" was well established from the Romances as the name of Arthur's castle. It was not, however, the name of Cadbury Castle in Arthur's day. The name "Camelot" was later grafted onto a location already known as a place to which Arthur "much resorted." In fact, Leland himself may be responsible for first applying the name Camelot to Cadbury Castle, because a later antiquarian, William Stukeley, reports that "Cadbury" was the name strongly preferred by the local residents when he visited the site in 1723. Although the hillfort was sometimes called Camelot in and after the Sixteenth Century, its original name is preserved in its alternative designation of Cadbury.

The key elements in the place name Cadbury are *cad*, which comes from the personal name Catavia or Cadwy, and *bury*, which is the Anglo-Saxon word for "fort." "Cadwy" is, of course, the name which the *Vita prima Carantoci* gives the man who was once Arthur's commanding officer. *Bury* is *castellum* in Latin or *dinas* in Welsh. The hillfort was thus originally called Castellum Cataviae or Dinas Cadwy, both meaning "fort of Catavia." When the Anglo-Saxons later conquered the area, they shortened Catavia's name and substituted their word *bury* for *castellum* or *dinas*. The post-Roman name Castellum Cataviae or Dinas Cadwy was thus anglicized into the modern "Cadbury," and the

ultimately gave rise to the modern discipline of archaeology.

hillfort was never really called Camelot, except in post-medieval writings.

Judging from the size of its garrison, Castellum Cataviae was the base where Aurelius stationed most of his elite cavalry troopers. The 1,000 or so soldiers quartered at the hillfort may seem like a tiny army by today's standards, but it was a major and potent fighting force in late Fifth and early Sixth Century Britannia. It was also a very expensive force to raise and support. The maintenance of six hundred or more full-time professional cavalrymen, plus their mounts, spare remounts, grooms, blacksmiths and other servants, as well as a company of permanent guard soldiers, required a major commitment of resources. The master of Cadbury Castle must have wielded power over, and drew upon the wealth of, more than just Dumnonia and the adjacent west country area. The reconstruction and reoccupation of the Cadbury Castle hillfort could have only been commissioned by Regissimus Aurelius.

The hillfort at Cadbury Castle was, moreover, part of a much larger military organization. The disposition of lesser forts in the region suggests a grand plan for the protection of the whole of southwest Britannia. The cavalry base at Cadbury Castle was the principal fort and command center of an extensive defensive system.

We can find another important fort in Aurelius's defensive system by following a well-known path from Cadbury Castle.

A track, locally referred to as "Arthur's Lane" or "Arthur's Hunting Causeway," runs twelve miles from Cadbury Castle to the hilltop site of Glastonbury Tor, next to the Somerset village of Glastonbury. Glastonbury Tor is the highest peak in a small cluster of hills dominating the low and level countryside of north and central Somerset. In Arthur's day, the surrounding area was marshland and the hill cluster formed a seasonal island. At high tide in the winter and spring most of north Somerset was flooded, and the Tor could be approached dryshod only from the east. Because of its commanding height of 518 feet above sea-level, Glastonbury Tor is clearly visible for twenty miles in all directions.

Glastonbury Tor, like Cadbury Castle, was occupied by a military force in the late Fifth and early Sixth Centuries. The archaeological evidence indicates that metal-working was conducted on the site and that large quantities of meat and imported Mediterranean wine were consumed there. The dwellers on the Tor were thus a company of well-equipped and well-fed aristocratic warriors. Such warriors formed the elite backbone of all post-Roman armies, both Romano-Briton and barbarian. Based upon its geographic location, the Glastonbury Tor garrison was employed by Aurelius.

An unobstructed line-of-sight runs directly from Cadbury Castle to Glastonbury Tor. The forces at the two hillforts could have easily communicated with each other by lighting signal fires at night, a proposition which has been successfully tested in modern times.

The post-Roman Britons were certainly aware of this possibility. The Roman army in Britannia had long used signal fires as a means of rapid long-distance communication. The best-known Roman signal fire network was operated by the watch towers on the modern North Yorkshire coast to alert the mobile army based at Eboracum (York) of seaborne Pictish invaders. Similar networks were in operation elsewhere in Britannia, including one running along Hadrian's Wall and another beside the road linking the military commander at Luguvalium Carvetiorum (Carlisle) with the Dux Britanniarum in Eboracum. The Welsh continued the practice: a mountain range in south Wales is called the Brecon Beacons from their one-time use as sites for signal fires. Because their Roman ancestors and their Welsh descendants both employed signal fires as a means of long-distance communication, the post-Roman Britons no doubt did so as well.

The line of sight, and probable line of signal-communication, from Cadbury Castle to Glastonbury Tor continues unobstructed from Glastonbury Tor to Brent Knoll on the Bristol Channel.

Brent Knoll is another isolated and solitary hill in Somerset, rising some 450 feet above sea-level. It lies just up the coast from Dunster and Carrum, where, according to the *Vita prima Carantoci*, Arthur was militarily active. In pre-Roman times, the Knoll was topped by earthwork defenses similar to those then found at Cadbury Castle, but on a much smaller scale. Brent Knoll has not yet been properly excavated, but artifacts from the late Roman and post-Roman periods have been found there.

Somerset folklore associates Arthur with Brent Knoll. William of Malmesbury preserves in his *De Antiquitate Glastoniensis Ecclesiae* (Concerning the Antiquity of the Glastonbury Community) a local belief that Arthur at one time sent a warrior named Ider ("Yder" in the Romances and "Edern" in the *Mabinogion*, but "Aeternus" in the original Latin) to fight three "giants" (i.e., bandit chieftains or pirate leaders) on Brent Knoll. Ider was slain in the fight, and the monks of medieval Glastonbury insisted that Arthur then donated Brent Knoll to their monastery in return for their prayers on Ider's behalf. Because local folk legend so strongly associates Arthur with Brent Knoll, we must conclude that Brent Knoll was another hillfort in Aurelius's defensive system.

The line of sight from Glastonbury Tor then continues unimpeded from Brent Knoll across the Severn River to the south coast of Wales, in particular to the hillfort of Dinas Powys near Cardiff in Glevissig (Glamorgan). "Dinas Powys" means "rural fort" in Welsh. The "rural area," or *powys*, in this case was the western Pagus of Civitas Silurum, whose capital was Venta Silurum (Caerwent). (The area about Venta Silurum itself was then, and is now, called Gwent.) According to the archaeological evidence, Dinas Powys was occupied in Arthur's time by a local ruler of some importance, although much lesser in status than the commander of Castellum Cataviae.

Another line of sight can be traced from Brent Knoll to Dunkery Beacon, a hill approximately thirty miles southwest of Brent Knoll and close to the site of Arthur's early encounter with Saint Carannog at Dunster. Dunkery Beacon rises some 519 feet over Exmoor near the north Somerset coast. The hill commands a view northward over the Bristol Channel and southward into the interior of modern Devon. The inland view from Dunkery Beacon was probably screened from Cadbury Castle and Glastonbury Tor by the Quantock Hills and Blackdown Hills. The view from Dunkery Beacon might have extended all the way down the Exe River valley to another site named Cadbury, which is situated about eight miles north of the Dumnonian Civitas capital of Isca Dumnoniorum (Exeter). The very name of Dunkery Beacon implies that the hill was once used as a signal fire station. The likelihood that Dunkery Beacon was a signal fire station, and

the association of nearby Dunster with Arthur, strongly suggest that Dunkery Beacon was one more link in Aurelius's chain of reoccupied hillforts.

A third line of sight can be traced from Brent Knoll to a mound called Cadbury Hill, which lies approximately twenty miles northeast of Brent Knoll in modern Avonshire. Cadbury Hill is located beside the town of Nailsea near the city of Bristol. Local legend insists that when Arthur and his knights return to this earth, they will issue forth from Cadbury Hill. Further excavation and study is required, but the Avonshire Cadbury was probably yet another military station in Aurelius's defensive scheme.

The hillforts of Cadbury Castle, Glastonbury Tor, Brent Knoll, Dinas Powys and Dunkery Beacon (and probably Cadbury Hill, Exeter's Cadbury and several as-yet unidentified sites) were, without a doubt, elements in a communications network linking the Romanized territories of southwest England and southeast Wales through the use of signal fires. The clear lines-of-sight between the hillforts and the evidence of their contemporary military occupation admit of no other interpretation. Moreover, the deployment of a large military force at Cadbury Castle necessarily implies the existence of a quick and reliable means of communication between Cadbury Castle and the other forts in the wider territory to be defended. The concentration of a large and powerful army at Cadbury Castle would have been sheer military folly otherwise, because it necessarily required stripping the vulnerable coastal areas of defenders. If, however, the elite mobile forces at Cadbury Castle were connected by signal fires with the whole region to be protected, then the central location of the hillfort made it possible for a veritable juggernaut to speedily descend upon any barbarian force foolish enough to wander into the region. Aurelius thus exploited the unobstructed views between the various hillforts in southwest Britannia to establish a Roman-style signal fire communications network as an integral part of his strategy for the protection of southwest Britannia.

These hillforts, and their employment as look-out posts, may lie behind one of the mysterious "Thirteen Treasures of the Isle of Britain" described in Welsh poetry and mentioned in the *Mabinogion* tale "The Dream of Rhonabwy." This Treasure is "The Mantle of Arthur in Cornwall: whoever was under it could not be seen, and he could see everyone." This description of the defensive arrangement in Cornovian Dumnonia would have naturally occurred to travellers who were astonished by the fact that their arrival was anticipated by unseen hilltop observers. The legend of a device which enables one to view others while remaining unseen could be a poetic description of the hillfort and signal station system which protected southwest Britannia.

The restoration of Cadbury Castle and other hillforts in southwest Britannia has been archaeologically dated to about A.D. 470. This date puts the construction of the elaborate defensive system in approximately the same time period as Aurelius's unfortunate expedition to Gaul in aid of the hapless Emperor Anthemius. Aurelius must have ordered the renovation of the forts soon after his return to Britannia from Gaul.

With this information concerning the refortification of southwest Britannia, we can reconstruct the progress of Arthur's career as he trod the path to leadership of Britannia.

## Arthur Rises to Command

After a quick victory over Dux Gorlois, a quick victory made possible by the continued loyalty of many Cornovians who did not join Gorlois in revolt, Aurelius undertook the military reorganization of the economically vital region of southwest Britannia. With Gorlois defeated and slain, Aurelius was free to alter the local defensive arrangements in Dumnonia to better suit the needs of the entire southwest region. To this end, Aurelius ordered the construction of a large and sophisticated military base at Cadbury Castle and of a number of lesser forts to serve as both lookout posts and signal stations. In order to implement his new military program, Aurelius was keen to recruit able and energetic cavalry officers to serve in the refurbished hillforts.

The most able and energetic of these cavalry officers was the son of one of Aurelius's Cornovian supporters in the war against Gorlois. Aurelius's supporter was a seasoned cavalry warrior named Artorius Castus who was descended from a long-ago Roman military hero. Aurelius recruited the young adult son of this notable warrior and assigned him a post in the new defensive system. The son of Aurelius's Cornovian supporter was, of course, Arthur.

In about A.D. 475, Arthur became a junior cavalry officer under Catavia, Aurelius's Magister Militum and commander of the key cavalry base at Cadbury Castle. The young Arthur proved to be an exceptionally capable officer, and he was soon given major assignments. In about A.D. 478, Arthur was awarded command of the small, but important, signal station and fort at Dunkery Beacon near

Dunster. Arthur's ability and loyalty made him the obvious choice for even more weighty military duties, and he rose ever higher through the ranks. Later, perhaps around A.D. 481, Aurelius appointed Arthur to the crucial position of Procurator Rei Publicae, the army's supply requisition officer.

Arthur pursued his new duties with extraordinary zeal and effectiveness. As a consequence, Arthur earned the eternal enmity of the monkish portion of the population and became the villain in a number of monastic stories. He also earned another promotion. When Catavia the Magister Militum died or retired in approximately A.D. 484, Arthur assumed his superior's former rank and command.

Aurelius then designated Arthur as his choice for succession to the high office of Regissimus Britanniarum. Aurelius made his designation in the manner of the old Roman Emperors by legally adopting the adult general. Hence Arthur, son of the Cornovian warrior Artorius Castus, also became the son and heir apparent of the Regissimus from Armorica. This dual heritage of Arthur confused medieval historians and gave rise to the fabulous legend of Arthur's conception during Aurelius's campaign against Dux Gorlois. Aurelius in time went on to his heavenly reward, and Arthur was in due course hailed by the Romano-Briton army as the new Regissimus Britanniarum.

When Geoffrey of Monmouth tells us that Arthur became "king" of Britannia at fifteen years of age, what he really means is that Arthur became Regissimus approximately sixteen years after Aurelius's campaign against Dux Gorlois. Because Geoffrey thought that Arthur was conceived during this campaign, he concluded that Arthur was a mere fifteen years old when he became Regissimus some sixteen years later. The passage of sixteen years from Aurelius's defeat of Gorlois puts Arthur's rise to the rule of Britannia around A.D. 490.

Long before he assumed the high office of Regissimus Britanniarum, Arthur was called upon to play a leading role in the military affairs of the Diocese. While still Aurelius's Magister Militum, Arthur took up the Romano-Briton red dragon banner and led Aurelius's forces in a series of major military campaigns.

## Chapter Twenty
## Artorius, Magister Militum per Britannias

The earliest surviving account of Arthur's career as Magister Militum per Britannias is found in Nennius's *Historia Brittonum*. In this work, Nennius identifies twelve battles in which Arthur commanded the Romano-Briton forces. The twelve battles of Arthur were those fought at the:

1. Mouth of the River Glein;
2. River Dubglas in the region Linnuis;
3. River Dubglas in the region Linnuis;
4. River Dubglas in the region Linnuis;
5. River Dubglas in the region Linnuis;
6. River Bassas;
7. Caledonian Wood;
8. Castle Gurnion, or,
   in some manuscripts, Castle Guinnion;
9. City of the Legion;
10. Shore by the River Tribruit;
11. Mount Breguoin or Bregomion, or,
    in some manuscripts, Mount Agned; and
12. Badon Hill.

Nennius tells us that Arthur emerged from each of these battles victorious.

Nennius's account of Arthur's victories closely resembles in form and style a battle-listing poem of the type that Celtic bards composed for their aristocratic employers. It is certainly based upon such a poem. Because none of Arthur's later combats, including the infamous Battle of Camlann, are mentioned in the *Historia Brittonum*, Nennius must have translated a poem which was originally composed during Arthur's lifetime - perhaps even for Arthur's own entertainment. Nennius's record of Arthur's wars is therefore entitled to a great deal of weight as an historical source. Unfortunately, the intended audience of the original poem was already quite familiar with Arthur's career, so Nennius gives only the scantiest of details for Arthur's early battles.

Nennius does not, for instance, confer any recognizable title upon Arthur. He only refers to Arthur somewhat ambiguously as "dux bellorum." Historians have long speculated as to what Roman military rank might lie behind "dux bellorum." Some have guessed that "dux bellorum" was a new title created in post-Roman Britannia especially for Arthur, a title which could translate quite well into modern English as "War Duke." *Bellum* is the Latin word for "war"; *bellorum* is the plural genitive form, meaning "of wars" or "of battles." The Latin word *dux*, however, besides being a high Roman military rank translatable as "Duke," could also simply mean "leader." In identifying Arthur as "dux bellorum," Nennius was not giving Arthur an official title, but simply indicating that Arthur was the *dux*, in the ordinary sense of "leader," who exercised overall command in battle.

Nennius also gives very obscure names for the sites of Arthur's battles. He calls these sites by the forgotten geographic names by which Arthur's contemporaries knew them, which makes it difficult for us today to locate them on a modern map. Ironically, the very difficulty of ascertaining the location of Arthur's battles is itself an excellent indication that Nennius's battle list is authentic. Battles are often fought at relatively insignificant places where two hostile armies just happen to meet on their way to more important destinations. In the days before national parks and battlefield memorials, such sites often faded back into the anonymity from which they had but momentarily emerged. We shall therefore have to struggle to identify the places where Arthur fought.

Geoffrey of Monmouth aids a great deal in locating many of Arthur's battles. He is, however, aware of only some of the battles listed by Nennius. He also misplaces one of the battles in time, wrongly attributing it to his fictitious "Utherpendragon." Geoffrey does nevertheless give us much invaluable information. Geoffrey provides a fair amount of detail for certain of Arthur's battles, which helps us to place all of Arthur's battles in their proper geographic and chronological context.

We should bear in mind that not all of the battles listed by Nennius were necessarily major conflicts. Some of them were no doubt minor skirmishes and are mentioned only because of their association with Arthur. Those battles of which Geoffrey has no knowledge certainly fall into this category. Even Arthur's minor combats are important to us in our efforts to reconstruct the course of his military career, however, so we shall endeavor to learn what we can about them.

Based upon our reconstruction of the events of Aurelius's reign, we can deduce with reasonable accuracy the years in which Arthur fought his twelve battles. If the first battle occurred soon after Arthur assumed the title of Magister Militum, it occurred around A.D. 485. The next four battles were obviously related and were probably fought the following year. The remaining battles then took place over the next several years, which indicates that warfare continued through the late A.D. 480's and early A.D. 490's. According to this reconstructed sequence of events, the last listed battle, the Battle of Badon Hill, occurred in about A.D. 493, which accords with other evidence we have

for the date of this Battle.

Geoffrey assigns all of Arthur's battles to the period after Arthur became "king" (i.e., Regissimus). In fact, most of Arthur's twelve battles were fought when Arthur was still Aurelius's Magister Militum. Because Geoffrey erroneously believed that Arthur became "king" at the youthful age of fifteen, he could not imagine Arthur having had a prior military career and he misconstrues Arthur's status when Arthur led the Romano-Briton army.

## The Battle at the Mouth of the River Glein

Geoffrey omits any mention of Arthur's first battle, the Battle of the River Glein. We must therefore rely upon place name analysis to locate this Battle. Unfortunately, "Glen," which is the form into which "Glein" evolved, is a common place name element in Britain. It is derived from the Celtic *glanos*, meaning "clean, holy, beautiful." Taking into account the relative Briton and Anglo-Saxon population centers in the late Fifth Century, two "Glen" sites emerge as possible locations. One possible location for the Battle is the River Glen in modern south Lincolnshire, and the other is the River Glen in modern Northumberland.

The Northumberland location could have been the site of a battle between Arthur and Octa's Bernician followers. A campaign so far from Aurelius's southern power base would, however, have been far too bold a venture to have been ignored by Geoffrey's sources. Also, for Arthur to have campaigned in modern Northumberland, he would have had to march across the entire length of the Dux Britanniarum's domain. Arthur's making such a journey is most improbable because the Dux at that time was unfriendly - if not outright hostile - to Aurelius. In view of the overall geopolitical situation, Arthur's first battle could not have been fought on the Northumberland River Glen.

The Lincolnshire site for Arthur's first combat, on the other hand, is favored not only by the process of elimination, but also by positive evidence. Lincolnshire was a likely place for a clash of arms between Arthur and the Anglo-Saxons because it was then divided between the Britons of Lindum Colonia (Lincoln) and their former laeti in Lindsey. In addition, the battles which immediately followed the Battle of the River Glein are located with certainty in the Lincolnshire area. The known location of these subsequent battles suggests that the earlier battle was fought in the same area as part of the same or a related campaign. The Battle of the River Glein was an incident in a prolonged war against the Anglo-Saxons settled in Lindsey along the modern Lincolnshire coast.

Lindsey had been settled by barbarians of the Angle tribe since the early Fifth Century. The Angles originally served as laeti in the employ of nearby Lindum Colonia, but they rebelled against their masters during the great Anglo-Saxon rebellion which followed the Massacre at the Cloister of Ambrius in A.D. 460. They ravaged the countryside about Lindum and they even burned down one of Lindum's town gates. The Angle population of Lindsey steadily increased in the years following their rebellion, and they began to encroach upon the adjacent Briton lands by the middle of the A.D. 480's.

Despite the damage suffered in the Anglo-Saxon rebellion, Lindum Colonia itself remained solidly in Briton hands. It stood as an obstacle to Angle expansion directly due west.

The Angles therefore moved in a southwesterly direction around Lindum towards modern Northampton. The natural path of expansion of the Lindsey Angles inevitably led to conflict in the southern part of modern Lincolnshire, wherein lies the River Glen.

In the Battle of the River Glein, Arthur probably fought and defeated an Angle raiding party that was probing new territory in advance of a more formal invasion or full-scale migration. The Battle must have been a minor skirmish in any case since it failed to receive mention in Geoffrey of Monmouth's sources. Nennius recorded the Battle of the River Glein only because it was Arthur's first victory - and a promising start to his career as Magister Militum.

Arthur soon saw much more serious fighting, probably only a year later in A.D. 486.

## The Battle of the River Dubglas

The next four battles named by Nennius are easily located. Nennius tells us that they all occurred by the River Dubglas in the region Linnuis. "Linnuis" is an early form of the modern place name Lindsey. The Battles in the Region Linnuis were obviously part of a major follow-up campaign to break the power of the Lindsey Angles.

Geoffrey gives a fairly detailed account of these four battles in the *Historia Regum Britanniae*. Unlike Nennius, who implies that all four battles were fought in a single campaign in the same geographic area, Geoffrey believes the first battle to belong to an entirely separate campaign fought beside the River Dubglas near Eboracum (York) in the same year that the other three battles were later fought in Lindsey.

Geoffrey's locating the Battle of the River Dubglas near Eboracum is credible. "Douglas," which is a later form of "Dubglas" (and the form used by Geoffrey), is a very common Celtic place name, meaning "black stream." One of the many rivers or streams flowing in the vicinity of Eboracum was no doubt once called "Dubglas" or "Douglas."

Nennius has certainly misinterpreted the Briton poem which he translated into the Latin prose of the *Historia Brittonum*. He has combined the several clashes of two separate campaigns into a single series of battles. A stanza concerning one year's scattered fighting was apparently misconstrued as describing multiple battles at the same site, and two separate geographic locations - the River Dubglas and the Region Linnuis - were erroneously fused into a single place. Geoffrey's version is detailed and credible, and it no doubt gives the correct account of the actual events. We shall therefore treat separately the Battle of the River Dubglas and the Battles in the Region Linnuis.

Geoffrey says the campaign of the River Dubglas began when Arthur marched north from Silchester (then called Calleva Atrebatum) to engage an army of Picts, Scots and Anglo-Saxons mustering near York (then called Eboracum). A new Anglo-Saxon leader named Colgrin commanded this mixed barbarian force.

Judging from the location of this and the other battles in which Colgrin participated, the barbarian commander was an heir of Icel (or Ickel or Hickel) and a leader of the Angles in Britannia. Colgrin was thus leader of the Angles of Anglia (modern Norfolk, Suffolk, Cambridgeshire and north Essex) as well as those of Lindsey. Colgrin does not appear in the official Angle royal genealogy,[113] but he

probably represents a branch of the dynasty which either died out or was ultimately disgraced and deposed from power. Regardless of what Colgrin's official status might have been, he clearly had charge of the military forces of the Angle nation in Britannia during Arthur's lifetime.

Geoffrey tells us that Arthur resolved to destroy the barbarian army gathering in the north of Britannia. As soon as Colgrin learned that Arthur was marching against him, he set out to meet the Britons head on. The two forces collided near the River Dubglas, not far from Eboracum. The resulting Battle of the River Dubglas was hard-fought, but Arthur gained the victory.

Astonishingly, the defeated barbarians then retreated for safety into the town of Eboracum.

Because the barbarian warriors sought, and received, refuge in the Dux Britanniarum's capital town, we can only conclude that the reigning Dux was Colgrin's ally and co-conspirator. The Dux had evidently recruited the assembling Picts, Scots and Anglo-Saxons for a planned invasion of south Britannia. Colgrin and the Angles must have joined the army massing at Eboracum pursuant to a military alliance between the northern Romano-Briton Dux and the ancient Icelingas dynasty. The Dux Britanniarum might have only half-heartedly supported the barbarian invasion which led to the Battle of Mount Damen in A.D. 472, but he was fully committed to the alliance with Colgrin which led to the Battle to the River Dubglas in A.D. 486. The Battle of the River Douglas was as much an incident in a civil war between north and south Britannia as it was a

---

113 This genealogy is actually for the kings of Mercia, not Lindsey or East Anglia, because of subsequent developments which we shall discuss later.

clash of arms in a barbarian war.

Arthur had obviously launched a preemptive strike against this Anglo-Briton coalition before all their forces could come together. He must have marched north very early in the spring, appearing unexpectedly outside Eboracum before the summer military campaign season was properly underway. Arthur's strategy succeeded and the Anglo-Briton army was defeated. After routing the enemy, Arthur placed Eboracum under siege.

While Colgrin was fighting Arthur at the River Douglas, Colgrin's brother Baldulf was away mobilizing additional Anglo-Saxon forces from a sea-coast area. This sea-coast area was presumably Deira, but could have been Lindsey. Baldulf was also awaiting a company of reinforcements due to arrive by ship under the command of "Duke Cheldric." "Cheldric" is a Germanic name, so the title "Duke" in this instance represents the Latin word *dux* in the ordinary sense of "leader." The overseas troops expected by Baldulf must have been mercenaries from Germania whom the Dux Britanniarum had hired.

Upon learning of his brother's defeat in the Battle of the River Douglas, Baldulf decided not to wait any longer for Cheldric and his mercenaries. He marched at once to the relief of Eboracum.

Geoffrey tells us that Baldulf commanded an extremely large army of 6,000 warriors. By way of comparison, 6,000 warriors was about the size of the Viking army which overran most of England in the Ninth Century. The army of Baldulf posed a very serious threat to Arthur's forces in the north.

Arthur did not break off the siege of Eboracum in response to this threat. He maintained the siege with only a part of his army and he sent the remainder to intercept the oncoming barbarians. Arthur sent 600 cavalry and 3,000 infantry under the command of Cador, the "Duke of Cornwall," to turn Baldulf back.

The numbers which Geoffrey gives for the Anglo-Saxon and Briton forces are credible. Although Baldulf's army of 6,000 warriors was large by the standards of the day, it was by no means improbably so. At the same time, the 600 horsemen whom Arthur sent to intercept the barbarians clearly represent two Romano-Briton cavalry units. In this instance, Geoffrey's sources seem to have given him accurate numbers for the size of the opposing armies.

Some historians believe that Cador, the "Duke of Cornwall" who commanded Arthur's intercepting force, is the same person as the Cadwy or Catavia who commanded Cadbury Castle. They base their belief upon the superficial similarity between the names "Cador" and "Cadwy." Their belief is ill-founded, however, because "Cador" is not a variation of "Catavia," but a Welsh form of the Roman personal name Cato. Their belief is also ill-conceived, because the dates associated with the two men cannot be reconciled. The original commander of Aurelius's principal fort must have been a very senior officer when the fort was refurbished and renamed for him in the early A.D. 470's. He was not likely to still be serving in the army a generation later - and certainly not as the subordinate of his former Procurator. The Cador or Cato who fought under Arthur in the A.D. 480's and A.D. 490's was a very different person from the Cadwy or Catavia who fought under Aurelius in the A.D. 460's and A.D. 470's.

Geoffrey, towards the end of the *Historia Regum Britanniae*, gives Cador the family name of Limenich. "Limenich" would be "Limenicus" in Latin, possibly meaning "guard" or "gatekeeper" (from *l i m e n*, meaning "threshold").[114] "Limenicus" is a plausible Roman *cognomen*. In the *Mabinogion* tale "Gereint and Enid," Cador appears as "Cadwr, son of Gwryon." The name of Cador's father would be "Varianus" in Latin, meaning "spotted." "Varianus" resembles a Roman *nomen*. Arthur's general was thus Cato Varianus Limenicus to his Roman colleagues.[115] We shall later see that Cador's son bore the Roman *praenomen* of Constantine, which makes his son's full Latin name Constantinus Varianus Limenicus. From the evidence of his name (and his son's name), Cador Limenich/Cato Varianus Limenicus came from a thoroughly Roman family.

The designation "Duke of Cornwall" indicates that Cador was a Cornovian leader from Dumnonia holding the high Roman military rank of Dux. Cador appears in the *Mabinogion* tale "The Dream of Rhonabwy," however, as "Cadwr" the "*earl* of Cornwall." Cador must have been later promoted to the even higher rank of Comes. In the Welsh tale, Cador had the honor of bearing Arthur's sword and arming Arthur for battle. These ceremonial

---

114 The real person Cato Limenicus might have later given rise to the similar-named Mador de la Porte ("Mador of the Gate"), a minor character in the Romances.

115 Alternatively, Cador's father might have been the Maurice Cador of "Cahors" who, according to Geoffrey, was slain in Gaul, apparently under the command of Aurelius/Riothamus. If so, then perhaps "Cato" was the family *nomen*, "Varianus" the family *cognomen* and Limenicus a more recently acquired second *cognomen*; in that case, Cador's full Roman name was Mauricius Cato Varianus Limenicus.

duties imply that, whatever his title, Cador held an especially high military status in Arthur's government. Geoffrey concurs, often depicting Cador in important, independent military commands under Arthur. When Arthur became Regissimus Britanniarum, he no doubt made Cador his Magister Militum.

Baldulf meanwhile hoped to catch Arthur, Dux Cador and the southern army besieging Eboracum by surprise. When he came within ten miles of the town, he even marched his troops at night in order that he might come upon the Britons unexpectedly. The barbarian failed in his objective. Instead, he himself fell victim to surprise. Cador ambushed the Anglo-Saxon relief force before it reached Eboracum. Cador attacked when the barbarians were still in road marching order, not yet properly deployed for combat. Cador easily routed the would-be rescuers of Eboracum.

Despite Cador's victory over Baldulf, Arthur abruptly broke off the siege of Eboracum and retired south.

Geoffrey explains Arthur's retreat by pointing out that the barbarian reinforcements under Cheldric had finally arrived. Geoffrey credits Cheldric with no less than 600 shiploads of warriors. That many ships would have carried about 20,000 warriors - a highly improbable number. Cheldric's force most likely consisted of only fifteen to twenty ships bearing 600 warriors: a much smaller force to be sure, but more than adequate, when joined to the survivors of Baldulf's army, to make Arthur's continued siege of Eboracum impractical. With substantial enemy forces active in the area, Arthur could not safely maintain the siege of a large and hostile walled Roman town.

Before pulling out, Arthur apparently attempted to bluff Colgrin and the Dux Britanniarum into capitulation. Geoffrey tells us that, after the arrival of Cheldric, Baldulf disguised himself as a minstrel in order to pass through the Briton lines and enter Eboracum. The barbarian leader would have only undertaken such a dangerous mission if he thought it important to inform Colgrin of the arrival of Cheldric and the recovery of his own forces from their defeat by Cador. Heartened by Baldulf's news of a friendly army operating in the vicinity, the defenders of Eboracum remained steadfast in their resistance to Arthur and were not intimidated into offering terms of surrender.

When Arthur broke off the siege of Eboracum, he withdrew south all the way to Londinium (London). Londinium occupied a strategic position in east-central Britannia astride several major Roman roads. From Londinium, Arthur could still move up rapidly to meet the Dux Britanniarum's anticipated invasion of south Britannia; he could also easily intercept any independent war parties which might come out of Anglia or Kent. In pulling back to Londinium, Arthur was not abandoning the fight against the Dux Britanniarum and his barbarians, but simply taking up a new position from which he could watch developments and then renew the war on his own terms.

Overall, the spring campaign of A.D. 486 must have been a disappointment to Arthur. Although he had twice defeated the barbarian allies of the Dux Britanniarum, he was unable to prevent the enemy forces from assembling and he failed to capture the Dux's capital of Eboracum. The northern allies had been taught to respect the martial prowess of the southern cavalry, but they were still far from subdued.

Arthur had to fight the Dux and his barbarian allies again the following summer.

## The Battles in the Region Linnuis

While Arthur was abiding in Londinium, a company of allied warriors from Armorica arrived in Britannia. Aurelius had obviously decided some time earlier to send for reinforcements from his Gallic homeland. The Regissimus must have foreseen the deterioration of the fragile peace which had prevailed in Britannia since his return from Gaul in A.D. 473. The fighting by the River Glein had likely provided disturbing confirmation of a new aggressiveness on the part of the Angles in Britannia. Aurelius therefore sent word to Armorica that he was recruiting soldiers, probably in A.D. 485. His word fell on receptive ears in Armorica, because the recent death of Aurelius's one-time opponent, the aggressive Visigoth King Euric, eliminated the immediate military threat to the Bretons in Gaul. If the Armorican volunteers left home soon after the winter of A.D. 485-486, they could have arrived in Britannia early in the summer of A.D. 486, just in time to join Arthur at Londinium.

The Armoricans were led by a commander named Hoel, son of Boudicius, upon whom Geoffrey graciously, but incorrectly, bestows the title "king." A modern rendering of "Hoel" would be "Howell," which seems to have been a common name among the Bretons. A "Howel, son of Emhyr of Brittany," who may or may not be the same person as the Armorican commander, appears in the *Mabinogion* tales "The Dream of Rhonabwy," "Peredur Son of Efrawg" and "Gereint and Enid." "Emhyr" was originally the Breton word for Emperor, but at some time it became a personal name. The misleading personal name of Howel's father in the Welsh tales might lie behind Geoffrey's conclusion that Hoel was royalty. Alternatively, "Emhyr" might not have been the name of Howel's father, but a confusion stemming from the fact that Howel's father, like Ambrosius Aurelianus the Elder, was a "purple-wearing" member of the Senatorial Class. In any case, Hoel was certainly not a king of Brittany who voluntarily left his own realm in order to fight under Aurelius in Britannia, but a member of a noble Roman family in Armorica. Hoel was a Romano-Breton aristocrat, and, as such, he was born and bred to noble pursuits, including horsemanship and the skills appropriate to cavalry warfare.

Geoffrey tells us that Hoel was Arthur's nephew, the son of Arthur's sister. Even allowing for the fact that Arthur was much older than Geoffrey believed, he still could not have been old enough to have had a nephew of sufficient age and experience to command an army. Geoffrey's source no doubt said that Hoel was "the king's" nephew, referring, of course, to Aurelius the Regissimus who had spent his youth in Armorica. Geoffrey, believing Aurelius to be dead and Arthur to be Regissimus, has mistaken a reference to Hoel's being the nephew of "the king" (i.e., Aurelius) for a statement that Hoel was the nephew of Arthur.

Hoel supposedly landed at Southampton with 15,000 warriors. The landing at Southampton, then called Clausentum, in the heart of Ambrosii territory is credible, but the large size given for Hoel's army is not. It reflects the hopeless medieval inability to deal with large numbers. Hoel did indeed land at Clausentum, but with less than a tenth of the troops attributed to him by Geoffrey.

Hoel's followers probably consisted of one unit of cavalry and one (understrength) of infantry, plus their support personnel. Hoel thus commanded about 300 cavalry and 800 infantry, with perhaps another 300 or so grooms and other servants. Although small by modern standards, such an army was a major force in Britannia in Arthur's time. Hoel's army was certainly large and powerful enough to become a decisive factor in Briton warfare when allied to Aurelius's soldiers from south Britannia.

Colgrin and Baldulf were not idle while Arthur and Aurelius awaited their Armorican reinforcements. Geoffrey tells us that the barbarian leaders marched south and invested Lincoln (i.e., Lindum Colonia) "in the province of Lindsey." Colgrin and Baldulf led their Angles from Lindsey and Anglia, as well as the other barbarian allies of the Dux Britanniarum, against Lindum Colonia.

The Angle leaders were no doubt also accompanied by a contingent of Eboracum Britons. Geoffrey does not mention the presence of Eboracum troops among the besieging forces, but we cannot put much weight on this omission. Geoffrey simply could not imagine Briton soldiers joining a barbarian host in an attack upon a Briton town. We, of course, now realize that the Britons were often divided against each other, and that such an occurrence was, sadly, far from uncommon. In this instance, we can be sure that Eboracum troops did indeed assist the barbarians. The Dux Britanniarum had a strong strategic interest in the fate of Lindum Colonia, so he must have sent at least some of his own troops to aid his barbarian allies and to advance his own cause.

The Dux Britanniarum had a strong interest

in the fate of Lindum Colonia because the town occupied a key position in east-central Britannia. Lindum sat at the juncture of the two main northbound Roman roads (later called the Fosse Way and Ermine Street) in the eastern half of Britannia.[116] The Pennine Mountains and the forests then standing in modern Nottingham and Derby diverted most northbound and southbound traffic onto these roads. Possession of the town was therefore crucial to the ability of the southern or northern regimes to meddle in each other's affairs. In fact, in Anglo-Saxon times, the town and its surrounding region were major points of contention between the barbarian kingdoms of Northumbria, based on Eboracum (then called Eforwig), and Mercia, located in central England. With Lindum Colonia in his hands, the Dux Britanniarum could open up the path of expansion for his Angle allies in Lindsey, shield his realm from interference by Aurelius's Romano-Briton regime, and project his own power into south Britannia.

Aurelius, for his part, had to preserve the independence of Lindum Colonia in order to protect the military security of south Britannia. He needed a sovereign town to stand as an obstacle to the expansionary plans of both the Dux Britanniarum and the Lindsey Angles. He therefore ordered Arthur to lead the newly combined Briton-Breton army to Lindsey to break the siege of Lindum Colonia.

Since Nennius places four battles in the region Linnuis, the ensuing campaign must have involved several large-scale engagements

---

116 Another, less important northbound road paralleled the Fosse Way through Danum (Doncaster), and yet another ran on the opposite side of the Pennine Mountains. According to the *Notitia Dignitatum*, Danum was garrisoned by one of the Dux's elite cavalry units (Equites Crispiani).

between the opposing forces. Even eliminating one of those engagements, the Battle of the River Douglas, leaves three major combats in which Arthur led his men against the besiegers of Lindum Colonia.

The outcome of this campaign was decisive. Arthur smashed the enemy host. In one day, which is to say in the final of the three Battles in the Region Linnuis, 6,000 Anglo-Saxons were slain, according to Geoffrey. Many of the barbarians were cut down or drowned in the nearby rivers as they tried to flee the victorious Romano-Briton horsemen. More likely, 6,000 Anglo-Saxons - and Eboracum allies and Eboracum Britons - were merely *defeated*, not literally slain, in the fighting. Even allowing for this exaggeration, the Battles in the Region Linnuis were a bloody disaster for the northern allies. It was in the rout and pursuit at the end of a battle that most casualties were inflicted in ancient and medieval combat, and the defeated northern army must have suffered grievous losses, perhaps half or more of its original strength.

When Arthur led his troops into warm quarters for the winter of A.D. 486-487, he should have been satisfied with his summer's work. He could not have been very pleased with the way the summer began because his spring campaign near Eboracum had failed in its objective of destroying the Ducal-barbarian conspiracy at its inception, although through no fault of his own. The Magister Militum had conducted a bold and daring offensive to forestall the gathering of hostile warriors, but the Briton forces were simply inadequate to maintain the siege of Eboracum and at the same time cope with the fully-assembled enemy army. Arthur therefore wisely, but no doubt reluctantly, withdrew to Londinium. Reinforced with Armorican allies, Arthur was, however, able to later resume the contest against the Dux and his barbarians. Arthur more than redeemed himself in the subsequent fighting. After a difficult and hard-fought campaign involving no less than three separate battles in Lindsey, the northern army was utterly destroyed and Lindum Colonia was saved.

Arthur's victory in the Battles in the Region Linnuis had far-reaching consequences. With the military might of the Lindsey Angles broken, the Britons of Lindum Colonia were able to maintain their independence for almost another century. Even then, the barbarians did not completely overwhelm the native Britons of the region. In the early Seventh Century, the ruler of Lindsey bore the Briton name of Caedbad, which indicates that persons of Briton, or at least of mixed Briton and Anglo-Saxon, blood continued to play an important role in Lindsey even after most of Britannia had fallen to the barbarians. In the same Century, at least one Anglo-Saxon governor of Lindum used the Roman title of *Praefectus Lindocolinae Civitatis* (Prefect of the Civitas of Lindum Colonia), which demonstrates a continuity of Roman governmental institutions. Because of the defeats inflicted by Arthur upon the Angles of Lindsey, the native population was able to deal with the barbarians of the region on a more equal footing and to preserve something of their Romano-Briton civilization. The Anglo-Saxon era Kingdom of Lindsey which later arose was thus more a merger of the two populations than a conquest of one by the other. Arthur effectively eliminated the Lindsey Angles as a military power, and in doing so he made it possible for the Britons of Lindum Colonia to survive and prosper long into the Anglo-Saxon

period.

## The Battle of the River Bassas

Arthur had little time to rest on the well-deserved laurels of his A.D. 486 campaigns. Probably the very next year, the Magister Militum had to fight another battle, this time at the River Bassas.

Geoffrey does not give us an account of the Battle of the River Bassas, and place name analysis offers little help in attempting to locate the campaign of A.D. 487. The most popular guess as to the meaning of "River Bassas" has been "the Bass," which is not a river at all, but a rock in the Firth of Forth near the modern town of North Berwick. In that case, the Battle would have been an action fought against Octa's followers in the north, or possibly against Pictish raiders. Alternatively, "River Bassas" could be a corruption of the name of the River Lusas in modern Hampshire, which would have been the site of a confrontation with a seaborne Anglo-Saxon raiding band. Neither battle site identification which relies solely upon place name similarity is satisfactory.

The Battle of the River Bassas must have been a minor struggle because it was not discussed in Geoffrey's sources. A campaign far to the north, in the Firth of Forth region, could have hardly been so unremarkable that it would have been ignored by Geoffrey's sources. Similarly, a pirate landing in Hampshire, in the heart of Ambrosii territory, would not have been omitted even if the invaders were few in number. The Battle of the River Bassas must have been an insignificant conflict which took place in a near and accessible, but relatively unimportant, place because it faded into obscurity notwithstanding Arthur's participation.

The most likely location for the Battle of the River Bassas is modern Lincolnshire. A punitive expedition against the Lindsey Angles would have been a natural follow-up to the destruction of their armies the summer before. It also would not have been noteworthy enough to gain immortality. Arthur's soldiers merely burned the barbarians' fields, slaughtered their herds and levelled their homes. It was hardly a glorious undertaking, but it was an ordinary and necessary part of ancient and medieval warfare; by such actions, an invader hoped to destroy his enemy's ability to maintain an army or wage war. The high point of the campaign, the Battle of the River Bassas itself, represented nothing more than the Lindsey Angles' pitiful attempt to resist the devastation of their lands.

We can even find a feasible site for the Battle of the River Bassas in modern northeast Lincolnshire. "River Bassas" could be a distortion of "Flumen Abus," the Roman name for the Humber River. When Arthur invaded Lindsey, the Angles could have chosen to make their stand on the shore near the mouth of the Flumen Abus/River Humber.

The hapless Lindsey Angles stood alone at the Battle of the River Bassas. Geoffrey reports that the Anglo-Saxons sailed to Germania after Arthur's next fight, the Battle of the Caledonian Wood. As we shall see, the circumstances of that Battle make such a journey highly unlikely. The "journey across the sea" must have actually been a much shorter trip from Lindsey to the other Anglo-Saxon lands on Britannia's eastern seaboard after the Battles in the Region Linnuis. The Anglia Angles went over the open waters of the Wash ("Metaris Aestuarium" to the Romans) separating Lindsey from Anglia, and the Eboracum Britons and their foederati traversed the estuary of the Humber River ("Abus Aestuarium") back to Deira. The warriors of Colgrin, Baldulf and the Dux Britanniarum, in other words, crossed the water as they retired to their own "German" territories in Anglia and Deira after the crushing defeats suffered at the hands of Arthur. The Anglia Angles and the Eboracum Britons abandoned their erstwhile allies in Lindsey to their fate.

Even so, the Angles of Lindsey, being a warrior race, did not meekly submit to Arthur's chastisement. They mustered whatever forces they could to oppose Arthur, but their resistance must have been feeble after the hard fighting and heavy losses of the previous year. Deserted by their kinsmen from Anglia and by their allies from Eboracum and Deira, the Lindsey Angles bravely met the Briton invaders near the River Abus, only to be run down and swept aside.

## The Battle of the Caledonian Wood

With his victory in the Battle of the River Bassas, Arthur brought the war against the Lindsey Angles to a successful conclusion. He was therefore able to campaign the next summer in a more remote part of Britannia. Arthur's next combat, the Battle of the Caledonian Wood, can be situated with confidence in the (then) forested area just north of Hadrian's Wall, between the towns of Luguvalium (Carlisle) and Alclud (Dumbarton).

The enemies whom Arthur fought in the Caledonian Wood were the Anglo-Saxons of the far north. These Anglo-Saxons included the barbarians who had gone north with Octa and the Frisians who put the "fries" element in the place name Dumfries.

Many historians have assumed that Arthur's opponents in the Battle of the Caledonian Wood were Picts, but the Picts are not otherwise known to have been militarily active outside their own territory after the middle of the Fifth Century. It is also not clear what the Picts would have been up to in the Caledonian Wood at this time. The far northern Anglo-Saxons, on the other hand, were then waging war against the Britons of Strathclyde and the Britons of Civitas Carvetiorum. This war was the war which Octa waged against Loth of Strathclyde and his former captors in Luguvalium (Carlisle). Unlike the Picts, the Anglo-Saxons were active in the vicinity of the Caledonian Wood and posed a direct threat to Aurelius's allies in Strathclyde and Civitas Carvetiorum.

Arthur's expedition to the Caledonian Wood was, in fact, the military assistance which Aurelius sent Loth of Strathclyde against Octa of Bernicia. Arthur's force was, in other words, the "British army" which Aurelius "put under Loth's command" (i.e., placed at his disposal). Arthur's seventh victory represents an effort to put an end to Octa's attacks upon Strathclyde and Civitas Carvetiorum.

Geoffrey thought that the Battle of the Caledonian Wood took place as Arthur pursued the Anglo-Saxons whom he had just defeated in Lindsey. In a sense, Geoffrey was right. Arthur was still fighting Anglo-Saxon barbarians who were actual, or at least potential, allies of his real enemy. Arthur's real enemy was, of course, the Dux Britanniarum. Geoffrey believed the Battle of the Caledonian Wood to be follow-up to the Battles in the Region Linnuis because his sources told him that Arthur fought Anglo-Saxons in the Battle of the Caledonian Wood and that Arthur's Caledonian Wood campaign was strategically connected to his earlier Battles in the Region Linnuis.

Arthur and his army, which no doubt included many allied troops from Civitas Carvetiorum, proceeded against the enemy by advancing along the old Roman road which ran north from Luguvalium. Arthur's objective was the Anglo-Saxon settlements situated in the area about the headwaters of the Rivers Clyde and Tweed. The Anglo-Saxons did not await the invaders, but marched out and attacked them on the road, inflicting many casualties. The Briton army did not break, however; it held steady and began to turn the tide of battle against the barbarians. Before a decisive Briton victory could be achieved, the Anglo-Saxons fled into the shelter of the nearby Caledonian Wood.

The Anglo-Saxons chose their refuge well. The forested terrain impeded the movement of Arthur's cavalry, depriving Arthur of his principal tactical advantage. Pursuit of the barbarians into the Wood was therefore out of the question. Not to be foiled by this development, Arthur methodically proceeded to besiege the Caledonian Wood itself.

At Arthur's direction, the Britons cut down many trees and used the felled trunks to erect barricades confining the Anglo-Saxons within a small portion of the Wood. Arthur's cavalry squadrons patrolled the circumference of the isolated forest, ready to cut down any barbarian who might attempt to make a break from the trees. The Anglo-Saxons soon found themselves surrounded in a place where they thought they would be safe. The barbarians must have been greatly surprised to find their refuge turned into their deathtrap.

After three days, the Anglo-Saxons succumbed to hunger and despair. They surrendered to Arthur.

The terms of surrender were harsh. The Anglo-Saxons were permitted to depart the area with their lives, but little else. They had to abandon their homesteads in far northwest Britannia, leaving all their goods behind. The defeated Anglo-Saxons no doubt migrated east, joining their fellow countrymen in Bernicia and Lodonesia. The far northwest of Britannia was, however, cleared of the barbarians. After Arthur's victory in the Battle of the Caledonian Wood, the far northern Anglo-Saxons were no longer able to pose a direct threat to Civitas Carvetiorum or to Strathclyde.

Arthur's victory in the Battle of the Caledonian Wood yielded another important military benefit. The probable year of the Battle is A.D. 488, which is also the year, according to the Anglo-Saxon Chronicle, that Aesc "received the kingdom" of Kent. Aesc, in other words, became king of Kent in A.D. 488. For Kent's third king to have assumed the throne in A.D. 488, Kent's second king, Octa, must have died in the same year. Octa was certainly slain in the Battle of the Caledonian Wood. He was no doubt in the far north visiting his northern realm of Bernicia and prosecuting his war against Loth and Luguvalium. When Arthur marched out of Luguvalium, Octa rushed to the assistance of his Dumfries area comrades - and to his death. Another favorable consequence of Arthur's great victory was thus the elimination of the troublesome Octa of Bernicia and Kent.

Geoffrey tells us that Octa was killed by "Utherpendragon" in the Battle of Verulamium. The "Utherpendragon" who killed Octa was Magister Militum Arthur, but the battle in which Octa died was the Battle of the Caledonian Wood. Geoffrey's failure to realize that "Utherpendragon" was a title and not a personal name, and his failure to realize that the Anglo-Saxons were a diverse people consisting of several different groups with their own leaders, caused him to muddle the circumstances of Octa's death. Geoffrey thus places Octa's death in the reign of his fictitious "Utherpendragon" before Arthur's time, and he places Colgrin in command of all the Anglo-Saxons in all the Battles fought by Arthur, including the Battle of the Caledonian Wood. Arthur was, of course, only one of the generals who held the title Utherpendragon, and Octa commanded the Anglo-Saxons of Bernicia and Kent at the same time that Colgrin commanded the Angles of Lindsey and Anglia. The truth is Octa was killed by Magister Militum Arthur in the Battle of the Caledonian Wood in A.D. 488.

Arthur's victory also achieved Aurelius's political objectives in the north. Not only did Arthur win a major military triumph and slay a dangerous barbarian enemy, he made a favorable impression upon the Briton rulers of the region. Civitas Carvetiorum and Strathclyde gladly renewed their alliances with the victorious southern army. In fact, the marriage of Aurelius's daughter Anna Ambrosia to Loth of Strathclyde was probably arranged at this time. We have dated the Battle of the Caledonian Wood to A.D. 488, when Anna was about thirteen years old. A political alliance contracted between Aurelius and Loth after the Battle of the Caledonian Wood could have been sealed by a wedding the following year, when Anna was about fourteen years old and of marriageable age. The rulers of Civitas Carvetiorum did not become so intimately connected to Aurelius, but they did become close allies of his regime. After Arthur's victory, both Civitas Carvetiorum and Strathclyde firmly aligned themselves with the

Regissimus of south Britannia, making the Caledonian Wood campaign a major political as well as military success.

## The Battle of Castle Gurnion

While Arthur and the Romano-Briton army were fighting the Anglo-Saxons of the far north, the Angles of Anglia decided to assert themselves in the south. Although the unsuccessful joint campaign with the Dux Britanniarum against Lindum Colonia and the military defeat of the Lindsey Angles in the Battle of the River Bassas were major setbacks to the Icelingas dynasty, the Angle heartland of Anglia (Norfolk, Suffolk, Cambridgeshire and north Essex) was as yet untouched by war. Anglia still constituted a strong power base from which future attacks against the Britons could be launched. Chagrined but not bowed, Colgrin and Baldulf were determined to wipe out the humiliation of their defeat in Lindsey. While Arthur was busy in the far north gaining allies against the Dux Britanniarum, the Angles of Anglia emerged as a military menace in their own right.

Colgrin and Baldulf probably raided westward from Anglia into central Britannia when Arthur and the Romano-Briton army were many miles away in the Caledonian Wood. They certainly conducted such raids in the years to follow. Another series of hard-fought campaigns was ultimately required over the next several years to suppress the resurgent Angle threat.

Arthur's base for operations against Anglia was the Roman town of Camulodunum, now called Colchester.

Camulodunum had once been a great town,
even for a brief time the capital of Roman Britannia, but it had fallen on hard times long since then. By the late Fifth Century, the town was a mere shadow of its former glory. Camulodunum nevertheless managed to avoid Anglo-Saxon conquest. The Romano-Briton population of the town was much reduced from earlier times, but it was still apparently adequate to defend the town's walls and preserve the town's independence against the Anglo-Saxons - although it had yet to face the full force of the newly expansionist Anglia. The struggling citizens of Camulodunum must have eagerly supported Arthur in his campaign to break the power of their dangerous neighbors, the Icelingas.

Arthur chose to make his campaign headquarters at Camulodunum because the town was strategically situated on the southern border of Anglia along the Roman road running from Londinium to the former Civitas capital of Venta Icenorum (Caistor-by-Norwich) in the heart of Anglia. Venta Icenorum had fallen to the Angles during the Anglo-Saxon rebellion of the early A.D. 460's, and it was the closest thing the barbarians had to a capital. Camulodunum was thus well placed to threaten the Angles, protect Arthur's store of supplies, keep open his line of communication to Aurelius at Venta Belgarum (Winchester), and provide a reasonably close refuge for the winter or in the event of misfortune.

The road from Camulodunum was only one of three available routes into Anglia, but it was the best route for Arthur because it traversed relatively good cavalry country. Two roads into Anglia ran due east from the midlands of modern England, but one crossed the great marsh known as the Fenlands, while the other passed through the rough and (then) thickly wooded terrain of western Anglia. A cavalry force riding over such ground could have been easily ambushed and cut to pieces. From Camulodunum, Arthur was able to march against Anglia across fairly open countryside. The Camulodunum road favored Arthur's mounted forces and offered fewer opportunities for the Angles to put up an aggressive defense.

Camulodunum also has very strong traditional associations with Arthur. The town has probably contributed more than any other single place to the legend of "King Arthur" because it has given us the name Camelot, applied to Arthur's fabulous capital in the Romances. "Camulodunum," stripped of its Latin word ending and shortened, becomes "Camulod," which in time evolved into "Camalot" and then "Camelot." Given the town's diminished condition and its proximity to hostile Anglia, Arthur is unlikely to have permanently resided in Camulodunum or made it his regular capital in the usual sense, but he certainly used it as a temporary military headquarters for his war against Anglia.

Marching out of Camulodunum, Arthur led his troops in an invasion of Anglia which culminated in his eighth victory at the Battle of Castle Gurnion, sometimes called the Battle of Castle Guinnion, in about A.D. 489. Geoffrey does not describe the Battle, so we must rely upon other evidence to determine the likely site and circumstances of this particular Battle.

The starting point for locating the Battle of Castle Gurnion is the word "castle." In the original Latin, "castle" is *castellum*, meaning "little fort." *Castellum* was the Roman term for a fort used to house troops other than legionaries (who resided in a *castrum* or "fort"). The search for the site of Arthur's eighth victory

should therefore focus upon finding a Roman fort with a name resembling "Gurnion" or "Guinnion."

By assuming that the "gu" in the spelling "Guinnion" should be a Welsh "gw," which corresponds to the Latin "v," the old Roman cavalry fort of Vinovia, now called Binchester, in modern Durham has been identified as a possible "Castle Guinnion." In A.D. 489, however, Vinovia was situated deep in the territory of the Dux Britanniarum, about twenty miles south of Hadrian's Wall. For Arthur to have fought at Vinovia, he would have had to lead his army through the heart of the Dux's domain, fighting past the Dux's forces. Such a confrontation between the southern Magister Militum and the northern Romano-Briton magnate would have been much too important to be neglected by Geoffrey's sources. Although justifiable on strictly linguistic grounds, the geopolitical circumstances of late Fifth Century Britannia weigh against Vinovia being the site of the Battle of Castle Gurnion/Guinnion.

The alternative spelling of the Battle's name, "Gurnion," points us to the correct location of the Battle. This spelling of the Battle's name suggests that the "u" should not be substituted with a Welsh "gw" or a Latin "v," but taken as a vowel. Taking the "u" in "Gurnion" as a vowel, we can find a "Castle Gurnion" in Anglia which is a feasible location for the Battle. The Battle of Castle Gurnion was fought at Gariannonum, now Burgh Castle, in modern Norfolk.

Gariannonum was a Saxon Shore fort, and thus a Castellum, on the east coast of Britannia. It had been one of the more northerly bastions of the Comes Litoris Saxonici (Count of the Saxon Shore). The Castellum was located about eighteen miles due east of Venta Icenorum in a heavily populated part of Anglia; the first Angles to settle in the area probably came to serve in the fort's garrison. Given its location, Castellum Gariannonum was a very likely site for a clash of arms between Arthur and the Angles of Anglia.

Castellum Gariannonum lay deep within Anglia, being roughly sixty miles from Camulodunum, so the Battle of Castle Gurnion would have occurred at the climax of a massive Briton invasion of Anglia. Arthur and the Romano-Briton army marched from their base at Camulodunum into the most thickly populated coastal region of Anglia, destroying the barbarian's homes and burning their fields as they went. Arthur must have set out with a large force early in the spring before the barbarians were ready. The Angles were not prepared for the war to be carried so aggressively onto their own soil, and they were slow to muster a response. Arthur moved rapidly and reached the Castellum Gariannonum area before the Angles were able raise sufficient forces to offer meaningful resistance. The Angles, surprised by the speed and ferocity of Arthur's attack, managed to bring the Magister Militum to battle only after he had progressed all the way to Castellum Gariannonum - and then they were soundly defeated.

The Battle of Castle Gurnion was a great victory for Arthur, but it was hardly the end of the Anglia War. One summer's raid and a single battle were not enough to destroy the Angles, nor could Arthur have realistically expected to have so easily eliminated the barbarian menace. It had taken six battles fought over three years to put down the Angles of Lindsey, and it would require several years of intense warfare to break the power of the more

numerous Angles of Anglia. We should classify the campaign of A.D. 489 as an important victory in the opening phase of a long war. The territory of the Angles was probed, their settlements damaged, the mettle of their warriors tested, and the long, slow process of destroying their military strength begun.

Arthur was unable to follow up this auspicious beginning to his Anglia War with a new offensive the following year. Another, more urgent danger unexpectedly arose to call Arthur and his warriors away to a far distant front.

## Armies in Post-Roman Britannia
## II

### Romano-Briton
Catavia, A.D. 475-484
  garrison of Castellum Cataviae    1,000
Cador, A.D. 486,
  Battle of the Eboracum Road    3,600
Hoel of Armorica, A.D. 486,
  arrival in Britannia    est. 1,100

### Anglo-Saxon
Baldulf, A.D. 486,
  Battle of the Eboracum Road    6,000
Cheldric, A.D. 486,
  mercenaries from Germania    600
Colgrin & Baldulf, A.D. 486,
  Battles in the Region Linnuis    6,000

## Chapter Twenty-One
## The Boar War

Arthur's next victory was achieved in the Battle of the City of the Legion. This Battle was the decisive combat of a hard-fought campaign which, for reasons we shall discuss, could be called "the Boar War." The Boar War represented the most serious military challenge yet faced by the Britons of the post-Roman period. Arthur's victory in the Battle of the City of the Legion would have certainly been his greatest accomplishment had it not been overshadowed by his even greater triumph a few years later in the Battle of Badon Hill.

### The City of the Legion

Post-Roman Britannia had three "Cities of the Legion," each of which has been proposed as the site of Arthur's ninth victory. One "City of the Legion" was Luguvalium (Carlisle), former capital of the Province of Valentia and still chief town of Civitas Carvetiorum. Another was Castrum Deva (Chester), former headquarters of Legion XX Valeria Victrix but virtually abandoned ever since Magister Militum Stilicho withdrew the Legion from Britannia in A.D. 402. The third was Isca Silurum (Caerleon), former headquarters of Legion II Augusta but then merely a minor town in Gwent. We shall examine each of these "Cities of the Legion" in turn.

The modern name of Luguvalium, "Carlisle," means "City of the Legion" in north Briton dialect.[117] This fact alone makes the town a candidate for the site of Arthur's ninth

---

117 Actually, we shall see, it probably means "City of the [plural] Legions."

---

victory. If, however, Arthur had campaigned so far in the north and so near such an important town, then at least some memory of the fighting would have survived. Yet we can find no mention of any such campaign in the *Historia Regum Britanniae* or any other early source. The military and political implications of a battle fought in the vicinity of Luguvalium would have been much too great for the battle to be so completely forgotten. Because we can find no record of a battle fought in the vicinity of Luguvalium, the northern town could not have been the site of the Battle of the City of the Legion.

Castrum Deva (Chester) was also once called "Caer Ligion" (City of the Legion) by the Britons. It appears a likely battle site on purely geographic grounds, its proximity to the Irish Sea suggesting the possible enemy. Once again, however, we can find no early tradition of a battle near the town. Although Castrum Deva itself was a minor town and did not play a major role in post-Roman affairs, any invasion of the Castrum Deva area would have been remembered at least by the Britons of the nearby Cornovian town of Viroconium (Wroxeter). Despite its location by the Irish Sea, Castrum Deva is not a strong candidate for the Battle of the City of the Legion.

Isca Silurum is yet another town once known as the "City of the Legion," its modern name of Caerleon being a Welsh version of "Carlisle." In its case, we do indeed find positive evidence in Welsh tradition identifying it as the "City of the Legion" where Arthur fought his Battle. A story in the *Mabinogion* tale "How Culhwch Won Olwen" describes an Irish invasion of south Wales that was opposed by Arthur. The invaders landed in Demetia and advanced eastward through Gower and

Glevissig all the way to Gwent and the area about Isca Silurum before they were stopped. The Welsh tradition preserved in "How Culhwch Won Olwen" indicates that Isca Silurum is the true "City of the Legion" where Arthur won his ninth victory.

Geoffrey of Monmouth also describes an Irish invasion of south Wales. He, like the storyteller of "How Culhwch Won Olwen," tells of the landing of an Irish army in Demetia and a successful Briton military response. He does not, however, credit the Briton victory to Arthur, but to his fictitious "Utherpendragon." The "Utherpendragon" whom Geoffrey says defeated an Irish invasion of south Wales was, of course, Magister Militum Arthur.

### Geoffrey of Monmouth's Account of the Boar War

From Geoffrey, we learn that an old enemy of Aurelius decided that the time was right to make one more attempt at power. Pascent, ruler of Builth and son of Vortigern, again plotted against the Regissimus Britanniarum.

Pascent had earlier conspired with the Irish of Demetia to undermine Aurelius's authority. A seaborne punitive expedition led by Catavia, Aurelius's first "Utherpendragon," against the Demetians soon split this alliance apart. Pascent then submitted to the new Regissimus, and Aurelius in return confirmed Pascent as ruler of Builth. Pascent and his would-be Demetian allies kept the peace, but they did not give up their ambition; they continued to nurse their animosity toward Aurelius. The resumption of the Builth-Demetia conspiracy led to the Battle of the City of the Legion.

Pascent would perhaps have been better advised to have initiated his insurrection in A.D. 488, when Arthur and his army were far away in the north. The timing of the revolt was not, however, under the Builth leader's control. The military forces under Pascent's command were limited, and he was dependent upon the recruitment of allies. For their part, Pascent's former collaborators in Demetia, having once suffered the wrath of Aurelius's army, were reluctant to again unilaterally support the rebel in his ambitious schemes. It took the arrival of reinforcements from Ireland to make a new revolt feasible. With Irish troops landing in Demetia to support him, and with Arthur at the opposite end of the island in Camulodunum (Colchester), Pascent apparently decided that A.D. 490 was a sufficiently propitious year in which to resume his rebellion.

The Irish leader who led an army in support of Pascent was none other than the Gillomanius, or Mannion, whom we have already met in connection with Geoffrey's description of "Utherpendragon's" first expedition to "Ireland." In fact, Gillomanius probably led the Irish forces only in the Boar War, and Geoffrey errs in identifying him as leader of the Irish defenders in the earlier conflict. Geoffrey, unaware that Demetia was a second "Ireland" located in Britannia, must have learned the name of the Irish chieftain from overseas who fought in the Boar War and mistakenly gave him command of the Demetian Irish in the prior campaign as well.

Geoffrey tells us that Gillomanius landed near Menevia, today called St. David's, in Demetia. He also says that "Utherpendragon" led the Briton army against the invaders because Aurelius was then lying ill at "Winchester" (i.e., Venta Belgarum). The royal army encountered the rebel Pascent and his Irish allies in Wales, and a ferocious combat ensued. Although the outcome of the conflict was long in doubt, "Utherpendragon" ultimately prevailed. Both Pascent and Gillomanius were slain in the fighting, and many Irish warriors were cut down as they fled toward their ships.

The *Mabinogion* tale "How Culhwch Won Olwen" gives a much more detailed account of the campaign of A.D. 490.

### The Mabinogion Account of the Boar War

"How Culhwch Won Olwen" is a curious medley of ancient pagan theology, post-Roman historical fact and sheer timeless fantasy. The tale freezes a moment in time when the slow process of grafting pagan mythology and medieval fiction onto Arthurian history was only just beginning. For example, the tale attributes to Arthur the ancient Celtic story of the quest to fetch a magic cauldron. An earlier version of the same story is found in the *Mabinogion* tale "Branwen Daughter of Llyr," in which the quest is undertaken by the mythological god-king Bran. Bran's magic cauldron is the first incarnation of the marvelous "Holy Grail," the sacred relic which played an important role in the medieval Romances. For our purposes, the most important part of the tale is the part which preserves in very elaborate - and very credible - detail the memory of a campaign which Arthur fought against Irish invaders who landed in Demetia and who marched on the Romanized territory of southeast Wales.

Arthur's opponent in the campaign described in the *Mabinogion* is not named Mannion or Gillomanius, but Twrch Trwyth. "Twrch" is the Welsh word for "boar," and

"Trwyth" is a Welsh corruption of the Irish word *triath*, also meaning "boar." The Irish chieftain who invaded Britannia was thus called "the Boar."

"The Boar," like "the Stallion" (Hengist) or "the Horse" (Horsa), is a *nom de guerre*, or warrior nickname. The boar, like the horse, was a noble animal much admired in warrior cultures; Arthur himself has been likened to a boar in the *Prophetiae Merlini* on account of his martial ferocity. Pigs and boars were particularly honored in Celtic tradition. Later Welsh storytellers offered a slightly different, and much less flattering, interpretation; in the "Culhwch" tale, Arthur is made to say of his enemy, "He was a king, but because of his sins God turned him into a pig."

From Geoffrey's account, we know that the Irish leader's personal name was Mannion. Combining the Latin *Historia Regum Britanniae* with the Welsh *Mabinogion*, we can deduce that the Irish king who led an army against Arthur in A.D. 490 was a renown warrior from Ireland called Mannion the Boar. From Mannion's nickname, we may call the conflict of A.D. 490 "the Boar War."

The *Mabinogion* confirms that Mannion the Boar did indeed come from Ireland and was not a local Demetian Irish warlord. In addition to saying so outright, the tale identifies "Twrch Trwyth" as the son of the ruler "Taredd" (pronounced "Tareth"), which is a corruption of "Tara," the name of the place where the Irish High Kings traditionally held court. Whether or not Mannion the Boar was really related to the royal family of Tara, the Welsh clearly remembered him as a nobly-born warrior from Ireland.

According to the *Mabinogion*, the Boar

War began when Arthur went to Ireland in order to fight "the Boar." Arthur's aggression provoked a retaliatory porcine invasion of Wales. The tale then depicts Arthur hurriedly leaving Ireland in hot pursuit of the Boar. Arthur's alleged provocation of the Boar War is a medieval addition to the original story. Arthur was hardly likely to have travelled outside Britannia while the Anglia War still raged, and he certainly would not have gone to Ireland - or anywhere else for that matter - for the purpose of making new enemies. On this point, we may disregard the *Mabinogion* account; Geoffrey is right on the mark in tracing the origin of Mannion's invasion to an alliance between the Irish leader and Pascent of Builth.

The *Mabinogion* goes on to fancifully describe the Irish invasion as if it were a wild pig hunt, with Arthur and his warriors seeking to slay "the Boar" and his "piglets." This presentation of the story, being an elaborate pun upon the enemy's nickname, must have been very amusing to the bard's audience who, at least in the early days of the tale's telling, were familiar with the true events. If we look past the storyteller's entertaining narrative, the tale preserves a very useful account of the fighting which took place in A.D. 490.

In the *Mabinogion* account, the Irish landed at Porth Cleis on the northern arm of the Demetian peninsula, which is near Menevia, modern St. David's. From there they advanced into the interior of Demetia, probably to join the main force of their Demetian allies before invading Briton territory. The arrival of the Irish was a mixed blessing to the Demetians, however, because hungry Irish warriors apparently slaughtered some cattle not belonging to them in the Milford Haven region. The combined Gaelic force then proceeded due east.

The Welsh storyteller depicts the Irish fighting for each step of their advance into Wales. In fact, opposition to the Irish would not have manifested itself until the invaders crossed over into the Briton territories of Gower and Glevissig. Gower was (and is) the peninsula just to the east of Demetia, and Glevissig was the Romanized territory along the Bristol Channel and the Severn Estuary from Gower up to Gwent. Gower and Glevissig are now called Glamorgan, and Gwent today again bears its post-Roman name. The first combat of the Boar War would have been fought at the crossing of the River Llwchwr (pronounced more or less as "Lucor" in modern English), which then formed the eastern border of Demetia and where the Welsh tale does indeed report a battle.

In the Battle of the River Llwchwr, the local Briton forces were swept aside and the Irish continued their advance into Gower. One of the Briton casualties reported by the *Mabinogion* was "Garwyli, son of Gwyddawg Gwyr," which could be translated as "Garwola, son of Wothauc, ruler of Gower."[118] The son of the Gower ruler probably fell in the Battle of the River Llwchwr. The Irish ravaged Gower and then entered Glevissig by crossing the River Tawy.

Scattered fighting and skirmishing occurred throughout Glevissig, as Irish warriors ranged across the countryside in search of booty and the local Romano-Briton gentry vainly resisted. The Gaelic fleet would have paralleled the army's course by sailing beside its route of advance along the south Welsh coastline. The proximity of the ships provided the Irish with both an emergency means of escape in the event

118 In Latin, his name would have been something like "Garvola, filius Votauci."

of defeat and an easy method of out-flanking the Glevissig-men whenever they attempted to block the Irish advance. Glevissig was devastated, after which the Irish began to move in a northeasterly direction, apparently to link up with Pascent and his rebels in Builth.

Sometime after the Battle of the River Llwchwr, a desperate plea for assistance must have been dispatched by the endangered citizens of Glevissig to Aurelius in Venta Belgarum (Winchester). This message was certainly carried by Aurelius's signal fire communications network in southwest Britannia. Aurelius then sent word to Arthur, ordering him to cancel his planned offensive against Anglia and to proceed with all haste to Glevissig instead. Arthur, who had probably already begun an advance into Anglia, promptly broke off his attack and, riding hard, headed west at great speed.

In order to have responded so quickly to the Irish invasion, Arthur could not have brought his infantry with him all the way from Camulodunum to Wales. The foot soldiers would have only slowed him down. Arthur must have left his infantry behind and travelled with only his cavalry.

The *Mabinogion* reports that, when Arthur arrived in Wales, he halted near the mouth of the Severn River to await the arrival of additional forces from Devon and Cornwall. These additional forces were, of course, the Cornovians of Dumnonia and the garrison at Castellum Cataviae (Cadbury Castle). Incidentally, in stating that Arthur halted near the mouth of the Severn River, the *Mabinogion* storyteller inadvertently admits that Arthur approached the battle area from the east, rather than chasing after "the Boar" from the west, as

he initially states. Arthur planned to rendezvous with his reinforcements at Isca Silurum or Caerleon, "the City of the Legion."

## The Battle of the City of the Legion

Arthur and his horse soldiers did not head straight to Isca Silurum from Camulodunum. Nennius, in another of his works, *De Mirabilibus Britanniae* (Concerning the Marvels of Britain),[119] reports that Arthur went to "Buelt" while "hunting" the "Troit Boar." Cabal, Arthur's dog, supposedly left his footprint on a stone atop a cairn in Builth when he accompanied his master there. The cairn is now dismantled and lost, but it was probably on a hill now called Corngafallt, not far from the town of Rhayader in what was then north Builth. "Troit Boar" is obviously a distortion of Twrch Trwyth, the *nom de guerre* of the Irish war leader Mannion. Nennius thus indicates that Arthur was in Builth sometime during the war against Mannion the Boar. Arthur's presence in Pascent's kingdom at this time can only mean that the Magister Militum detoured through Builth on his way to Gwent in order to take the life of the Briton traitor Pascent.

Because we can find no account of any fighting in Builth, Arthur must have moved so rapidly and arrived in the rebel realm so suddenly that he caught Pascent completely by surprise. Facing little or no opposition from the unprepared Builthmen, the Magister Militum was able to seize and unceremoniously kill the treacherous ruler. According to the *Mabinogion*, Arthur then sent "the men of Brittany"

---

119 Some historians doubt that Nennius wrote *De Mirabilibus Britanniae*; they believe it was mistakenly ascribed to him by a medieval editor. For convenience, we shall nevertheless refer to the work as his.

(i.e., Hoel and his Armoricans) to intercept the Irish army still en route to their planned link-up with Pascent, while he, with the remainder of his mounted soldiers, rode on to Isca Silurum to meet the troops whom he had summoned from Dumnonia and Castellum Cataviae.

Mannion the Boar saw no reason to continue to push into the interior of Britannia now that Pascent had been killed. He probably preferred to fight on the relatively open south Welsh coast in any case, where he could re-establish close contact with his fleet and more easily deal with Briton resistance. At the same time, the Armorican cavalrymen whom Arthur sent to block the Irish advance were no doubt making repeated hit-and-run assaults on the Irish army. They would have ambushed Irish foraging parties, attacked small bands which became separated from the main force and generally badgered the invaders. The rugged terrain and the swift mobility of the Breton horsemen made it difficult for the Irish foot soldiers to cope with these tactics. Mannion soon grew weary of the continual harassment, and his troops began to lose heart. Deprived of their Builth co-conspirator and facing spirited opposition from Arthur's soldiers, the Irish abandoned their advance into central Wales and headed back to their ships by the Gwent shore.

The Irish force had meanwhile split up. Perhaps deceived by the lack of effective resistance early in the invasion, one of Mannion's sub-chieftains, comically referred to as a "piglet," had gone off on his own. This "piglet" represents the contingent of Irish warriors from Demetia. The Demetian warriors abandoned the advance into Builth and headed west in order to wreck havoc in the vicinity of Cardigan.

The Cardigan area, or Ceredigion as it was then called, had recently fallen into the hands of Cunedda's son Ceredig, for whom it was renamed. Ceredig or his heir probably led his followers in an attack upon the Irish kingdom in a deliberate effort to divert the Demetian forces away from Mannion's main army of invasion. All Cunedda's descendants were at least nominally allied to Aurelius by virtue of Aurelius's marriage to Ygerna, and the leaders of Ceredigion seem to have been especially close to Aurelius; as we shall see, a future ruler of Ceredigion was probably then serving in Arthur's army. Moreover, the Britons of Ceredigion had as much to fear from Mannion the Boar and his Demetian allies as did the Britons of Gower, Glevissig and Gwent. In any event, the departure of the Demetian "piglet" left Mannion short of troops. Having finally encountered the elite cavalry of the Romano-Briton army, Mannion must have realized that he was engaged in a much tougher fight than he had bargained for, and he no doubt regretted the departure of his Demetian allies.

Mannion and the main group of Irish warriors, enraged by the gadfly attacks of the Armorican cavalry, continued to head straight for the Gwent coast. The Magister Militum was ready and waiting for them. He had his Romano-Briton horsemen with him, and his reinforcements had just arrived from Dumnonia and Castellum Cataviae. The Armoricans probably rejoined Arthur even as the Irish charged into battle. The great confrontation between Arthur and Mannion took place somewhere between Lake Lliwan and the River Wye, in the vicinity of Isca Silurum, the Welsh "City of the Legion."

The Irish were routed.

Arthur owed his victory to the fact that his

elite mounted troops struck before the conspiring Irish and Builthmen could join forces. The signal fire communications network established by Aurelius, the prompt response of Arthur and the extraordinary efforts of the Romano-Briton cavalry soldiers had turned back the most serious threat to Britannia since the days of Vortigern.

The campaign was not yet over, however. One more battle had to be fought before Arthur could claim complete victory.

### The Battle on the Shore by the River Tribruit

The *Mabinogion* relates that the Boar, after most of his "piglets" (i.e., sub-commanders) had been slain, took to the sea. The Irish warlord and some of his followers apparently managed to fight their way back to their ships. When Mannion set sail, he did not seek safety; he sought revenge. The *Mabinogion* tells us that the Boar decided to vent his anger on "Cornwall" while Arthur was still in Wales.

Mannion's target was certainly Arthur's permanent headquarters at Castellum Cataviae in Cornovian Dumnonia. Mannion knew that he could deal a serious blow to Arthur's prestige and authority if he destroyed Arthur's chief military base. The hillfort was an especially tempting target at this time because most of its garrison troops were away with Arthur at Isca Silurum.

Nennius identifies the location of Arthur's tenth victory as the shore or strand by the River Tribruit, which refers to the beach at the mouth of the River Brue in modern north Somerset. "Tribruit" is an early form of "Ribroit," which is another name for the River Brue. Some historians believe that the Battle on the Shore by the River Tribruit was fought somewhere in the Scottish lowlands, but we have no credible explanation for Arthur's presence in that region at this time. The Somerset location also has traditional associations with Arthur; local legend claims that Arthur's sword Excalibur was thrown into the River Brue after Arthur's death. The River Brue or Ribroit in modern Somerset is undoubtedly the River Tribruit by whose shore Arthur won his tenth victory.

After escaping defeat in the Battle of the City of the Legion, Mannion the Boar sailed his fleet directly across the Severn Estuary, landing on the beach at the mouth of the River Tribruit/River Brue. From there, a brief march to the east along the banks of the River would have brought him into the center of modern Somerset and into the heart of Aurelius's western defenses. The River Brue even passes close by Glastonbury on the direct route toward Castellum Cataviae. Mannion obviously hoped to destroy Castellum Cataviae, and perhaps Glastonbury as well, and then escape before Arthur could react.

Mannion did not take into account the effectiveness of Aurelius's signal fire communications network. The mouth of the River Brue and the seaward approaches to the river were well within sight of the lookouts posted in the small fort atop Brent Knoll. Word of the second Irish landing should have been on its way to Arthur as soon as the Irish ships came into view of the Somerset shore. Gathering his weary warriors for one more herculean effort, Arthur and the Romano-Briton cavalry rode out after the Irish leader.

Not realizing the danger they were in, the Irish might have rested a day or so beside their ships on the beach near the mouth of the River Brue. Alternatively, they might have begun an advance into Somerset, but fell back toward their ships when they spotted Arthur's approach. In either case, Arthur attacked them on the beach by the river. On this beach, Arthur and Mannion fought the Battle on the Shore by the River Tribruit.

The Irish were surprised and dismayed by the sudden, unexpected appearance of the Romano-Briton cavalry. The Irish really had no chance and the resulting combat was not much of a contest. According to the early Welsh poem *Cath Palug* (Clawing Cat), enemy warriors fell by the hundred in the Battle. Arthur again defeated the Irish invaders and again drove them into the sea, but this time the Irish did not escape until after Mannion the Boar himself had been slain.

Arthur thus brought the Boar War to a triumphant conclusion.

Arthur paid dearly for his success. According to the *Mabinogion*, Arthur's army suffered many casualties in the Boar War. One of these casualties was "Osla Big Knife," whom we have identified as the Anglo-Saxon leader Eosa. Osla drowned while fighting the Boar near the mouth of the Severn River. The *Mabinogion* also reports the loss of a soldier named Gwydre, whom it identifies as Arthur's own son. Arthur and the Romano-Briton army had saved Britannia, but at enormous cost in the blood of heroic warriors.

## Arthur Becomes Regissimus Britanniarum

After the valiant efforts and hard fighting of the campaign against Mannion the Boar, Arthur and his troops had well earned a rest - a rest, however, which they were probably denied. Arthur, at least, still had much to do that year, because while the Magister Militum and his army were waging war in Gwent, Aurelius, the Regissimus Britanniarum, died.

Geoffrey tells us that Aurelius died when "Utherpendragon" was away fighting in south Wales, and that "Utherpendragon" then succeeded Aurelius as "king." Geoffrey did not know that "Utherpendragon" was a military title rather than a name, so he did not realize the significance of this statement which he found in one of his sources. The "Utherpendragon" or Magister Militum who returned from the battlefield as Regissimus Britanniarum was Arthur.

## Chapter Twenty-Two
## Artorius, Regissimus Britanniarum

While Arthur battled Mannion the Boar in Wales, the Angles did not sit idly by in Anglia. They sought to avenge their defeat of the previous year in the Battle of Castle Gurnion by attacking the Britons. The Angles marched down the ancient Icknield Way, striking deep into Briton territory. Aurelius mustered the Briton troops still available, and he fought the barbarian invaders at Verulamium (St. Albans).

### The Battle of Verulamium

We have already discussed the Battle of Verulamium in connection with the end of the Age of Ambrosius. Aurelius attacked the barbarians in the town, but was driven off. The next day, when the Anglo-Saxons made an attempt to break out of Verulamium, the Regissimus engaged and defeated them. After much hard fighting, Aurelius won a great - his last - victory.

Geoffrey of Monmouth identifies the barbarian leaders at the Battle as Octa and Eosa, but it must have been Colgrin and Baldulf who commanded at Verulamium. Octa was already dead, having fallen in the Battle of the Caledonian Wood some two years earlier, and Eosa/Osla was then serving with Arthur in Wales, where he fell in the Battle of the City of the Legion. Geoffrey is correct in his belief that Octa and Eosa were killed before Arthur became "king," but he is wrong as to the exact circumstances of their deaths. Geoffrey knew that Octa and Eosa both died before Arthur became Regissimus and that they both fell in battle, but he assumed that they had been slain together and he therefore identifies the wrong pair of leaders in the Battle of Verulamium.

Colgrin and Baldulf, on the other hand, were militarily active both before and after the Battle of Verulamium. They could have also made the short journey down the Icknield Way from Anglia to attack Verulamium much more easily than Octa could have made the longer journey from Bernicia, or the shorter but more dangerous journey past Londinium from Kent. Colgrin and Baldulf certainly had a compelling reason to launch an invasion of Britannia in A.D. 490 since they were then locked in a war to the death with Arthur. The Icelingas leaders must have eagerly seized the opportunity presented by the absence of Arthur and the Romano-Briton army to invade Briton territory and inflict damage upon their enemy. Colgrin and Baldulf would not have missed this fight.

Aurelius deserves enormous credit for turning back Colgrin's and Baldulf's invasion. The circumstances in which he won his victory make his achievement especially commendable. He fought against hardened Anglo-Saxon warriors with only such of his infantry and rear area troops as could be spared from the Boar War. There are, however, limits to what even Aurelius could do with such an army, and he was unable to follow up his battlefield success with a vigorous pursuit of the enemy. As a result, most of the barbarian warriors escaped, including the leaders Colgrin and Baldulf. The Angles were therefore capable of fielding large and effective armies in the years following the Battle. We do not insult Aurelius if we insist that the Battle of Verulamium was not nearly the slaughter of the barbarians which Geoffrey describes.

Aurelius gained his last victory at the cost of

his life. The strain of the campaign on the unwell Aurelius sapped his strength, and he did not long survive his defeat of the Angles. Ironically, in drawing Arthur away to Wales and in causing Aurelius to take the field against the Angles, Pascent did, albeit indirectly, cause the death of his enemy. Pascent thus finally gained vengeance against his father's slayer.

We can be certain that Aurelius's death and Arthur's rise to the rule of Britannia occurred in A.D. 490. Geoffrey tells us that Arthur was only fifteen years old when he became "king," which means Arthur became Regissimus Britanniarum fifteen years after the date on which Geoffrey *thought* that Arthur was born. Geoffrey thought that Arthur was conceived during Aurelius's Dumnonian campaign against Dux Gorlois, which places Arthur's putative fifteenth birthday and his rise to the position of Regissimus approximately sixteen years after the defeat of Gorlois. Based upon the known dates for Aurelius's Continental expedition, we have derived a date for his Dumnonian campaign of A.D. 474. Adding sixteen years to the date of Aurelius's campaign against Dux Gorlois gives us A.D. 490 for Aurelius's demise and for Arthur's elevation to the high office of Regissimus Britanniarum.

## Arthur Becomes Regissimus Britanniarum

Geoffrey tells us that "Utherpendragon" (i.e., Arthur, the Magister Militum) returned to "Winchester" (i.e., Venta Belgarum) after the death of Aurelius to assume the government of Britannia. Later, Geoffrey tells us that Arthur was "crowned" in "Silchester" (i.e., Calleva Atrebatum). After the hard-fought Boar War, Arthur must have gone first to Venta Belgarum to arrange Aurelius's funeral, and then to various other towns and forts in south Britannia to test the reaction to his rise to power. The new Regissimus had to pay final honors to his predecessor, receive pledges of loyalty from the Magistrati of the southern Civitates, confirm the allegiance of the scattered military garrisons and generally take into his hands the reins of government. He finally felt comfortable enough in his position to formally assume the title of Regissimus Britanniarum when he arrived in Calleva Atrebatum. If Arthur made a circuit of south Britannia along the Roman road network by first going south and then proceeding in a generally counter-clockwise direction, Calleva would have been the final stop on his inaugural journey. Arthur must have spent the winter of A.D. 490-491 travelling across his domain and taking steps to ensure that his new-found regal authority rested upon a sound political foundation.

The Angle problem meanwhile continued to demand attention, and Arthur might have temporarily moved his political court, as well as his military headquarters, to Camulodunum. From Camulodunum, Arthur could both run his kingdom and keep a close watch upon his barbarian enemies. The former capital town was connected by a good road system to the rest of Britannia, and it occupied a strategic position from which Arthur could respond quickly to a military threat from either Anglia or Kent, the two principal barbarian kingdoms in south Britannia.[120] Camulodunum, or "Camelot," thus could have truly been, at least for a brief time, Arthur's capital - as claimed by the Romances.

Despite his occupation of Camulodunum, Arthur was probably not militarily active during

---

120 Kent, now ruled by Aesc, might have already been showing signs of resurgence.

the first campaign season of his reign, the summer of A.D. 491. Arthur still had much politicking to do in order to tighten his grip on power, because he surely knew that he could not take the support of all the local leaders in south Britannia for granted. He also had to rebuild his army, because the elite Romano-Briton cavalry must have been seriously depleted by the constant warfare of the past several years, especially the long marches and hard fighting of the Boar War. Arthur was too preoccupied, and his military forces too exhausted, to undertake a major offensive against the Angles in A.D. 491.

Arthur did not abandon the war against Anglia. He planned a new military campaign, probably for the very next year.

### The Battle of Mount Agned near Breguoin

The eleventh victory listed by Nennius is the Battle of Mount Breguoin, sometimes written as "Mount Bregomion." On strictly linguistic grounds, historians have proposed several different "Breguoin" sites. Among the proposed sites are Bremenium (High Rochester), an abandoned Roman army fort north of Hadrian's Wall, and Bravonium (Leintwardine), a small Cornovian town in modern Herefordshire. Even Bremetennacum (Ribchester), the former Sarmatian cavalry base, has been suggested. None of these sites could have been the battleground, however, because we cannot ascertain why or whom Arthur would have fought at any of those places - especially the far northern site. Given that Arthur was still at war with the Angles, the Battle of Mount Breguoin must have been fought somewhere in Anglia.

A feasible site for the Battle can be found in modern Suffolk. "Breguoin" or "Bregomion" is probably a corruption of "Combretovium," the name of a small town in Anglia, its prefix "com" having dropped off.

Combretovium was the Roman town now called Baylham, which is located about five miles north of modern Ipswich. The town lies on the Roman Road connecting Camulodunum (Colchester) with Venta Icenorum (Caistor-by-Norwich). A battle there would have been a natural occurrence in Arthur's resumption of the war against Anglia. A small hill somewhere in the vicinity of the town of Combretovium is probably the "mount" where the Battle was fought.

The Battle of Mount Breguoin is called the Battle of Mount *Agned* in some manuscripts, so the original battle poem consulted by Nennius must have referred to a battle on a mount *near* Breguoin, with "Agned" being the name of the mount. The original description of the Battle was probably something like "bellum in monte qui dicitur Agned ad [com]Bretovium," meaning "battle on the mount which is called Agned near [com]Breguoin." The name of the town was later confused with that of the mount, resulting in two different names for the same battle.

On strictly linguistic grounds, "Mount Agned" has been identified as Mount Angned, now Edinburgh Castle, in Scotland. The old Welsh poem *Cath Palug* (Clawing Cat) also mentions a battle "on the borders of Eidyn," which clearly refers to the Edinburgh area. Mount Angned does not lie near a likely "Breguoin" site, however, so the *Cath Palug* reference must be to another battle which Arthur later fought near modern Edinburgh. "Agned" was probably a common ancient Celtic place name, like "Douglas" and "Glen." Several hills could have borne that name, including one beside modern Edinburgh and another beside the Roman town of Combretovium.[121] The Battle of Mount Agned near Breguoin did not take place at Mount Angned near modern Edinburgh, but at an unknown Mount Agned near Roman Combretovium.

Combretovium is only about twenty-one miles up the road from Arthur's temporary capital of Camulodunum. It is not nearly as far into Angle territory as Arthur had penetrated just three years earlier when he defeated the Angles in the Battle of Castle Gurnion. Although the Battle is listed as a victory for Arthur, the actual outcome must have been more ambiguous. If Arthur had thoroughly defeated the barbarians, he would have followed up his victory by advancing deeper into Angle territory. In that case, another battle further north in Anglia would have been reported. The Angles must have been ready for Arthur this time, bringing him to battle soon after he entered Anglia.

Alternatively, Arthur simply might not have intended to fight a decisive battle in A.D. 492. If Arthur was not ready to renew the Anglia War, he might have advanced only far enough into Anglia to draw the attention of the Angles and keep them from raiding westward into Briton territory. Having distracted the barbarians from an invasion of central Britannia, Arthur immediately withdrew his forces because they were not yet prepared for the resumption of full-scale warfare.

In either event, Arthur's invasion force was turned back or pulled out before a definitive victory could be achieved. Whether its inconclusive outcome was due to Angle preparedness or Briton lack of preparedness, the Battle of Mount Agned near Breguoin was not an auspicious beginning to the reign of Regissimus Arthur.

---

121 And yet a third in modern Dorset. Geoffrey reports that the ancient Briton King Ebraucus built a fort on a Mount named Agned and later called Maiden Castle. Although Edinburgh Castle was once called Castle of the Maidens, Geoffrey probably means the Dorset Maiden Castle in this instance because Geoffrey also tells us that King Ebraucus made war upon Gaul. Ebraucus probably built the Dorset Mount Agned as a base of operations for his Gallic war.

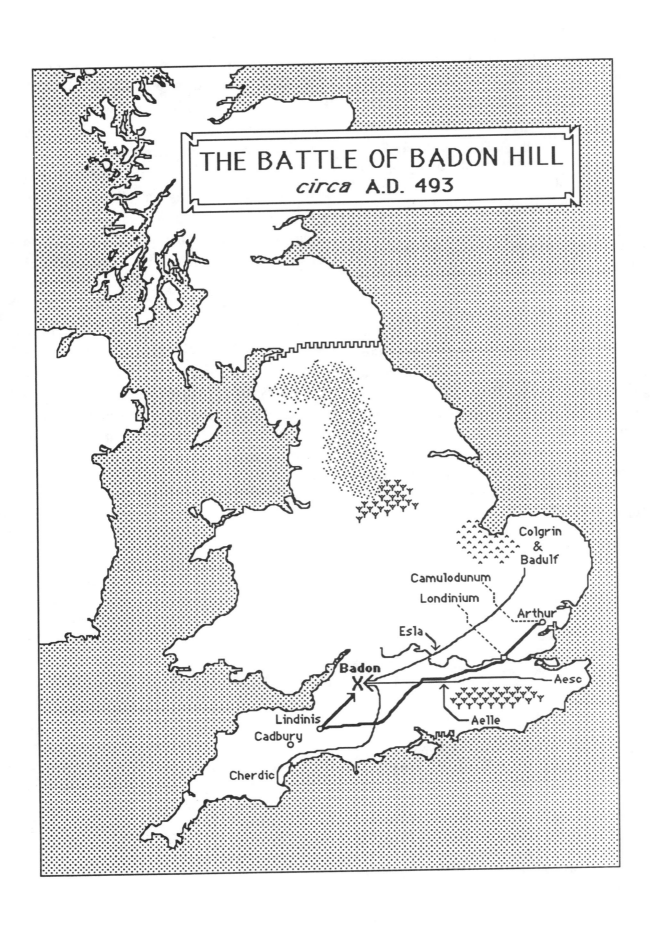

THE BATTLE OF BADON HILL
*circa* A.D. 493

Colgrin
&
Badulf

Camulodunum

Londinium

Arthur

Esla

Badon
X

Aesc

Lindinis

Aelle

Cadbury

Cherdic

## Chapter Twenty-Three
## The Battle of Badon Hill

Even if the outcome of the Battle of Mount Agned near Breguoin was not entirely satisfactory to Arthur, the overall military situation still favored the Britons in their war against Anglia. Arthur's victories had stymied all enemy attempts to upset the strong Romano-Briton strategic position, and Arthur's army was steadily regaining its strength and effectiveness, as amply demonstrated by the quality of its future performance. Arthur was also able to maintain the initiative in the war because most of its principal battles were fought in Anglia; until then, the only major battle fought on Briton territory was the Battle of Verulamium, which was fought when Arthur was away in south Wales. So long as Arthur preserved his army intact and so long as he restricted the fighting to Angle rather than Briton soil, he would have eventually worn the enemy down. In repeated invasions of Anglia, Arthur could have destroyed more and more of the Angles' farms and homes until the barbarians' very ability to wage war was shattered.

If the Angles hoped to survive as a military power in Britannia, they would have to take the offensive and carry the fight to Arthur. An aggressive thrust deep into Briton territory by a large barbarian army might overwhelm the Romano-Briton military forces and devastate the areas in southwest Britannia from which Arthur drew his cavalrymen and supplies. The Angle leaders were up to the challenge. Colgrin and Baldulf led their followers and allies in a massive attack upon Arthur with the aim of eradicating Briton power in a single, massive bloody stroke.

The climax of this great barbarian offensive was the crucial and decisive Battle of Badon Hill.

The Battle of Badon Hill has generated no end of historical controversy: Where was it fought? When was it fought? Who fought there? How was it fought? What was its significance? We have more positive and reliable information about this one Battle of Arthur's than we do for all his other battles combined, but greater information seems to have only generated greater controversy. Now that we have reconstructed the events which preceded and led up to the Battle of Badon Hill, we can finally put most of this controversy to rest; we can finally come to a true and full appreciation of the importance of this Battle in history.

### Locating the Battle of Badon Hill

The earliest surviving reference to the Battle of Badon Hill is found in *De Excidio Britanniae*. *De Excidio Britanniae* was written by the monk Gildas just a generation after the Battle was fought. Gildas refers to the Battle as *obsessio Badonici montis* (siege of Badon's mount).

Gildas's description of the Battle as a "siege" and his use of the word *mons* (*montis* being the genitive form), the Latin term used to describe hillforts, have misled historians and archaeologists for many years into looking for a reoccupied hillfort in which the Anglo-Saxons could have besieged Briton defenders. Gildas was not, however, a military technician, and he did not use the word "siege" in the specialized sense too readily attributed to it. In addition, the word *mons* did not always or necessarily imply a hillfort; it could also mean an ordinary hill. In fact, as we shall see, the Battle of Badon Hill was not a formal siege, but an open field battle in which one side simply held the high ground, and it was not fought at a hillfort, but upon an ordinary hill.

We shall therefore deliberately describe the conflict as a *battle*, not a siege, and we shall name its site as Badon *Hill*, not Fort Badon nor even Mount Badon.

We should nevertheless bear in mind that the hill upon which the Battle was fought was not necessarily itself named Badon. In fact, the exact Latin used by the earliest reporters of the Battle suggests otherwise. "Badon" would be *Bado* in Latin; the term *Badonicus* used by Gildas literally means "pertaining to Badon." (*Badonici* is the genitive form, consistent with *montis*.) Similarly, Nennius refers to the Battle as that of *Mons Badonis*, meaning the mount *of* Badon, not Mount Badon.[122] If the name of the hill itself was Badon, the Latin phrase would have been *Mons Bado*.[123] The *Annales Cambriae* (Annals of Wales) does not even refer to the hill at all; it calls the conflict *Bellum Badonis*, meaning simply "Battle of Badon." The efforts of many generations of historians to find a hill called Badon were as misguided as their efforts to find a suitable place for a siege to have occurred.

Geoffrey of Monmouth places the Battle of Badon Hill in the vicinity of the town of Bath,

then called Aquae Sulis. Although long disregarded by historians, Geoffrey's location for the Battle is correct.

The very name of the Battle site, Badon Hill (or, more accurately, Badon's Hill), suggests the area about modern Bath. A Latin territorial name like "regio Badonis" (region of Badon) or "Civitas Badonis" (Civitas of Badon) would have become "Caer Vadon" in Welsh, with the "d" pronounced like the Anglo-Saxon (or modern English) "th." In time, the Welsh word pronounced "Vathon" would have evolved into the Anglo-Saxon "Bath," a corruption readily suggested by the ruins of the Roman baths found in the old town. Several early English documents do indeed indicate that "Bath" and "Badon" were variant spellings of the same word. Place name analysis thus supports Geoffrey's identification of the area about Aquae Sulis as the site of the Battle of Badon Hill.

The area about Aquae Sulis is also a site that makes sense in military terms. The southwest of Britannia, in which Aquae Sulis is located, was a relatively prosperous region in Arthur's day and the region from which the post-Roman regimes in south Britannia drew a great deal of their wealth and army recruits. When the Anglo-Saxons finally did prevail over the south Britons, it was in a post-Arthurian military resurgence in the late Sixth Century beginning with a series of important victories moving in the general direction of Aquae Sulis. Any serious barbarian effort to destroy the power of Arthur and his government would have to bring war and destruction to the part of Britannia in which Aquae Sulis lay.

Later, when the Britons (or, more accurately by then, the Welsh) attempted to stage a recovery of their fortunes in the late Seventh

---

122 The exact phrase used by Nennius is *bellum in monte Badonis*, meaning "battle on the mount of Badon." The word *monte* is in the ablative case, as required by the Latin preposition *in*; *Badonis* is in the genitive case, which calls for the insertion of the English preposition "of" between the word mount and the name Badon.

123 Or, more precisely, *bellum in monte Badone*.

Century, they did so by invading this very same part of Britannia, which they still called Badon. The *Annales Cambriae* reports the occurrence of a "Second Battle of Badon" in its entry for the year A.D. 665 or A.D. 667. Based upon other Welsh sources, it seems that the Briton leader Morgan or Morcant led Welsh forces in an attack upon the Anglo-Saxons. Morgan had earlier united under his sole rule all of Glevissig and Gower, which were then renamed Glamorgan after him, so his army was obviously drawn from southeast Wales. The Welsh were less successful this time around, and Morgan lost his life in the ill-fated venture. The exact location of the Second Battle of Badon is not specified, but, given the location of Morgan's kingdom, it must have been in the general vicinity of Aquae Sulis.

Any one of a number of low hills near Aquae Sulis could have been the mount upon which the first Battle of Badon Hill was fought. In ancient and medieval battles, combatants often sought an advantage by occupying the high ground; even a slight rise in the terrain could serve this purpose. The area about Aquae Sulis is provided with several hills which would have made satisfactory battlefield positions.

## Dating the Battle of Badon Hill

Gildas has done us a disservice in describing the Battle of Badon Hill as a "siege," thereby generating a great deal of confusion as to its true location, but he is much more helpful when it comes to establishing the date of the Battle. Gildas tells us that the Battle of Badon Hill was fought in the same year in which he was born. From Gildas's statement, we can determine the date of the Battle with a high degree of confidence.

From the internal evidence of *De Excidio Britanniae*, through references to contemporary events, we know that Gildas wrote around A.D. 540. He certainly completed his work before A.D. 549, the year in which King Maelgwn of Gwynedd, mentioned as a living monarch in *De Excidio*, died of plague. At the same time, Gildas could not have been a young man at the time of his writing. Only an experienced and respected man would have been allowed the leisure time, or would have had the knowledge, to write a work such as *De Excidio*. More importantly, only such a person would have been permitted to criticize powerful reigning monarchs, as Gildas does in the latter part of his work. Since Gildas wrote *De Excidio* in the A.D. 540's, and on the likely supposition that he was then close to the age of fifty, the Battle of Badon Hill must have been fought sometime in the A.D. 490's.

Gildas also makes an ambiguous reference in *De Excidio* to forty-four years and one month having passed. Most historians interpret Gildas to mean that he was born, and the Battle of Badon Hill fought, forty-four years and one month before he wrote *De Excidio*. Others understand him to mean that the Battle was fought approximately forty-four years after the Adventus Saxonum, the arrival of the Anglo-Saxons in Britannia. Although this latter interpretation reflects the minority opinion, we should not dismiss it too quickly because it has been endorsed by no less a distinguished scholar than Venerable Bede. Bede is highly respected as an historian, and he worked with sources and information no longer available to us. For our purposes, however, the correct interpretation is almost irrelevant. Whether Gildas meant that the Battle of Badon Hill was fought forty-four years before he wrote, or forty-four years after the arrival of the Anglo-Saxons, the resulting date for the decisive clash of arms would not be substantially different.

If Gildas meant that the Battle was fought approximately forty-fours years prior to the date of his writing, then the Battle of Badon Hill - and Gildas's birth - should be dated to the early or middle A.D. 490's. According to the *Annales Cambriae*, Gildas died in A.D. 570 or A.D. 572. It is therefore extremely unlikely that Gildas was born before A.D. 490. If Gildas was born, and the Battle of Badon Hill fought, in, say, A.D. 493, then the monk would have been a long-lived, but plausible, seventy-seven to seventy-nine years old at the time of his demise.

If, on the other hand, Gildas meant that the Battle took place forty-fours years after the Adventus Saxonum, then the Battle of Badon Hill was still fought around A.D. 493. Bede places the Adventus Saxonum in A.D. 449, which is the date of the formal repudiation by the Anglo-Saxons of Kent of their foederati treaty with the Britons. Assuming Gildas would have likewise seen the loss of Romano-Briton authority over the Anglo-Saxons, and not merely the Britons' first employment of barbarian mercenaries, as the proper incident by which to mark the Adventus Saxonum, then we derive a date for the Battle of Badon Hill of A.D. 493.

The date of A.D. 493 for the Battle of Badon Hill fits very nicely with our reconstructed chronology for Arthur's military career. From the date of A.D. 490 determined for Arthur's ninth and tenth victories in the Battle of the City of the Legion and the Battle on the Shore by the River Tribruit, which is based upon the passage of sixteen years from Aurelius's defeat of Dux

Gorlois, it follows that Arthur's twelfth victory in the Battle of Badon Hill was just a few years later, in the early A.D. 490's. For this reason, but mostly out of deference to Venerable Bede, we shall accept A.D. 493 as the date of the great Battle of Badon Hill.

If A.D. 493 is in error for the Battle of Badon Hill, then it is too early rather than too late. A date after A.D. 493 would imply that Arthur had abandoned, at least for a time, his plan to destroy Anglia. A temporary cessation of the war is a realistic possibility because Arthur could have required more than a single year to rebuild his army and resolve internal political matters. In that case, a number of minor skirmishes were probably fought between the Britons and the Angles in the years preceding the Battle. Colgrin or Baldulf might have even won one or more engagements, thus rehabilitating their martial reputation. A date after A.D. 493 would have also allowed the Icelingas leaders more time to conspire with their fellow barbarians in Britannia before launching their massive attack upon the Britons. All things considered, the Battle of Badon Hill was probably fought in A.D. 493, but could have been fought a little later, perhaps as late as A.D. 496.

The only objection to placing the Battle of Badon Hill in the A.D. 493 to A.D. 496 time period is the *Annales Cambriae*, which places the Battle in the year A.D. 516 or A.D. 518. The *Annales Cambriae* is clearly mistaken, however, because its date is well outside the range which can be confidently established through the reliable contemporary testimony of Gildas. The *Annales Cambriae* could have erred in any of a number of ways, causing it to put the Battle more than two decades after its proper time.

The most likely source of error lies in the form in which many post-Roman and early medieval chronicles, including the *Annales Cambriae*, were kept. They were written as margin notes on Easter Tables, the computational charts used to calculate the date upon which the holy day of Easter would fall in any given year. Because the date of the religious observance of Easter varied from year to year, Churchmen found it helpful to prepare and keep Tables over a period of many years. The typical Easter Table was based upon a cycle of nineteen years. The scribes keeping the nineteen year Easter Tables would from time to time jot down notable events that occurred during the year next to the appropriate line on the Easter Tables. The *Annales Cambriae* is a collection of margin notes from several different nineteen year Easter Tables.

When the margin notes from the various Easter Tables were assembled and transcribed into the *Annales Cambriae*, the copyist erroneously attributed the Badon Hill entry to a later Easter Table. This error resulted in the Battle of Badon Hill being dated nineteen years too late. Thus, the Easter Table margin note which should have been the 53rd entry in the *Annales Cambriae* was erroneously copied onto the 72nd line. Subtracting nineteen years from the date given in the *Annales Cambriae* places the Battle of Badon Hill in A.D. 497 or A.D. 499.

Even after correcting the systematic nineteen year dating error, we must regard the *Annales Cambriae* date as only approximate. When margin notes were made on Easter Tables, they were often not lined up precisely with the year to which they relate. Sometimes all the entries for a five year period were lumped together,

sometimes an entry for one year spilled over onto the lines for other years, and sometimes a scribe was simply careless in placing the entry in an ambiguous location. As if to illustrate the nature of the problem, the surviving version of the *Annales Cambriae* contains errors in its enumeration of the years, which is why two different years are associated with most events dated from the *Annales*. In addition, the different Easter tables from which the *Annales Cambriae* was drawn could have employed different calendar systems because Latin chroniclers did not always begin the new year on the same day; some chroniclers used the Roman New Year (January 1), as we do, while others used the feast of the Annunciation (March 25), the Roman tax assessment (or indiction) date (September 1 or 24),[124] Christmas (December 25), the start of Advent (the four week period preceding Christmas) or Easter itself. The *Annales Cambriae*, corrected, thus gives us a range of about A.D. 490 to A.D. 499 for the date of the Battle of Badon Hill, which is consistent with the time period we have determined from an examination of Gildas's contemporary statements.

An entirely different type of error might have occurred if the Battle of Badon Hill entry was taken from a chronicle employing the modern *Anno Domini* (Year of the Lord) or A.D. dating system. The A.D. dating system did not become standard until after the post-Roman period, due to the influence of Venerable Bede's *Historia Ecclesiastica*, which was written about A.D. 731. Until then, most chroniclers did not count the years beginning with the year of Christ's birth, but with the year in which He

---

124 The Indiction was a period of fifteen years. At the start of every Indiction, the tax rolls were reviewed and updated.

began His Public Life (A.D. 28) or the year of His Passion (A.D. 30). If, therefore, one of the Easter Tables consulted by the compiler of the *Annales Cambriae* was precociously kept on an *Anno Domini* basis, the compiler might have mistakenly assumed that it was kept on the Public Life dating system and erroneously added 28 years to the date given in the original record. Reversing this error would result in dating the Battle of Badon Hill to A.D. 488 or A.D. 490, which, taking into account the other factors discussed above, is also consistent with the A.D. 493 to A.D. 496 time frame.

The date of A.D. 493 for the Battle of Badon Hill therefore remains substantiated, despite the confusion caused by the *Annales Cambriae*.

The earliest references to the Battle of Badon Hill thus indicate that the Battle was fought in the vicinity of the modern town of Bath, then called Aquae Sulis, and that it was fought in, or soon after, A.D. 493. As to the question of who fought against Arthur in the Battle of Badon Hill, we must turn to Geoffrey of Monmouth and archaeology for the answer.

### The Great Anglo-Saxon Uprising

Geoffrey of Monmouth identifies Colgrin and Baldulf as the principal barbarian commanders at the Battle of Badon Hill. The presence of the ambitious and aggressive Icelingas leaders suggests (as we would expect) that the Angles of Anglia were the chief planners and instigators of the campaign which led to the Battle. By drawing upon the prestige of the ancient and revered Icelingas dynasty, Colgrin and Baldulf lured the Angles and other Anglo-Saxons in Britannia into a grand barbarian coalition for the purpose of dealing Arthur's southern Romano-Briton realm its death-blow.

Although the sad fate of the Lindsey Angles must have weakened the political standing of the Icelingas in Britannia, subsequent developments were more favorable. In A.D. 490, the Angles were able to penetrate deep into Britannia, even briefly occupying the town of Verulamium and bringing about the death of Aurelius, the then-reigning Regissimus Britanniarum. In A.D. 491, and possibly over the next several years if we accept a later date for the Battle of Badon Hill, they were able to conduct unanswered raids onto Briton territory while Arthur was busy securing his hold on the Romano-Briton government. Then, around A.D. 492, the army of the new Regissimus was turned back from an invasion of Anglia. These successes, limited or ambiguous though they might have been, wiped out at least some of the shame of the Icelingas' earlier failure. By A.D. 493, or soon thereafter, Colgrin and Baldulf were ready to carry the war to Arthur, and they initiated a bloody contest which plunged all south Britannia into war.

The Angles of Anglia were not the only Anglo-Saxons to rally to the Icelingas standard. Although the barbarian army at Badon Hill must have been predominantly an Angle force led by representatives of the traditional Angeln dynasty, it also included many warriors from several other Anglo-Saxon groups serving under their own leaders. Among the Anglo-Saxons who took up arms against the Britons were the Kentishmen under their new Aescingas dynasty, a contingent of barbarians who had recently arrived in modern West Sussex and some of the hitherto loyal Anglo-Saxon foederati of the upper Thames region.

Aesc, the third king of Kent, had firmly

established himself and his Aescingas dynasty in power in the oldest Anglo-Saxon kingdom in Britannia by the time Arthur became Regissimus. Aesc apparently wished his new dynasty to be a dynamic and aggressive one, for he named his son and heir-apparent Eormenric. "Eormenric" (or "Hermanric") is not an Anglo-Saxon name; it is a Gothic name. "Eormenric" was the name of the great warrior king of the Goths who carved out a mighty empire for himself between the Baltic and Black Seas more than one hundred years before Aesc's day. The Anglo-Saxons held the Gothic King Eormenric in special awe, for he appears in their poems *Beowulf*, *Widsith* and *D e o r* (or *Deor's Lament*), where he is noted for his savagery, but also for his great wealth and military power. The Kentish ruler's selection of such a name for his son is a telling insight into his own ambitions; he obviously had grandiose plans for his own kingdom and dynasty. Aesc would have lent an eager ear to any proposed action which seemed likely to break the power of the Britons and open up opportunities for him to push his own borders westward toward Londinium.

Welsh tradition supports the inference of Kentish participation in the great barbarian uprising. The relatively late *Mabinogion* tale "The Dream of Rhonabwy" identifies "Osla Big Knife" as the Anglo-Saxon commander in the Battle of Badon Hill, notwithstanding that the earlier *Mabinogion* tale "How Culhwch Won Olwen" depicts Osla as an ally of Arthur and reports him killed in the Boar War.[125] The

"Rhonabwy" tale reflects a true folk memory of Kentishmen having fought at Badon Hill, and the storyteller has simply gotten the Kentish leader's name wrong. A careless scribal error has certainly altered the original and correct "Ossa," the Briton form of "Aesc," into the erroneous but more familiar "Osla." "The Dream of Rhonabwy" in identifying "Osla" as the Anglo-Saxon leader at Badon Hill, indicates that Aesc (or Ossa) joined Colgrin and Baldulf in the fight against Arthur.

A small contingent of Anglo-Saxons from modern West Sussex also participated in the great anti-Briton campaign. Aelle, the first king of what is today West Sussex, is traditionally regarded as the first "Bretwalda" (Ruler of Britannia). "Bretwalda" was the title conferred by the early Anglo-Saxons upon the foremost king among them. The early Anglo-Saxon chroniclers do not tell us what Aelle did to earn this distinction, but it must have been quite extraordinary because the small size and isolation of his kingdom made him a most unlikely candidate for this high honor. Aelle's participation in the Badon Hill campaign must have been what gained him sufficient prestige to merit the title Bretwalda - especially since he seems to have been the only major barbarian leader who survived the campaign with both his life and his territory intact. In order to have won his unusual prominence among his barbarian contemporaries, Aelle must have led his warriors from Sussex into battle against Arthur.

Many of the upper Thames Anglo-Saxon foederati, who had until then remained loyal to the Britons, also chose this time to assert themselves by waging war upon Arthur. Anglo-

---

125 "Culhwch" survives in a Fourteenth Century copy of an early Eleventh Century manuscript, whereas "Rhonabwy" exists in a Sixteenth Century copy of an early Thirteenth Century manuscript. The oral versions of both tales are much older than the manuscripts, but

"Rhonabwy" is still not quite as ancient as "Culhwch," parts of which could have been composed as far back as the Eighth Century.

Saxon warriors were first introduced into the upper Thames region almost a hundred years earlier to serve as soldiers in the employ of the Roman army supply depot at Dorciconium (Dorchester-on-Thames). By the late Fifth Century, the barbarian settlers had come to dominate Dorciconium and the surrounding territory, and they established their own flourishing Anglo-Saxon realm in the region. Until the very end of the Fifth Century, the upper Thames Anglo-Saxons lived in peace with, and remained steadfast allies of, their Briton neighbors. They probably served the Ambrosii after the collapse of Roman Imperial government in Britannia, and then the Curia of the nearby Civitas based upon Glevum Colonia (Gloucester) after the Battle of Wallop. Archaeology tells us that many upper Thames foederati succumbed to the temptation to declare their independence toward the end of the Fifth Century by turning against the Britons for the first time.

The distribution of Germanic artifacts in south Britannia indicates that a large Anglo-Saxon population suddenly withdrew from parts of the upper Thames region just before the start of the Sixth Century. The abruptness and thoroughness of the area's depopulation is extraordinary. The upper Thames Anglo-Saxons would not have abandoned their homes willingly, so they must have joined Colgrin and Baldulf at the Battle of Badon Hill and lost their lands as a consequence.

These disparate Anglo-Saxon factions - the Angles of Anglia, the Kentishmen of Aesc, the followers of Aelle and the disloyal upper Thames foederati - came together just before the end of the Fifth Century for the express purpose of destroying the Romano-Briton regime headed by Arthur. This barbarian coalition posed a greater danger to the survival of post-Roman Britannia than did Drust macErp, Hengist of Kent or Mannion the Boar. The outcome of the apocalyptic confrontation between the Anglo-Saxon conspirators and the Romano-Briton Regissimus at Badon Hill decided the fate of Britannia for the next two generations.

As for the events of the Badon Hill campaign itself, Geoffrey of Monmouth gives an account that is both plausible and enlightening.

## The Badon Hill Campaign

According to the *Historia Regum Britanniae*, the fighting which led to the Battle of Badon Hill was precipitated by the landing in southwest Britannia of a large seaborne Anglo-Saxon army. Geoffrey believed this army to have been commanded by the Angle brothers Colgrin and Baldulf, whom he thought had just been defeated in the Battle of the Caledonian Wood. This mistaken belief was a result of Geoffrey's imagining all the barbarians in Britannia to constitute a single nation under a single set of leaders, as well as his tendency to link events occurring over several years into a compressed narrative. Because Geoffrey knew that the barbarians defeated in the Battle of the Caledonian Wood had been expelled from their far northwest Britannia homeland, he assumed that they headed for Germania, and because he thought that the Battle of Badon Hill was fought very soon after the Battle of the Caledonian Wood, he assumed that the barbarians changed course at sea in order to land instead in southwest Britannia and fight at Badon Hill.

Geoffrey might not be very far off the mark. Although the Battle of the Caledonian Wood was, as we have seen from our analysis of the victories listed by Nennius, several years and several combats removed from the Battle of Badon Hill, it is nonetheless likely that at least some of the Anglo-Saxons vanquished in the Caledonian Wood did indeed turn up at Badon Hill, and that barbarian reinforcements from the Continent did indeed make an amphibious invasion of southwest Britannia.

Geoffrey tells us that the seaborne invaders landed near modern Totonesium Portus (Totnes) in south Devon. They advanced generally northward, ravaging the countryside and slaying the inhabitants as they went. The Continental Anglo-Saxons apparently sailed along, and raided, the south Devon coast after they arrived in Britannia. They then beached their ships on the Dorset shore and, except for a small contingent of warriors detached to guard the ships, they marched inland toward Aquae Sulis. Arthur, distressed by news of the barbarian invasion, once again had to break off a planned expedition into Anglia and once again had to race off toward the opposite end of the Diocese.

Geoffrey actually states that Arthur cancelled a foray against the Picts and Scots. The targets of Arthur's contemplated invasion were surely the Angles of Anglia, not the marauders of the far north. Geoffrey's source must have told him that Arthur cancelled a campaign against "the barbarians," whom Geoffrey mistakenly concluded were the far northern variety since Geoffrey had just placed Arthur in the Caledonian Wood and all the Anglo-Saxons on ships sailing to Germania.

The barbarian army which lured Arthur away from Camulodunum was soon heavily reinforced. A major invasion so deep into Briton territory could not have consisted of just a single amphibious force from the Continent, but must have inevitably drawn in the discontented barbarians already resident in Britannia. It would have attracted in particular the support of the Angles who were then embroiled in a war against Arthur and who could have easily travelled overland to the battle area. The Badon Hill campaign was in essence a widespread uprising of the Anglo-Saxons in Britannia, even if this uprising was launched in collaboration with a foreign invasion.

After the seaborne force of Continental adventurers landed in south Devon, Colgrin and Baldulf marched from Anglia toward Aquae Sulis by way of the ancient Icknield Way. Although the Anglia end of the trail crossed rough and marshy ground, the Angle infantry was less handicapped by the difficult terrain than was Arthur's cavalry. Moreover, the barbarians reached relatively open country soon after leaving their own territory. The western end of the Icknield Way lay in the region of the upper Thames River, and there the rebel Anglo-Saxon foederati joined the Angle host.

The Kentishmen took a different path to Badon Hill. They advanced by the Harrow Way, an ancient track running just south of, and roughly parallel to, the Thames River. Aelle and his contingent of Anglo-Saxons from modern West Sussex probably joined the Kentish force somewhere along this route. At some point, the combined army of Kent and Sussex turned north to rendezvous with the Angles, perhaps after linking up with the amphibious force from the Continent.

All four Anglo-Saxon armies - the seaborne invaders who landed at Totonesium Portus, the warriors of Anglia who marched down the Icknield Way, the former foederati from the upper Thames region, and the men of Kent and

Sussex who advanced by the Harrow Way - savagely wasted the Briton territory through which they passed. Their objective was to destroy the economy upon which Arthur's Romano-Briton horse soldiers depended, as well as to seize plunder for themselves. The barbarian allies all came together somewhere in the vicinity of Aquae Sulis.

Geoffrey says that the barbarians "besieged" Aquae Sulis. The Anglo-Saxons certainly did not conduct a full-blown, formal siege in the medieval sense. They might have undertaken a simple blockade of the town while they ravaged the surrounding countryside, but they did not make a serious effort to reduce the town. The Anglo-Saxons were more interested in scouring the region for booty than in attacking a fortified and defended town. Geoffrey was probably misled by Gildas's use of the word "siege" to describe the Battle of Badon Hill. In any case, the main fighting did not occur at the town. The "siege" of Aquae Sulis, if it took place at all, was a most casual affair.

Arthur had meanwhile gone to Dumnonia to gather troops, and from there he moved against the barbarians "besieging" Aquae Sulis. Once he realized where the Anglo-Saxon armies were headed, Arthur must have sent word for all available Briton forces to meet him at some convenient place. The Roman town of Lindinis, now called Ilchester, would have been a natural rendezvous point because it lay at the junction of several major roads crossing southwest Britannia. Lindinis was thus accessible to the Romano-Briton soldiers deployed throughout the southwest, including Arthur's fellow Cornovians in Dumnonia, the garrison at Castellum Cataviae (Cadbury Castle) and Aurelius's supporters in the Venta Belgarum

(Winchester) area. Lindinis was also only about thirty-two miles south of Aquae Sulis by road; from Lindinis, it was a relatively short march to the battle area. When Arthur and his army approached the large barbarian force camped outside Aquae Sulis, there could not have been any doubt in the minds of the gathering warriors that the most important and decisive battle since the arrival of the Anglo-Saxons in Britannia was about to be fought.

Geoffrey claims that Arthur marched against the barbarians with only a part of his forces because Hoel of Armorica, and presumably the Bretons who had come with him to Britannia in A.D. 486, were away at Alclud (Dumbarton). Geoffrey places Hoel in Alclud much too early in time. Arthur would not have dispatched an important commander or a large contingent of his best troops to a remote town while the Anglia war still raged. Even if Arthur did not anticipate the great barbarian attack of A.D. 493, he certainly realized that the Angles were a dangerous enemy and that he would need all his forces to face them. Hoel did indeed lead a detachment of soldiers to Alclud, but only much later, when Colgrin and Baldulf no longer posed a threat to south Britannia.

Arthur probably had at his disposal some 900 to 1200 cavalry (three or four troops) plus about 3,000 to 4,500 infantry (four to six companies). Geoffrey tells us that Cador later led 10,000 men against the barbarians who fled the Battle, which suggests that the Romano-Briton army at Badon Hill consisted of ten units. Despite what Geoffrey says, Hoel's Armoricans certainly formed one of Arthur's cavalry units. Also, despite the archaeological evidence of upper Thames treason, a contingent of loyal foederati formed at least one of Arthur's infantry companies. Excavation of Anglo-

Saxon sites in the upper Thames region indicates that only some of the upper Thames Anglo-Saxons were expelled from the region in the late Fifth Century; the barbarians who stayed must have remained loyal to the Britons. Moreover, a leader from the region with the Germanic name of Boso later appears in the *Historia Regum Britanniae* as an ally of Arthur; Boso must have been the leader of a group of loyal foederati. The Regissimus thus commanded a substantial cavalry wing and at least some high quality infantry when he marched against the Anglo-Saxon enemy. By the standards of the day, Arthur led a very large and powerful army to Badon Hill.

The Anglo-Saxons were even more numerous, probably in the neighborhood of 10,000 warriors. Given the importance of the Badon Hill campaign, the barbarians would have deployed the largest army they could muster; they would have deployed almost their entire military strength in south Britannia The total Anglo-Saxon population in the former Roman Diocese at this time is currently estimated to have been about 100,000 persons. After allowing for troops left behind on home guard duty and for neutral or pro-Briton villages, a barbarian population of this size could have fielded an offensive force of about 10,000 warriors. The composition of the Anglo-Saxon force would have been something like 5,000 Angles, 3,000 Kentishmen, 500 disloyal upper Thames foederati, 1,000 Sussex warriors and 500 Continental barbarians.

Outnumbered by about 10,000 Anglo-Saxons to his approximately 6,000 Britons, or perhaps by even worse odds, Arthur would have to rely upon the mobility of his cavalry and the brilliance of his own genius in order to prevail in the upcoming confrontation.

Geoffrey tells us that Archbishop Dubricius addressed the Romano-Briton army on the eve of the Battle of Badon Hill, urging them to victory. The Archbishop's exhortation is a detail which Geoffrey might have supplied from his own imagination; a medieval historian could not imagine any Christian force going into combat, especially against pagans, without clerical blessing. In fact, the words which Geoffrey puts into the Archbishop's mouth were those used in Geoffrey's day to send Crusaders into battle. On the other hand, Dubricius or some other Church official probably did address the troops on the night before the Battle. The Britons must have realized how serious the situation was and how crucial the outcome of the Battle of Badon Hill would be; a little religious encouragement at this juncture would have been very appropriate, and could have been an important boost to morale.

As the Briton army neared Aquae Sulis, the Anglo-Saxons assumed a defensive posture. They drew up in their customary shieldwall battle formation. The barbarian infantrymen thus stood shoulder to shoulder in a dense mass, with each soldier's shield touching, and slightly overlapping, his neighbor's. They presented a strong and solid line to the Britons. Thus deployed, the Anglo-Saxons were difficult to dislodge, and virtually impossible to overrun. As long as the Anglo-Saxon army retained its discipline and cohesion, it was indomitable. The Regissimus launched repeated attacks upon the barbarians in hopes of disorganizing the Anglo-Saxon shieldwall, but without success.

As darkness fell, the armies broke off combat. The Battle was not over, however, for both sides intended to resume the fight the very next day.

The Anglo-Saxons withdrew in good order to a nearby hill, where they camped for the night. This hill could have been any one of the many mounds or spurs in the neighborhood of Aquae Sulis (Bath). It did not have to be a particularly tall hill, nor did its slopes have to be especially steep, in order to afford meaningful protection against attack. Even a moderately gentle ascent would weaken the impact of an infantry or cavalry charge and would give the Anglo-Saxon defenders an important edge. The hill to which the Anglo-Saxons withdrew was called Badon's Hill, and it was where the outcome of the Battle would be determined.

Arthur knew that the best hope of a Briton victory lay in an attack upon the barbarians when they were not in their traditional shieldwall array. Although the Anglo-Saxons were redoubtable foot soldiers, even the best warrior afoot could not prevail one-on-one against a trained cavalryman. In a tight formation, especially one as formidable as that used by the Anglo-Saxons, a disciplined unit of infantrymen could hold off innumerable mounted assaults. If, however, an attack was made when the defenders were not formed up in proper style, the horsemen could easily run down the individual foot soldiers. At any time during the press and confusion of combat, the Anglo-Saxon shieldwall might become disordered, leaving the barbarians momentarily vulnerable before they could reform their ranks. The ability to perceive and appreciate the fleeting opportunity to launch a successful attack in the middle of an ongoing battle, and the instant availability of a mobile strike force capable of hitting fast and hard before this opportunity passed, would be the keys to Romano-Briton victory on Badon Hill.

Early the next morning, Arthur led his men against the encamped Anglo-Saxons atop Badon Hill. The Regissimus probably hoped to catch the barbarians before they were ready for the day's combat, but he was soon disappointed. The Anglo-Saxons were prepared to resume the struggle and they vigorously defended their position. The barbarians even counter-attacked the Britons as they struggled up the slope. The aggressiveness of the enemy and the disadvantage of the ascent took its toll on the Britons, and Arthur's soldiers suffered many casualties in the assault. The Britons nevertheless persisted. After much strenuous fighting, they finally reached the level surface at the top of the Hill. Once they gained the summit of Badon Hill, the Britons were able to fight the barbarians on more equal footing.

The Battle was far from over, for the Anglo-Saxons rallied on the crest of the Hill and joined shoulder-to-shoulder to repulse the Britons. The Britons had gained a toehold on Badon Hill, but they were still unable to overcome the stout defense of the beleaguered Anglo-Saxons. The combat raged through most of the morning and afternoon. It began to look as if the barbarian army would survive intact, capable of renewing the fight on yet another day.

The Anglo-Saxons had been severely battered, however, and they were weary. They apparently faltered, and their redoubtable battle formation wavered. Arthur judged the circumstances right for a final, all-out attack. The Regissimus had planned for such an event, because he had held back a small reserve of elite cavalry under his own command. These horsemen were still fresh and eager to fight. The time had come to commit them to combat. Gathering his best riders about him, Arthur personally led a last desperate cavalry charge directly into the heart of the barbarian army.

The Anglo-Saxons broke.

This one cavalry charge alone resulted in several hundred barbarian casualties. Geoffrey credits Arthur with having killed 470 Anglo-Saxons, Nennius with 940, and William of Malmesbury with 900. Although all three historians speak in terms of Arthur himself causing all these enemy casualties, Arthur did not literally dispatch each and every one of the Anglo-Saxon warriors with his own hand. The original meaning was that the barbarians were slain by the Briton troops under Arthur's command. Geoffrey's number (470) probably represents the number of barbarians slain in the crucial cavalry charge which Arthur personally led, while the larger numbers (900-940) probably represent total barbarian losses in the whole day's combat. Many hundreds more of the invaders must have been slaughtered the next day, when the vengeful Britons pursued and cut down the fleeing Anglo-Saxons.

Among the dead were Colgrin and Baldulf. The Icelingas brothers might have been killed in Arthur's decisive cavalry charge, but they more likely fell in the wild and bloody fighting which accompanied the retreat of the barbarians from Badon Hill.

Geoffrey's narrative accounts for only two days of strife, but the *Annales Cambriae* implies that the Battle of Badon Hill lasted three days. More precisely, the *Annales Cambriae* states that, at the Battle of Badon, Arthur bore the Cross on his shoulder for three days. The *Annales Cambriae* entry means that the Regissimus had emblazoned a Christian cross emblem upon the shield which he carried during three days of combat. The "missing" third day must have been the day following the struggle

atop Badon Hill, which the Romano-Briton forces spent hunting down the routed barbarians. Geoffrey apparently did not feel it necessary to relate the details of the scattered fighting which followed the main portion of the Battle, so he skipped over this stage of the campaign, discussing only the most exciting first two days of combat.

Geoffrey does, however, relate the fate of one particular group of Badon Hill combatants. Cheldric, who had earlier participated in the A.D. 486 campaign near Eboracum (York), appears again at the end of Geoffrey's account of the Battle of Badon Hill. Cheldric appears this time leading the remnant of his warband, and probably other Anglo-Saxon survivors as well, in retreat from the Badon Hill disaster.

Cheldric apparently commanded the seaborne invaders who had landed at Totonesium Portus, because he headed right for the Anglo-Saxon ships beached on the Dorset shore. Arthur was not about to let the barbarian adventurer escape quite so easily; he sent his Magister Militum Cador in pursuit. Cador raced ahead of the barbarians, beat them to their Dorset anchorage and seized their fleet. He then turned back to harass the retreating Anglo-Saxons. Cheldric must have realized that Cador had captured his vessels, because he turned eastward, making for the territory of his allies in West Sussex and Kent.

The hard riding and fierce combats of the Badon Hill campaign seem to have wearied the victorious Romano-Briton cavalrymen almost as much as the defeated Anglo-Saxon warriors, for Cador suddenly gave up the chase. Some, at least, of Cheldric's followers must have therefore reached safety in West Sussex or Kent. Many of them probably settled there. But not

Cheldric. Cador broke off his pursuit only after Cheldric had been killed.

Arthur, meanwhile, led a follow-up action against the main body of Angles as they attempted to flee back over the Icknield Way to Anglia. Geoffrey does not report on Arthur's leading any such action, but we know he must have done so. Only by pursuing the routed barbarians could Arthur have reaped the full fruits of his victory at Badon Hill and brought the Anglia War to a successful conclusion. A vigorous pursuit of the defeated Angles would have taken a heavy toll of the barbarians and deprived them of the ability to make war for a long time - a very effective means of imposing peace upon a warlike nation. Arthur knew that if he allowed the Angle survivors to escape, he would only have to fight them again at a later time, and certainly in less favorable circumstances. Although the reconquest of the heavily populated Anglia was not feasible, the destruction of Anglia's armed forces and the slaying of its generals was now within Arthur's grasp. Arthur achieved final victory in the Anglia War by pursuing and slaying the Angles as they fled Badon Hill, in the process destroying the military might of the barbarian Kingdom of Anglia.

## Consequences of the Battle of Badon Hill

The importance of Arthur's victory in the Battle of Badon Hill cannot be overestimated. The unsuccessful military challenge to the Regissimus Britanniarum cost the Anglo-Saxons an entire generation of warriors and two important leaders, Colgrin and Baldulf. It also dealt a serious blow to the martial pride of the Anglo-Saxons, no small thing to a warrior people. More than half a century would pass

before the Anglo-Saxons of Britannia were again able to mount an effective challenge to Briton rule of the Diocese.

Gildas tells us that the peace of Badon Hill endured through the date of his writing *De Excidio Britanniae* in the middle of the Sixth Century. Archaeology confirms the prolonged post-Badon pause in the Anglo-Saxon advance. Even the Anglo-Saxon Chronicle agrees; except for a few exceptional victories and advances by the West Saxons of modern Hampshire, the Chronicle records no barbarian successes until A.D. 547. The exceptional West Saxon victories were also, we shall see, made in special and unique circumstances. The Anglo-Saxons were able to hold on to their principal and most heavily-populated territories along the east coast of Britannia - specifically, Lindsey east of Lindum Colonia (Lincoln), modern Norfolk and Suffolk, the eastern half of Kent, and modern Sussex - but they were unable for almost two generations to expand beyond those territories.

Archaeology even finds traces of barbarian withdrawal from certain parts of Britannia soon after the Battle of Badon Hill. Modern north Essex, modern Cambridgeshire, and the area north of the River Thames near modern Oxford were deserted by the Anglo-Saxons in the late Fifth Century. These areas were not reoccupied by the barbarians until well into the Sixth Century. The Anglo-Saxons would not have left their farms and homes voluntarily, so they must have been compelled to do so at sword point.

Arthur no doubt insisted upon the expulsion of the Anglo-Saxons from these districts in order to push the hostile barbarian populations further back from the economic center of his realm. He also wished to make an example of the defeated Anglo-Saxons, a vivid and unforgettable demonstration to the other barbarians in Britannia of the high price to be paid for opposing his Romano-Briton regime. Arthur's soldiers must have burned and slashed their way through the Anglo-Saxon settlements, creating a zone of utter devastation along the frontier with Anglia and in the territory of the disloyal upper Thames foederati.

Many barbarians left Britannia altogether after the Battle of Badon Hill. Considerable numbers of Anglo-Saxons are known to have relocated from Britannia to Gaul and other places on the Continent in the late Fifth/early Sixth Century. Some Saxons even returned to their ancestral homeland in Germania. The large Anglo-Saxon population which had settled in south Britannia during the Fifth Century was now confined to a limited area and began to suffer from overcrowding. Prevented from expanding onto Briton soil by fear of Arthur, many Anglo-Saxons sought more promising prospects outside the Diocese.

Procopius of Caesarae, a contemporary Roman historian living in Constantinople, reports on this reverse Anglo-Saxon migration. He interviewed a number of Angles who had accompanied a Frankish embassy to the eastern Roman capital sometime between A.D. 534 and A.D. 548. From these barbarians, he learned the state of affairs in Britannia. Procopius writes that there were then three nations in Britannia:[126] the Britons, the Angles, and the Frisians. By "Frisians," Procopius must mean the barbarians of Kent, many of whom, like Hengist, had come to Britannia via Frisia in modern Holland. The Britons were ruled by the successors to Arthur, the Angles by the Icelingas, and the "Frisians" by the Aescingas. The other Anglo-Saxon realms in Britannia were ignored by Procopius, either because they were subordinate to the three principal nations, such as the still-loyal upper Thames foederati were to the Britons and the Lindsey Angles were to the Icelingas, or else because they were simply too small to matter. Procopius declares that every year each of the three nations sent forth emigrants to the Continent in order to relieve overpopulation. The Briton emigrants were, of course, headed to join their fellow countrymen in Armorica, but the migratory Angles and Kentishmen no doubt left the island in order to pursue martial opportunities denied them in Arthur's Britannia.

Despite the continued departure of Britons to Armorica, which could have only undermined Arthur's efforts to rebuild the Diocese, Arthur's victory in the Battle of Badon Hill brought peace and prosperity to post-Roman Britannia. The most eloquent testimonial to the high degree of security established by the defeat of the combined barbarian armies at Badon Hill is the fact that many of the hillforts which had been refurbished and reoccupied in the preceding decades were once again abandoned between A.D. 500 and A.D. 550. Protection from barbarian raiders and immunity from foreign attack contributed directly to the economic well-being of Arthur's subjects. The suppression of the Anglo-Saxons meant that Briton farmers could till their fields and raise their livestock undisturbed, and that Briton tradesmen could travel across the Diocese in relative safety. As a result, urban populations ceased to decline and a strong internal economy developed. Arthur gave Britannia a new and meaningful chance for long-term survival.

---

126 Procopius actually refers to Britannia as "Brittia," which is apparently what the Angles called it; he might not have realized that by "Brittia" the barbarians meant the former Roman Diocese.

Lucius Artorius Castus, Regissimus Britanniarum, won a great and magnificent victory in the Battle of Badon Hill. He restored, in very real sense, the stability, order and glory of the Roman Empire in one small part of Europe. For this outstanding and extraordinary achievement, he deserves a prominent place in history.

## Armies in Post-Roman Britannia III

### Romano-Briton

Arthur, A.D. 493

| | |
|---|---|
| Battle of Badon Hill | est. 6,000 |
| Briton cavalry | 900-1,200 |
| Briton infantry | 2,400-3,200 |
| foederati infantry | 800-1,600 |

### Anglo-Saxon

Colgrin & Baldulf, A.D. 493

| | |
|---|---|
| Battle of Badon Hill | est. 10,000 |
| from Anglia & Lindsey | 5,000 |
| from Kent | 3,000 |
| from Upper Thames | 500 |
| from Sussex | 1,000 |
| from Germania | 500 |

## Chapter Twenty-Four
## The Demetian War

Geoffrey of Monmouth claims that Arthur and Cador headed north to join Hoel at Alclud immediately after the Battle of Badon Hill. Geoffrey is wrong. He has mistakenly compressed together in time two events which occurred several years apart. Arthur still had many tasks to perform in south Britannia before he could even think of marching north.

Arthur's first priority was to confirm the achievements of his victory in the Battle of Badon Hill. He had to replace the losses which his army suffered in the Battle, oversee the repair of the damage which the barbarians did in their raids and invasions, and enforce the expulsion of the Anglo-Saxons from the border regions. He also had to take steps to ensure the full restoration of order and stability after almost a decade of constant warfare. In particular, he had to reassert the dominance of his government over local rulers all over south Britannia and suppress the general lawlessness which must have flourished while he was preoccupied with the fight against the Anglo-Saxons. Arthur no doubt led his soldiers on occasional military forays against free-lance barbarian raiding parties and lawless native bandit gangs, but he did not lead them into the north of Britannia. If Arthur had gone north immediately after the Battle of Badon Hill, he would have thrown away most of the hard-won gains of the Battle.

Arthur, instead of heading north, returned to Dumnonia to govern his realm from Castellum Cataviae (Cadbury Castle). He probably ordered the construction of the "Palace" within the hillfort enclosure at this time. He certainly ordered the digging of the foundation for a cruciform church. Somerset legend reports that every Christmas Eve and every June 24 (Feast of Saint John the Baptist), the ghosts of Arthur and his warriors travel along the causeway from Cadbury Castle to Glastonbury. This legend reflects a true memory of trips which the Regissimus regularly made in his lifetime in order to celebrate religious holidays at the Glastonbury monastery, trips which the new church was intended to make unnecessary. Arthur planned to make Castellum Cataviae the military, political and religious capital of south Britannia.

While at Castellum Cataviae, Arthur plotted the downfall of the last remaining hostile barbarian kingdom in south Britannia. This kingdom continued to threaten the security of Arthur's realm even after the destruction of Anglo-Saxon armed might in the Battle of Badon Hill. Arthur could not consider his work in south Britannia complete until he had overthrown the Irish kingdom of Demetia in southwest Wales.

Demetia had repeatedly conspired against the Romano-Briton government of south Britannia. The first conspiracy was thwarted by the Stonehenge Expedition, Catavia's surprise raid on Demetia, and the second was forestalled by the death of Gorlois in the Siege of Dimilioc, but the third was stopped by Arthur in the Battle of the City of the Legion only after a hurried and arduous campaign. Demetia's co-conspirators, Pascent of Builth, Gorlois of Dumnonia and Mannion the Boar of Ireland, had all been slain, but the Gaelic kingdom itself was as yet undefeated. The Demetian Irish were deadly enemies of Arthur's Romano-Briton government, and he could not ignore the danger they posed to his regime.

## Brychan of Brycheiniog

Before Arthur could come to grips with Demetia, he had to contend with the minor Irish realm of Brycheiniog. Brycheiniog is the area about the modern town of Brecon in southeast Wales. It was more recently called Breconshire and is today the southernmost part of the shire of Powys. Brycheiniog was militarily important in Arthur's day because it lay just to the east of Demetia and between Glevissig and Builth.

Local legend claims that the name of the region and town of Brycheiniog/Brecon was taken in the early Sixth Century from an Irish chieftain called Brychan. The traditions of the Cardigan area confirm the Brecon stories in this matter, asserting that Brychan's father landed in Wales toward the end of the Fifth Century and that he was associated with the king of Demetia. Brychan and his father must have landed with Mannion the Boar at Menevia and then fought under him in the Boar War. Brychan obviously survived the War and chose to remain in Britannia. The Irish king of Demetia granted Brychan and his followers the territory that became known as Brycheiniog so they could defend his eastern border against the Britons.

Brychan's small kingdom was well placed to protect his sponsor in Demetia. Brycheiniog (or Breconshire) is mountainous country, not easily traversed. The town of Brecon itself, called Cicutio by the Romans, lies at the intersection of the three Roman roads which cross the rugged terrain of south Wales. Even a small military garrison based in the town would be able to block the direct overland invasion route into Demetia.[127] With Cicutio in Irish hands, a

---

127 The other major road intersection in south Wales was to the northeast of Demetia at Llandovery, called Alabum by the Romans; Alabum was guarded by

Romano-Briton army of conquest could move against Demetia only from the southeast along the Glevissig and Gower coast, where the Demetian defenders could anticipate its route and use their fleet to harass its flank and rear. Brychan had, moreover, assumed an aggressive posture toward his Briton neighbors, conducting raids into the region about Cardiff in Glevissig. Thus, even if the Britons invaded by the southeast coastal route, they still ran a serious risk of being assailed by Brycheiniog warriors along their line of march. So long as Brychan of Brycheiniog remained loyal to Demetia, an attack upon the Irish kingdom was simply not feasible.

An important incident recounted in the *Vita Cadoci* (Life of Cadoc), composed around 1100, reveals how Arthur successfully dealt with the Brycheiniog problem.

According to the *Vita Cadoci*, Gwladys, daughter of Brychan and future mother of Saint Cadoc,[128] fell in love with Gwynnlyw, ruler of the small Romano-Briton realm of Cardiff in Glevissig. Gwladys's name is now usually written "Gladys" and is probably a Welsh derivative of the common Roman female name Claudia; her lover's name would have been "Vannlivus" in Latin and is probably a Roman family name meaning "blue fan" (although it was later re-latinized as "Gundleus").

The Irish princess and the Romano-Briton king wished to wed, but Brychan opposed the marriage. The young pair therefore decided to elope. As Gwladys/Gladys and Gwynnlyw/

---

another Irish garrison allied to Demetia.

128 Brychan's family seems to have been inclined to the religious life; he had a number of saintly offspring, including two daughters, Saints Keyna and Eluned, who were renown for their pious virginity, and a son, Saint Cynog, who became a martyr for the Faith.

Vannlivus made their way south to Cardiff, they encountered Arthur and two companions, Kei and Bedwyr, playing dice. Arthur supposedly lusted for the young maiden himself, but was reminded by his comrades that he had a duty to aid those in distress. Arthur then (we may presume with reluctance) allowed the Irish-woman and her paramour to pass. When Brychan and his warband later appeared in hot pursuit of Gladys and Vannlivus, Arthur and his colleagues barred the way, thereby enabling the fleeing lovers to make good their escape and their elopement.

Arthur must have colluded with Brychan's daughter and her Glevissig suitor in arranging the flight and marriage. Despite what the *Vita Cadoci* says, it is extremely unlikely that Arthur just happened to be in the right place at the right time to cover Gladys's and Vannlivus's escape. When the inevitable "rescue" party set out after the eloping couple, it plunged right into an ambush prearranged by Arthur with Gladys and Vannlivus. Arthur thus played the role of a dynastic Cupid, employing his military might to facilitate a marital alliance between the Romano-Briton Kingdom of Cardiff and the Irish Kingdom of Brycheiniog.

Once Gladys and Vannlivus were wed, Brychan became, much against his will, the ally of Glevissig, and, by extension, of Glevissig's patron, Regissimus Arthur. The Irish warlord would have been hard-pressed to find an honorable excuse to make war upon his own son-in-law, especially since it seems Gladys went willingly into Vannlivus's arms. Celtic women in general, and Irish women in particular, were quite independent in matters of the heart, so Gladys probably did, as the *Vita Cadoci* claims, choose to elope in defiance of her father. In addition, Brychan would have been reluctant to undermine the military security of Glevissig after the marriage, because he would only be depriving his own grandchildren, Gladys's sons and daughters, of their political inheritance. Arthur cleverly took advantage of an existing *affaire de coeur* to resolve his military problem and forcibly bind the interests of Brycheiniog to those of his ally in Cardiff.

Brychan should not have been too angry over the perfidious plot hatched by Gladys, Vannlivus and Arthur. In the short-run, Brychan was humiliated by the marriage forced upon him: a rare case in which the bridegroom's sponsor, not the bride's father, toted the "shotgun" (or, in this case, the sword) at the wedding. In the long-run, however, the alliance between Brycheiniog and Glevissig was beneficial to the Irish dynasty. Whereas Brychan's sponsors in Irish Demetia were soon defeated and overthrown, his own realm endured and continued to be ruled by his heirs for many generations to come. Because of the wedding of Gladys and Vannlivus, Brycheiniog was not attacked by Arthur, and Brychan's descendants remained in power long enough to qualify as one of the traditional honored ruling dynasties of Wales.

The wedding between the Irish Gladys and the Romano-Briton Vannlivus probably took place around A.D. 504. By A.D. 504, Arthur should have completed the expulsion of the Anglo-Saxons from the upper Thames and border regions, and he should have managed to restore order in his realm; he should, in other words, have had time to spare to meddle in Welsh marital politics. Arthur's military offensive against Demetia would have followed a few years later, in A.D. 508 or A.D. 509.

Arthur himself did not command the invasion force which finally conquered the Irish kingdom. He conferred this honor instead upon a Romano-Briton subordinate and a barbarian mercenary.

## Marcellus Agricola Stator, Tribunus Demetarum

According to Brecon tradition, the Romano-Briton officer who undertook the conquest of Demetia was named Marchel. "Marchel" is a Welsh form of the Roman individual name Marcellus.

A Marchel/Marcellus is associated with Arthur, Kei and Bedwyr in the Welsh Triads. The Triads claim that the four men unsuccessfully attempted to steal some pigs belonging to the king of Cornwall and guarded by the Cornish hero Tristan. Tristan is a genuine historical figure, but from a slightly later period, so the incident described in the Triads is clearly fictitious. Although the Triad reference is not to be taken literally, it does reflect a genuine tradition which recognizes Marcellus as one of Arthur's most trusted lieutenants.

Brecon tradition also avers that Marcellus was accompanied in his invasion of Demetia by "Tewdrig, son of Teithfallt." "Tewdrig" is a Welsh rendering of the Gothic name Theodoric, whereas "Teithfallt" is a Welsh version of the Gothic name Theudebald. Theodoric, as Tewdrig, later appears in Cornish folklore as a sea captain who defended "Cornwall" (i.e., Dumnonia) against Irish pirates. The name and pedigree of the warrior dispatched to Demetia with Marcellus tell us that Arthur hired Gothic mercenaries, and this warrior's subsequent activities in Dumnonia tell us that these mercenaries were sailors.

The last time the Goths played a role in Briton history, it was as the anti-Roman Visigoths who attacked and defeated Aurelius in the Battle of Dol. The Visigoths had fallen on hard times since then, and the bringer of these hard times was Clovis, the king of the Franks who had overthrown Syagrius, the Rex Romanorum of north Gaul. In A.D. 507, Clovis and his Franks attacked the Visigoths in Gaul, defeating them and driving them into Hispania.

The Visigoths are known to have had ships operating in the Bay of Biscay before their defeat by Clovis. The Visigoths had no further need for a navy after they abandoned Gaul, and they disbanded their fleet. Some of the Visigoth sailors were apparently unwilling to forsake the maritime life; they decided to seek their fortune in Britannia instead. With the recent destruction of the Anglo-Saxon armies in the Battle of Badon Hill no doubt in mind, the Visigoths wisely came to Arthur's realm as allies, not as raiders. Part of the Visigoth navy sailed to Britannia under the command of Theodoric, and it offered its services to Arthur.

Theodoric's arrival allowed Arthur to consider a seaborne invasion of Demetia. Although Arthur had ships of his own - the tale "How Culhwch Won Olwen" even gives the name of his flagship as Prydwen (Fair Face) - he did not have a fleet large enough to commit to, or expendable enough to risk in, a major naval undertaking against the Demetian Irish, who also had a fleet. The Regissimus could afford to be more aggressive with mercenary warships. With a Visigoth fleet at his disposal, Arthur could contemplate a combined land and sea invasion of Demetia, hammering his enemy on two fronts.

Arthur probably ordered Marcellus and Theodoric to undertake the invasion of Demetia in A.D. 508 or A.D. 509, a year or so after the Visigoths were expelled from Gaul and Theodoric's fleet arrived in Britannia. Marcellus marched with a Romano-Briton land army from Glevum Colonia (Gloucester) into Demetia from the east, traveling along the Cicutio (Brecon) road through newly-friendly Brycheiniog. At the same time, Theodoric sailed with his Visigoth mercenary fleet around the Demetian coast, raiding the Irish coast from bases in Glevissig. Brecon tradition actually implies that Theodoric invaded Demetia by the same overland route which Marcellus took, but it also indicates that the two commanders did not travel together. A later storyteller has obviously fused together two different wings of the invasion. The most effective use of the military resources which Theodoric brought with him to Britannia was in a naval capacity, and Arthur was not one to waste any tactical advantage. Faced with a two-pronged invasion, the Demetian Irish were unable to mount an effective defense: if they brought all their forces to bear against one enemy, they would leave themselves vulnerable to the other.

The Demetians did not give up without a struggle, and Marcellus had to fight two battles as he advanced from mountainous Brycheiniog into the Demetian lowlands. Marcellus is said to have lost one hundred men in each battle. Losses of this magnitude would have represented a large percentage of Marcellus's force, which could have only numbered a few thousand combatants. The statement concerning Marcellus's heavy losses is probably not a literal casualty count, however, but simply a poetic way of saying that the invasion was strongly resisted and hard-fought. Marcellus battled his way to Porth Mawr, near modern Saint David's, where he linked up with Theodoric.

The fall of Porth Mawr marked the successful conclusion of the Demetian War. Porth Mawr was then a major town, being the principal port for voyages between Demetia and Ireland. Porth Mawr has declined in significance since Arthur's day due to a recession of the sea, but in the early Sixth Century it was still an important harbor. It was, for example, the point from whence Saint Patrick is traditionally believed to have sailed to Ireland. The town was thus a natural target for both the landward and seaborne invasion forces. In taking Porth Mawr, Arthur's forces seized a key military objective and isolated the Demetian dynasty from possible overseas Irish assistance.

In commemoration of his victory, Marcellus conferred his name upon the fort of Caer Farchell, just four miles east of Porth Mawr. Caer Farchell was originally called Castellum Marcelli (Fort of Marcellus/Marchel), which the Welsh later corrupted into "Caer Farchell." An even greater monument to the success of Marcellus's expedition is the change in the names which appear in both the Irish and Welsh versions of the Demetian king list: whereas Demetia's Fifth Century monarchs bore Irish names, its Sixth Century monarchs bore Roman and Briton names.

The first ruler of Demetia after A.D. 500 was called Aircol map Triphun, which is Welsh for "Agricola, son of Tribunus." "Agricola" was a Roman family name derived from the Latin word for "farmer." "Tribunus" was a Roman military title which seems to have been particularly popular in post-Roman Britannia: Venerable Bede and the near-contemporary *Vita Germani* describe the military leader of a Briton town visited by Saint Germanus in A.D. 429 as being *tribuniciae potestatis* (of tribunical authority), while Venerable Bede and Geoffrey of Monmouth, working with Romano-Briton sources, anachronistically refer to Julius Caesar's subordinate general as "Tribunus" Labienus. The new Demetian ruler thus had the Roman family name of Agricola and was associated with the common Roman military rank of Tribunus.

We are not told who this Agricola was, where he came from, or why he was made governor of the conquered Irish kingdom. It would have been most odd, however, if Marcellus, who commanded the Regissimus's army in the invasion and who left his name on a fort in the liberated territory, was not rewarded with the rule of Demetia. Marcellus and Agricola therefore must have been the same person, with "Marcellus" being his *praenomen*, or individual name, and "Agricola" his *nomen*, or family name. He could have even been related to the Bishop Agricola who was accused in A.D. 428 of "reviving" the Pelagian heresy in Britannia. The Agricola who rose to the rule of Demetia was no doubt Arthur's companion Marcellus, identified by his family name.

"Tribunus" was obviously the title used by Marcellus Agricola when he assumed the government of liberated Demetia. Medieval Welsh genealogists, who were unfamiliar with Roman army ranks, later mistook the title Tribunus for the name of Marcellus Agricola's father, much as they mistook the title Utherpendragon for the name of Arthur's father.

"Tribunus" was an important, but junior, military rank. It fell below Comes and even Dux in priority. In the late Roman period, "Tribunus" was the title often bestowed upon commanders of small infantry units, garrison troops and barbarian foederati. It was, for example, the title conferred upon the Alamanni King Fraomar in A.D. 372 when he officered a company of his countrymen in Roman service. A higher status was accorded commanders of legions, cavalry units and naval flotillas, who all bore the title "Praefectus." "Tribunus" may therefore seem a rather strange designation for the ruler of a major kingdom.

Demetia was, however, still a barbarian Irish realm even after the Romano-Briton reconquest. Marcellus had overthrown Demetia's Irish ruling dynasty, but its population remained heavily Irish. The Demetian Irish maintained strong cultural and commercial ties to Ireland for many generations after the reconquest. The strength of the Irish element in Demetia is reflected in its many surviving Irish place names and in its many contemporary monuments bearing both Latin and Irish (but not Briton) inscriptions. Demetia might have been an important part of Britannia, but its barbarian population diminished its prestige as far as the Romano-Briton aristocracy was concerned. To their way of thinking, Irish Demetia did not merit a ruler with the high rank of Rex (king), nor even of Comes or Dux or Praefectus. In the Roman military hierarchy, "Tribunus" was the appropriate title for the ruler of Demetia, who was essentially an army officer appointed to govern a barbarian tribe.

In the *Historia Regum Britanniae*, Geoffrey of Monmouth refers to the ruler of Demetia as "King Stater." The royal designation was nothing more than an assumption on Geoffrey's part, based upon his knowledge that later Demetian rulers did assume this high dignity. The name Stater, however, suggests a plausible Roman *cognomen* of Stator, meaning "stander" (in the sense of "steady" or "standfast"). The

"King Stater" identified by Geoffrey as ruler of Demetia was Arthur's army officer, Marcellus Agricola Stator, Tribunus Demetarum (Tribune of the Demetians).

Theodoric, Marcellus's co-commander and Arthur's admiral in the Demetian campaign, also continued to serve the Regissimus after the reconquest of the Irish kingdom. According to Cornish tradition, Theodoric later fought another Irish army, this time a band of pirates led by an chieftain named Fingar. After an unsuccessful attempt to raid Brittany, Fingar landed with 770 men at Hayle Bay near St. Ives in Cornwall. A second pirate leader with the Briton name of Guiner was to meet Fingar there. Before the two pirate leaders could join forces, Theodoric managed to defeat them each in turn. Arthur had obviously ordered Theodoric and his Visigoth sailors to patrol the Dumnonian coast against seaborne raiders, and they seem to have ably discharged this duty.

The patrol of Dumnonian waters by Theodoric's Visigoth fleet relieved much of the military pressure on the region. Dumnonia's long seacoast and proximity to Ireland made it vulnerable to Gaelic onslaught, but a friendly naval force operating in the area was an effective deterrent to overseas attack. With Dumnonia under the protection of Theodoric's warships, the land forces stationed in the region could be reduced, freeing Romano-Briton soldiers for service elsewhere in Britannia. Because of the added security provided by the Visigoth fleet, Arthur was able to withdraw troops from Dumnonia for an extended campaign in far north Britannia.

Before we accompany the Regissimus on his northern adventures, however, we shall examine certain aspects of his reign in south Britannia.

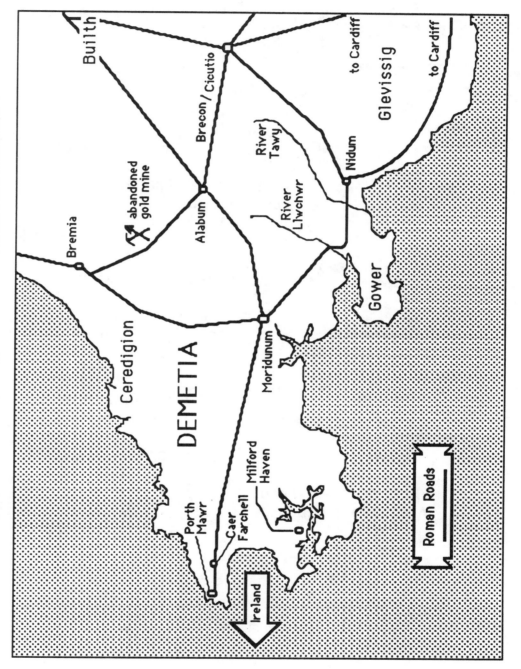

The Kingdom of Demetia
in the Time of
Tribunus Marcellus Agricola Stator
*circa* A.D. 505

Roman Roads

DEMETIA

Ceredigion

Bremia

abandoned
gold mine

Alabum

Builth

Brecon / Cicutio

River
Tawy

River
Llwchwr

Nidum

to Cardiff

Glevissig

to Cardiff

Gower

Moridunum

Porth
Mawr

Caer
Farchell

Milford
Haven

Ireland

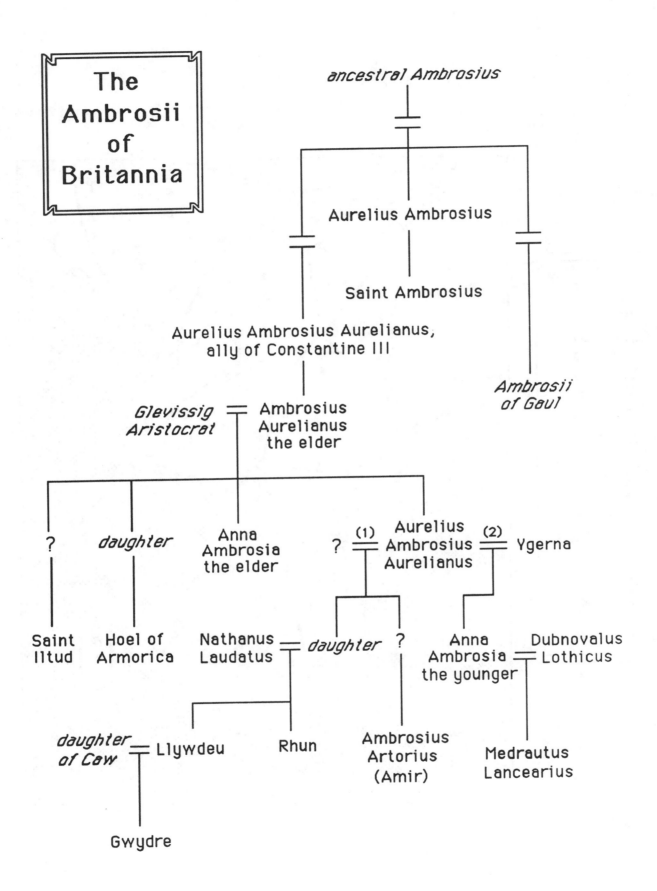

The
Ambrosii
of
Britannia

*ancestral Ambrosius*

Aurelius Ambrosius

Saint Ambrosius

Aurelius Ambrosius Aurelianus,
ally of Constantine III

*Ambrosii
of Gaul*

*Glevissig
Aristocrat* — Ambrosius
Aurelianus
the elder

? — *daughter* — Anna
Ambrosia
the elder

? —(1) Aurelius
Ambrosius
Aurelianus (2)— Ygerna

Saint
Iltud

Hoel of
Armorica

Nathanus —
Laudatus — *daughter* — ?

Anna
Ambrosia
the younger — Dubnovalus
Lothicus

*daughter
of Caw* — Llywdeu

Rhun

Ambrosius
Artorius
(Amir)

Medrautus
Lancearius

Gwydre

# The Artorii of Britannia

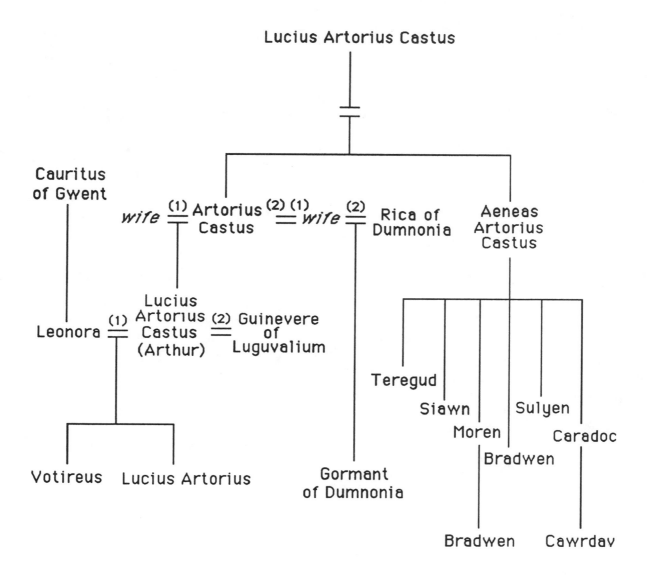